# Keynes's General Theory After Seventy Years

This is IEA conference volume no. 147

# Keynes's General Theory After Seventy Years

Edited by

Robert W. Dimand

Robert A. Mundell

and

Alessandro Vercelli

© International Economic Association 2010

All rights reserved. No reproduction, copy or transmission of this publication may be made without written permission.

No portion of this publication may be reproduced, copied or transmitted save with written permission or in accordance with the provisions of the Copyright, Designs and Patents Act 1988, or under the terms of any licence permitting limited copying issued by the Copyright Licensing Agency, Saffron House, 6-10 Kirby Street, London EC1N 8TS.

Any person who does any unauthorized act in relation to this publication may be liable to criminal prosecution and civil claims for damages.

The authors have asserted their rights to be identified
as the authors of this work in accordance with the Copyright,
Designs and Patents Act 1988.

First published 2010 by
PALGRAVE MACMILLAN

Palgrave Macmillan in the UK is an imprint of Macmillan Publishers Limited, registered in England, company number 785998, of Houndmills, Basingstoke, Hampshire RG21 6XS.

Palgrave Macmillan in the US is a division of St Martin's Press LLC,
175 Fifth Avenue, New York, NY 10010.

Palgrave Macmillan is the global academic imprint of the above companies and has companies and representatives throughout the world.

Palgrave® and Macmillan® are registered trademarks in the United States, the United Kingdom, Europe and other countries.

ISBN-13: 978–0–230–23599–1 hardback

This book is printed on paper suitable for recycling and made from fully managed and sustained forest sources. Logging, pulping and manufacturing processes are expected to conform to the environmental regulations of the country of origin.

A catalogue record for this book is available from the British Library.

A catalog record for this book is available from the Library of Congress.

10  9  8  7  6  5  4  3  2  1
19 18 17 16 15 14 13 12 11 10

Printed and bound in Great Britain by
CPI Antony Rowe, Chippenham and Eastbourne

# Contents

*List of Figures* vii

*Acknowledgments* viii

*Notes on Contributors* ix

Introduction 1

1 Whose Keynes? 8
  Roger E. Backhouse and Bradley W. Bateman

2 The *General Theory* in Keynes's Biographies 28
  Maria C. Marcuzzo

3 The Legacy of Keynes as Public Intellectual 43
  Sherry D. Kasper

4 Mr Keynes and the "Liberals" 63
  Alessandro Vercelli

5 Corporatism and Keynes: His Views on Growth 91
  Edmund S. Phelps

6 Keynes, Art and Aesthetics 101
  Gilles Dostaler

7 Keynes and the Social Sciences: Contributions Outside of Economics, with Applications to Economic Anthropology and Comparative Systems 120
  Mathew Forstater

8 Keynes' Enduring Legacy 133
  Richard N. Cooper

9 The Principle of Effective Demand: The Key to Understanding the *General Theory* 136
  Colin Rogers

| 10 | Getting Rid of Keynes? A Reflection on the Recent History of Macroeconomics<br>*Michel De Vroey* | 157 |
|----|----|----|
| 11 | Aggregate Demand, Employment and Equilibrium with Marginal Productivity: Keynesian Adjustment in the Craft Economy<br>*Edward J. Nell* | 197 |
| 12 | Keynes's Approach to Money: What can be Recovered?<br>*L. Randall Wray* | 222 |
| 13 | Keynes's Revolutionary and "Serious" Monetary Theory<br>*Paul Davidson* | 241 |
| 14 | Preliminary Draft: Was There a (Methodological) Keynesian Revolution?<br>*Sheila C. Dow* | 268 |
| 15 | What Keynesian Revolution? A Reconsideration Seventy Years After *The General Theory*<br>*Robert W. Dimand* | 287 |

*Index*   312

# List of Figures

**Figures**

| | | |
|---|---|---|
| 4.1 | Labour market and effective demand | 74 |
| 11.1 | Adjustment in the craft economy | 205 |
| 11.2 | Behavior of profits | 206 |
| 11.3 | Consumption moves with Investment | 211 |
| 11.4 | Adjustment in the mass production economy | 213 |
| 11.5 | Effects of interest on saving and investment | 215 |
| 11.6 | The Central Bank's interest rate determines employment | 215 |

# Acknowledgments

We are very grateful to the Monte dei Paschi di Siena for its generous sponsorship of the International Economic Association conference "Keynes's General Theory After Seventy Years", July 3 to 6, 2006, to the University of Siena for its support of the conference, and to Valerie Natzios and Robert Mundell for their wonderful hospitality at the Palazzo Mundell in Santa Colomba, where the conference was held. In addition to the more formal papers collected here, the participants in the conference had the great treat of hearing C. Lowell Harris's recollections of how Keynes's *General Theory* was received at Columbia University in 1937, when Professor Harris began his graduate studies there. We thank Fay Sun for her work on the index to this volume. Thanks are also due to Siena for being Siena: in addition to the seventieth anniversary of the publication of Keynes's *General Theory*, the conference also marked the centenary of Keynes's visit to Siena, and one can easily understand why he was so delighted with Siena and Tuscany.

# Notes on Contributors

**Roger E. Backhouse** is Professor of the History and Philosophy of Economics at the University of Birmingham. His books include *The Ordinary Business of Life/The Penguin History of Economics* (Princeton University Press/Penguin Books, 2002), *The Cambridge Companion to Keynes* (co-edited with Bradley W. Bateman, Cambridge University Press, 2006), and *The History of the Social Sciences since 1945* (co-edited with Philippe Fontaine, Cambridge University Press, 2010).

**Bradley W. Bateman** is the provost and executive vice-president of Denison University. He is the author of *Keynes's Uncertain Revolution* and co-editor (with Roger Backhouse) of *The Cambridge Companion to Keynes*. His work on the religious influences on American economics has appeared in many journals, including the *Journal of Economic Perspectives*, *History of Political Economy*, and the *Journal of the History of Economic Thought*. He is working on a book on the religious influences in the formation of American economics in the late Nineteenth and early Twentieth Century and how the discipline subsequently became secularized.

**Richard N. Cooper** is Maurits Boas Professor of International Economics at Harvard University. He taught at Yale University from 1963 to 1977, and was in public service on several occasions, including as Under-Secretary of State for Economic Affairs, chairman of the Federal Reserve Bank of Boston, and chairman of the National Intelligence Council.

**Paul Davidson** is Visiting Scholar at the New School for Social Research, Bernard Schwartz Center for Economic Policy Analysis. He is the editor of the *Journal of Post Keynesian Economics*, the author of *John Maynard Keynes* (Palgrave Macmillan, Great Thinkers in Economics, 2007), the author, co-author, or editor of 21 other books, and the author of more than 200 articles.

**Michel De Vroey**, Professor at the University of Louvain, Belgium), is the author of *Involuntary Unemployment: The Elusive Quest for a Theory* (Routledge, 2004). He is working on a book on the history of macroeconomics, a subject on which he has published extensively. He held visiting positions at Paris-Sorbonne, Duke University, Clemson University, and the University of British Columbia.

**Robert W. Dimand** is Professor of Economics at Brock University and Adjunct Professor at McMaster University, Canada. He is the author of *The Origins of the Keynesian Revolution* (Elgar and Stanford University Press, 1988), co-author of *A History of Game Theory, Vol. 1: From the Beginnings to 1945* (Routledge, 1996), co-editor of *A Biographical Dictionary of Women Economists* (Elgar, 2000) and editor of *The Origins of Macroeconomics* (10 volumes, Routledge, 2004). He has been a visiting professor at Connecticut College and the Universities of Paris II (Assas-Panthéon) and Dijon. He is currently writing the volume on James Tobin in the Palgrave Macmillan series Great Thinkers in Economics.

**Gilles Dostaler** is Professor of Economics at the Université du Québec à Montréal, Canada. He specializes in the history of economic thought. He wrote extensively on Keynes, Hayek, Marx, and other prominent thinkers. He has published, among other works, *Economic Thought since Keynes* (with Michel Beaud, Edward Elgar, 1995, and Routledge, 1997), *Le libéralisme de Hayek* (La Découverte, 2001), *Keynes and his Battles* (Edward Elgar, 2007), *Capitalisme et pulsion de mort* (with Bernard Maris, Albin Michel, 2009), and *Keynes par-delà l'économie* (Thierry Magnier, 2009).

**Sheila C. Dow** is Professor of Economics at Stirling University. She is co-editor (with Alexander Dow), of *A History of Scottish Economic Thought* (Routledge, 2006), and author of *Economic Methodology: An Inquiry* (Oxford University Press, 2002), *The Methodology of Macroeconomic Thought* (Elgar, 1996) and other publications in methodology, history of economic thought, Post Keynesian economics, monetary theory, and regional finance. She is Director of SCEME, an associate editor of the *Journal of Economic Methodology*, and special advisor on monetary policy to the UK House of Commons Treasury Select Committee.

**Mathew Forstater** is Associate Professor of Economics and Black Studies at the University of Missouri–Kansas City and Director of the Center for Full Employment and Price Stability at UMKC. He is the author of *Little Book of Big Ideas: Economics* (ANC Books, 2007) and co-editor (with L. Randall Wray) of *Keynes for the Twenty-First Century* (Palgrave Macmillan, 2008).

**Sherry Davis Kasper** is a Professor of Economics at Maryville College, Tennessee. She is the author of *The Revival of Laissez-Faire: A Case Study of its Pioneers* (Elgar, 2002). Her recent work focuses on the role of economists as public intellectuals and civility in intellectual discourse.

**Maria Cristina Marcuzzo** holds a First Degree in Philosophy (University of Milan) and MSc in Economics (London School of Economics). She is Professor of Economics at the University of Rome La Sapienza and is currently president of the European Society for the History of Economic Thought. She has worked on classical monetary theory (co-author of *Ricardo and the Gold Standard*, 1991) and on the Cambridge School of Economics (co-editor of *The Economics of Joan Robinson*, 1996, and of *Economists in Cambridge*, 2005, and author of several articles in various journals). She is currently editing a collection of her papers on Keynes.

**Robert A. Mundell**, Professor of Economics at Columbia University, won the Royal Bank of Sweden Prize in Economic Science in Memory of Alfred Nobel (the Nobel Prize in Economics) in 1999. His many publications include *International Economics* (Macmillan, 1968), *Monetary Theory: Inflation, Interest, and Growth in the World Economy* (Goodyear, 1971), and "A Reconsideration of the Twentieth Century" (Nobel Lecture, *American Economic Review*, 2000).

**Edward J. Nell** is Professor of Economics at the New School for Social Research in New York. He has taught at Wesleyan University and the University of East Anglia and has been a visiting professor at the Universities of Bremen, Paris, Rome, Siena, Orleans, and Nice. A Fellow of the Lehrman Institute, a Bard Center Fellow, and fellow and teaching member of the Centro di Studi Economici Avanzati, he is the author of *Rational Economic Man* (with Martin Hollis, 1975), *Prosperity and Public Spending* (1988), *Keynes After Sraffa* (1990), and *Transformational Growth and Effective Demand* (1992), and the editor of *Growth, Profits and Property* (1980) and *Free Market Conservatism* (1984).

**Edmund S. Phelps**, born in 1933 in Chicago, received his B.A. from Amherst in 1955 and his Ph.D. from in 1958. After appointments at Yale and Pennsylvania he joined Columbia in 1971. He founded the Center on Capitalism and Society in 2001. He won the 2006 Nobel Prize in Economics. In 2009 he was named Chevalier of the Legion of Honor and received the Premio Pico della Mirandola and the Kiel Global Economy Prize, and a Phelps Chair was established in his honor at the Universidade de Buenos Aires. In 2001 he was honoured with a Festschrift conference and volume.

**Colin Rogers** has a Doctorate of Commerce from the University of South Africa and is currently an Associate Professor of Economics at the School of Economics, University of Adelaide, South Australia. His research interests focus on the foundations of monetary theory, the international monetary system and the economics of Keynes. His publications, including *Money, Interest and Capital: A Study in the Foundations of Monetary Theory* (Cambridge University Press, 1989) and a chapter in *A "Second Edition" of the General Theory* (ed. Harcourt and Riach, Routledge, 1997), have stressed the importance of the principle of effective demand for understanding the integration of money and real forces in Keynes's *General Theory*.

**Alessandro Vercelli** is Professor of Economics at the University of Siena. He is the author of *Methodological Foundations of Macroeconomics: Keynes and Lucas* (Cambridge University Press, 1991) and co-editor of *Macroeconomics: A Survey of Research Strategies* (Oxford University Press, 1992).

**L. Randall Wray** is a Professor of Economics at the University of Missouri-Kansas City as well as Research Director, the Center for Full Employment and Price Stability (at UMKC), and Senior Scholar at the Levy Economics Institute of Bard College, NY. A student of Hyman P. Minsky while at Washington University in St. Louis, Wray has focused on monetary theory and policy, macroeconomics, financial instability, and employment policy. He is the author of *Understanding Modern Money: The Key to Full Employment and Price Stability* (Elgar, 1998) and *Money and Credit in Capitalist Economies* (Elgar, 1990) and the editor of *Credit and State Theories of Money* (Elgar, 2004). Wray received a B.A. from the University of the Pacific and an M.A. and Ph.D. from Washington University in St. Louis.

# Introduction

John Maynard Keynes never ceases to fascinate macroeconomists, whether they see themselves as his disciples, as his opponents, or as eclectics drawing insight both from him and from earlier competing or complementary traditions. The questions that Keynes raised – about the stability of the economy, the economic role of government, the proper institutional framework of the world economy, and the relation of economic decisions to an uncertain future – remain as vital as when he posed them. The economics of Keynes thus meets Joseph Schumpeter's criterion for great ideas: most ideas disappear in a period varying from an after-dinner hour to a generation, but the great ones keep coming back, not as unidentifiable strands of a cultural heritage but in recognizable form.

The publication in February 1936 of John Maynard Keynes's *General Theory of Employment, Interest and Money* marked the emergence of modern macroeconomics from the earlier heritage of monetary theory and business cycle analysis. Subsequent macroeconomics, including approaches that rejected Keynes's conclusions, was shaped by the questions that Keynes posed and by the way he tried to answer them: what determines aggregate output and employment? Is the economy self-adjusting? Do the government have a responsibility to use counter-cyclical monetary and fiscal policy to stabilize economic fluctuations, or is the government itself the source of instability? How does a monetary economy differ from a barter economy? Keynes's legacy and the nature of the "Keynesian revolution" remain fiercely contested: was his revolution in economy theory, in methodology, in public policy, or in pre-analytic vision?

The seventieth anniversary of the publication of Keynes's *General Theory* coincided with the centenary of his only visit to Siena. With financial support from the Banca Monte dei Paschi di Siena, the International Economic Association and the University of Siena sponsored an international conference to reconsider "Keynes's *General Theory After Seventy Years*" at the Palazzo Mundell in Santa Colomba, Siena, from July 3 to 6, 2006. Keynes scholars and leading macroeconomists from half a dozen countries gathered to reflect upon Keynes, his impact as a public intellectual, and the contested legacy of *The General Theory*.

Bradley Bateman of Denison University in Ohio and Roger Backhouse of the University of Birmingham raise the issue "Whose Keynes?" Drawing on study of Keynes that culminated in *The Cambridge Companion to Keynes* (2006), which they edited, Bateman and Backhouse skeptically assess the competing efforts of "successive generations of Keynesians, post Keynesians, neo-Keynesians, and new Keynesians" to invoke Keynes's authority, and especially that of *The General Theory*, in support of their own projects and ideas. They find that "One of the main reasons why there has been so much disagreement over who Keynes belongs to is that economists have been trying to do something that Keynes himself was not trying to do, and perhaps was trying to avoid" – create a new orthodoxy.

Keynes differs from other "defunct economists" in having lived a life so rich, complex, and interesting that it has been the subject of several major biographies that are both scholarly and widely read, serious contributions to knowledge and highly entertaining, from the first biography by his friend Roy Harrod to more recent works by Don Moggridge and, in three volumes, Robert Skidelsky. It is difficult to imagine the general public not only buying, but also reading, three large volumes on the life, loves, and ideas of any economist other than Keynes – or that a volume of biography on another economists would bear the subtitle, "The Economist as Savior." Maria Cristina Marcuzzo of the University of Rome "La Sapienza," who is the guiding force of a large-scale research project on the correspondence of the Cambridge economists, critically examines the differing ways in which Keynes's biographers have presented *The General Theory*: Moggridge writing as a professional historian of economic thought, Harrod as an economist with his own research program, Skidelsky as an historian of twentieth-century Britain.

The ballerina Lydia Lopokova, whose marriage to Maynard Keynes brought her into contact with many economists, wrote to her mother-in-law about economists, "Great many of them are most tiresome, no wide outlooks, no touch with life, and no great ideas. They should not rule the country, except Maynard, who is more than economist" (quoted by Skidelsky 1988, p. 161). No "ivory tower" scholar, Maynard was indeed "more than economist." The next two chapters look at the wider role of that very political economist. Sherry Davis Kasper of Maryville College in Tennessee considers Keynes's career as a public intellectual, and explores why "only a few of the next generation of economists followed in his lead, and probably only Friedman was successful in changing public opinion to the extent that Keynes did." Reminding us of Keynes's dictum that "A study of the history of opinion is a necessary preliminary to the emancipation of the mind," Alessandro Vercelli of the University of Siena maintains that the much-criticized category of the "classics" introduced by Keynes in the *General Theory* as the target of his criticisms aims to emphasize a common thread in the leading economists after Adam Smith: the adherence to the fundamental principles of economic liberalism including the acceptance of Say's law that excludes the possibility of a macroeconomic market failure. Keynes rejected Say's law and introduced this new kind of market failure. Keynes did not reject, however, the other fundamental principles of classical liberalism. Although Keynes and his followers have been often accused of having abandoned the basic tents of economic liberalism, Professor Vercelli argues that the *General Theory* should be interpreted as a radical updating of economic liberalism to cope with the new problems raised by the evolution of market economies, the crucial importance of which had been underlined by the Great Depression of the 1930s.

Edmund S. Phelps of Columbia University, winner of the 2006 Royal Bank of Sweden Prize in Economic Science in Memory of Alfred Nobel, writes on "Corporatism and Keynes: His Views on Growth." Phelps focuses on Keynes's early "corporatist" dissatisfaction with free-market capitalism, a topic closely related to that of Vercelli's chapter. Phelps dissents strongly from the view of Keynes and Frank Ramsey that work is everywhere an inferior good, and that the work week would shrink to next to nothing as societies approach Ramseyan bliss.

Neither Keynes's interests nor his influence was limited to economic science, narrowly defined. Gilles Dostaler of the University of Quebec at Montreal, author of *Keynes and His Battles* (2007), presents Keynes as a writer on art and beauty with his own views on aesthetics and, counting literature as an art, as an artist in his own right. Mathew Forstater of the University of Missouri at Kansas City looks at Keynes's contributions and influence in social sciences beyond macroeconomics: anthropology, sociology, and political science, with particular attention

to economic anthropology and comparative systems. Forstater reminds us that

> Keynes was a political economist, or to use Heilbroner's term a "worldly philosopher." He took what we would today call a more "interdisciplinary" approach, not because it was a fad, but because, on the one hand, he recognized the dangers of overspecialization in the social sciences and, on the other, he saw this as the only way to approach solving complex, real world problems.

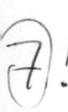

The distinguished international monetary economist Richard N. Cooper of Harvard University, whose Penguin volume of readings on *International Finance* is in the library of everyone in the field, emphasizes five aspects of Keynes's legacy to macroeconomics, four positive but one, the closed-economy framework of *The General Theory*, negative. He brings out what macroeconomics owes to Keynes by turning to Alfred Marshall's testimony before the Royal Commission on the Depression in Trade and Industry in 1886, testimony that was strikingly intelligent and observant but which nevertheless "lacked what we economists have come to take for granted, namely an overall view of the interactions among the major components of the economy, such as investment, consumption, and the trade balance."

Colin Rogers of the University of Adelaide stresses Keynes's principle of effective demand as the key to understanding the revolutionary message of the *General Theory*. Keynesians, old and new, who have accepted *The General Theory* as a special case of classical economics rather than as a revolution in economic theory have

> paved the way for the repudiation of study of the economy as a whole in favor of a return to microeconomic analysis, the representative agent and equilibrium real (non-monetary) business cycle theory.... The principle of effective demand, as a key insight of Keynes's Monetary Analysis, finds no home in any form of Keynesian Real Analysis

Michel De Vroey of the Catholic University of Louvain raises the question whether modern macroeconomics has in fact moved beyond Keynes, or whether it has merely evaded some of his questions and forgotten its debt to him on other questions. To explore this question about the unfolding of macroeconomics from Keynes to the present day,

Professor De Vroey uses a grid of analysis that combines two distinctions: the Marshall–Walras divide between two alternative neoclassical research programs and the distinction between the Keynesian conceptual apparatus and the Keynesian policy cause. "Have macroeconomists really got rid of Keynes?" he asks. "As far as the conceptual apparatus is concerned, the answer is yes (but if Keynes is out, Marshall is still in!)" but not with regard to the Keynesian policy cause. However, "a mellowing of the Keynesian cause has occurred over the years, a shift away from the aim of demonstrating market failures, in particular involuntary unemployment, to the less ambitious goal of bringing imperfections to the forefront."

In his essay on "Aggregate Demand, Employment and Equilibrium with Marginal Productivity: Keynesian Adjustment in the Craft Economy," Edward J. Nell of the New School for Social Research explores Keynes's analysis of the labor market. Keynes insisted that wages are set in money terms, rather than real, while accepting the "first classical postulate" that the real wage equals the marginal product of labor (rejecting the "second classical postulate" that the utility of the real wage equals the marginal disutility of labor). "But," asks Nell, "if the market operates with money wages, how exactly does the real wage adjust to the marginal product? If the real wage adjusts in the labor market, why is full employment not established? And when there is unemployment in 'equilibrium', why is it so deep and persistent?" His answer, drawing on Keynes's lectures, stresses that the real wage can be equal to the marginal product of labor at many levels of employment, and that, with investment and consumption moving together, fluctuations in investment set off destabilizing movements rather than a process of adjustment back to a unique equilibrium.

Two essays discuss Keynes's *General Theory* as a theory of a monetary economy. L. Randall Wray, of the University of Missouri at Kansas City and the Levy Economics Institute, argues that Keynes (1936) offered two contradictory approaches to money: a money supply and demand equilibrium model in Chapters 13 and 15, since incorporated in conventional macroeconomics textbooks, and a liquidity preference approach to asset prices in Chapter 17. Wray argues that it is the Chapter 17 analysis that is consistent with Keynes's general approach and that "is critical to our understanding of the role money plays in causing unemployment." Paul Davidson of the New School for Social Research, editor of the *Journal of Post Keynesian Economics* and author of the volume on *John Maynard Keynes* (2007) in Palgrave Macmillan's series on Great Thinkers in Economics, draws attention to the statement by Arrow and Hahn

(1971, p. 357) that "if a serious monetary theory comes to be written, the fact that contracts are made in terms of money will be of considerable importance." Davidson argues that Keynes's monetary theory, unlike any earlier monetary theory, qualifies as "serious" by the Arrow and Hahn criterion, and that Keynes made a revolutionary break with preceding economics. Keynes's analysis, with the possibility of involuntary unemployment, does not require that money wages are fixed, but only that the economy is a monetary one, with contracts made in terms of money.

Sheila C. Dow of the University of Stirling concludes that "on balance, there has not been a Keynesian revolution at the level of methodology that is consistent with Keynes's approach to economics." Nonetheless, she raises the possibility that economic thinking may yet

change in the way Keynes had advocated, with formal argument being treated as only partial alongside other (incommensurate) forms of argument. There are significant difficulties in incorporating into rationality axioms the type of behavior which these new types of evidence [from experimental and behavioral economics] are suggesting, just as it has proved impossible to incorporate model uncertainty, in its true sense, into a modeling framework. Keynes's "way of thinking" addressed the actual behavior and actual knowledge problems we face in a non-deterministic social system. If these are really to be taken seriously as economics moves forward, and Keynes's thinking taken on board, then there is still scope for a methodological Keynesian revolution.

Although macroeconomics could and did draw on a rich and diverse heritage of monetary economics and business cycle analysis, Robert Dimand of Brock University argues that Keynes's *General Theory*, both through Keynes's own contributions and through his work of synthesis, was crucial to the emergence of modern macroeconomics. Keynes, and not just his subsequent interpreters, provided a usable macroeconomic framework, with roles for the goods market (income–expenditure) and money market equilibrium conditions, for expectations, uncertainty, and volatile investment, and for an analysis of why the labor market may not clear (especially the dynamic analysis of Keynes's Chapter 19) and nominal shocks can have real consequences. All four elements are indispensable to his framework. To pick any one as Keynes's "central message" obscures the powerful synthesis they jointly comprise. Much had been written before *The General Theory* on unemployment and much on the short-run non-neutrality of money (not least by Keynes himself), but *The General Theory* gave macroeconomics a new focus on the determination of equilibrium levels of income and employment, a focus distinct from focus of interwar business cycle analysis or the quantity theory of money. There was indeed, Dimand concludes, a Keynesian revolution in economics.

## References

Arrow, Kenneth J. and Hahn, Frank H. 1971. *General Competitive Analysis*. San Francisco: Holden-Day, and Edinburgh: Oliver & Boyd.
Backhouse, Roger E. and Bradley W. Bateman, eds. 2006. *The Cambridge Companion to Keynes*. Cambridge, UK: Cambridge University Press.
Davidson, Paul. 2007. *John Maynard Keynes*. London and Basingstoke: Palgrave Macmillan.
Dostaler, Gilles. 2007. *Keynes and His Battles*. Cheltenham, UK, and Northampton, MA: Edward Elgar.
Keynes, John Maynard. 1936. *The General Theory of Employment, Interest and Money*. London: Macmillan.
Skidelsky, Robert. 1988. "Some aspects of Keynes the man," in Omar F. Hamouda and John N. Smithin, eds., *Keynes and Public Policy After Fifty Years*, Vol. 1. Aldershot, UK: Edward Elgar.

# 1
# Whose Keynes?[1]

*Roger E. Backhouse and Bradley W. Bateman*

> The *General Theory* is no one's property.
> – Skidelsky 1992, p. 541

## 1. Introduction

Many economists have laid claim to Keynes's legacy, creating successive generations of Keynesians, post-Keynesians, neo-Keynesians, and new Keynesians. Paradoxically, one of the reasons for this proliferation of claimants who denounce others as either pretenders or bastard progeny is the very success of the Keynesian revolution. For decades, macroeconomics was dominated by Keynesian economics. For example, as late as 1971, Robert Barro could take the view that Keynesian economics was "the only ball game in town" (Snowdon and Vane 1994, p. 269). Some people want to claim Keynes's authority for themselves because the immense success of the Keynesian revolution makes his authority extremely desirable. Others take Keynes as their target because to knock him down is to establish their own credentials more effectively than would be possible by attacking anyone else. But to claim his mantle, economists have to reinterpret what his revolution was in their own terms. This has led to many Keynesian revolutions each of which has its own Keynes.

The first stage in recovering Keynes's legacy is thus to ask what the Keynesian revolution was for the different groups who redefined it: What did they want from him and what constructive use did they make of his ideas? The chapter starts by doing this. Here, note that we need to consider not just those Keynesians who have praised his work but also anti-Keynesians who have claimed his work in order to affect a counter-revolution. For example, James Buchanan and Richard Wagner (1997) claim to have understood Keynes better than the Keynesians: by doing this they define a particular Keynes and a particular Keynesian Revolution for themselves.

The chapter then uncovers Keynes's own view of his legacy, suggesting that one of the reasons for why it was possible for there to be so much confusion about the nature of Keynes's message is that Keynes (unlike most Keynesians) did not try to manage his own legacy in detail; there were a few points to which he attached great importance but, beyond that, he was content to let people develop his theories as they wanted. The reason for this lies in his hostility to orthodoxies and to rigid doctrines, something that is incompatible with most of the Keynesianisms that emerged in the half-century after the publication of the *General Theory*. The roots of this hostility to orthodoxy can in turn be traced to attitudes deeply rooted in Keynes's life and values.

## 2. The Keynesian revolutions

The first large-scale interpretation of the Keynesian Revolution was probably Lawrence Klein's well-known *Keynesian Revolution* (1944[1968]). As the first dissertation chaired by Paul Samuelson, Klein's book served a useful purpose as the formal statement of what the Keynesian Revolution meant to the emerging Keynesian mainstream. Samuelson was one of the chief architects of the neoclassical synthesis that was beginning to emerge in the 1940s as Keynes's insights about the operation of the macroeconomy were translated into a theoretical framework compatible with the marginalist, utility maximizing framework of neoclassical economics and with the new econometric methods that were being developed. Thus, for Klein, the Keynesian Revolution was a breakthrough in multiple-equation modelling of a national economy. These equations gave the structural framework for the statistical estimation of macroeconomic models that could be used for engineering the fine tuning of the economy.

This understanding of macroeconomic management had first emerged in its modern guise a few years earlier with Abba Lerner's *Economics of Control* (1944). It was complemented by the work of other Keynesians such as Alvin Hansen who used his fiscal policy seminar at Harvard to train new PhDs in the nuances of fiscal fine tuning. For all of these American Keynesians, Keynes was simultaneously the author of fiscal fine tuning and a complex engineering model of the economy.

In this Keynesian Revolution, Keynes had meant to instigate a revolution in economic modelling that leant itself to a revolution in economic policy making. Keynes had meant for his work in the *General Theory* (JMK VII) to enable the kind of specification of a macroeconomy that Hicks, Harrod and Samuelson undertook when they incorporated his ideas about the economy into a simple general equilibrium model. And if Keynes himself had not engaged in the statistical specification of that model, it was certainly the direction to which he had pointed, as all those who had done the modelling work agreed on some form of activist fiscal policy, and the model specification was obviously necessary for the scientific work of making the correct fiscal policy recommendations

The early Keynesianism of Lerner, Hicks, Harrod and Samuelson soon gave way to a different form of modelling with roughly the same policy objectives. Beginning with the work of Oskar Lange and Franco Modigliani in the 1940s, a new interpretation of Keynesian economics began to emerge, based on the idea that Keynesian economics was about what happened when, for some reason, markets fail to come to equilibrium at their optimum levels. The theoretical framework for this analysis was Walrasian general equilibrium theory. Starting from that framework, these economists tried to solve the theoretical puzzle of how there could be unemployment when competition tended, so it was believed, to equilibrate supply and demand in all markets. Perhaps unemployment arose because the equations for general equilibrium were inconsistent, making it impossible for all markets to be in equilibrium simultaneously. The most comprehensive development of this perspective came in Don Patinkin's *Money, Interest, and Prices* (1956), which sought to provide a theory of how a monetary economy would behave out of equilibrium. Though wage stickiness was central to Patinkin's Keynesian economics, he pointed to a more complex vision of "what Keynes really meant". Out of equilibrium, demand for labour would not be given by the Walrasian demand functions but would depend on realised sales of commodities. The failure of markets to clear created disequilibrium and thereby opened up new problems that did not arise when markets were in equilibrium.

Robert Clower (1965) took this argument a stage further. Clower argued that Keynes could not have been working with Walrasian demand functions for commodities (though he did not realise this, this paralleled Patinkin's argument about demand for labour). This was used as the basis for two new interpretations of Keynesian economics. Axel Leijonhufvud argued that Keynesian economics was "economics without the auctioneer" – it was about what happened when there was no one to coordinate decisions. However, the failure of the interest rate to coordinate savings and investment was as important as what happened in commodity markets – Keynesian unemployment was the result of an inter-temporal disequilibrium in a world where there was no mechanism to coordinate different agents' decisions. Leijonhufvud approached his task explicitly through trying to reclaim Keynes from the Keynesians, the title of his main work being *On Keynesian Economics and the Economics of Keynes* (1968). The second new interpretation came from Robert Barro and Herschel Grossman (1971), who took the argument in a very different direction, ignoring Leijonhufvud's arguments about inter-temporal coordination and interpreting Keynesian economics as being about what happened when both commodity prices and wage rates were rigid. This led to the "general disequilibrium" literature that grew up in the 1970s and 1980s.

One of Leijonhufvud's claims in *On Keynesian Economics and the Economics of Keynes* had been that Keynesian economics was about what happened when quantities adjusted more quickly than prices: that the revolutionary aspect of Keynes's economics was his reversal of the Walrasian assumption that prices adjusted much more quickly than quantities. In the mid-1970s, Clower and Leijonhufvud came to the conclusion that this was a mistake. In the place of their original Keynes, they found a Keynes who worked within Marshall's analytical framework. Like Marshall, this Keynes understood equilibrium in a way that was very different from the way it was understood in Walras. Keynes became the economist who provided an alternative not to Marshall but to Walras: the entire neoclassical synthesis, as well as the "general disequilibrium" literature had got Keynes wrong according to this point of view.

In the face of the collapse of the authority of Keynesian economic policy during the stagflation of the 1970s, when Keynesian policy was seen as incapable of simultaneously offering solutions to inflation and recession, yet another Keynesianism arose, post-Keynesianism. Like Leijonhufvud, the members of this school of Keynesians believed that it was our understanding of Keynes that was wanting, not Keynes's own work. Led by Joan Robinson, G. L. S. Shackle and Paul Davidson, this group of Keynesians believed that Keynes's greatest insight about the economy had been the radical uncertainty of the future. When summing up his work, in response to his critics, Keynes had written, "I accuse the classical economic theory of being itself one of those pretty, polite techniques which tries to deal with the present by abstracting from the fact that we know very little about the future" (JMK, XIV, p. 115). In the absence of meaningful probabilities, behaviour could not be governed by rational calculation but was driven by animal spirits, a spontaneous urge to do something rather than nothing. Keynes was, thus, the one who had challenged the very foundations of economic theory.

The post-Keynesians used this insight about human ignorance to provide a new explanation of persistent unemployment. Faced with radical uncertainty, economic agents often acted in sub-optimal ways that generated unemployment as people sought to avoid unnecessary risk. For this group of Keynesians, the "true" Keynesian Revolution was authored by the Keynes of his well-known 1937 summing up in his *Quarterly Journal of Economics* article, "The General Theory of Employment" (JMK vol). From this point of view, all the careful modelling of the original American Keynesians and the sophisticated work of the macroeconomics of disequilibrium Keynesians missed the point. Keynes had really meant to tell us that the economy cannot be modelled in the way orthodox Keynesians were insisting on modelling it. The models themselves were not useful in the way that traditional Keynesians had assumed because of the unpredictable responses to an uncertain future.

However, the poor economic performance of the 1970s led other economists to reject Keynes as fundamentally mistaken. In doing this, they constructed other versions of Keynesianism, some of them profoundly unsympathetic to Keynes. One of these was presented in James Buchanan's and Robert Wagner's *Democracy in Deficit: The Political Legacy of Lord Keynes* (1977). For Buchanan and Wagner, Keynes was an elitist, anti-democrat, with a naïve understanding of politics, who had erred unforgivably in undercutting what they termed the "old time religion" of balanced budgets (highly questionable given Keynes's own attitude towards budget deficits – cf. Bateman 2005). The Keynesian Revolution was all too real for these critics: it was a terrible policy revolution based on ill-conceived economic analysis. This Keynesian revolution amounted to a kind of economic treason and deserved to be cut off at the knees.

Another, equally hostile, interpretation was the one put forward by Lucas, who argued that Keynesian economics was based on misconceptions about the relationship between policy makers and the economic agents whose behaviour they were analysing. The Keynesian revolution had been about creating models of the economy based on empirical generalisations that were flawed and, as a consequence, had failed. The most dramatic expression of this was by Robert Lucas and Thomas Sargent (1978, p. 49 as quoted by Snowdon and Vane, p. 270):

For the applied economist, the confident and apparently successful application of Keynesian principles to economic policy which occurred in the United States in the 1960s was an event of incomparable significance and satisfaction. These principles led to a set of simple, quantitative relationships between fiscal policy and economic activity generally, the basic logic of which could be (and was) explained to the general public, and which could be applied to yield improvements in economic performance benefiting *everyone*. It seemed an economics as free of ideological difficulties as, say, applied chemistry or physics, promising a straightforward expansion in economic possibilities.

From Lucas's perspective, Keynesian economics is about simple, quantifiable models of fiscal (not monetary) policy, the application of which is unproblematic to its practitioners. Lucas and Sargent went on to argue that this theory was clearly wrong.

That these predictions were wildly incorrect, and that the doctrine on which they were based is fundamentally flawed, are now simple matters of fact, involving no novelties in economic theory. The task which faces contemporary students of the business cycle is that of sorting through the wreckage, determining which features of that remarkable intellectual event called the Keynesian Revolution can be put to good use, and which others must be discarded.

Lucas claimed that if the economy were modelled correctly, with agents taking full account of all the information available to them about what the government was doing, stabilization policy would be impossible. From this point of view, the Keynesian Revolution was based on a confusion of observed regularities with underlying stable parameters in the economy.

Alongside these many versions of Keynesianism lay the long-established view that Keynesian economics was about wage stickiness. In the days of the neoclassical synthesis, this interpretation had been present, but it was always seen as incomplete, there being extensive debate on other possible explanations such as the liquidity trap and problems with investment. In the 1970s, these other concerns about slopes of IS and LM curves faded into the background, leaving wage stickiness as the sole explanation of unemployment. New Keynesians' sought to provide explanations of this, resorting to devices such as long-term or implicit contracts, asymmetric information, and imperfectly competitive labour markets. If New Keynesians' explanations of wage stickiness were rejected, Keynesian economics was rejected too, leaving the field open for theories that allowed no place for the notion of involuntary unemployment (see De Vroey 2004). For those in this camp, Keynes was the economist who theorised about the effects of wage stickiness.

Thus, between 1936 and the end of the century, there emerged many different Keynesian revolutions, each of them with their own Keynes, either claiming his authority as supporting their own theories, or else interpreting him so that their ideas could be presented as successfully challenging his work.

## 3. Keynes's management of his legacy

Keynes often claimed that his work was revolutionary, and after the publication of the *General Theory*, he actively engaged with several of those who were creating what was to become Keynesianism. What one sees in these many engagements is an effort to encourage others to extend his own insights using their new theoretical frameworks.

The most well known is probably his correspondence with Hicks on the chapter that set out what became the IS–LM model. After the *General Theory*, Hicks and others, such as Harrod, were working to incorporate Keynes's model in a general equilibrium framework. Hicks shared his preliminary work with Keynes who responded that he liked what Hicks was doing and encouraged him to continue. Keynes did this even though Hicks specified his model so as to remove the possibility of including expectations, but he did not suggest that this made Hicks's work illegitimate or unworthy of pursuing. Quite the contrary. After reading a draft of Hicks's chapter, Keynes wrote to him that he "found it very interesting and really have next to nothing to say by way of criticism" (JMK XIV, p. 79).

Keynes's correspondence with Abba Lerner reveals the same kind of encouragement. Keynes knew Lerner, a student at LSE, from a year that Lerner had spent as a Rockefeller fellow at Cambridge in the 1930s, and he had given his approval to a sophisticated reworking of the basic model of the *General Theory* in Lerner's review of the book in 1936. By the time of World War II, Lerner had emigrated to the United States where he continued to develop his model of the macroeconomy. Lerner's model was sophisticated, but mechanical, and allowed him to characterise economic management as a simple process akin to driving an automobile. Keynes heard this very mechanistic model expounded during one of his wartime trips to the United States, and found it simplistic as regards policy making and the potential for using government budget deficits to spur the economy. Still, as Colander (1984) has shown, Keynes kept open his channels of communication with Lerner and never discouraged him in his model building, per se. His only qualms regarded the value of the parameters in Lerner's model; he did not criticise Lerner's theoretical efforts.

This list of colleagues whose work he encouraged could be extended. Moggridge (1986, p. 361) draws attention to similar remarks made to Robert Bryce, Brian Reddaway, Roy Harrod and Joan Robinson, correctly noting that these authors were presenting very varied interpretations of the book, almost all of which fell into the category that Joan Robinson later labelled "bastard" Keynesianism. Keynes's ease in encouraging others in their work shows a clear desire on his part to establish his legacy through the development and extension of his work, rather than in demanding some kind a strict adherence to the original form of his ideas. Nowhere in the voluminous correspondence after the publication of his magnum opus does he tell anyone that they must adhere exactly to the form of his models in the *General Theory*. Keynes even took a relaxed attitude to his claim to have effected a revolution in economic theory. Harrod, in 1937, wrote a chapter in which he remarked, "Mr Keynes has not effected a revolution in fundamental economic theory but a re-adjustment and a shift of emphasis"; Keynes's response was to say that he was shortly to present a paper in Stockholm and that he would like to present Harrod's instead of his own (JMK XIV, p. 84; cf. Moggridge 1986, p. 361).

Another story from Keynes's last year shows a different side to his attempts to cultivate his legacy. In conversation with Friedrich Hayek in 1946, Keynes told Hayek that if it were necessary, that he could easily turn the main message of his work, should that be necessary.

> Later, a turn in the conversation made me ask him whether he was not concerned about what some of his disciples were making of his theories. After a not very complimentary remark about the persons concerned, he proceeded to reassure me by explaining that those ideas had been badly needed at the time he had launched them. He continued by indicating that I need not be alarmed; if they should ever become dangerous I could rely upon him again quickly to swing

round public opinion – and he indicated by a quick movement of his hand how rapidly that would be done. But three months later he was dead.

(Hayek 1995, p. 232)

The implication here may be that Keynes's real concern with his legacy rested more in his ability to influence the policy agenda, rather than in a single theoretical message.

This attitude is consistent with his approach towards the emerging field of national income accounting. Keynes was sceptical about the possibility of quantifying economic behaviour but nonetheless encouraged James Meade and Richard Stone in their work on calculating national income. He used such methods in his wartime work on the British budget. But though some of this work, such as calculating the inflation gap and the amount of money that had to be withdrawn from circulation to close the gap (through taxes, compulsory saving or other measures), could be seen as supporting a "hydraulic" Keynesianism, he did not interpret his results in any narrow way.

His attitude here also reflects something that Moggridge (2006) has identified in Keynes's management of his publishing contracts. In circulating his ideas in the United States, Keynes was willing to take risks, even foregoing the protection of copyright, in order to get things into print quickly and to make a greater impact. When he published pieces in the United States, he could not get copyright for them unless the works were physically printed in the United States. Rather than lose the time necessary to reset the type on the other side of the Atlantic, Keynes had his works printed in Britain from the plates that had been made there and then shipped the sheets to the United States for binding.

In the case of American copyright, it was clearly more important to Keynes to have influence, or to influence public opinion, than it was to protect his income stream. His legacy seemed to him to flow more from his ability to impress people with fresh analysis than from a single set of ideas, in a particular form, in place for all time.

## 4. Keynes and orthodox religion

Despite Keynes's use of the rhetoric of revolution after the publication of the *General Theory*, he was not trying to foment just one of the theoretical revolutions that others have attributed to him. He attached great importance to certain intuitions about capitalist society – for instance, the fact of persistent involuntary unemployment, the unstable and erratic behaviour of investors and the possibility of government intervention to improve economic performance – but beyond that he was happy to let others formalise his ideas in different ways and within different theoretical frameworks. This is almost certainly why Keynes was willing to risk his American copyright for his opinion pieces and policy analyses; what mattered to him was his ability to drive home these main points. He had wanted to develop the analytical framework in the *General Theory* to give his insights and policy recommendations more warrant, but they appeared perfectly comfortable to have people develop alternative forms of the theory. If they held on to the fundamental insight that involuntary unemployment was not only possible, but could be represented as an equilibrium position for a capitalist economy, he was happy to have others develop alternative forms of theoretical warrant for the insight.

He would, no doubt, have sympathised entirely with Paul Samuelson's outburst against the "unreconstructed Keynesians" he met at the hundredth anniversary celebrations of Keynes's birth:

> I actually did not like a certain note that I thought I detected at the hundredth anniversary of Keynes's birth, celebrated at the holy of holies, King's College, Cambridge. Person after person got up, walked the sawdust trail and said: 'I am just as firm a Keynesian as I ever was. I am an unreconstructed Keynesian.' And I finally exploded and said: 'We don't want unreconstructed Keynesians. We want people who will carry the scientific analysis further.'

In fact, Keynes was explicit that he did not value holding onto old theoretical constructs when one's basic insights about the economy had changed. By 1937, he was already looking to move on from the *General Theory*, as he explained in a letter to Joan Robinson. He encouraged her go ahead with her book, which he described as "practically following my *General Theory*", but then wrote, "I am gradually getting myself into an outside position towards the book, and am feeling my way to new lines of exposition" (JMK XIV, p. 150). In correspondence with Richard Kahn, Keynes referred to the efforts of Dennis Robertson and A. C. Pigou to hold onto their old theories in the face of their new-found support for public works projects as "a sort of Society for the Preservation of Ancient Monuments" (ibid., p. 259).

This attitude on Keynes's part represents more than simple pragmatism or some kind of petulance with those who disagreed with him.

It follows from his early experience in Bloomsbury where he learned to develop strong opinions while always refusing to hold them up as a new orthodoxy. His friend Roger Fry (1920, p. 188), for example, explained why he never considered a subject finished in words that could have been used by Keynes: "I have always looked on my system with a certain suspicion. I have recognised that if it ever formed too solid a crust it might stop the inlets of fresh experience". They never considered any subject settled. One of the central tenets that underpinned the work of the members of Bloomsbury was the effort to debunk myths and undercut dogma. This trait is evident in their painting, in their novels, in their biographical writings, and in their social commentary. Craufurd Goodwin (1999, 2006) has probably made this feature of Bloomsbury most evident and he has certainly gone further than anyone in demonstrating how the ideal of reason over dogma was as a central to Maynard Keynes's work as it was to that of any other member of Bloomsbury. "Keynes found that the political economy of Great Britain, extending from the nineteenth century into the twentieth, like the rest of British culture cried out for liberation from dogma and superstition" (Goodwin 1999, p. 431). The importance of avoiding dogmatism in economic matters was very clearly expressed in his reaction to an interview published in the *New Statesman* in 1934:

> [George Bernard] Shaw and Stalin... look backwards to what capitalism was, not forward to what it is becoming. That is the fate of those who dogmatise in the social and economic sphere where evolution is proceeding at a dizzy pace from one form of society to another.
> 
> (JMK XXVIII, pp. 32–3)

It was a few weeks after this that he wrote the famous letter to Shaw in which he said that he was writing a book that would "largely revolutionise... the way the world thinks about economic problems" (JMK XXVII, p. 42). However, he immediately observed the theory would be mixed with politics, feelings and passions, and that he could not predict what the outcome would be.

Keynes reluctance to respond to detailed criticisms made by reviewers of the *General Theory* was also characteristic of Bloomsbury. They often did not respond to critics: they just smiled. This was often viewed as snobbery and implying disrespect, which only made the critics angrier. So too with those who worked hard to criticise the *General Theory* (not to mention Hayek, who had been immensely frustrated over Keynes's failure to respond to his earlier criticisms of the *Treatise on Money*).

This reluctance to respond to critics, which Virginia Woolf explored in her novels, may have stemmed from Quaker pacifism (pervasive in Bloomsbury), but it is also consistent with their belief that they should set their ideas free in the world, not letting them become hardened into any orthodoxy.

This desire is evident in the introduction to the *General Theory* when Keynes says that his intention is to help his readers in the "struggle of escape from habitual modes of thought and expression". When Keynes refers to escaping from habitual modes of thought, he immediately makes it clear that the barriers to escape arise from the way that dogma has been ingrained in us. "The difficulty lies, not in the new ideas, but in the escaping from the old ones, which ramify, for those brought up as most of us have been, into every corner of our minds" (JMK VII, viii). Indeed, Keynes explicitly compares Ricardian economics (classical economics) to a religion. "Ricardo conquered England as completely as the Holy Inquisition conquered Spain" (ibid., p. 32) and "One refers to the analogy between the sway of the classical school of economic theory and that of certain religions".

But while Keynes was concerned to place the persistence of involuntary unemployment at the centre of economics, he was intellectually honest in not demanding that the manifestation of this insight be handled in only one way. He refused to be dogmatic about the form of the model that would carry his concerns into the next generation of modellers. In this sense, he seems to also demonstrate an adherence to another Bloomsbury tenet, the respect for and encouragement of creativity. For it is striking that in each of the cases in which he dealt with a younger economist who was trying to expand upon his model in the *General Theory* or re-formulate it, Keynes was generous in his praise and encouraged the efforts.

In this sense, Keynes may have been willing and eager to foment many revolutions, rather than a single one. What he really demanded of economics was that it provide solutions to contemporary economic problems. In his own generation, those problems were recession, depression, unemployment and unnecessary human suffering. If he had a dogmatism, it was that the ultimate value in economics lies in its ability to help humankind beyond these problems to the kind of abundance that he often wrote was the world's real economic destiny. But his sense of revolution against the dogmas that precluded action against economic hardship simply did not extend to a sense on Keynes's part that he had authored a single, "true" revolution. His theoretical eclecticism, his encouragement to others and his open and liberal stance in the face of immense opposition to his work all indicate a man who eschewed dogma. Avoidance of dogma involved being creative and open-minded, but modest at the same time. Thus as well as writing about creating a revolution, he could also write, "If economists could manage to get themselves thought of as humble, competent people, on a level with dentists, that would be splendid!" (JMK IX, 332).

## 5. Keynes and economic theory

Keynes's attitude to the revolution he was attempting to achieve is of a piece with his attitude towards economic theory. There are at least two dimensions to this. The first is that he regarded economics as a "diagnostic" science (Hoover 2006). After World War I, he was a part-time academic, much of his career being spent in government service, economic journalism and portfolio management; thus, a high proportion of his energy was devoted to influencing public opinion. His economics was always driven by a concern with policy. When it came to economic theory, his aim was therefore not to construct a theory for its own sake but to use theory in the service of policy. If existing theoretical tools were serviceable, he used them; if not, he sought to develop new ones. Thus in his early work, such as the *Tract on Monetary Reform* (1923, JMK IV), we see him defining a policy problem and then drawing on such conventional theoretical tools as would allow him to provide a diagnosis and prescribe a cure. He should be seen not as trying to emulate Newton or Einstein but as a doctor or physician, diagnosing problems with the economic body and prescribing solutions. For this purpose, he needed neither theoretical sophistication nor elegance but merely effective theories.

The other dimension to Keynes's attitude towards economic theory is that, as one might perhaps expect from an artist, he attached great importance to intuition (Moggridge 1992, pp. 551–71; Skidelsky 1992, pp. 539–48; Backhouse 1997). One started with intuition or vision – what he called "the grey fuzzy woolly monster" in one's head (Skidelsky 1992, p. 539) and then sought to make this more precise. This meant that the broad structure of an argument would come first and the details would be worked out later. However, whilst he attached importance to these details, and to the clarity that they brought into the argument, he believed that it was impossible to be perfectly precise. The world was vague and complex and could not be captured in a precise model. Keynes explained this towards the end of the *General Theory*

(JMK VII, pp. 297–298; Rymes 1989, p. 101, cf. Backhouse 1997; Hoover 2006).

> It is a great fault of symbolic pseudo-mathematical methods of formalising a system of economic analysis... that they expressly assume strict independence between the factors involved and lose all their cogency and authority if this hypothesis is disallowed; whereas, in ordinary discourse, where we are not blindly manipulating but know all the time what we are doing and what the words mean, we can keep 'at the back of our heads' the necessary reserves and qualifications and the adjustments which we shall have to make later on, in a way in which we cannot keep complicated partial differentials 'at the back' of several pages of algebra which assume that they all vanish. Too large a proportion of recent 'mathematical' economics are merely concoctions, as imprecise as the initial assumptions they rest on, which allow the author to lose sight of the complexities and interdependencies of the real world in a maze of pretentious and unhelpful symbols.

What was most important to Keynes was the overall vision of capitalism, in which economies could get stuck, for long periods of time, in positions of mass unemployment and where management of the level of aggregate demand was a crucial aspect of government activity. He did not encapsulate this vision in a simple model, thus demonstrating that he saw virtue in the construction of economic theory, even if he fully understood its limits. The *General Theory* is replete with mathematical language and argumentation, but its use is strictly limited in two ways. The first is that Keynes offers an intuitive, informal theoretical account of the main relationships (the marginal propensity to consume, the marginal efficiency of capital, liquidity preference and the determinants of the money wage rate). In these informal accounts, he brings in arguments and ideas that could not be represented in the mathematics. Thus, although he was familiar with models of saving such as the one developed by his colleague Frank Ramsey, and with mathematical theories of investment, he chose not to use them. The second is that he did not provide a formal mathematical model of the system *as a whole*: the *General Theory* contains all the components of the IS–LM model, which neatly sums up important ideas in the book, but Keynes chose not to provide this summary because he believed that it would lead to a playing down of ideas that were not expressed in the mathematics.

The main reason why most mainstream economists have been blind to this is that, roughly contemporaneously with the *General Theory* (which arguably contributed to this movement, even if this was not Keynes's intention), economic theory became seen as concerned with modelling (e.g., Morgan 2003 has argued that after the Second World War economics became a "modelling science"). To construct an economic theory became, in the post-war period, to an extent that was not true of the interwar period, to construct an economic model: a logical apparatus, usually represented by equations or a diagram that could be manipulated to generate conclusions. To use an economic theory became to derive the formal, mathematical properties of an economic model. Economists stopped thinking about economic theories as broader, less precisely specified constellations of beliefs about the economy. As a result of this shift, it became hard to see that Keynes was not thinking in this way. As with Milton Friedman, a generation later, Keynes consciously used mathematical arguments to illustrate and develop propositions about a world some of whose *relevant* characteristics could not be represented by the mathematics; and just as Friedman was criticised for not having a theory, so Keynes was criticised for being vague and imprecise.

One of the critics who accused him of being imprecise was Joan Robinson (1973, p. 261). She pointed out that one can argue from assumptions (A) to conclusions (C) or vice versa. A correctly worked-out argument is represented by what she calls the "equilibrium line" that goes from assumptions to conclusions and vice versa. Robinson claims that the *General Theory* is an imperfect version of this: it "has got the equilibrium line in it but Keynes did not rub out all the other lines before he published the book". Her complaint is exactly that Keynes's refused to let go of all those "necessary reserves and qualifications and the adjustments which we shall have to make later on" in order to produce a simple, pared-down model. Many of the other lines of reasoning that Robinson believed should have been rubbed out are an integral part of Keynes's theoretical strategy. Robinson's "equilibrium line" is the equivalent of a theoretical model, and Keynes was not willing to confine himself to such a way of arguing. A more complex picture was necessary in order to express his intuitions about a complex economic world.

However, whilst Keynes did not confine himself to a simple, modern model (the "equilibrium line"), it is important that there still was a model there. For many policy purposes, the model was serviceable. The inflation gap, a theory comparable with the quantity theory in its simplicity, could be used to analyse wartime inflation, and Keynes was happy to produce quantitative estimates of the tax and expenditure policies necessary to avoid inflation. Thus, one can argue that he accepted Hicks's IS–LM model as a representation of a significant part of his argument (perhaps even the "equilibrium line", though there is no necessity to accept this) at the same time as believing that it was not the whole, and that other elements in the *General Theory*, not necessary to derive the IS–LM model, were vital in explaining his vision. He could thus praise IS–LM whilst at the same time writing his *Quarterly Journal of Economics* article. The reason Keynes could behave in this way was that he was engaging in pragmatic, diagnostic theory, not seeking to create the very general theory, honed to the form of a post-war model, that interpreters of the Keynesian revolution have tried to force upon him.

In his lectures during the Michaelmas term, 1933, when he was working out the argument of the *General Theory* in front of his students, he made his approach to theory very explicit.

> What degree of precision is desirable in economics? There is a danger of falling into scholasticism, "the essence of which is treating what is vague as what is precise". A generalisation to cover everything is impossible and impracticable.... Even mathematical thinking is not in terms of *precise* concepts but 'fluffy gray lumps', afterwards you can perhaps discover the *nature* of these 'fluffy gray thoughts' although you can never write it down quite precisely the reason for this is that you are trying to express your theory for those who can't think.
> (Rymes 1989, p. 101; passages in quotation marks are direct quotations of Keynes as noted in Lorie Tarshis's notes)

This coincides quite closely, of course, with Keynes's remark (quoted above) that his intuitions were "the grey fuzzy woolly monster".

This picture of Keynes as an economic theorist is consistent with Austin Robinson's (1947, p. 43) assessment of Keynes's claims to greatness: (1) Keynes had linked academic theory to practical problems of policy at a time when they were in danger of drifting apart; (2) he integrated theoretical and statistical work and (3) he forced Robinson and his contemporaries continually to question the assumptions underlying their theories. Robinson also provides a clue as to how the interpretation being offered here can be reconciled with Keynes's claim to be offering a "general" theory. Keynes's insistence on the need for a general theory was not so much arguing the case for a new "correct" theory as serving to question assumptions that would otherwise have been taken for granted, such as that having more of one thing implied having less of something else (ibid., pp. 44–5). Keynes's own theory may have been more general than "classical" theory, but there was no suggestion in his mind that it was *the most* general theory: generality had been achieved only at the level of his intuition. Robinson found the consistency in Keynes's career to lie in his having placed a set of objectives, pre-eminent among which was full employment of resources, at the heart of the policy agenda.

## 5. Conclusions

One of the main reasons why there has been so much disagreement over who Keynes belongs to is that economists have been trying to do something that Keynes himself was not trying to do, and perhaps was trying to avoid. Keynes was trying to force economists to focus on the problems of mass unemployment and the level of aggregate demand as something central to economics, not something peripheral, that was to be covered by "ad hoc" modifications. He spoke of a "general" theory not because be believed he could offer a completely general theory but because he wanted to challenge economists to question basic assumptions rather than dealing with uncomfortable facts by making ad hoc modifications that contradicted their own basic premises. In doing this, he offered a wealth of new ideas about how theory might be extended. However, what many of his interpreters have tried to do is to push his ideas into a new system that can provide an alternative to the "classical" theory against which he railed. This has typically involved taking a package of his ideas and integrating them into a new system. But this is not what Keynes was trying to do: instead of constructing a new "Keynesian" system, he was trying to refocus the discipline by creating the environment for new, creative theorizing along more helpful lines. In this sense, he was treating his fellow economists in much the way he had treated many of his Bloomsbury friends, as a supporter and patron of new, path-breaking work.

In fact much of Keynes's best work is suffused with the values he learned as a member of Bloomsbury. He is iconoclastic, attempts to shatter myths and seeks to start a new branch of creative work based on different premises than those of his immediate predecessors. But while many variants of Keynesianism have picked up easily on his rhetoric of revolution and his clear desire to nudge his fellow economists in a new direction, few have understood that his work was also informed by the Bloomsbury value of not wishing to establish a new orthodoxy. He wanted to shatter the myths of the "classical theory", but he did not wish to establish a new myth. His openness to the improvisations of others on his basic themes is very much in the vein of a confident artist who has turned the branch and started a new school of painting or sculpture. He knows that others will pick up on his suggestions and develop them in ways that are very different from his own, and he is happy for this to happen. Though he wanted to influence others, he would never have expected anyone to produce exact replicas of his work: that is something that no artist would want.

Seen in this light, Keynes had a method and a self understanding that are foreign to the thinking that came to dominate economics in the post-war period. He did build models, but he did not adopt the pared-down sense of what modelling was about that characterised post-war economics. Theory was, for him, much broader. By trying to make Keynes into a modeller in the post-war sense, and by assuming that he wanted to prescribe what was *the* correct way to think about economic problems – which, if successful, would mean establishing a new orthodoxy – many economists have missed the essence of what Keynes did and how he understood himself.

## Acknowledgements

This chapter follows on from Backhouse and Bateman (2006). We acknowledge our great debt to the contributors of that volume. We thank David Colander and Craufurd Goodwin for comments on early drafts of this essay. At the conference at Santa Columbo, several participants made interesting comments, not all of which we were able to use in revising. We especially thank Sherry Kasper, Colin Rogers, Ned Phelps, Bob Dimand, Matt Forstater, Randy Wray and Sheila Dow.

## Bibliography

Backhouse, R. E. 1997. The rhetoric and methodology of modern macroeconomics. In *Reflections on the Development of Modern Macroeconomics*, ed. B. Snowdon and H. R. Vane, Cheltenham: Edward Elgar: 31–54.
Backhouse, R. E. and Bateman, B. W. (eds.) 2006. *The Cambridge Companion to Keynes*. Cambridge: Cambridge University Press.
Barro, R. J. and H. I. Grossman. 1971. A general disequilibrium model of income and employment. *American Economic Review* 61: 82–93.

Bateman, B. W. 2005. Scholarship in deficit: Buchanan and Wagner on John Maynard Keynes. *History of Political Economy* 37(2): 185–90.

Buchanan, J. and R. Wagner. 1977. *Democracy in Deficit: The Political Legacy of Lord Keynes*. New York: Academic Press.

Clower, R. W. 1965. The Keynesian counterrevolution: A theoretical appraisal. In *The Theory of Interest Rates*, ed. F. H. Hahn and F. P. R. Brechling, London: Macmillan: 103–25.

Colander, D. 1984. Was Keynes a Keynesian or a Lernerian? *Journal of Economic Literature* 22: 1572–5.

De Vroey, M. 2004. *Involuntary Unemployment: The Elusive Quest for a Theory*. London: Routledge.

Fry, R. 1920. *Vision and Design*. London: Chatto and Windus.

Goodwin, C. D. W. 1999. Economic man in the Garden of Eden. *Journal of the History of Economic Thought* 22(4): 405–32.

——— 2006. The art of an ethical life: Keynes and Bloomsbury. In *The Cambridge Companion to Keynes*, ed. R. E. Backhouse and B. W. Bateman, Cambridge: Cambridge University Press.

Hayek, F. A. (ed.) 1995. *Contra Keynes and Cambridge*. The Collected Works of F. A. Hayek, ed. S. Kresge, vol. 9. London: Routledge. (Edited by Bruce Caldwell.)

Hoover, K. D. 2006. Doctor Keynes: Economic theory in a diagnostic science. In *The Cambridge Companion to Keynes*, ed. R. E. Backhouse and B. W. Bateman. Cambridge: Cambridge University Press.

JMK. *The Collected Writings of John Maynard Keynes* ed. D. Moggridge and E. Johnson. 30 vols. London: Macmillan.

Keynes, J. M. (JMK) 1971–1989. *The Collected Works of John Maynard Keynes*. 30 vols. London: Macmillan.

Klein, L. R. 1968. *The Keynesian Revolution*. 2nd Ed. London: Macmillan. First edition, 1944.

Leijonhufvud, A. 1968. *On Keynesian Economics and the Economics of Keynes*. Oxford: Oxford University Press.

Lerner, A. P. 1944. *The Economics of Control*. New York: Macmillan.

Lucas, R. E., and Sargent, T. J. 1978. After Keynesian macroeconomics. In *After the Phillips Curve: Persistence of High Inflation and High Unemployment*, Boston, MA: Federal Reserve Bank of Boston, 49–72.

Moggridge, D. E. 1986. Keynes and his revolution in historical perspective. *Eastern Economic Journal* 12(4): 357–69.

——— 1992. *Maynard Keynes: An Economist's Biography*. London: Routldege.

——— 2006. Keynes and his correspondence. In *The Cambridge Companion to Keynes* ed. R. E. Backhouse and B. W. Bateman. Cambridge: Cambridge University Press.

Morgan, M. S. 2003. Economics. *The Cambridge History of Science, Vol. 7: The Modern Social Sciences*. ed. Theodore M. Porter and Dorothy Ross. Cambridge: Cambridge University Press.

Patinkin, D. 1956. *Money, Interest and Prices*. Evanston, Il: Row, Peterson.

Robinson, E. A. G. 1947. John Maynard Keynes, 1883–1946. *Economic Journal* 57: 1–68.

Robinson, J. V. 1973. *Collected Economic Papers*. Vol. 4. Oxford: Basil Blackwell.

Rymes, T. K. (ed.) 1989. *Keynes's Lectures, 1932–35: Notes of a Representative Student.* London: Macmillan.

Skidelsky, R. 1992. *John Maynard Keynes, Volume 2: The Economist as Saviour, 1920–1937.* London: Macmillan.

Snowdon, B., Vane, H. and Wynarczyk, P. 1994. *A Modern Guide to Macroeconomics.* Aldershot: Edward Elgar.

Snowdon, B., and Vane, H. R. (eds.) 1997. *A Macroeconomics Reader.* London: Routledge.

# 2
# The *General Theory* in Keynes's Biographies

*Maria C. Marcuzzo*

> It may both be true that many things said by Keynes [in the *General Theory*] had been said, or could have been said, in the old terminology, and that his scheme has temped its users into certain errors, and yet remain also true that, on the whole and on balance, his scheme is far superior
>
> – Harrod (1951: 465)

> I must remind the reader that the book is probably the least clear of Keynes's contribution to economics
>
> – Moggridge (1992: 557)

> There are many different ways of telling the story of the *General Theory of Employment, Interest* and *Money*, and many different stories to be told about it.
>
> – Skidelsky (1992: 537)

## Premise

It is perhaps fitting to mark the 70th anniversary of the *General Theory* (*GT*)[1] with an assessment of what we have learned about this work from the vast research undertaken by three biographers of Keynes whose researches on his chapters and correspondence mark them out among scholars for their extraordinary scope and thoroughness. I will compare the analysis of the *GT* in Keynes's three major biographies (Harrod 1951; Moggridge 1992; Skidelsky 1992) in order to assess the views presented there on the genesis of the book, the development of its main ideas and the various "versions" which have been produced ever since. Once set in the context of Keynes's life, does the book prove more intelligible, and if so, in what respects? Can we detect different interpretations of its meaning and significance? On posing these questions and comparing these three biographers' approaches to the subject matter, one should bear in mind that Harrod holds a peculiar position among the three. On the one hand he knew Keynes and participated in the process which led to the *General Theory* (he was also one of the people Keynes entrusted the proofreading to), while on the other hand he could not have full command of the Keynes's chapters, most of which were still uncatalogued and unpublished when he set about writing the biography. Moggridge, of course, enjoyed a very different position since, in his capacity as editor of the *Collected Writings* of J. M. Keynes, he was responsible for much of dating and ordering of the relevant papers, letters and manuscripts. Skidelsky, on the other hand, while claiming that his purpose was to "rescue Keynes from the economists", dedicated considerably more pages to the *GT* than the other two biographers,[2] although largely taken up with the reactions to the book and the criticism it came in for.

In comparing and assessing the biographers' narratives I divide my account into three sections: 1. Origin and purpose; 2. Development and influences and 3. Interpretations and controversies. In the final section I draw some conclusions.

## 1. Origin and purpose

All three biographers agree that the origin of the *GT* is to be found in Keynes's dissatisfaction with his *Treatise on Money*, coupled with an urge to find remedies to the worldwide high level of unemployment. However, they stress different aspects in the scenario against which the book is set and should be placed.

Harrod draws attention to the *readership* the book targeted: "His aim ... was to convert his professional colleagues. He judged that a direct appeal to the people would be in vain, unless it could be reinforced by the majority of economists speaking with one voice" (Harrod 1951: 461). In this respect, the *GT* is presented as a work of persuasion, like many others by Keynes, but with a particular public in mind. Harrod's characterization is indeed borne out by Keynes's warnings in the final pages of the book against being "slaves of some defunct economist" or the danger of "gradual encroachment of ideas" (CWK VII: 383).

Who were the "professional colleagues" he was intent on converting? Certainly D. H. Robertson and F. A. Hayek, who – if judged against their review of the *Treatise on Money* – had proved to him that they "had not in the least understood what he had tried to say" (Harrod 1951: 435), but also A. C. Pigou, L. Robbins and H. Henderson, the professional economists, the representatives of "sound principles" (Mini 1996: 331) with whom Keynes was in constant contact.

According to Harrod the support Keynes was receiving from his closest (and younger) colleagues, R. F. Kahn and J. Robinson, sharpened the contrast with the economists who failed to see what he was getting at, despite his efforts to impress his meaning on them. Perhaps after all they were hardly to be blamed, one could argue, since he was breaking new ground and "raising a dust" (CWK XIII: 548). We know that Harrod, too, from the very outset, when the writing of the *GT* was still being written, was very critical of Keynes's insistence on emphasizing differences between his approach and what he labelled "classical thought". In his biography he volunteers an explanation of Keynes's irreverence towards the established view, as a psychological reaction "to the frustrations he had felt, and was still feeling, as the result of the persistent tendency to ignore what was novel in his contribution" (Harrod 1951: 451).

By "classics" Keynes meant the tradition stemming from Marshall, including that inheritance from British Political Economy which had been filtered into it; this tradition was embodied in the work and teaching of Pigou and Robertson and most of Keynes's colleagues at his Faculty in Cambridge. Keynes was exposed to the views of his fellow economists also in his capacity as editor of the *Economic Journal*, Secretary of the Royal Economic Society and in his multifarious academic and non-academic endeavours. Most aptly it has been said that

> Keynes was an educator. His classroom was England and the world, and his tools were the newspaper article, the pamphlet, the letter to *The Times*, the radiobroadcast, the committee testimony and, occasionally, the technical books and journal articles addressed to economists. In pursuit of this mission, he gained knowledge by participating in economic committees, by questioning those in authority, by partying and conferring with statesmen, bankers, politicians and those 'in the know'.
> 
> (Mini 1995: 49)

He was well acquainted with the ethos of the profession and in disagreement with most of it, especially in the late 1920s and early 1930 when important issues, such as rationalization of the cotton industry, trade and exchange rate policy and remedies for unemployment were being debated. He censured the majority of the economic profession for their inability to change habits of mind which, when added to the "habits and instincts of the ordinary man, bred into him for countless generations" (CWK IX: 327), made engagement in experiments conducive to practical results even more difficult.

Economists did not enjoy top ranking in Keynes's scale of values and appreciation,[3] but to persuade them he had to meet them on their own ground. The sense of frustration Keynes was experiencing is borne out in many instances during the drafting of the *GT* and in the aftermath, offering some support for Harrod's interpretation. A famous letter to Lydia, in October 1933, gives us a glimpse into Keynes's state of chagrin: "Are all the economists mad except Alexander [R. F. Kahn] and me? It seems to me so, yet it can't be true" (quoted in Moggridge 1992: 566).

For his part, Skidelsky insists on another of Keynes's main concerns, namely the threat facing civilization, i.e. freedom and democracy, with the rise of the two totalitarianisms of the 1930s: "The General Theory was projected against the background not just of the world depression, but of its political and social repercussions: specifically, the spread of communism and fascism" (Skidelsky 1992: 440). There is no doubt that in the 1930s Keynes was shocked at the discovery that many of his friends were turning to Marx, and that on many occasions he voiced his aversion to Marx and his economic theory. His opposition to fascism is equally beyond question; the Preface to the German edition of the *GT* cannot be interpreted as implicit support of the Nazi economic experiment (Schefold 1980). Still, it is difficult to assess how strongly he felt the seriousness of the threat and to what extent he was endeavouring to get through to a readership that was politically committed to a totalitarian creed.

Certainly, in the book he praised the advantages and virtues of capitalist individualism: "The authoritarian state system of today seem to solve the problem of unemployment at the expense of efficiency and of freedom... it may be possible by a right analysis of the problem to cure the disease whilst preserving efficiency and freedom" (CWK VII: 381). However there are passages in which individualism is portrayed as the culprit of many failures in market economies,[4] so perhaps it was in the realm of economic, moral and civil liberties, that Keynes was pursuing his agenda, in many respects at variance with traditional liberal stances (see Dostaller 1998; Vercelli 2010). The threat was not only the dangers of advancing totalitarianisms, but also those deriving from excessive much reliance on the market system. While Keynesian policies are wrongly characterized as synonymous with government intervention, his cure of "socializing investment" to sustain aggregate demand can rightly be adduced as evidence of his mistrust of market mechanisms (Bateman 2006). How much anti-liberal *politics* and how much anti laissez-faire *economics* is behind the GT is perhaps still an open question.

Moggridge, on the other hand, draws attention to Keynes's deep dislike of those premises in economics which are found out to be false or ill-conceived: "[his] emphasis on assumptions or premises also provides a large part of the explanation of why he abandoned his *Treatise on Money* so quickly" (Moggridge 1992: 555). Indeed many instances can be found in the GT of Keynes's argumentative logic against "the classical theory" based on the accusation of holding "tacit assumptions [that] are seldom or never satisfied" (CWK VII: 378) such as the "illicit assumption" that "the wage bargain determines the real wage" (ibid.: 13) or their "fallaciously supposing" that an act of individual saving leads to an act of investment (ibid.: 21). This aversion to false premises applied to his own theory as well, and this may explain why Keynes was at times found to be inconsistent with his previously held views.

What, then, was so wrong with the assumptions of the *Treatise* that Keynes, within a year of its publication, felt he had to abandon them? I have argued elsewhere (Marcuzzo 2002) that basically he had misgivings about the Fundamental Equations, i.e. the assumed independence of the price level of consumption goods from that of investment goods, which came under fire both from his opponents (Pigou and Robertson) and from his closer associates (Kahn and Sraffa). However, astonishing as his readiness was to accept the need to revise his assumptions (and eventually to discard the Fundamental Equations), in the end he could not resist presenting his new book as a "natural evolution" in his line of thought (CWK VII: xxii).

He laboured to make his former approach appear compatible with the latter and was always careful to indicate *where* exactly his new argument departed from the old. First, there was the change in the definition of income (ibid.: 61); second, there was a new mechanism for output adjustment (ibid.: 77); and third there was determination of the equilibrium level of output at less than full employment (ibid.: 77–8). Thus, reinterpreting his former approach based on the Fundamental Equations in the light of the latter, based on Effective Demand, Keynes claimed to have established compatibility between his two books (see Marcuzzo 2003). Moggridge argues that "one should accept Keynes's retrospective account of how he came to his conclusions" (Moggridge

1992: 559). However I feel that in the case of these two books he was stretching the continuity of his approach a bit too far.

## 2. Development and influences

Thanks to his editorship of Keynes's *Collected Writings*, Moggridge was better placed to provide the most detailed account of the development of Keynes's ideas towards the *GT* and trace out the stages through which concepts and argument took various forms and final shape. His narrative is extremely accurate and well grounded on evidence coming from drafts, correspondence, table of contents and lecture notes, only a part of which is published in vols. XIII and XIXX of the *Collected Writings*. There are alternative reconstructions – as found in the literature (see Patinkin 1973, 1996) – but Moggridge's is to be considered the benchmark chronology.

The five years spanning from the publication of the *Treatise* to that of the *General Theory*, can be divided into three time-legs. The first dates from comments and criticism on the *Treatise* (autumn 1930) to the early material for the new book and lectures (spring 1932). The second spans from the Easter Term 1932 lectures, which were attended by members of the "Circus", to the summer 1933, when the writing of the new book was well under way. The final stage runs from the 1933 Michaelmas Term lectures and the contemporary fragments of versions of the *GT*, when the principle of effective demand was clearly expounded, to the final touches to the proofs in December 1935.

Disagreement among scholars about the development of Keynes's ideas towards the *GT* can be grouped into two headings, namely the list of steps leading to it and the evidence agreed upon to support it. Perhaps the issue which has attracted more attention is *when* Keynes arrived at the formulation of the principle of effective demand. Most commentators (Dimand 1988: 167; Moggridge 1992: 562; Patinkin 1993: 656) agree that by Michaelmas term 1933 the conception of effective demand had been accomplished; more disputed is whether the supporting argument, namely that a change in investment causes a change in saving, was present even in the 1932 drafts. For instance, Moggridge's dating of these fragments was questioned by Patinkin (1975, 1993) on the grounds that description of the equilibrating role of changes in output does not appear in the November 1932 lecture notes (Rymes 1989). I have argued elsewhere (Marcuzzo 2002) that I have not found enough evidence to support Patinkin's claim.

Skidelsky's account follows the same line as Moggridge's, but he makes an important methodological point in passing:

> [the] scholarly obsession with timetabling the *flow* of intellectual invention... also reflects an agenda which is not historiographical or methodological. Involved are the linked questions of the relative value of *Treatise* and the *General Theory* and the whole corpus of Keynes's writings; the relationship between Keynes's work and that of the that of the other monetary economists of his day; and what the "main point" of the General Theory was.
> (Skidelsky 1992: 444–5)

In fact when it comes to tracing out the influence of his fellow economists in the process which led Keynes toward the *GT*, nuances in the accepted chronology become marked historiographical differences. Skidelsky, like Harrod,[5] plays down the importance of the Circus[6] and gives more credit to Kahn and Hawtrey. Moggridge, on the contrary, takes the view that:

> Kahn certainly deserves Keynes's glowing acknowledgement in the Preface to the General Theory. Yet the surviving materials show that Keynes was in control. He chose the destination and the main route. His colleagues and collaborators tried to keep him from unnecessary logs, and to improve his sketch map for his successors – but not always successfully.
> (Moggridge 1992: 569–70)

Harrod's narrative is intertwined with autobiographic threads, since he was directly involved in the process of commenting on the *GT*, from the early stages through the proofs. "My main endeavour" – he claims – "was to mitigate his attack on the 'classical' school... [in particular] in regard to his allegation that the traditional theory of interest did not make sense" (Harrod 1951: 453). In the biography he defends the point which he had made at the time, namely that Keynes was "in some confusion about what the classical position really was" and that he claimed "for his definition of the marginal efficiency of capital more originality than can be accorded to it" (ibid.).

There are two questions here. The first is how accurately the biographer – who happens to be contemporary with his subject – is able to recount the process of development of ideas at the time and to assess the nature of his own contribution; the second is whether his argument about Keynes's theory of interest rate stands up to criticism.[7] On these two issues the literature provides us with a good deal of evidence. Daniele Besomi has convincingly argued that Harrod's role as commentator upon the *GT* in the making, if judged against the extant correspondence, shows that "at several crucial stages in the evolution of Keynes's thought Harrod was unaware of the developments taking place" (Besomi 2005: 92). Moreover the exchange they had between June and September 1935 on the proofs "bear witness to the incompatibility of their viewpoints" (ibid.: 98), both in terms of methodology and substantive issues.

On the question of the rate of interest, there is no agreement in the literature as to whether Keynes had entirely freed himself from the basic marginalist ideas about the decreasing ordering of investment projects because of diminishing returns and the inverse relationship between investment and interest rate.[8] It seems to me that Harrod acknowledges "the importance of expectations in this connection" (Harrod 1951: 453), but he misses Keynes's point about the "conventional" nature of the interest rate which qualifies it as a monetary phenomenon, unlike the classical theory which anchors it to the productivity of capital.

Moggridge does not address this issue – simply noting that by 1933 Keynes "had the glimmerings of the marginal efficiency of capital, as distinguished from marginal productivity of capital" (Moggridge 1992: 561); Skidelsky devotes quite a few pages to the topic, concluding that "The fundamental unity between Keynes's liquidity-preference theory of interest and the rest of his ideas in the *General Theory* lies at the instinctive, or visionary level" (1992: 563). Thus, against conceptual difficulties, interpretation of the theory shifts towards interpretation of the man, which is not an uncommon outcome in biographies.

## 3. Interpretations and controversies

The underlying ambition which I found common to Harrod, Moggridge and Skidelsky (and perhaps to any biographer) is to find a key to Keynes's mind and understand how it worked. In doing so they came to stress different qualities of his intellect and personality both in general and in the *GT* in particular.

Harrod's point is Keynes's *consistency*. "I detect" – he wrote – "a most remarkable consistency in the development of his theories and practical proposals, from his early studies in the Indian currency to the *General Theory*" (1951: 467). Consistency here is seen as a feature of Keynes ever ready to change ideas, in the pursuit of truth, to open up new paths, to give himself up to new discoveries.[9] Many words are spent defending

Keynes from the charge of being inconsistent throughout his work and in his policy promoting. Moreover, Harrod seems to be interpreting consistency as continuity, thus embracing the thesis which lately has gained a lot of favour in the literature (see Davis 1994), when he states that "the careful student is able to trace a natural evolution of ideas from his early writings to the great system set out in the *General Theory*". No clues, however, are given to the reader about the elements which could be brought in to confirm or disconfirm the "continuity" thesis.

Moggridge lays great emphasis on Keynes's *intuition* in general, and specifically on working out the *GT*: "in the development of particular idea for the *General Theory* it is clear that he had intuitively grasped the essentials of many of them quite early" (Moggridge 1992: 552). Moggridge insists that for Keynes "intuition ran ahead of analysis", and that for him economics required "appeal to intuitions", not proofs as in mathematics, alluding here to the wider issue of the methodological differences in natural and moral sciences to which Keynes attached great importance.

In the same vein, but in a slightly different sense, Skidelsky points out to the *artistic* aspect of Keynes, in particular as far as the *GT* is concerned; he described it as "as work of art and imagination as well as economic logic [...] an invitation to thought rather than a machine for solving crises" (1992: 538).

These differences in characterizing Keynes's intellect add to their shared belief that the driving force behind it was an urge to persuade and a deep involvement in policy-making.[10] In a related chapter (Marcuzzo 2008) I examined the central role of persuasion in Keynes's work as a means to change the environment within which individuals operate – so that moral and rational motives become the spring of action of the collectivity as a whole – and to induce behaviour to conform to goals that were attainable only by moving beyond individualistic motivation or utilitarian calculation. As Samuel Brittan aptly noted, Keynes "never lost hope that morality and permeation of ideas could be relied upon to disseminate enlighten thinking after, at worst, a lag of generation" (Brittan 2006: 182).

There is no doubt that the *GT* is better portrayed as a study in *persuasion* rather than in *policy making*, offering a set of recipes or rules to be followed in all circumstances. Skidelsky warns against the dangers of "reading off Keynesian policy prescriptions from a single book" (1992: 319) and in particular the misreading of the *GT* as a eulogy of fiscal policy. He argues, however, that notwithstanding Keynes's own resistance to "premature formalisation of his theory [...] the reduction of theory to model was inseparable from its triumph as a tool of policy" (ibid.: 548)

Harrod's viewpoint on the role of models in economics was very far from Keynes's, as is borne out by the exchange they had on this matter (see Besomi 2005). He does not attempt to present the main propositions of the *GT* in model-like form and mentions only in passing that at the time he had "supplied a diagram purporting to reconcile the classical theory with [Keynes's] theory" (Harrod 1951: 453). In a footnote, however, he mentions his *Econometrica* article (Harrod 1937) said to be "a summary account of the doctrines of the *General Theory*, for consideration by professional economists" (ibid.).

Moggridge takes pains to present Keynes as not putting "great faith in the simple-minded application of ideas from particular models" (Moggridge 554), but does not commit himself to any "interpretation" of the *GT*, thereby coming in for criticism from some reviewers (see Blaug 1994; Dimand 1993). We have, however, other sources to evaluate his position. Unlike the case of Harrod, with whom Moggridge in very few cases disagrees over matters of facts and interpretation – apart from the trenchant line in a footnote referring to "Harrod's general attempt to make Keynes's views conform with it" (1992: 573n) – he took issue with the way in which Skidelsky dealt with many aspects of Keynes's life and work in general and the *GT* in particular (Moggridge 2002a, 2002b). The verdict is clear-cut: "Skidelsky's treatment of the General Theory is post-Keynesian" and shows "a lack of engagement with the literature on nineteenth-century economics" (2002a: 640, 642). Keynes – in Moggridge's view – was disposed to accept the formalisation of his theory "in terms of a simple three-equation, two identity model" as formulated on more or less similar lines by Hicks, Lange, Reddaway, Champernowne, Harrod, Meade and Lerner (ibid.: 641). This assertion has him siding more with Harrod than with the Post-Keynesians (and Kahn and Joan Robinson for that matter) in not rescuing the *GT* from its subsequent developments.

Finally, Moggridge claims that "Skidelsky has been overly preoccupied" (ibid.: 653) with Harrod's biography, implying perhaps that he was not preoccupied with his. In fact there are not many "Moggridge" entries in the index to the three volumes by Skidelsky and I am not aware that Skidelsky responded to Moggridge's criticism of his trilogy. On the contrary, an entire section in the last chapter of the third volume by Skidelsky (2000) is devoted to Harrod's biography and how it was received at the time of its publication, with no comments, unfortunately, on Harrod's analysis of the *GT*.

## Some concluding remarks

We have seen that there are many layers in the readings of the *GT* by Keynes's biographers, to which one could also add the various assessments their accounts were received in the literature. All three biographies prompted a great many reviews by professional economists and historians, who naturally had critical remarks to make on some aspects of them. Pollard (1994: 140–1) rightly points to the different evaluation of the *Treatise on Money* vis-à-vis the *GT* in Skidelsky and Moggridge; while the former maintains that Keynes's "classical achievement" is the 1930 book, the latter gives the highest marks to the 1936 book. Laidler (2002: 102) argues that "Skidelsky manages to place more emphasis on the heterodox element in Keynes's economic thought than the overall record perhaps justifies". Dimand (1993: 996) criticizes both Skidelsky and Moggridge for not making "proper use" of Rymes (1989) as "rich source of insights into the writings of the General Theory", and argues that in general Keynes's most important book is not given the full treatment it deserves in Moggridge's biography. Also Blaug (1994: 1210) observes that, surprisingly, Moggridge "declines to enter into a discussion of the what-Keynes-really meant literature". Harcourt and Turnell (2005: 4937), on the other hand, with reference to Skidelsky, claim that "Readers with little or no prior knowledge of why the *General Theory* was so significant [...] will go away with a clear idea of its momentous importance and impact at the time it was written."

It seems to me that, having compared the accounts of the *GT* in these three biographies, we may conclude that they differ in some important aspects. The first is what we can term their biographical style. Moggridge is the professional historian of economic thought who is looking for evidence, context, dating and, as it were, steps back from the tasks of both textual exegesis and modelling. Skidelsky is more engaged in producing a narrative which is historically accurate, but which also digs into the personality of his author, searching for clues to access his inner feelings, motivations and even unconscious drives. Harrod is the "official" biographer, mindful of the responsibility of portraying his author according to the sensibility of his time, but he is also the affectionate admirer of the master who was his contemporary. The second aspect is what we can call their expertise, or even comparative advantage, in approaching the subject. Moggridge is the professional historian of economic thought, knowledgeable about facts, circumstances and people, who set up the necessary framework to place the *GT* within the development of economics as a discipline. Harrod is the economist, engaged in his own research program which differed in scope and content from Keynes's, who is trying to convey the *GT* to a general public, but bearing also in mind the professional reader. Skidelsky is the historian with a superb command in story-telling, very versed in twentieth-century British culture, who is attempting to give his readers a summary of the book, taking care of its enduring fascination, the reactions it prompted and the controversies it still produces.

It would be vain to conclude this comparison by giving marks to each of the biographers in the attempt to establish which of them best performed the task of presenting the *GT* both to the practitioner of the subject and to the layman. In an article of some years ago Gerrard (1991: 286) argued that we should not be "worrying about the multiple interpretations" of the *GT* since its continuing achievement consists precisely in the "ability to generate a diversity of research program". Similarly, perhaps, we should have no worries about being confronted with further attempts to frame the *GT* within the life of John Maynard Keynes[11] as long as new material is brought to the fore. Changing readings of the *General Theory* have always been monitored in the professional literature (see recently Dimand 2009) either by reinstating what was believed to be its true meaning and message, or by denouncing its supposed failures and misgivings (see De Vroey 2004). The contribution of biographers – to place the book in its context, both in the life of Keynes and in his times – is not a minor task of scholarship, although not exhaustive. This should also be kept under scrutiny, to monitor what needs to be discarded or abandoned in their accounts. In the future additional evidence from various people's papers, correspondence and manuscripts may turn up, supporting or disproving the present historical reconstructions; in history, as in science, there are no results that cannot in principle be revised.

The layers of interpretation of the book – the original text, Keynes's own account, the biographer's story, and the heaps of reviews assessing them all – thus make appraisal of it on the occasion of the 70th year since publication a complicated, but no less intriguing and enticing undertaking.

## Notes

1. In 2006 a number of events were held to celebrate the anniversary of the *General Theory* and commemorate Keynes's death ten years later; this burst of activity took a heavy toll on scholars who had perhaps too readily accepted the invitation to take part in them, untroubled by the danger of repetitions and overlapping in what they had to say. This was certainly my case, as I later

discovered that by taking part in these celebrations I had committed myself to writing 3 chapters on Keynes in a very short period of time. I have tried my best to make this chapter a complement to rather than a substitute for the other two companion pieces (Marcuzzo 2006, 2008).
2. In Moggridge the *GT* is covered in two chapters amounting to 53 pages, while the two chapters devoted to it in Skidelsky come to 87 pages.
3. See Keynes's often quoted remark: "The study of economics does not seem to require any specialised gifts of an unusually high order. Is it not, intellectually regarded, a very easy subject compared with the higher branch of philosophy and pure science? Yes good, or even competent, economists are the rarest of birds. An easy subject at which very few excel" (CWK X: 173).
4. See for instance what he wrote in 1933: "The decadent international but individualistic capitalism, in the hands of which we found ourselves after the War, is not a success. It is not intelligent, it is not beautiful, it is not just, it is not virtuous – and it doesn't deliver the goods" (CWK XXI: 239).
5. "in the writing of the book itself, his main pillar of support was Mr. Richard Kahn" (Harrod 1951: 451).
6. "Despite much 'pooled memory' to the contrary, the Circus seems to have played a relatively minor part in the development of the *General Theory* [...] the most important effect of the Circus discussion was to reinforce the impetus Hawtrey gave Keynes to working out a short-period theory of output [...] much more important than Circus's collective contribution to Keynes's progress was Kahn's personal contribution" (Skidelsky 1992: 447).
7. One reviewer of Harrod's biography acutely remarked that one has "to disentangle three things: (1) Harrod's account of Keynes's economics; Harrod's own recent economics; and Keynes account of Keynes's economics" (Wright 1952: 392).
8. Pasinetti (1977: 60) argues that the ordering of investment projects cannot be assimilated to the marginal reasoning of neoclassical vintage, being closer to the Ricardian principles of ordering of land on the basis of degree of fertility; on the contrary Bonifati and Vianello (1998: 103) argue that Keynes remains faithful to the marginalist tradition according to which as the rate of interest decreases more capital – intensive production processes are adopted as an effect of the "scarcity" principle.
9. "There is little doubt that he would not have rested content in the position that he had achieved in 1935 anymore than Ricardo, whose mind was also continually moving forward, would have rested content with the last edition of the *Principles*" (Harrod 1951: 473).
10. "Keynes was passionately concerned with policy; so were most of those who took up the *General Theory*" (Skidelsky 1992: 617).
11. For a very recent one see Dostaller (2007).

# References

Bateman, B. (2006), Keynes and Keynesianism, in R. Backhouse and B. Bateman (eds), *Cambridge Companion to Keynes*, Cambridge: Cambridge University Press, pp. 258–71.

Besomi, D. (2005), A goodwilling outsider. The correspondence between Keynes and Harrod, in M. C. Marcuzzo and A. Rosselli (eds), *Economists in Cambridge. A Study Through their Correspondence, 1907–1946*, London: Routledge.
Blaug, M. (1994), Recent Biographies of Keynes, *Journal of Economic Literature* 32: 1204–15.
Bonifati, G. and Vianello, F. (1998), Il saggio d'interesse come fenomeno monetario e il saggio di rendimento del capitale impiegato nella produzione, in M. C. Marcuzzo and N. De Vecchi (eds) *A cinquant'anni da Keynes: Teorie dell'occupazione, interesse e crescita*. Milan: Unicopli.
Brittan, S. (2006), Keynes's political philosophy, in R. Backhouse and B. Bateman (eds), *Cambridge Companion to Keynes*, Cambridge: Cambridge University Press, pp. 180–98.
Davis, J. B. (ed.) (1994), *The State of Interpretation of Keynes*, Boston: Kluwer Academic Publisher.
De Vroey, M. (2004), *Involuntary Unemployment: The Elusive Quest for a Theory*, London: Routledge.
Dimand, R. (1988), *The Origins of the Keynesian Revolution*, Aldershot: Edward Elgar.
Dimand, R. (1993), Review of Moggridge and Skidelsky, *The Canadian Journal of Economics* 26: 993–9.
Dimand, R. (2009), What Keynesian Revolution?, Chapter 15 of this volume.
Dostaller, G. (1998), Néolibéralisme, keynésianisme et traditions libérales, *Cahiers D'épistémologie*, Cahier n° 9803, UQAM: Montréal.
Dostaller, G. (2007), *Keynes and His Battles*, Cheltenham: Elgar.
Gerrard, B. (1991), Keynes's *General Theory*: Interpreting the interpretations, *Economic Journal* 101: 276–87.
Harcourt, G. C. and Turnell, S. (2005), On Skidelsky's Keynes, *Economic and Political Weekly* Nov 19: 4931–45.
Harrod, R. F. (1937), Mr. Keynes and Traditional Theory, *Econometrica* 5: 74–86.
Harrod, R. F. (1951), *The Life of John Maynard Keynes*, London: Macmillan.
Keynes, J. M. (1971–1989), *The Collected Writings* (CWK), D. Moggridge (ed.), London: Macmillan.
CWK, VII, *The General Theory of Employment, Interest, and Money*.
CWK, IX, *Essays in Persuasion*.
CWK, X, *Essays in Biography*.
CWK, XIII, *The General Theory and After: Preparation*.
CWK, XXI, *Activities 1931–1939 World Crises and Policies in Britain and America*.
Laidler, D. (2002), Skidelsky's Keynes: A review essay, *The European Journal of the History of Economic Thought* 9: 97–110.
Marcuzzo, M. C. (2002), The collaboration between J. M. Keynes and R. F. Kahn from the *Treatise* to the *General Theory*, *History of Political Economy* 34: 421–47.
Marcuzzo, M. C. (2003), From the fundamental equations to effective demand: "natural evolution" or "change of view"?, in P. Arestis, M. Desai and S. Dow (eds), *Methodology, Microeconomics and Keynes: Essays in Honour of Victoria Chick*, vol. 2, London: Taylor and Francis, 26–38.
Marcuzzo, M. C. (2006), Keynes and Cambridge, in R. Backhouse and B. Bateman (eds), *Cambridge Companion to Keynes*, Cambridge: Cambridge University Press, pp. 118–35.

Marcuzzo, M. C. (2008), Keynes and persuasion, in M. Forstater and L. R. Wray (eds), *Keynes for the 21st Century: The Continuing Relevance of the General Theory*, London: Palgrave Macmillan, 2008, pp. 23–40.

Mini, P. V. (1995), Keynes' Investments: Their relation to the *General Theory*, *American Journal of Sociology* 54: 47–56.

Mini, P. V. (1996), Maynard Keynes: An economist's biography, A Review Article, *American Journal of Economics and Sociology* 55: 327–35.

Moggridge, D. (1992), *Maynard Keynes: An Economist's Biography*, London: Routledge.

Moggridge, D. (2002a), Skidelsky on Keynes: A Review Essay, *History of Political Economy* 34: 633–55.

Moggridge, D. (2002b), "Rescuing Keynes from the Economists"?: The Skidelsky Trilogy, *European Journal for the History of Economic Thought* 9: 111–23.

Pasinetti, L. (1977), *Sviluppo economico e distribuzione del reddito*, Bologna: Il Mulino.

Patinkin, D. (1975), The Collected Writings of John Maynard Keynes: From the *Tract* to the *General Theory*, *Economic Journal* 85: 249–71.

Patinkin, D. (1993), On the Chronology of the *General Theory*, *Economic Journal* 103: 647–63.

Pollard, S. (1994), New Light on an Old Master, *Economic Journal* 104: 138–53.

Rymes, T. K. (1989), *Keynes's Lectures, 1932–1935*. Ann Arbor: University of Michigan Press.

Schefold, B. (1980), The General Theory for a Totalitarian State? – A note on Keynes' preface to the German edition of 1936, *Cambridge Journal of Economics* 4: 175–6.

Skidelsky, R. (1992), *John Maynard Keynes: The Economist as Saviour 1920–1937*, London: Macmillan.

Skidelsky, R. (2000), *John Maynard Keynes, Volume 3: Fighting for Britain, 1937–1946*. London: Penguin.

Skidelsky, R. (2002), *John Maynard Keynes. Fighting for Britain, 1937–1946*, London: Macmillan.

Vercelli, A. (2010), *Mr. Keynes and the "Liberals": A Suggested Interpretation*, Chapter 4 of this volume.

Wright, D. M. (1952), Review of Harrod, *The American Economic Review* 42: 392–5.

# 3
# The Legacy of Keynes as Public Intellectual

*Sherry D. Kasper*

Today the name John Maynard Keynes usually evokes thoughts of his book *The General Theory* and the revolution in macroeconomic theory and policy it inspired in the United States. Yet, in his 22, April 22, 1946 obituary, the *New York Times* only refers in passing to *The General Theory* in a long list of Keynes's books, instead focusing on him "as a political and social economist who influenced both specialists and general public" (*New York Times*, 1946). Much of the *Times'* tribute is devoted to Keynes's impact as the author of *The Economic Consequences of the Peace* (1919). He "first won public attention" with his departure from the Paris Peace Conference and publication of the book three months later:

> The book created a storm of controversy but was so widely in demand that it ran five editions the first year and was translated into eleven languages.[1] Lord Keynes was not again associated with the British government in any official capacity until the spring of 1940, by which time much of what he had prophesied had come true.
> 
> (New York Times 1946)

The book's "sensation" was due in part to its revealing portrait of the conference, but the *Times* also noted "its lucid literary style". Subsequently its ideas captivated US President Franklin Delano Roosevelt.

It is tempting to rely on several easy explanations for the *Times'* focus on *The Economic Consequences*. Clearly, the timing of Keynes's death, a mere 10 years after the publication of *The General Theory* and at the beginning of the Keynesian Revolution played a role. Likewise, the audience for a *New York Times* obituary called for a more general tribute, because it was written for the public rather than a small group of economic theorists. Nonetheless, the 1946 emphasis on Keynes as communicator of ideas to general audiences begs clarification, particularly because a careful study of his life and works reveals that he took on this role as a critical responsibility for the academic economist.[2]

Contemporary expression describes individuals, like Keynes, who communicate erudite ideas to a general audience as "public intellectuals". This term appears to have entered the language after World War II. Many attribute its coinage to sociologist C. Wright Mills, who in *The Causes of World War Three* charged academics to abandon their middle class lives and "act as political intellectuals... as public intellectuals" (Mills 1958, p. 135). Russell Jacoby became a noted popularizer of the phrase in his book *The Last Intellectuals: American Culture in the Age of Academe*, defining these individuals as "writers and thinkers who address a general and educated audience" (Jacoby 1987, p. 5). Richard Posner in his 2001 book *Public Intellectuals: A Study of Decline* concurred with Mills about the political content of the work: "the [public] intellectual writes for the general public, or at least for a broader than merely academic or specialist audience, on 'public affairs' – on *political* matters in the broadest sense of the word, a sense that includes cultural matters when they are viewed under the aspect of ideology, ethics, or politics..." (Posner 2003, p. 23). Economist R. Glenn Hubbard added a criterion of effectiveness to his definition: "It is when experts speak meaningfully to an audience broader than their colleagues that they enter the realm of public intellectual" (Hubbard 2004, p. 392). Thus, as we explore the legacy of Keynes as public intellectual, we will draw on these definitions and concentrate on his work that included a broadly defined political aspect of some consequence and that is effectively addressed to a general and learned audience.

## Keynes as Public Intellectual

Keynes began his careers as economist and public intellectual at the same time. Upon earning a degree in mathematics from Cambridge in 1905, he spent one term studying economics with Alfred Marshall. He entered the British Civil Service in 1906, working in the India Office. He returned to Cambridge as a lecturer in economics in 1908 and soon after published his first article for a general audience in *The Economist*. He described this event in a letter to Duncan Grant in February 1909:

> Oh, I don't think I told you that I've taken to Journalism. Last Tuesday night I received a letter enclosing an article about "Shippers,

Bankers and Brokers" from the Economist...and asking if I would write a letter on it "suggestive and provocative" as soon as possible. I seized my pen and had dispatched a reply within an hour and a half of opening the request. Today I open my Economist and find it, a column long, in the leading position, and the Editor [F. W. Hirst] writes to say that he will treat it as a contribution. So I shall get at least a guinea.

(Keynes in Skidelsky 1983, pp. 206–7)

Keynes apparently liked seeing his ideas in print, because he let Grant in on his plan: He would send Hirst an article he had written for the *Economic Journal*, "Recent Economic Events in India", and sell himself as "an occasional correspondent on Indian affairs" (Keynes in Skidelsky 1983, p. 207). He went on that year to act as an advocate of free trade, writing articles in the *New Quarterly* and the *Cambridge Daily News*, speaking at the Cambridge Union, and giving campaign speeches for Hilton Young and Edwin Montagu during the election of 1909 (Skidelsky 1983, pp. 206, 228 and 241–2).

*India Currency and Finance* was the first book Keynes wrote for a general audience. In 1912, the India silver scandal led an anonymous Indian writer in *The Times* to allege political corruption and the House of Commons to call for an investigation of the Indian Monetary System. Keynes initially responded by writing a letter to *The Times* to refute points made by the "Indian Correspondent". An official in the Indian Office subsequently characterized his comments as "the best statement on our side that has yet appeared" (Skidelsky 1983, p. 273). Keynes then temporarily stopped work on his probability manuscript and turned earlier lectures given at the London School of Economics and Cambridge into a short book to explain how the Indian Monetary System functioned. Since the book was both "expert and respectable", Keynes was invited to serve on the Royal Commission on Indian Currency and Finance (Skidelsky 1983, p. 274).

In August 1914, England declared war on Germany. Prior to returning to government work in the Treasury in 1916, Keynes continued advocating his positions on wartime financial issues in *The Morning Post* and *The Economist*. His public-intellectual work began again when he left the Paris Peace Conference in June 1919 in despair, convinced that the terms of the proposed treaty would create massive economic problems for post-World War I Europe. Five months later he published *The Economic Consequences of the Peace*, once again an outsider writing for the general public on a political issue of consequence.

Throughout the 1920s, Keynes continued to establish his credentials as public intellectual, speaking on issues of the day that ranged from a the peace treaty and war debts, to a return to the gold standard, postwar price fluctuations and the onset of the Great Depression. He gave up his lectureship at Cambridge in 1919 to spend weekdays in London working on "publicist and political activities" (Patinkin 1987, p. 38). He became an economic journalist, writing over 300 articles in popular publications, including the *New Statesman*, *The Manchester Guardian* and *The Economist* (Patinkin 1987, p. 38). He joined forces with Cambridge-trained economist Hubert Henderson in reviving the *Nation* to popularize the positions of the Liberal Party (Skidelsky 1992, pp. 22, 134). He wrote hundreds of letters to editors of newspapers and weeklies. And despite his embarrassment over his voice and physical appearance, Keynes continued to speak to the public – speeches, radio addresses and sessions at the Liberal party's summer schools. This decade of work culminated in the 1931 publication of *Essays in Persuasion*, a collection of what Keynes considered his most important work as public intellectual, all of which he wrote "*in a hurry*, desperately anxious to convince his audience in time" (Keynes 1931, p. vi, emphasis in original).

In the 1930s, Keynes moved away from his public-intellectual work, concentrating instead on developing economic theory. In 1930, he published *A Treatise on Money*, a book he had written alongside his journalistic endeavours during the 1920s. Ultimately, he was not satisfied with the book. He began working out the ideas that culminated in *The General Theory*, a book that as Keynes notes in his introduction he had written for an academic audience:

> At this stage of the argument, the general public, though welcome at the debate, are only eavesdroppers at an attempt by an economist to bring to an issue the deep divergences of opinion between fellow economists which have for the time being almost destroyed the practical influence of economic theory, and will, until they are resolved, continue to do so.
> 
> (Keynes 1936, p. vi)

After publication of *The General Theory*, Keynes continued his public-intellectual work on a smaller scale. For example, his 1939 pamphlet on *How to Pay for the War* influenced the discussion about controlling inflation. But he was sick with heart disease by this time, and he focused his waning energy on fighting the financial World War II and setting up the world monetary system after the war (Skidelsky 2000).

Keynes's talents were in great demand, and he put a great deal of energy and effort to communicating with the public about momentous issues of his times. The unanswered question remains: Why did he decide to allocate his time to serving as a public intellectual? In the pre-*Economic Consequences* years, Skidelsky argued that Keynes used public-intellectual work in two ways. Initially, he aimed "to display his professional competence" as an economist (Skidelsky 1983, p. 206). Once World War I began, he "wanted an occupation connected with the war", and "his writing" provided this job until he went to the Treasury (Skidelsky 1983, p. 293). Elizabeth Johnson stated that Keynes's withdrawal from the Paris Peace Conference signified his transformation into advocacy: "[H]e gave up his influential role behind the scenes and emerged into the limelight as a publicist and propagandist. For the rest of his life he was to be occupied with successive attempts to persuade the world to come round to his own way of thinking" (Keynes 1977, p. 3). Skidelsky offered a slightly different explanation that added a translator aspect to Keynes's public-intellectual work. With publication of *The Economic Consequences*, Keynes followed:

> a pattern which had already started with Indian Currency and Finance – that of interpreting the official minds for the educated public, and bringing the force of enlightened opinion to bear on political action. The view he would expound, as in his earlier book, was that of the informed insider, but one who was just ahead of the possibilities of action.
>
> (Skidelsky 1983, pp. 377–8)

Keynes's own words provide partial support for the interpretation of Skidelsky as translator and advocate. In essence, Keynes stated that that enlightened, private individuals like him had a duty to change public opinion so that political leaders could implement appropriate policy changes. Keynes also added an evolutionary dimension to his justification. With World War I, he believed that capitalism had moved to a crucial stage in its development. To insure its survival, changes in the relationship between the government and the economy had to occur, which required the intervention of specialists as public intellectuals. We will discuss each of these two aspects in turn.

Keynes's first explanation for his interest in public-intellectual work highlighted its potential for advocacy. As Keynes explained to Grant in 1909, after publishing his first journalistic article, to continue: "[to] offer myself... as an occasional correspondent on Indian affairs... would give me an anonymous pulpit for anything on the subject which would come into my head" (Keynes in Skidelsky 1983, p. 207). When he described to economist Herbert Foxwell why he wrote *Indian Currency*, his explanation highlighted his expertise: "But their [the India Office] difficulty is that none of them connected with the place who make speeches understand the currency" (Keynes in Skidelsky 1983, p. 273). When he wrote *The Economic Consequences*, his justification continued with its emphasis on expertise and advocacy and added duty, both on an emotional and a philosophical level. Just before he left the Peace Conference, he had offered his services to Jan Smuts, another British representative to the Conference, to help him explain the peace treaty to the public and initiate a protest against it. When Smuts decided to sign the Treaty, Keynes took on the leading role as educator and dissenter. Immediately, he began writing *The Economic Consequences*, suggesting through comments to his mother that his impetus to return to public-intellectual work was an emotional response to the Treaty: "I was stirred into it by the deep and violent shame which one couldn't help feeling for the events of Monday [when Allies ended discussions about charging reparations]" (Keynes in Skidelsky 1983, p. 377). Later in comments to a reviewer, he stated: "I have come bluntly to feel that the best thing in all circumstances to speak the truth as bluntly as one can" (Keynes in Skidelsky 1983, p. 382).

In *The Economic Consequences* his self-assessed, ineffective participation as Treasury representative to the Paris Peace Conference had convinced Keynes that he could not change "the deliberate acts of statesmen" ([1919] 1971, p. 188). As a result, he wrote the book with the exalted purpose to "change *opinion*... [through] the assertion of truth, the unveiling of illusion, the dissipation of hate, the enlargement and instruction of men's hearts and minds" ([1919] 1971, p. 188 emphasis in original). With this book, not only did he hope to influence a "new generation [who] has not yet spoken,... [but also] the formation of the general opinion of the future" ([1919] 1971, p. 188). Twelve years later in the Preface to *Essays in Persuasion*, Keynes reiterates this point: "... it was in a spirit of persuasion that most of these essays were written, in an attempt to influence opinion" (Keynes 1931, p. v).

Keynes's adoption of a strategy to change opinion from the outside rather than policies on the inside rested on two primary foundations: (1) the ways in which humans made predictions and (2) the role of statesmen versus specialists in utilizing these forecasts. He first presented these ideas in the context of his response to Paris Peace Conference.[3] According to Keynes, a fundamental characteristic of humans was "to become habituated to [their] surroundings" believing what they observed and experienced was a permanent, rather than temporary, form of social organization (1931, p. 3). In reality, social conditions change. Since they rely on habitual understandings of their environment, reasonable humans made errors about forecasting the future effects of policy changes in changing economic circumstances:

> The secular changes in man's economic condition and the liability of human forecast to error are likely to lead to mistake in one direction as in another. We cannot as reasonable men do better than base our policy on the evidence we have and adapt it to the five or ten years over which we may suppose ourselves to have some measure of prevision.
>
> (1931, p. 14)

Keynes drew on these ideas to explain why the public was demanding what he viewed as illogical and potentially destructive war reparations. The public perceived incorrectly that the well-endowed Germany, to which they had become habituated before the war, would be paying reparations, rather than the actual, economically devastated Germany that existed after the war (Keynes 1931, pp. 14–7).

In a chapter entitled "The Change in Opinion" in *A Revision of the Treaty*, his 1921 sequel to *The Economic Consequences*, Keynes explained how modern democracies caused statesmen to advocate policies based on the bad forecasts of their constituents:

> It is the method of modern statesmen to talk as much folly as the public demand and to practice no more of it than is compatible with what they have said, trusting that such folly in action as must wait on folly in word will soon disclose itself as such, and furnish an opportunity for slipping back into wisdom' (Keynes 1931, p. 46). Thus, one explanation for Lloyd George's actions during the Paris Peace Conference was the democratic statesman's requirement to meet 'the demands of the mob' (1931, p. 47). In contrast, 'private individuals [like Keynes] are not under the same obligation to sacrifice veracity to the public weal'; in addition, they can "speak and write freely" (1931, p. 48).

In "My Early Beliefs", an essay written in 1938 but published posthumously in 1949 after his death, Keynes attributed his feelings of "obligation" to speak the truth to the pivotal influence of *Principia Ethica* on his generation of undergraduates at Cambridge. Keynes stated that his generation accepted Moore's notion of religion as "one's attitude towards oneself and the ultimate" (436; vol. 10). Their religion became the struggle to develop good states of mind, which "consisted in communing with objects of love, beauty and truth", to ask the right questions so that they could apply a logical calculus to answer them, and to remain faithful to "the calculus and mensuration and the duty to know *exactly* what one means and feels..." (Keynes [1933]1972, pp. 438, 440, 442). Keynes believed that this "religion" ultimately was limiting and one geared to the young, as it led him and his fellows to live solely in the present, engaging in a life of "passionate contemplation" rather than a life of action ([1933] 1972, p. 445). At the same time, late in his life, Keynes admitted his continuing religious faith in the essential rationality of humans, and he drew on this belief to explain why he continued to engage in public-intellectual work:

> I still suffer incurably from attributing an unreal rationality to other people's feelings and behaviour (and doubtless to my own). There is one small but extraordinarily silly manifestation of this absurd idea of what is 'normal', namely the impulse to protest – to write a letter to The Times, call a meeting in the Guildhall, subscribe to some funds when my presuppositions as to what is 'normal' are not fulfilled. I behave as if there really existed some authority or standard on which I can successfully appeal if I shout loud enough – perhaps it is some hereditary vestige of belief in the efficacy of prayer.
>
> ([1933] 1972, p. 448, emphasis in original)

In summary, Keynes seems to have believed that a knowledgeable private individual possesses a moral responsibility to persuade essentially rational people of the truth, if they are relying on ill-formed opinions derived from bad forecasts.

To Keynes the responsibility to serve as public intellectual seemed to become especially important when social organization was at a crucial stage in its evolution. Keynes believed that this was the state of capitalism after World War I. Initially, he attributed this evolution to the devastating impact of postwar fluctuations in the value of money. In *The Economic Consequences*, he noted that inflation had caused some producers to earn windfall profits causing in the public mind, the constructive entrepreneur of an earlier era to turn into a detested profiteer. In addition, he observed that as "the real value of currency fluctuates wildly from month to month, all permanent relations between debtors and creditors, which form the ultimate foundation of capitalism, become so utterly disordered as to be almost meaningless; and the process of wealth-getting degenerates into a gamble and lottery" (1931, pp. 77–8). In the 1923 *Tract on Monetary Reform*, he highlighted the negative impact of inflation on savings of the middle class and its subsequent alteration of the distribution of income among classes. In Keynes's estimation, this loss of financial security would inevitably "modify the social psychology" of saving for a middle-class individual "who neither spent nor 'speculated,' who made 'proper prevision for his family', who sang hymns to security and observed most straitly the morals of the edified and the respectable injunctions of the worldly-wise" (1931, p. 91). With price fluctuations affecting class relations, speculative behaviour and income redistribution, Keynes believed that the "social and economic order of the nineteenth century" was breaking down (1931, p. 79).

By 1924 Keynes moved to study how changes in the profit motive had affected the evolution of capitalism. He observed that modern humans did not behave as the natural law principles underlying *laissez faire* presumed. For example, divine intervention did not insure that private and social interests coincide, nor was self-interest always enlightened. Rather modern capitalism "depend[ed] upon intense appeal to the money-making and money-loving instincts of individuals" (1931, p. 319). As a result, he believed that "the moral problem of our age is concerned with the love of money, with the habitual appeal to the money motive in nine-tenths of the activities of life" (1931, p. 308).

Clearly by the end of the 1920s, Keynes was discouraged by capitalism, by the loss of its moral underpinnings and the dislocations caused by the lengthening slump. Yet, as his work with popularizing the ideas of the Liberal Party demonstrated, he never wanted to abolish the capitalist system. In fact, by the end of the decade, he evinced great optimism that the economic problem of scarcity could be solved.[4] This optimism pervades his 1930 essay "The Economic Possibilities for Our Grandchildren". He reiterated these sentiments as the "central thesis" of the *Essays in Persuasion*:

> the profound conviction that the Economic Problem, as one may call it for short, the problem of want and poverty and the economic struggle between classes and nations, is nothing but a frightful muddle, a transitory and an unnecessary muddle. For the Western World already has the resources and the techniques, if we could create the

organization to use them, capable of reducing the Economic Problem, which now absorbs our moral and material energies, to a position of secondary importance.

Thus the author of these essays...still hopes and believes that the day is not far off when the Economic Problem will take the back seat where it belongs, and that the arena of the heart and head will be occupied, or re-occupied, by our real problems – the problem of life and human relations, of creation and behavior and religion.

(1931, p. vii, emphasis in original)

It is important to note how Keynes's public-intellectual work affected his economics. Late in his life, Sir Alec Cairncross, a student in the 1930s, reported how his teacher described the advent of his original ideas:

I remember particularly a lecture in 1933 when [Keynes] tried to convey how new ideas were born. Never did they arrive, he said, with the hard edges that later critics came to attribute to them when trying to define their terms. Ideas were apt to be like fluffy balls of wool with no fixed outline, and the relationship between concepts when first perceived was likely to be equally woolly. Keynes mistrusted intellectual rigor of the Ricardian type as likely to get in the way of original thinking, and saw that it was not uncommon to hit on a valid conclusion before finding a logical path to it.

(Cairncross 1996, p. 76)

Patinkin reiterated this point. For example, the public works programs Keynes recommended in *The General Theory* appeared first in 1924 articles in *Nation and Anthenaeum* and in a pamphlet jointly written with Hubert Henderson "Can Lloyd George Do It?" for the 1929 election (Patinkin 1987, p. 33). Likewise, Skidelsky has argued that many of Keynes's ideas "sprang from what he called 'vigilant observation' of the world around him" (1992, p. 174). For example, the first time he described the economy as "stuck in a rut" was in 1924 articles in *The Nation* (Skidelsky 1992, p. 184). Keynes's public-intellectual work provided an important mechanism for this vigilant observation. In the *Essays in Persuasion*, one can observe Keynes grappling with many of the ideas that will eventually lead to his "struggle of escape from habitual modes of thought and expression" underlying the General Theory (Keynes 1936, p. viii).

## Keynes's Legacy as Public Intellectual

A legacy has a dual meaning: something that is handed down and something that remains from a different generation. So, what instruction did Keynes, as public intellectual, hand down to a different generation of American economists? He stated the following:

- Economies and their supporting institutions change.
- The public makes forecasts based on their habitual understanding of the social organization, including the economy and its supporting institutions.
- In democracies, policy makers must follow the demands of public opinion.
- A specialist has an ethical obligation to participate in public discourse to change ill-formed public opinion so that statesmen in democratic societies can change policies.

Several implied features of this legacy are also important to note:

- Unlike the general public, specialists possess enlightened self-interest and will work to change public opinion for the good of all.
- The specialist has a vision of the future towards which the change in public opinion is oriented – in his case, Keynes wanted to preserve capitalism but realized that the government must become more involved for this to occur.
- Public-intellectual work can stimulate the specialist to develop new theory.

What remains of Keynes's legacy in America as a public intellectual stands out in stark contrast, because, many of its essential qualities seem lost. Reflect first on the early years of the Keynesian Revolution. Young people who encountered Keynes at Cambridge in the early 1930s brought the Keynesian Revolution to America, initially to Harvard. Canadian undergraduates Robert Bryce and Lorie Tarshis were captivated by what they learned attending Keynes's lectures and reading and discussing papers in his Political Economy Club. Bryce returned to Harvard in 1935 for two years of graduate study and spread these ideas in a student discussion group he organized. In 1938 Tarshis wrote *An Economic Program for American Democracy* with other younger Harvard economists, a book that even intrigued Franklin Roosevelt. In 1937

Alvin Hansen, in his 50s, was appointed the Littauer Professor of Economics at Harvard. He made the unusual decision to change his mind about economic theory and became one for the few older leaders of the Keynesian Revolution. He played a pivotal role by running a seminar about Keynesian economics with John Williams, a gathering that soon forged links between Harvard professors and Washington policy makers (Colander and Landreth 1998, pp. 4–9). As David Colander and Harry Landreth described: "By the early 1950s the economics journals were filled with Keynesian models, the Committee for Economic Development (CED) had signed on, Samuelson's text book was published and would become the model for future texts, and the three-part revolution was essentially complete" (1998, p. 9).

Note that Colander and Landreth interpret the American Keynesian Revolution as having three parts, which they categorize as theoretical, political and pedagogical (1998, p. 9). No mention is made of a revolution in the way that young American economists talked to the public. In fact, when thinking of economists who acted as public intellectuals during the years of the Keynesian consensus, only John Kenneth Galbraith stands out as an individual with ties to Keynesian economics. The other economist notable in this regard is Milton Friedman, who played a pivotal role in the counter-revolution to Keynesian economics and policy, in part by communicating with the public through books, magazine and newspaper articles and a television show.

Two discussions about public intellectuals, one specific to Keynes and the other general to economists, are also instructive about the loss of the Keynesian legacy of public intellectual. First, in his investigation, Posner presented Keynes and *The Economic Consequences* as a dead model of a public-intellectual effort. He describes the book an exemplar of good work: "[It] is written at a level that a general audience would have no difficulty comprehending and is as much a political, in places a journalistic, work as a work of economic scholarship" (Posner 2003, p. 21). Yet, unlike modern examples, the book was "prescient" and "influential.... It foresaw the economic dislocation that the Versailles Treaty...would visit on Germany and Europe generally; and while it did not persuade the victorious powers to revise the treaty, it may have helped to avert a repetition of the treaty's mistakes after World War II" (Posner 2003, pp. 21–2). Thus, Posner seems to agree that the Keynesian legacy has vanished.

A more recent example of the lost legacy occurred in a session at the 2004 meetings of the American Economic Association. Hubbard categorized modern public intellectuals as filling three roles. Translators provide clear and simply exposited explanations of economic ideas, drawing on both their expertise and ability to communicate. Outreach public intellectuals draw on longstanding programs of research to explain the relevance of economic ideas for the broader political and social context. Symbolic public intellectuals speak to issues broader than the discipline (Hubbard 2004, pp. 392–3).

Keynes's public-intellectual work certainly would have met the standards of the translating and the symbolic roles. Obviously, he could not serve in the outreach role as his public-intellectual work predated his program of research. In the later article, Hubbard did not set out the criteria for success as public intellectual in a symbolic role, but in his AEA presentation, he jokingly said: "Need not apply". Thus, Hubbard also seemed to believe that it was not possible to aspire to the level of symbolic public intellectual, the legacy that Keynes certainly left; these individuals cropped up, but could not be produced following the instructions of Keynes.

So if Keynes left economists with directives for becoming public intellectuals, why did so few take on this role during the years of the Keynesian consensus? Further, why are public intellectuals no longer prescient or influential, as Posner claims, or why does Hubbard not recommend economists to apply for symbolic status? A beginning explanation focuses on three factors: (1) the change in media outlets, (2) the specialization of knowledge (3) and the increase in the cynicism of society's thinkers.

An obvious answer for the loss of public intellectuals of the type of Keynes is the rapid increase in media outlets to communicate with the public, at the same time academics have lost the skills necessary to accomplish this exchange successfully. For example, in a recent forum on the future of the public intellectual, sociologist Herbert Gans noted that modern media outlets demand numerous "quote-suppliers to legitimize the media" that are filling time on cable TV stations, radio and the Internet ("Future", *The Nation*, 2001). Gans called these individuals disciplinary public intellectuals, "the people who apply the ideas from their disciplines to a general topic", similar to the level of outreach described by Hubbard. The criterion for success is to write and speak clearly, unfortunately "a rarity in the academy" (Gans in "Future"). Posner agreed with Gans's point, noting that success in communication among academics required much time and study and a radically different skill set than that which would make academics successful public intellectuals (2003, p. 57). As a result, even as the media demands more experts, in fact, very few academics can move effectively beyond the translator role described by Hubbard.

Interestingly, even in the 1920s, Keynes already viewed new media outlets as providing an opportunity for public intellectuals to change public opinion. For example, in an article in *The Radio Times*, he commented that radio broadcasting seemed "one of the best opportunities now available of doing something for the political education of a big public" (1977, p. 474). The growth of the press had led to extensive coverage on political speeches, but not in a way that politicians could "expound his ideas before the big public in coherent or continuous argument" (1977, p. 474). To offset this tendency, Keynes recommended using radio broadcasts as a means of spreading "political information and argument" with the goal of providing a more comprehensive coverage of the big ideas to the public (1977, p. 475). Unlike modern academics, he possessed the skills to do so.

Why do so few modern academics have the ability to communicate clearly to the public? In their studies of the decline of public intellectuals, Jacoby and Posner pointed to the specialization of knowledge. In essence, this trend caused "the habitats, manners, and idiom of intellectuals [to] transform" since the heyday of Keynes in the 1930s (Jacoby 1987, p. 6). Consider the milieu in which Keynes lived while he wrote *The Economic Consequences* as described by Posner:

> A person of Keynes's ability today would not have accrued the governmental experience that Keynes acquired by 1919..., would not have hobnobbed with the leading political figures of the day, would not possess Keynes's intellectual breadth, and would be a specialist, a technician, disinclined to address large issues of foreign and security affairs in terms intelligible to a lay audience. The minuteness of the English educated elite in Keynes's day also fostered an ease of movement across its various departments.
>
> (Posner 2003, p. 22)

Skidelsky's description of Keynes's life confirms this picture of his environment – he had a remarkable opportunity and capacity to move from the lawns of Cambridge to the halls of government to the financial edifices of the City to the editorial offices of newspapers and weekly magazines to the communal homes of the Bloomsbury group.

After World War II, the habitats of American intellectuals became universities.[5] They began to leave what 1950s public intellectual Irving Howe and later Jacoby called bohemia, "fragile urban habitats of busy streets, cheap eateries, reasonable rents, and decent environs" (Jacoby 1987, pp. 28, 82). Bohemian urban centers, such as New York's

Greenwich Village and San Francisco, had nurtured public intellectuals, providing them with an enriched, fluid environment to develop and exchange a breadth of ideas. When urban renewal, slums, expressways and suburbs damaged bohemia, the intellectuals dispersed. As Jacoby noted: "The difference [in habitat] is critical: a hundred artists, poets, and writers with families and friends in ten city blocks mean one thing; scattered across ten states and ten university towns, they mean something else" (1987, p. 28). Or, in other words, they lost the "common intellectual culture" that enabled Keynes to move so easily among so many groups (Posner 2003, p. 55).

As American intellectuals moved to the universities, their manners and idiom also changed. To achieve material success and professional stature, academics now had to write for each other in specialized journals and monographs using the often-arcane language of their specialized disciplines (Jacoby 1987, p. 6; Posner 2003, pp. 56–7). In the process, they shifted discussion to different issues using a distinct language from that of the general public.

Economists were no exception. Their conventions of rhetoric changed. Few would describe modern economists in the way that Skidelsky described Keynes as a writer who possessed "the indispensable civil servant's gift for producing crisp, lucid memoranda at a moment's notice" and "spoke like an angel with the knowledge of an expert" (1983, p. 299; 1992, p. 3).

Their methods of analysis transformed. Unlike Keynes, they focused their efforts on developing skills as mathematical theorists and econometricians. They often worked from the tools provided by Keynesian wunderkind Paul Samuelson in his 1947 *Foundations of Economic Analysis*, what Robert Lucas later called "the bible for his generation of economists" (1999, p. 146). In the process, the uncertainty implicit in Keynes's ideas about forecasting was removed from most macroeconomic models, first through assumptions of adaptive expectations and later rational expectations. In addition, mainstream economists virtually abandoned the interwar pluralism in economic theory that included the evolutionary analysis Keynes drew on to justify his work as public intellectual.[6]

The audience for economic work narrowed. By 1970, Nobel laureate Wassily Leontief was chastising his fellow economists for abandoning "the wider public" in favor of constructing sophisticated models that had limited application to real problems and became quickly outmoded (1985, p. 272). He predicted this trend would continue, because young economists were quickly learning that they could "advance their careers by building more and more complicated mathematical models" (1985, p. 284). In the early years of the Keynesian Revolution, economists followed Keynes in considering policy makers, if not the public, as an important segment of their audience. They aimed to answer the questions policy makers were asking and made their work accessible to these individuals. But by the early the 1980s, Lucas, the new classical economist who helped lead the Keynesian counter-revolution, even criticized this practice as non-scientific:

> There's a feeling, and I guess I've helped encourage it, among a lot of younger people that politics and the political role that economists play has had a very bad effect on macroeconomics. A lot of older economists seem to me to be solely concerned with politics, as opposed to scientific matters. People are asking the wrong questions; they are taking questions from Washington, rather than thinking about what's puzzling them or taking more scientific points of view.
> (Lucas in Klamer 1983, p. 52)

Note that with this recommendation, Lucas turned what Keynes learned from his public-intellectual work on its head. For Lucas, intellectual rigor activates original thinking, not the "fluffy balls of wool with no fixed outlines" that came in part from his public-intellectual work and ultimately inspired Keynes to develop the general theory.[7]

In 2001, Stephen Carter of Yale Law School offered a third explanation for the demise of the Keynesian legacy – a cynicism in America about the possibility of the pursuit of truth. He argued that:

> there's no sense that there are truths and ideas to be pursued. There are only truths and ideas to be used and crafted and made into their most useful and appropriate form. Everyone is thought to be after something, everyone is thought to have some particular goal in mind, independent of the goal that he or she happens to articulate. And so, a person may write a book or an article or make an argument, and people wonder, they stand up in the audience and they say, 'So, are you running for office, or are you looking for some high position?' There's always some thought you might be after something else.
> ('Future' 2001)

Certainly the success of public choice theory helped to create a degree of this cynicism. Nobel Laureate James Buchanan and others had developed influential models that suggested policymakers made decisions to enhance their own self-interest rather than to serve the public interest, in contrast to how Keynes had assumed the expert behaved when communicating to change public opinion. But also present in Carter's view of modern public discourse is a loss in the belief that the truth and ideas can be pursued. This depiction stands in stark contrast with the Utopian vision that guided the public-intellectual work of Keynes. He worked from a basic truth – that capitalism was the best system to promote efficiency and freedom and, if correctly engineered by the specialists, it could be harnessed in such a way to solve the economic problem of scarcity in a mere hundred years.

## Implications of the Lost Legacy

Early in his life Keynes, a man of many talents, took on the role of public intellectual with seemingly missionary zeal. He believed that the world was changing, and thinkers of his caliber had an ethical responsibility to use their abilities to correct ill formed public opinion so that statesmen would have the political base to alter policy. Yet, only a few of the next generation of economists followed in his lead, and probably only Friedman was successful in changing public opinion to the extent that Keynes did. What has society gained and lost from the demise of the public intellectual of Keynes's type?

The movement of American intellectuals to the university is certainly a key factor in this story. While damaging to the intellectual habitat that nurtured Keynes, this change was not all bad. In the 1950s, Lionel Trilling characterized this movement as a sign of cultural progress, because public intellectuals were no longer the poor and living on the fringes of society, but rather financially secure and active participants in intellectual discourse (Jacoby 1987, p. 78). Furthermore, the increase in universities resulting from the democratization of education after World War II allowed women and religious and ethnic minorities access to institutions of higher learning. This occurrence certainly is positive, because a more broadly representative population now has the possibility to expand the "common intellectual culture" described by Posner. In Keynes's time, one gets the sense that the public discourse in which he participated took place among a small group of the elite.

Nonetheless, the movement of American intellectuals to the university also caused a greater specialization of knowledge, a trend that has decreased the pool of thinkers available for public-intellectual work. First, unlike Keynes, economists cannot develop their skills as translators of economic ideas, because they will not keep their jobs, and, hence, their financial security and professional stature. Second, unlike Keynes, current standards of practice limit access to public-intellectual work to those who have longstanding programs of research. Keynes did not complete his serious research until after many years of work as an effective public intellectual. His success as one of the original economic thinkers of the twentieth century makes one question what novel and potentially life-changing ideas the society is missing due to these changing conventions of practice.

As he left the Treasury, Keynes toasted economists as the trustees of the possibility of civilization. It seems only remotely possible that a modern American economist would evince such bravado, and it perhaps it is this aspect of the lost legacy that is most dismaying. Today, just as at the end of World War I and during the Great Depression, the modern world needs original thinkers. It needs people that can inform the public about the momentous issues of the day so that a more civilized world will become possible.

## Acknowledgements

The author thanks Roger Backhouse, Bradley Bateman, Philip Cardinale, Kara Kasper and participants in the conference on "Keynes General Theory after Seventy Years" for helpful comments on earlier drafts of this chapter.

## Notes

1. The first English printing sold out in 48 hours. In the United States, the first printing of 20,000 sold out immediately and established success of new publisher Harcourt Brace and Howe. It was translated into German, French, Dutch, Flemish, Danish, Swedish, Italian, Spanish, Roumanian, Russian, Japanese and Chinese. Five months after its publication in May 1920, 100,000 copies were sold (Keynes 1977, pp. 15, 51).
2. Richard J. Kent also notes Keynes's importance as a public intellectual: 'Keynes was as much a public intellectual as he was an economist,' emphasizing in particular 'his appearances as lecturer' (Kent 2004, p. 195).
3. Because Keynes was finishing the *Treatise on Probability* in the years after World War I, it seems reasonable to conjecture that his ideas in this project came to bear on his thinking about the formation of public opinion as he wrote and talked about impact of the Treaty of Versailles. While interesting and important, Keynes's discussions about probability were nuanced and complex and explication of them will take this essay away from its focus on the legacy of Keynes of public intellectual. Interested readers should review Skidelsky's summary of this discussion in the Keynes's biography (1992, pp. 82–9).

4. Keynes provided some hints about the source of this optimism in "My Early Beliefs" where he stated that his generation was more resilient than subsequent ones and that his King's group at Cambridge was always more cheerful than those at Trinity ([1933] 1972, pp. 436, 441). Skidelsky argued that Keynes's optimism came from his economic analysis that the capitalist system "was not sick but unstable," and a that a revival of "animal spirits" could end the slump (1992, p. 279).
5. For example, Jacoby noted that the number of college teachers grew ten times from 1920 to 1970, while population of the United States only doubled (1987, p. 14).
6. The term "interwar pluralism" comes from the work of Mary S. Morgan and Malcolm Rutherford (1998).
7. See Kasper (2002) for extended discussion of changes in American macroeconomic theory during the twentieth century.

## References

D. C. Colander and H. Landreth, eds. (1998) *The Coming of Keynesianism to America: Conversations with the Founders of Keynesian Economics*. Cheltenham, UK, and Brookfield, VT: Edward Elgar.

A. Cairncross (1996) "John Maynard Keynes," *The Economist*, April 20–26, 75–6.

"The Future of the Public Intellectual: A Forum" (2001), *The Nation*, February 12, http://www.thenation.com/doc/20010212/forum.

R. G. Hubbard (2004) "The Economist as Public Intellectual," *Journal of Economic Education* Fall: 391–4.

R. Jacoby (1987) *The Last Intellectuals: American Culture in the Age of Academe*. New York: Basic Books.

S. D. Kasper (2002) *The Revival of Laissez-Faire in American Macroeconomic Theory: A Case Study of the Pioneers*. Cheltenham, UK, and Northampton, MA: Edward Elgar.

R. J. Kent (2004) "Keynes's Lectures at the New School for Social Research," *History of Political Economy* 36:1, 195–206.

J. M. Keynes ([1919] 1971) "The Economic Consequences of the Peace," in *The Collected Writings of John Maynard Keynes*, D. Moggridge, ed., Vol. II. London: Macmillan, and New York: Cambridge University Press, for the Royal Economic Society.

J. M. Keynes (1931) *Essays in Persuasion*. London: Macmillan.

J. M. Keynes ([1933] 1972) "Essays in Biography," full text with additions in *The Collected Writings of John Maynard Keynes*, D. Moggridge, ed., Vol. X. London: Macmillan, and New York: Cambridge University Press, for the Royal Economic Society.

J. M. Keynes (1936) *The General Theory of Employment, Interest and Money*. New York: Harcourt Brace Jovanovich.

J. M. Keynes (1977) "Activities 1920–1922: Treaty Revision and Reconstruction," in *The Collected Writings of John Maynard Keynes*, E. Johnson, ed., Vol. XVII. London: Macmillan, and New York: Cambridge University Press, for the Royal Economic Society.

J. M. Keynes (1981) "Activities 1922–1929: The Return to Gold and Industrial Policy," in *The Collected Writings of John Maynard Keynes*, D. Moggridge, ed., Vol. XIX. London: Macmillan, and New York: Cambridge University Press, for the Royal Economic Society.

A. Klamer (1983) *Conversations with Economists*. Totowa, NJ: Rowman and Allan.

W. Leontief (1985) "Theoretical Assumptions and Nonobserved Facts," in *Essays in Economics*, W. Leontief, ed., New Brunswick, NJ: Transaction Books, 272–82.

R. E. Lucas, Jr. (1999) "Interview," in *Conversations with Leading Economists: Interpreting Modern Macroeconomics*, B. Snowdon and H. R. Vane, eds., Cheltenham, UK, and Northampton, MA: Edward Elgar.

M. S. Morgan and M. Rutherford, eds. (1998) *From Interwar Pluralism to Postwar Neoclassicism*. Durham, NC: Duke University Press, Annual Supplement to *History of Political Economy*.

C. W. Mills (1958) *The Causes of World War Three*. New York: Simon and Schuster.

*New York Times* (1946) "Lord Keynes Dies of Heart Attack," *New York Times*, April 22, www.nytimes.com/pages/obituaries/index.html.

D. Patinkin (1987) "John Maynard Keynes," in *The New Palgrave: A Dictionary of Economics*, J. Eatwell, M. Milgate, and P. Newman, eds., Vol. 3. London: Palgrave Macmillan, 19–41.

R. A. Posner (2003) *Public Intellectuals: A Study of Decline*. Cambridge, MA: Harvard University Press.

R. Skidelsky (1983) *John Maynard Keynes, Hopes Betrayed, 1883–1920*, Vol. 1. New York: Viking.

R. Skidelsky (1992) *John Maynard Keynes, The Economist as Savior, 1920–1937*, Vol. 2. New York: The Penguin Press.

R. Skidelsky (2000) *John Maynard Keynes, Fighting for Freedom, 1937–1946*, Vol. 3. New York: Viking Penguin.

# 4
# Mr Keynes and the "Liberals"

*Alessandro Vercelli*

> A study of the history of opinion is a necessary preliminary to the emancipation of the mind. I do not know which makes a man more conservative – to know nothing but the present, or nothing but the past
>
> – Keynes, 1926, *The End of Laissez-Faire*

## Introduction

In the *General Theory* (1936; henceforth GT), Keynes conflated the long and variegated tradition of mainstream economists since Adam Smith into a single category: the "classics".[1] This extreme simplification has never been accepted by Keynes's critics or most of his followers, as this wide and apparently indiscriminate category blurs fundamental distinctions between different pre-Keynesian schools of thought. In particular it even blurs the basic and widely held distinction between the classical economists, in the usual meaning of proponents of a labour theory of value (such as Smith, Ricardo and Mill), and the neoclassical economists who supported the marginal utility theory of value (as Marshall, Walras and Pareto). Keynes was of course fully aware of this and other crucial distinctions and his decision to ignore them in the GT was inspired by the desire to stress something crucial that he believed was shared by mainstream economists since Adam Smith. The common thread emphasised by Keynes in the "classical" tradition may be summarised by the following propositions:

i) In a perfect-competition market equilibrium, the allocation of resources is optimal and social welfare is maximised (the so-called invisible hand argument);

ii) A capitalist market economy is able to self-regulate itself in the sense that it recovers promptly equilibrium whenever it is displaced from it;
iii) In principle, the state should therefore avoid interfering with the spontaneous operation of the market;
iv) There are limits to markets that may distort the allocation of resources and require motivated and circumscribed public intervention to allow them to do their job;
v) In a competitive market economy the possibility of macroeconomic disequilibrium between aggregate demand and supply is excluded by the principle that James Mill and David Ricardo called "Say's law".

These propositions may be found with different emphasis and phrasing in the writings of "classical" economists since Adam Smith, notwithstanding their deep disagreements on value theory and other important theoretical issues. What is common to "classical" economists according to Keynes is not their analytical approach but their vision of the market and its basic policy implications, what we could call their shared view of "economic liberalism" (see Appendix).

The relationship between Keynes and the "classics" has been extensively discussed since the first reviews of the GT, mainly from the point of view of the analytical and methodological differences (starting with the influential "Mr Keynes and the 'classics': a suggested interpretation" by Hicks, 1937). It has always been clear that the crucial issue at stake behind these theoretical and methodological questions is a thorough assessment of the properties of markets and their policy implications, but this has rarely been made fully explicit. In this chapter, we intend to revisit some of these controversial issues from the point of view of the different policy philosophies distinguishing Keynes and the "classics". In this view the "classics" are seen as the "liberals", i.e. exponents of economic liberalism before Keynes, in order to stress the policy philosophy side of the debate. By policy philosophy, we mean more than the policy implications of economic analysis, as we want to capture their common rationale, but less than political philosophy as we focus exclusively on the economic policy side of the latter.

Before going on, we have to clarify the distinction between *laissez-faire* and "economic liberalism". We define *laissez-faire* as a general prescription in favour of unfettered markets lacking sound theoretical foundations, while we define "economic liberalism" as a set of descriptive and policy assertions on the properties of markets and their limits based on state-of-the-art economic theory. Keynes emphasised this distinction and underlined that it had been stressed by all the best economists since the late 19th century (Keynes, 1926). He complained, however, that this distinction had not been understood and adopted by public opinion, politicians and many economists of lesser rank who were still under the influence of traditional *laissez-faire*.

Throughout his career Keynes did much to weaken the influence of *laissez-faire* with his fellow economists and in the public opinion at large. Already in the early 1920s he felt it necessary to reassert that traditional *laissez-faire* had come to an end (e.g. Keynes, 1923, 1925, 1926). He repeated the same concept on many occasions in his scientific and popular writings. On the other hand he never denied his own acceptance of the basic principles of economic liberalism. However, Keynes always regarded economic liberalism as an evolving doctrine that had to be continuously updated to cope with new developments in theory and facts. In his masterpiece he aimed to provide a major contribution to its updating not to its demise as some interpreters wrongly believed (Keynes, 1936). His innovations were soon considered inconsistent with the tenets of sound liberalism by a few economists (Hayek and Friedman are early examples). This thread of criticism against mainstream Keynesism progressively grew in the 1960s and 1970s, leading eventually to its profound crisis in the 1970s.

In this chapter we would like to assess whether and in what sense Keynes and his followers deviated from the tenets of economic liberalism or contributed to its updating. We start from a bird's eye view of the evolution of liberalism before Keynes (Section 2). We then consider whether and in what sense Keynes may be regarded as a liberal (Section 3). In Section 4 we explore the relationship between liberalism and the orthodox Keynesism of the 1950s–1970s (the so-called neoclassical synthesis). In Section 5 we analyse the downfall of the neoclassical synthesis from the point of view of the growing difficulties of its liberal stance and the successful reaction of the new classical economists. In Section 6 we discuss why the breakdown of the neoclassical synthesis in the 1970s was conducive to the revival of an updated form of *laissez-faire*. Section 7 concludes. In the Appendix we try to clarify further the differences between *laissez-faire* and alternative paradigms of economic liberalism by discussing their basic assumptions.

Since the topic of this chapter is too wide to manage without simplifications, we limit the analysis from the temporal and methodological points of view as much as possible (see Borghesi and Vercelli, 2008, for a more extended analysis). Thus we focus on a well-defined historical period going from publication of the GT to the anti-Keynesian counter-revolution of the 1970s, excluding the war period and the early post-war reconstruction that were heavily marked by specific extra-economic events. In addition, the crucial relationship between innovation in economic theory and its implications for economic liberalism is examined mainly from the point of view of the interaction between the cognitive attributes of economic agents and their reaction to policy interventions.

## Economic liberalism before Keynes: A bird's eye view

Adam Smith is usually considered the first scholar to provide rigorous economic foundations for liberal ideas concerning economic policy. He introduced the basic ideas that would characterise political economy and economic liberalism. First, he saw the market as a coherent system, or "machine", expressing the "obvious and simple system of natural liberty" in the economic field (Smith, 1776, p. 651). This was the great innovation underlying Smith's novel conception of political economy as an autonomous scientific discipline based on systematic investigation of its subject-matter. In other words, he conceived economic theory as providing an *ideal machine*, we would say today a *model*, representing the *real machine* underlying a market economy.

Second, he introduced the crucial distinction between the ideal model of a market that corresponds to "perfect freedom" (in the sense conveyed today by "perfect competition") and real markets.

Third, he clarified that the properties of a market depend on the prevailing system of prices: the ideal market is characterised by natural prices while real markets are characterised by market prices. The system of natural prices that characterise the ideal model is seen as an equilibrium towards which market prices gravitate. This equilibrium is regarded as dynamically stable, because, as long as there is a gap between market prices and natural prices, self interest tends to reduce the gap. Self interest is thus the centripetal force of the market system and plays the same role as gravity in Newtonian celestial mechanics (Skinner, 1974, p. 7).

In the first three of the five books of the *Wealth of Nations*, Adam Smith argued that a perfectly competitive market allocates resources between alternative uses in the best possible way, maximising the welfare of people. This argument happened to be labelled as the "argument of the invisible hand", although Smith introduced this expression only in the 4th book of his masterpiece. He coined it to stress that private interests and the interests of society are reconciled by the market, despite the fact that individuals pursue their own private interests and are unaware of the extent to which they contribute to the social interest. This implies that the state should, as a general rule, avoid any unnecessary interference with free enterprise and free movement of goods, services and factors of production in space. In other words, the liberal policies advocated by Smith aimed to approach this desirable state of affairs (i.e. competitive equilibrium) as close as possible although Smith entertained no illusions on the concrete possibility of fully eliminating the gap between real markets and the ideal model of perfect competition.

Smith advocated free movement of goods, services and factors of production (labour and stock or capital), both within and between national boundaries. In particular, he emphasised the right of individuals to reside wherever they wished.

In Smith, as in all classical economists, exaltation of the "providential" role of the market was never divorced from lucid awareness of its shortcomings. Therefore, the liberalism of classical economists, or "classical liberalism" as we call it here, did not deny an important economic role for the state. The invisible-hand argument implied only that interference of the state in the economy should be considered an exception, not the rule, and that any violation of this rule should be thoroughly justified. In the 4th and 5th books of the *Wealth of Nations*, Smith discusses in some detail the general cases in which state intervention is justified. In particular, he argued that the state has to assure the best possible environment for the full expression of economic freedom by promoting justice, liberty and equality, as well as by introducing and preserving free competition in the markets. Economic freedom, in particular, presupposes personal and property security that the state has to insure by providing adequate military defence from external threats and internal defence from crime. This requires efficient administration of justice to be kept independent of government pressure, as well as an efficient system of education based on far-sighted cultural policy. Smith also attributes to the state the task of designing and managing a system of taxation to finance public expenditure or reduce inequality, and confers a certain responsibility for monetary policy to avoid fraud and inflationary pressures. Finally, the state has to provide efficient infrastructure for economic activity, especially the transport network.

After Smith, there were notable advances in the classical school only in single aspects of the general argument. Ricardo developed the point of view of classical liberalism and spread its influence among economists, policy-makers and public opinion. His point of view was narrower than that of Smith but he went deeper on some points, especially issues concerning international trade. *The Principles of Political Economy and*

*Taxation* (1817) introduced his celebrated theory of comparative costs which provided the first rigorous argument on the benefits of free trade between countries. We may say that in Ricardo the standard of analytic rigour was for the first time approaching that required today in scientific research.[2] On the basis of this and other important contributions to economic theory, such as his theory of rent, he conducted an influential campaign in favour of free trade, advocating the abolition of the *Corn Laws*, introduced in England in 1815 to protect farmers and landowners from cheap grain imports by heavy import tariffs. Though the Corn Laws were eventually abolished only in 1846, the influence of Ricardo and his pupils and followers was deep in gradually shifting the British economic policy towards a free-trade inspiration.

At the beginning of the 19th century, Bentham added an important ingredient to classical liberalism: utilitarianism (Bentham, 1952–54). This approach opposed the view maintained by Locke, the Physiocrats and Adam Smith himself, that free markets achieve a natural order created by God and should not be perturbed by the State (ibidem). For Bentham and the utilitarians, neither the status quo nor any definition of natural order could be considered sacred, and government intervention was justified whenever utilitarian calculus proved that such intervention could increases the happiness of society (on this point see, e.g. Robbins, 1952, and Schotter, 1985). The generalised adoption of Benthamite utilitarianism by most classical economists since the early 19th century put the debate about the limits of unfettered markets on a sound scientific basis underpinned by a thorough evaluation of the costs and benefits of state intervention in single areas.

The synthesis between classical economics (in the Ricardian version) and Benthamite utilitarianism was first systematically sketched by James Mill, mentor and pupil of Ricardo. *The Principles* of Ricardo dominated the intellectual scene until mid-century when John Stuart Mill published a new synthesis of the classical school updated from a utilitarian point of view in his *Principles of Political Economy* (Mill, 1848). Mill clearly restated the general principle of classical liberalism: "*laisser-faire*, in short, should be the general practice; every departure from it, unless required by some great good, is a certain evil" (ibidem, p. 314).

Then he defined the cases in which these departures may be considered justified (particularly in book 5 of his masterpiece). The "natural" liberty of individuals is passionately defended from any unjustified interference on the part of the state, provided that it does not jeopardise the liberty of other individuals and therefore also the security, stability and prosperity of society (Mill, 1859, p. 141). On the basis of this approach, Mill did not hesitate, however, to add important new areas of legitimate state intervention, such as the conservation of the natural environment (ibidem, p. 148).

A major breakthrough in the analysis of the invisible hand argument came only with Walras's general equilibrium model. He was able to represent the general system of transactions that characterise a certain competitive economy under "pure" conditions, showing that the system has an equilibrium that achieves the optimal allocation of resources. In addition, in his analysis of "tâtonnement" he offered an argument to corroborate the plausibility of the dynamic stability of general equilibrium. The potential of general equilibrium theory for advancing economic liberalism began to be developed by Pareto, successor of Walras in Lausanne, who was a fervent liberal militant in his youth (Pareto, 1906).

Classical liberalism extended its influence into the first two decades of the 20th century. The *Principles of Political Economy* by Mill was still the most popular textbook of economics at the end of the 19th century in English-speaking countries, when it was gradually overtaken by the *Principles of Economics* (1891) by Marshall. Though Marshall is considered a major exponent of the "marginalist revolution" in economic theory, his liberalism maintained quite strict continuity with classical liberalism:

> Ricardo and his followers developed a theory of the action of free enterprise (or, as they said, free competition), which contained many truths, that will be probably important so long as the world exists.
> (Marshall, 1891, p. 10)

Writing at the end of the 19th century, however, he recognised the negative implications of *laissez-faire* that had emerged in the earlier part of the century when:

> free competition, or rather, freedom of industry and enterprise, was set loose to run, like a huge untrained monster, its wayward course. The abuse of their new power by able but uncultured businessmen led to evils on every side; it unfitted mothers for their duties, it weighed down children with overwork and disease; and in many places it degraded the race. (ibidem, p. 9)

Marshall was therefore attracted by the opportunity of bringing "free enterprise somewhat under control, to diminish its power of doing evil and increase its power of doing good" (ibidem, p. 10).

The new approach to liberalism foreshadowed by Marshall was characterised by two main novelties. First, the boundaries between the scope of markets and legitimate state intervention were discussed not in terms of limits to state interference in the economy but to unfettered markets. This new attitude reflected the change in orientation of economists and public opinion in favour of free markets and the progressive accumulation of observations on market failures. Second, he was prepared to extend the scope of state intervention in the market beyond the limits of classical liberalism, provided the new roles attributed to the state were the fruit of free and democratic deliberation based on sound economic arguments. Marshall himself suggested a clear historical explanation of both novelties. While classical economists were reacting to the negative implications of traditional mercantilist interventionism, the enlightened liberal economists at the turn of the century were reacting to the experience of the negative consequences of insufficiently regulated free markets.

Though the point of view of what we may call *updated liberalism* was already quite clear in Marshall, its rigorous foundations only emerged in subsequent generations of economists in the second and third decades of the 20th century. For the sake of simplicity we only stress the crucial role of the two best pupils of Marshall: Pigou and Keynes.

Summing up, traditional liberalism, as codified by the great classical economists (Smith and Ricardo) at the end of the 18th century and developed by their followers (in particular John Stuart Mill and Marshall) in the 19th century, underlined the virtues of free markets but never forgot their limits. The founding fathers of classical liberalism were fully aware of the crucial importance of a thorough analysis of the limits to markets in order to understand where they had to be supplemented by state intervention.

In the 1920s and 1930s two crucial steps were made towards understanding the limits of competitive markets and how to remedy them. Pigou, in his milestone *The Economics of Welfare* (1920), elaborated on ideas sketched by Marshall, clarifying a fundamental reason for market failures: the existence of economic *externalities*, i.e. costs or benefits that cannot be reckoned by the market. At the same time he pointed out how to remedy them in principle (internalisation of externalities through subsidies or taxes). Pigou thus provided microeconomic foundations not only for welfare economics but also for the welfare state, previously supported with passion but weak foundations by political figures such as Lord Beveridge and political movements such as the Fabian Society. A few years later Keynes's *General Theory* (1936) provided the macroeconomic foundations of market failures and policies required to mend them. These two fundamental contributions were in a sense complementary and were later merged in a model of liberalist regulation (called in this essay *welfarist liberalism*), that spread after World War II until the 1970s. Its success was fostered by the soaring power of trade unions in the 1950s and 1960s, as the growth of big firms increased membership of trade unions, and declining unemployment increased their strength.

## Was Keynes a liberal?

This is a question that Keynes himself raised not only in the well-known essay "Am I a liberal?" (1925) but on many other occasions throughout his life. His own answer has always been a positive answer, but we can detect an evolution in his position. He started as a very convinced supporter of traditional principles of free trade claiming that: "free trade is based on fundamental truths that, when exposed with the necessary qualifications, cannot be questioned by anyone who understands the meaning of words" (Keynes, 1923, p. 87).

Until he conceived and started to write the GT, Keynes's position was not substantially different from that of the "classics". He insisted on the necessity of abandoning *laissez-faire* and updating economic liberalism, but this was in line with the attitude of all leading economists since the 1870s (Robbins, 1952).

A radical change of attitude towards classical liberalism emerged clearly, and was emphasised by Keynes, only once he was writing the GT. We can speculate that it was to stress the novelty of his own position that he introduced the new category of the "classics" that was meant to encompass the leading economists belonging to the liberal tradition since Adam Smith. What Keynes wanted to emphasise in the GT was the possibility of macroeconomic failure revealed by the existence of involuntary unemployment. Before the GT, structural unemployment was not considered to be the fault of the market but of interference on its working by trade unions and public intervention. Keynes, on the contrary, wanted to demonstrate that the dire phenomenon of structural unemployment is a macroscopic market failure, much more important than the allocative (or microeconomic) market failures considered so far:

> When 9,000,000 men are employed out of 10,000,000 willing and able to work, there is no evidence that the labour of these 9,000,000

men is misdirected ... It is in determining the volume, not the direction, of actual employment that the existing system has broken down.

(Keynes, 1936, p. 379)

The emphasis on this new kind of market failure did not imply the demise of economic liberalism: "the result of filling in the gaps in the classical theory is not to dispose of the 'Manchester System', but to indicate the nature of the environment which the free play of economic forces requires if it is to realise the full potentialities of production" (ibidem).

Keynes was aware that it could be contended that "the central controls necessary to ensure full employment will ... involve a large extension of the traditional functions of government" but he stressed that "there will still remain a wide field for the exercise of private initiative and responsibility" (Keynes, 1936, pp. 379–80).

If the extension of state intervention to macroeconomic equilibrium is regarded as a reduction of individual liberty, two fundamental objections put forward in the GT are worth considering:

i) Structural unemployment is redefined by Keynes as *involuntary unemployment*, i.e. as a restriction of the options set available to individuals. Its removal through state intervention is thus meant to increase the liberty of individuals. As we show in Figure 4.1, the set of possible choices in the market of labour in the absence of macroeconomic market failures is delimited by the short side of demand and supply of labour, so that the maximising behaviour of economic agents selects full employment equilibrium. The main purpose of the GT, clearly announced since the second chapter, was to show that the set of options in the market of labour is restricted as a consequence of macroeconomic failures. Employment is thus exogenously determined according to the "principle of effective demand". Employees select within the restricted set of options the point characterised by the maximum possible real wage, that is the point where effective demand crosses the labour demand curve defining the level of unemployment equilibrium. On the basis of this argument we may say that any measure of macroeconomic policy that succeeds in relaxing the effective demand constraint, expands the liberty of economic agents at the same time.

ii) This macroscopic but circumscribed enlargement of the functions of government is considered by Keynes "as the only practicable means of avoiding the destruction of existing economic forms in their entirety and as the condition of the successful functioning of individual initiative" (ibidem, p. 380). In other words a full-employment macroeconomic policy was seen as a necessary condition for preserving market capitalism and economic freedom.

In the light of these considerations it is clear that the intention of Keynes in the GT was not to undermine economic liberalism but to rescue and update it in a period of profound crisis. This underlines the continuity between Keynes's and "classical" liberalism. Economic liberalism, by its very nature, never failed to update its analysis and prescriptions by taking account of the evolution of economic facts and economic theory. From this point of view we may say that Keynes's liberalism is nothing but a further updating of this tradition of thought. On the other hand, though thoroughly circumscribed, the discontinuity between the liberalism of Keynes and that of the classics is not at all minor, since in the tradition of economic liberalism no one before Keynes recognised the possibility of *macroeconomic* failure. Its introduction, however, is not foreign to the spirit of economic liberalism, provided its theoretical foundations are sound. In the GT, Keynes struggled to show that acknowledgement of the existence of this crucial macroeconomic failure had been inhibited by mainstream economists' acceptance of Say's law. Did he succeed? We cannot provide here a full-length discussion of this vexed question (for a recent critical survey see De Vroey, 2004). We may, however, try to clarify a line of reasoning that plays a crucial role in Keynes's revolutionary theory, as well as in the subsequent history of its fortune and misfortune.

If uncertainty is considered a crucial reason for "unemployment equilibrium", as sustained by Keynes, the same uncertainty seems to raise doubts on the possibility, or at least the opportunity, of state intervention in the market (Kerstenetzky, 2007). In fact, it has been contended that sound interventions require reliable forecasts of agents' reactions in an environment modified by policy (Lucas, 1981). Keynes was fully aware of this problem: "in such matters it is rash to predict how the average man will react to a changed environment" (1936, p. 377). He uses this argument to deny the possibility of controlling the economy through monetary policy. Keynes's multiplier shifts the analysis to the real side of the economy where state intervention may directly affect the aggregates of the economy. When other policy strategies fail to bring about full employment by affecting the marginal propensity to consume or the volume of private investment, the state may use the last-resort strategy of increasing public expenditure in order to reduce involuntary

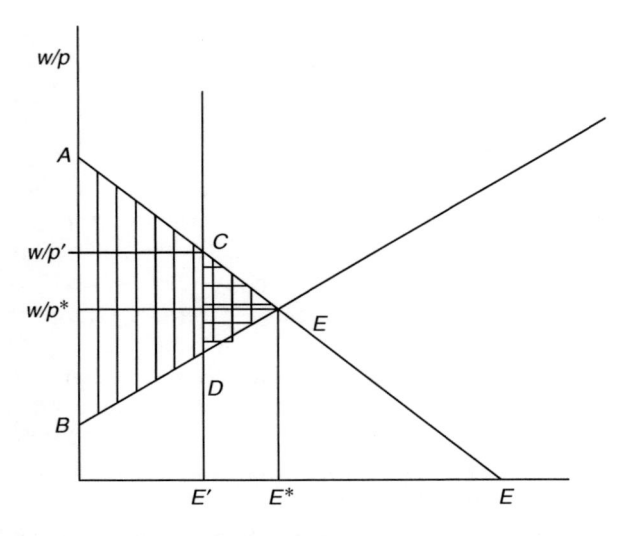

*Figure 4.1* Labour market and effective demand

unemployment through the multiplier. The Keynesian revolution is ultimately based on his peculiar cognitive assumptions. Keynes's economic agents have to make choices in situations of hard (or strong) uncertainty. They are aware of their ignorance about future events and the probability distributions of their occurrence. Their expectations are conceived in terms of non-additive probabilities or elude any probabilistic formulation altogether. In such situations economic agents rely on conventions leading to herd behaviour. They may suddenly change expectations or rules of conduct and this translates into unpredictable shifts in the main functions of the model (liquidity preference and marginal efficiency of capital). This prevents the market from self-regulation and makes any attempts of monetary policy unreliable.

We may wonder why Pigou's microeconomic updating of liberal tenets was accepted without particular scandal by most liberal economists, while Keynes's macroeconomic updating was considered outrageous even by open-minded liberal economists such as Pigou himself. We may speculate that the main pillar of economic liberalism since Adam Smith has been the confidence in the power of market prices to allocate economic goods between alternative uses in the best possible way, clearing markets and maximising social welfare. Pigou's microeconomic updating did not really question the crucial power of the price system but only defined its limits. If the market is the best social computer, as emphasised by Hayeck during the famous debate on the limits of socialism in the 1930s, Pigouvian market failures do not depend on the intrinsic weakness of the computer (the market) but only on its incomplete inputs (the data set). On the contrary, Keynes's alleged macroeconomic market failure questions the power of the market price system in a much more radical way. Microeconomic equilibrium in all other markets is considered to be consistent with persistent disequilibrium in a crucial aggregate market, such as the market of labour. Keynes does not deny that money wages may subside in situations of excess supply of labour. He claims, however, that this does not necessarily increase consumption or investment, if it is taken as a sign of depression (Vercelli, 1991).

## The neoclassical synthesis and "welfare liberalism"

After the death of Keynes, mainstream Keynesian economics aimed at a rigorous synthesis between "classical" economics in the neoclassical version based on general equilibrium theory and Keynes's own theory, trying to preserve his policy conclusions rather than the theoretical and methodological peculiarities of his approach. The Keynesian model was conceived as a special case of a "classical" model specified in general equilibrium terms, but a special case considered particularly relevant for the real world. Hicks indicated the direction to follow in his celebrated review article "Mr Keynes and the classics" (Hicks, 1937). Samuelson (1947) and Patinkin (1956) provided sophisticated foundations in terms of general equilibrium theory. Modigliani (1944) and Tobin (1958) elaborated the monetary part. Harrod (1939) opened the way to a macroeconomic theory of growth of Keynesian inspiration developed by Solow (1956). Samuelson (1939) and Goodwin (1951) worked out a theory of cyclic fluctuations based on the interaction between multiplier and accelerator. Generally speaking, Keynesian results were obtained under particular assumptions on the parameters of the model that were claimed to be more realistic. The focus shifted mainly to econometric models of Keynesian inspiration, intended to support the decision process of public authorities and big firms (Klein and Goldberger, 1955).

Whatever we think of the neoclassical synthesis from the theoretical and methodological points of view, from the point of view of economic liberalism this school of thought allowed an operational synthesis of analysis and policy concerned with both microeconomic and macroeconomic failures. Under the influence of the neoclassical synthesis, applied liberalism took on a different physiognomy that synthesised the two quite different versions of updated liberalism by Pigou and Keynes. Taken together, the analysis of microeconomic failures by Pigou and of macroeconomic failures by Keynes provided the foundations for building a welfare state consistent with the basic tenets of updated liberalism. We may call this form of applied economic liberalism "welfarist liberalism" to distinguish it from the preceding and subsequent forms of liberalism. By pursuing the research programme outlined above, this approach promised to reconcile private and social interests. Combining the advantages of individualism with social concerns, it rapidly became the mainstream macroeconomic school in the 1950s and 1960s.

This highly successful synthesis, however, was only obtained at the cost of abandoning the deepest and most original insights of the GT (see Section 3). The cognitive assumptions attributed to economic agents by Keynes cannot be dealt with under the constraints of a general equilibrium model that may only introduce uncertainty in its weakest form of known and fully reliable additive probability distributions over the relevant variables.

Under these assumptions, the equilibrium described by the model may only be a full employment equilibrium, unless we introduce specific assumptions: rigid or sticky prices that give a peculiar shape to the crucial functions of the model. A case in point is the liquidity preference curve that is assumed to become flat after a certain threshold of money supply, so that its special shape frustrates the potential role of the rate of interest in restoring economic equilibrium. Even before Keynes, no one denied that a classical model could generate unemployment equilibrium under the assumption of rigid prices. This approach, however, was in contrast with the claim that Keynesian theory (in all its variants including the neoclassical synthesis) was more realistic than traditional classical theory. In fact many observers would agree that, in the real world, prices are generally neither fully flexible as assumed by the "classical" theory nor fully rigid. The neoclassical synthesis explored a different approach to reach Keynesian-like results without necessarily assuming rigid prices. This view emphasised out-of-equilibrium behaviour, showing that, under quite general assumptions, we cannot rely on a sufficiently rapid convergence towards full employment equilibrium (Patinkin, 1956). This gives macroeconomic policy a role in accelerating the process of convergence to full-employment equilibrium. On the contrary, Keynes did not develop the dynamic side of the new theory, believing it to be of secondary importance for his policy philosophy. His assumptions on the characteristics of a monetary economy, however, imply that its dynamic behaviour is complex. In both variants (rigid prices or complex dynamics) the success of Keynesian policy has to rely on the ability of policy authorities to understand the specific functional form of the structural relations of the economy, assuming they do not vary as a consequence of policy interventions.

Keynesian macroeconomics was originally seen as the "economics of depression", not incidentally worked out during the *Great Depression* of the 1930s. Its scope was easily extended to the period of post-war reconstruction and steady growth of the 1950s and, to some extent, to the more troubled 1960s. When serious inflationary tensions re-emerged in the early 1960s, Keynesian economists had to introduce a way of dealing with inflation into the model. The Phillips curve provided the missing equation linking involuntary unemployment with inflation (Phillips, 1958). Theoretical reasons and empirical evidence suggested that a growing economy creates inflationary tensions before hitting what Keynesians called the full-employment barrier. This phenomenon was considered to be at the root of the observed trade-off between unemployment and inflation. This trade-off was interpreted by a few prominent Keynesian economists as a stable curve offering a menu of policy choices. The introduction of the Phillips curve into the model seemed to provide a way to extend the validity of Keynesian theory even to cases of inflation, but this solution presupposed invariance of the Phillips curve to changes in policy rules. Accelerating inflation in most industrial countries in the late 1960s and early 1970s due to increasing conflict in industrial relations and labour markets, and the stagflation of the 1970s showed that the trade-off was not stable. Econometric studies of the period showed that the short-run Phillips curve was progressively shifting upwards becoming increasingly steep. Explanation of this empirical phenomenon and its policy implications was the object of a hot dispute between the Monetarists and the Keynesians. The latter tried to stabilise the curve by adding new variables, while their opponents rejected this strategy because the behaviour of economic agents was not invariant to changes in policy rules. The outcome of this harsh scientific battle was a clear defeat of the neoclassical synthesis and its consequent demise. A different specification of disequilibrium dynamics or updated foundations for partial rigidity of prices could have rescued the essential part of Keynesian theory and did in fact underlie the revival of Keynesian theory a few years later (mainly since the late 1980s). This story, however, goes beyond the limits of this chapter. We want to emphasise here that defeat of the neoclassical synthesis came about because Keynes's own methodological principles had been abandoned. In the GT Keynes emphasised that the reaction of wage earners to policy interventions was intrinsically irregular and unpredictable because of the cognitive constraints analysed above. In his opinion, money wages tended to increase in proximity to full employment, at a rate that depended on the characteristics of the economy. Keynes's version of the trade-off cannot thus be conceived as a stable menu for policy choices. Similarly, within Keynes's own conceptual framework the wage-unemployment trade-off cannot be stabilised simply by adding further variables in the model.

## The emergence of New Classical Economics

Starting from "classical" foundations, the neoclassical synthesis could only obtain Keynesian results by assuming rigid prices or disequilibrium dynamics. The battle over the Phillips curve was inconsistent with the assumption of rigid prices since it was about variations in money wages or nominal prices. As far as disequilibrium dynamics is concerned, Phelps (1967) and Friedman (1968 and 1969) argued that any attempt at improving on the long-run market equilibrium represented by the natural unemployment rate could only worsen the situation by accelerating inflation. This argument was found convincing by most economists, many of whom shifted to the anti-Keynesian camp.

In the 1970s the monetarist victory in the battle over the Phillips curve determined the demise of Keynesian economics as hegemonic school in macroeconomics. The new orthodox school, soon called New Classical Economics (henceforth NCEcs), was initially presented as a more sophisticated version of monetarism ("monetarism mark 2" as Tobin called it) but in a few years it emancipated from the strictly monetarist assumptions and presented itself mainly as a new methodology different from traditional Keynesism and monetarism. The NCEcs aimed to provide rigorous foundations for macroeconomics based on *General Equilibrium Theory* in the most updated version of Debreu (1959). Since this version was based on axiomatic foundations, unlike previous versions that relied on dynamic foundations (Samuelson, 1947), Lucas assumed that disequilibrium dynamics could be skipped altogether. He also assumed complete flexibility of prices, implying that equilibrium was only consistent with full employment. The crucial concept of unemployment equilibrium became unintelligible in this conceptual framework. As for the cognitive assumptions, Lucas was the first to recognise that if one builds economic theory on foundations based on the GE model with uncertainty (Debreu, 1959), one has to assume that the economic agents entertain rational expectations. In such a world, in the absence of any source of price rigidity or disequilibrium dynamics, Keynesian problems concerning insufficient effective demand could not even be conceptualised.

In the New Classical world, macroeconomic policy became impossible or unreliable. According to a few early contributions, economic policy is impossible because economic agents compensate well-understood effects of policy interventions in order to keep their desired results (thesis of the impossibility of economic policy). Quite soon Lucas demonstrated that the behaviour of economic agents depends on the policy environment so that the effects of a change of policy rules are not predictable and may have perverse consequences (Lucas, 1981). This argument, that came to be called the "Lucas critique", became immensely influential and determined a profound crisis of Keynesism and welfarist liberalism. The approach suggested by Lucas was conceived in such a way as to exclude, at least prima facie, the existence of market failures. This counterfactual implication of his theory is clearly questionable and was immediately criticised. It eventually gave rise to alternative, more robust, versions of Keynesian ideas. The Lucas critique, however, immediately seemed a compelling attack not only on the Keynesian version of liberalism but more in general on any form of liberalism inconsistent with mere *laissez-faire*. Even if we assume that market failures may arise and that the state is benevolent, there is no guarantee that new policy interventions will improve the status quo.

It is ironic that the argument underlying the Lucas critique plays a crucial role in the GT but was retorted against Keynesian approach. The anti-Keynesian implications of the Lucas critique rely on the crucial assumption that private agents have rational expectations while the policy authorities do not. It is not clear why the Lucas argument should not be applied to any kind of strategic behaviour, even in the private sector, as assumed by Keynes. In this case we need a theory that assumes strong uncertainty and complex dynamic behaviour. This is exactly the point of view of Keynes who tried courageously to build its foundations. However, even in the hypothesis that in the real-world private agents are liable to strong uncertainty and complex behaviour, Lucas claimed that scientific analysis, by definition, should ignore these aspects and focus on rational, stationary, predictable behaviour (Lucas, 1981). This is particularly true of policy-oriented economic analysis since only in this case may policy interventions be consistent with democracy. For both scientific and policy reasons, the role of the state should shrink to the most simple and compelling tasks where we can rely on the rational adaptation of economic agents. This line of reasoning is liable to objections. First, the idea of science looming in Lucas's argument is unconvincing and inconsistent with updated ideas of science put forward by the most prestigious historians and philosophers of science. Hard uncertainty and complexity are crucial aspects of the phenomena studied in most scientific disciplines, including natural sciences. Second, the boundary between complex and simple phenomena (e.g. stationary and non-stationary stochastic processes) is unlikely to be stationary. Therefore, even robust evidence in favour of the stationarity of a certain time series based on past observations, does not guarantee that it will remain stationary in the future. Third, to be consistent with the argument of Lucas we should restrict the analysis to a very narrow subset of issues studied by our disciplines. On the contrary methods devised for simple issues characterised by stationarity and soft uncertainty are routinely applied to complex issues characterised by non-stationarity and hard uncertainty; however, this approach produces misleading results (Vercelli, 2002 and 2005).

## The revival of *laissez-faire*

The anti-Keynesian counter-revolution did not limit itself to sweeping away the novelties of Keynesian liberalism, but it was also instrumental in triggering a revival of *laissez-faire* that the liberal tradition had in fact rejected much before Keynes. According to this view, that has often been misleadingly called *neoliberal*, market failures are nonexistent or otherwise their extension and size is quite limited. In any case, it is considered axiomatic that state interventions meant to avoid or mitigate market failures would produce state failures with worse consequences. This new point of view claims sound foundations in the recent evolution of economic theory. As for macroeconomic failures, we have seen that the criticisms by Friedman and Lucas are questionable, if referred to the assumptions of the GT itself rather than to those of the neoclassical synthesis, particularly as far as the complex dynamics of the economic system and the cognitive assumptions attributed to economic agents are concerned.

Of course, if market failures require some amount of regulation, the failures of regulation are no less harmful. Both experience and theoretical analysis of bureaucratic and political processes have shown that regulatory failures are systematic and may even be worse than market failures. In addition, failures of regulation are much more visible than the market failures they are supposed to mend. Disillusionment about the efficiency of regulation has been so strong in the light of the experience of the 1950s and 1960s that an irrational faith in the power of unfettered markets has spread, particularly since the 1970s. The ensuing process of deregulation has dismantled some degenerated forms of regulation, but it has gone too far, demolishing also necessary forms of regulation such as those that set environmental, health, humanitarian and ethical standards. In addition, the relationship between regulators and regulated agents has proved to be a sort of evolutionary game: the regulated agents always try to elude the rules set by the regulators who must therefore continuously update them. A continuous process of re-regulation must therefore accompany the process of deregulation meant to dismantle obsolete or inefficient rules in order to introduce efficient rules in the evolving context. The mistrust in regulation, however, has gone so far as to cloud the necessity of market regulation. Of course market regulation must be kept to a minimum in order to avoid the disruptive potential of regulation failures but cannot be altogether absent. Finally, we cannot deny that the same reasons that cause failures of state regulation lead to no less disruptive failures in deregulation (Russia is a case in point: see Stiglitz, 2002).

The prophets of the *neoliberal* counter-revolution ignored the arguments on the limits of real markets accumulated not only by *updated liberalism* but also by *classical liberalism* that demonstrated the necessity of active regulation of markets in order to optimise their contribution to social welfare. In this essay, I limit myself to briefly examining the crucial contributions of two eminent economists who have been regarded, correctly or incorrectly, as founding-fathers of neoliberalism.

The micro-foundations of the *neoliberal* stance are often explicitly or implicitly based on a broad interpretation of the Coase theorem (Coase, 1960). According to this view, market failures occur only when property rights are not well defined, as in the case of environmental commons. Thus the remedy suggested is quite different from that of *updated* and *welfarist* liberalism. This new explanation was not seen by the neoliberal followers of Coase as an additional explanation of market failures, that could well be considered consistent with those pointed out by updated liberalism, but as the ultimate cause of market failures that, in principle, substitutes all the other explanations analysed by classical and updated liberalism. To the best of my knowledge, the reason why the other causes of market failures were ignored by this stream of thought has never been spelled out with thorough scientific arguments. This exceedingly broad interpretation of the Coase theorem led to a very simplistic policy rule of markets regulation: "let us define property rights on all goods, including public goods (such as for example environmental goods); unregulated markets will solve all the other problems by themselves". This was a very radical departure not only from updated liberalism but also from classical liberalism. All the areas assigned to the state by classical liberalism, including education, were considered better left to unregulated markets. In addition, one particular aspect of the Coase theorem – it does not matter to whom property rights are attributed (polluter or polluted, rich or poor, etc.) – was interpreted as if distributional problems were immaterial for social wealth.

Friedman proposed macroeconomic foundations against updated liberalism from the early 1950s onwards by arguing that countercyclic policies are harmful for the economy, at least in the long run, as they tend to increase the structural inflation rate and the natural rate of unemployment (Friedman, 1969). His approach shares a few aspects of the dynamic methodology of Keynes and Pigou descending from the influence of Marshall, that focuses on the crucial role of disequilibrium dynamics, but this is turned against Keynes. The main argument is that any attempt to stabilise the economy is bound to increase its instability by feeding inflationary expectations. The whole argument, however, is based on a severe undervaluation of the intrinsic instability of unfettered markets in a sophisticated monetary economy (Vercelli, 2000, and the literature therein cited).

A few years later, Lucas provided different, and much more radical, macroeconomic foundations for the neoliberal stance by assuming that the economy is always in a state of perfectly competitive equilibrium. Provided the model based on this assumption mimics reality sufficiently well, all deviations from the perfectly competitive paradigm (disequilibrium, oligopoly, monopoly, etc.) are considered irrelevant for economic analysis as a *scientific* discipline (for a criticism, see Vercelli, 1991). Under these assumptions, Lucas proved that what is generally defined as Keynesian countercyclic economic policy is impossible, or at least completely unreliable, as its actual results are affected in an unpredictable way by the structural instability of a monetary economy and are bound to increase the hard uncertainty of economic agents. Lucas argues that disequilibrium concepts, such as unemployment and out-of-equilibrium dynamics, are meaningless, but this leaves the economists without any method for detecting market failures and remedying them.

Friedman advocated a fixed monetary policy and systematic deregulation. In this view the only structural intervention considered sound is therefore privatisation. While Lucas did not deny some scope for further structural policies meant to increase the efficiency of free markets, both denied the utility of active counter-cyclic regulation of competitive markets. Since the late 1970s the macroeconomic school of new classical economists inspired by Lucas has ousted both the Keynesian school and Friedman's monetarism, becoming the mainstream school of macroeconomics in line with the simultaneous rise of neoliberalism.

As we have seen in the above brief analysis of the contributions of economists who have been considered prophets of neoliberalism, their departure not only from the updated liberalism of Keynes and Pigou, but also from the classical liberalism of Smith and Ricardo, was very radical. Active economic regulation of markets was in principle completely ruled out. In this view deregulation and privatisation would mark a transition period to the golden age of unfettered, perfectly competitive, free markets. The role of the state is reduced to defining and defending property rights.

## Concluding remarks

Since the early reviews of the GT Keynes has been often accused of abandoning the tradition of liberal economic thought and paving the way to a dangerous new form of statism or collectivism. He always denied this interpretation, claiming that his innovative contributions to economic theory and policy were intended to update economic liberalism to avoid the collapse of market capitalism. We have to recognise, however, that Keynes laid himself open to this criticism by overemphasising the discontinuity between the liberal tradition of the "classics" and his updated version of economic liberalism centred around a disruptive macroeconomic market failure (unemployment equilibrium). This discontinuity was greatly reduced from the analytical point of view by his mainstream followers who suggested the outlines of a neoclassical synthesis. Their policy prescriptions accepted the extension of collective action to macroeconomic regulation, coordinating it with the updated classical liberalism of Pigou and with the idea of welfare state that had its own tradition. The neoclassical synthesis provided thus robust foundations to what we have called welfarist liberalism that dominated the policy philosophy of industrialised countries well into the 1970s. Its growing difficulties since the late 1960s raised increasing criticism against the Keynesian paradigm. In the 1970s the conviction that the Keynesian revolution had deviated from the main road marked out by "classical" theory and its policy implications became widespread, causing the demise of the neoclassical synthesis and a temporary but serious setback for Keynesian thought. In this chaper we argued that the new version of "classical" economics suggested in the 1970s erected a protective belt around the kernel of "classical" thought, making it impossible to reject the neglect of macroeconomic market failures. The argument laid down by the influential Lucas critique attributed to Keynes the epistemic assumptions of the neoclassical synthesis that are, however, completely different from those held by Keynes himself. The new policy philosophy emerging as a consequence of the anti-Keynesian counter-revolution was not a revival of the sophisticated and balanced liberalism of the "classics" but a cruder *laissez-faire* long rejected by economic liberalism.

Our knowledge of market properties and limits is still limited, even in the case of perfect competition and much more so in the case of real markets. Our knowledge of market and state failures and their relative size and policy implications is therefore also limited. We have to return to the tradition of systematic in-depth exploration of these issues that was typical of the great tradition of economic liberalism to which Keynes belonged, rejecting the simplistic and misleading philosophy of *laissez-faire* revived by the Keynesian counter-revolution. In particular, we have to study the behaviour of the system of prices as a system characterised by complex dynamics, attributing cognitive assumptions, consistent with such a complexity and the ensuing strong uncertainty, to economic agents.

## Appendix

In this Appendix we discuss the different concepts of economic liberalism mentioned in this chapter. We first distinguish *laissez-faire* and *economic liberalism*.

We define *laissez-faire* as an approach to economic policy that denies any positive role to the regulation of markets or state intervention. When its arguments are based on economic theory, their foundations lack acceptable rigour. On the other hand we define "economic liberalism" as an approach to economic policy based on sound theoretical arguments based on state-of-the-art economic theory.

The different streams of economic liberalism are characterised by the following propositions:

1. *Existence of a market gap*. Between real markets and the ideal perfect-competition market there is a gap that is quite relevant for economic theory and economic policy, for many reasons. First of all,

the *uncertainty* intrinsic to the workings of markets raises serious problems because it is often endogenous and/or inconsistent with the usual axioms of decision theory under uncertainty (Savage, 1956). It implies that the expectations of economic agents are in general neither correct nor rational (Shiller, 2000; Vercelli, 2002). Moreover, when information is imperfect or asymmetric, competitive equilibrium is not Pareto-efficient (Greenwald and Stiglitz, 1986).

Markets are *incomplete*; most future markets are absent and cannot be easily established. What is worse, it can be proved that markets cannot be made complete. In any case, the optimal intertemporal allocation of resources cannot be achieved by real markets: since most future markets do not exist, the more expectations refer to the distant future the more they are liable to be systematically incorrect.

Also *transaction costs* are often quite sizeable. In particular, the effort necessary to match demand and supply may bring about significant material costs, such as travel and immaterial costs, involved in the gathering and processing of information about the relevant characteristics of potential demand and supply. The existence of these costs is sufficient to jeopardise the ability of a competitive market to achieve optimal allocation of resources (see Arrow and Hahn, 1999, for a recent assessment of the problem).

*Externalities* are particularly important in real markets because, by definition, incomplete markets cannot record all the costs and benefits of economic decisions, and property rights on goods and resources are not always well defined, as is typical with many environmental resources (water, air, biodiversity, etc.)

A few important markets are also fairly *unstable* from three different points of view (see Vercelli, 1991, for a discussion of different concepts of instability). Competitive markets tend to be *institutionally* unstable in the sense that they tend to lose their competitive nature through exploitation of scale and scope economies, or discretionary power in disequilibria, or monopolist and oligopolist practices. In addition markets may be *dynamically* unstable in the sense that they do not recover equilibrium easily when are displaced by a shock. Finally, markets may be *structurally* unstable in the sense that a small shock may alter the qualitative characteristics of their dynamic behaviour.

2. *Invisible hand postulate.* The equilibrium of a perfectly competitive market allocates resources between alternative uses in the best possible way by efficiently coordinating the decisions of rational agents and maximising social wealth.

From Adam Smith to contemporary welfare economics, this proposition has received increasingly rigorous foundations that have progressively clarified the virtues of markets and their limits. These limits are expressed in the following propositions.

3. *Shortcomings of the invisible hand.* Even an ideal model of perfect competition has strictly limited power in coordinating the decisions of economic agents. In particular, the invisible hand by itself cannot solve distributive problems, in the sense that the distribution of income, wealth and resources brought about by the market does not necessarily correspond to a desirable standard (ethical or of other nature). In addition equilibrium is not necessarily unique or stable.

4. *Foundations of liberal policies.* Liberal policies aim to eliminate the market gap, or at least reduce it as far as possible. Their ultimate foundations rely on the foregoing postulates but require a further postulate, namely that, at least in principle, there is a monotonous correlation between the size of the market gap and the losses of social welfare brought about by this gap. This postulate is generally not made explicit but is logically necessary to justify liberal policies aiming to reduce the market gap. However, this apparently plausible postulate is not much more than an act of faith. First, it is not clear how to measure the market gap. Real markets deviate from the ideal model on many mutually independent dimensions. There is no reason to believe that the correlation between single market gaps, or any aggregate measure of them, and welfare losses is monotonic. There could be trade-offs between the single dimensions of the gap that would prevent a sound aggregation in a comprehensive measure of market gap. Although this is the weakest postulate of economic liberalism, it is needed to draw unambiguous policy conclusions from knowledge concerning the economic and welfare properties of ideal and real markets. We have to maintain full awareness of its weakness in order to avoid degeneration of arguments on these complex issues in ideological statements.

5. *Limits to liberal policies.* There are serious limits to how much the gap between real markets and the ideal perfect-competition market can be reduced. As we have seen in Section 1, markets cannot be altogether completed, externalities cannot be fully internalised, transaction costs may be reduced but not fully eliminated, information may become less asymmetric but not homogeneous, and so on. Moreover, economic agents operating in real markets are boundedly rational and not always self-seeking decision makers (see, e.g. Agarwal and Vercelli, 2005).

We are now in a position to define in a more rigorous way the different concepts of liberalism analysed in this chapter. Classical and updated liberalism accept the five propositions listed above. From the logical point of view pursued in this Appendix, the distinction between these two types of liberalism is secondary, corroborating the thesis of their profound continuity advanced in this chapter. As maintained in Section 1, updated liberalism is characterised by a different rhetoric orientated to define the limits of the market rather than its superior virtues, and a cautious and motivated extension of the role of the state to new fields.

If, on the contrary, we compare classical and updated liberalism with neoliberalism, we see a sharp distinction that corroborates the present thesis of a discontinuity with the previous tradition of economic liberalism. Neoliberal exponents, in fact, typically accept propositions 2 and 4 but, unlike classical liberalism and updated liberalism, do not accept propositions 3 and 5 on the limits of the invisible hand and of liberal policies. As for proposition 1, the gap is not denied but its importance is played down. Neoliberal exponents, for example, typically believe that monopolistic or oligopolistic deviations from perfect competition in a certain market may be much less important than they seem at first sight to the extent that the market in question remains "contestable" (Baumol et al., 1982). Similarly they deny the soundness of the distinction between strong and week uncertainty, and the empirical relevance of other distinctions emphasised above, such as the distinctions between equilibrium and disequilibrium, bounded and unbounded rationality and so on (Vercelli, 2005). As for proposition 3, the Paretian approach to welfare adopted by most liberal economists since the 1950s implies that the optimality of market equilibrium is conditional on a given initial distribution. According to a common belief in classical and updated liberalism the market performs well when the initial distribution is sufficiently fair, such as to allow all economic agents access to all major options. Neoliberal exponents typically deny this requirement, maintaining that redistributive policies are inconsistent with free market individualism. As for proposition 5, neoliberal exponents typically believe (i) that markets can be completed, e.g. by introducing a congruous number of Arrow securities; (ii) that transaction costs can be reduced at will through institutional reform to enhance the transparency of business decisions or through technological innovations based on ICT; (iii) that externalities may be reduced by defining property rights on free goods, and so on.

The economic policy implications vary according to the different attitudes towards the above propositions. Acceptance of propositions 1, 2 and 4 promotes liberalisation of markets and is the common denominator of the different variants of economic liberalism. Collectivism and statism deny the general validity of proposition 2. The limits of the invisible hand and liberal policies are denied or played down by neoliberal exponents. Thus they deny the benefits of countercyclic policies or interventions directed at internalising externalities. Likewise they reject redistributive policies aimed at equalising wealth and fighting poverty.

Both classical and updated liberalism accept a stronger version of proposition 1 that requires cautious application of competitive theory to real markets. Finally, they both accept proposition 3 on the limits of perfect-competition markets and proposition 5 on the limits to policies directed at reducing the market gap, but updated liberalism accepts a stronger version of the two that expands the scope of state intervention.

## Notes

1. In order to avoid confusion between the usual meaning of *classic* and the particular meaning of Keynes, we write the latter in quotation marks throughout this chapter.
2. This does not imply that his argument was fully correct. John Stuart Mill soon observed that effective exchange ratios not only depend solely on cost conditions but also on demand functions (Mill, 1848).

## References

Agarwal, B., and A. Vercelli, 2005, *Psychology, Rationality and Economic Behaviour: Challenging Standard Assumptions*, Basingstoke and New York: Palgrave Macmillan.

Arrow, K. and F. Hahn, 1999, Notes on Sequence Economies, Transaction Costs, and Uncertainty, *Journal of Economic Theory*, 86(2), pp. 203–18.

Baumol, W.J., J.C. Panzar, and R.D. Willig, 1982, *Contestable Markets and the Theory of Industry Structure*, New York: Harcourt Brace Jovanovich.

Bentham, J., 1952–54, *Jeremy's Bentham's Economic Writings*, 3 vols., ed. W. Stark, London: George Allen and Unwin.

Borghesi, S. and A. Vercelli, 2008, *Global Sustainability. Social and Environmental Conditions*, Basingstoke and New York: Palgrave Macmillan.

Coase, R.H., 1960, The Problem of Social Cost, *Journal of Law and Economics*, 3, pp. 1–44.

Debreu, R., 1959, *The Theory of Value: An Axiomatic Analysis of Economic Equilibrium*, New York: John Wiley and Sons.

De Vroey, M., 2004, *Involuntary Unemployment: The Elusive Quest for a Theory*, London: Routledge.

Friedman, M., 1968, The Role of Monetary Policy, *American Economic Review*, 58, pp. 1–17.

Friedman, M., 1969, *The Optimum Quantity of Money and Other Essays*, Chicago: Aldine.
Goodwin, R.M., 1951, The Nonlinear Accelerator and the Persistence of Business Cycles, *Econometrica*, 19(1), pp. 1–17.
Greenwald, B. and J.E. Stiglitz, 1986, Externalities in Economics with Imperfect Information and Incomplete Markets, *Quarterly Journal of Economics*, 101(2), pp. 229–64.
Harrod, R.F., 1939, An Essay in Dynamic Theory, *Economic Journal*, 49(1), pp. 14–33.
Hicks, J.R., 1937, Mr Keynes and the "Classics": A Suggested Interpretation, *Econometrica*, 5(2), pp. 147–59.
Kerstenetzky, C., 2007, Hayeck and Popper on Ignorance and Intervention, *Journal of Institutional Economics*, 3, pp. 33–53.
Keynes, J.M., 1923, Free Trade, *The Nation and Atheneum*, 24 November and 1 December.
Keynes, J.M., 1925, Am I a liberal?, *The Nation and Athenaeum*, 8 and 15 August, 1925.
Keynes, J.M., 1926, *The End of the Laissez-Faire*, London: Hogart Press.
Keynes, J.M., 1936, *The General Theoryof Employment, Interest and Money*, London: Macmillan.
Klein, L. and A.S. Goldberger, 1955, *An Econometric Model of the United States, 1929–1952*, Amsterdam: North Holland.
Lucas, R.E. Jr., 1981, *Studies in Business-Cycle Theory*, Boston: MIT Press.
Marshall, A., 1891, *Principles of Economics*, London: Macmillan.
Mill, J.S., 1848, *Principles of Political Economy*, London.
Mill, J.S., 1859, *On Liberty*, Boston: Ticker and Fields.
Modigliani, F., 1944, Liquidity Preference and the Theory of Interest and Money, *Econometrica*, 12, pp. 45–88.
Pareto, V., 1906, *Manuale di Economia Politica*, Boringhieri, Torino, 1948.
Patinkin, D., 1956, *Money, Interest and Prices*, New York: Harper and Row.
Phelps, E., 1967, Phillips Curves, Expectations of Inflation and Optimal Unemployment over Time, *Economica*, 34, pp. 254–81.
Phillips, A.W., 1958, The Relation Between Unemployment and the Rate of Change of Money Wage Rates in the United Kingdom, 1851–1957, *Economica*, 25, pp. 283–99.
Pigou, A.C., 1920, *The Economics of Welfare*, London: Macmillan.
Ricardo, D., 1817, *The Principles of Political Economy and Taxation*, London: G.Bell.
Robbins, L., 1952, *The Theory of Economic Policy in English Classical Political Economy*, London: Macmillan.
Samuelson, P.A., 1939, Interaction Between the Multiplier Analysis and the Principle of Acceleration, *Review of Economics and Statistics*, 21, pp. 75–8.
Samuelson, P.A., 1947, *Foundations of Economic Analysis*, Cambridge: Harvard University Press.
Savage, L.J., 1956, *The Foundations of Statistics*, New York: Dover.
Schotter, A., 1985, *Free Market Economics: A Critical Appraisal*, New York: St. Martin's Press.
Shiller, R.J., 2000, *Irrational Exuberance*, Princeton: Princeton University Press.
Skinner, A.A., 1974, *Adam Smith and the Role of the State*, Glasgow: University of Glasgow Press.

Smith, A., 1776, *An Inquiry into the Nature and Causes of the Wealth of Nations*, Oxford University Press, 1976.
Solow, R., 1956, A Contribution to the Theory of Economic Growth, *Quarterly Journal of Economics*, 70(1), pp. 75–94.
Stiglitz, J., 2002, *Globalization and its Discontent*, London: Penguin Books.
Tobin, J., 1958, Liquidity Preference as Behaviour Towards Risk, *The Review of Economic Studies*, 25(2), pp. 65–86.
Vercelli, A., 1991, *Methodological Foundations of Macroeconomics: Keynes and Lucas*, Cambridge: Cambridge University Press.
Vercelli, A., 2000, Structural Financial Instability and Cyclical Fluctuations, *Structural Change and Economic Dynamics*, 11, pp. 139–56.
Vercelli, A., 2002, Uncertainty, Rationality and Rearning: A Keynesian Perspective, ed., S.C. Dow and J. Hillard, *Keynes, Uncertainty and the Global Economy*, vol. 2, Elgar: Cheltenham, pp. 88–105.
Vercelli, A., 2005, Rationality, Learning and Complexity, in Agarwal, B., and A. Vercelli, 2005, pp. 58–83.

# 5
# Corporatism and Keynes: His Views on Growth

*Edmund S. Phelps*

Of the main contests in twentieth-century political economy, the contest between capitalism and corporatism still matters. And it matters quite a lot, as I believe the recent economic record of continental western Europe helps to confirm.[1] My discussion here of the economic thought of John Maynard Keynes will focus on his early "corporatist" dissatisfaction with the market – a dissatisfaction that ran deeper than the Pigovian critique of *laissez faire*, later known as the "free market" system.

## Intellectual currents in Keynes's day

Before we can discuss Keynes in relation to corporatism and capitalism we have to ask: What do they mean now? And in what ways did their meaning differ in Keynes's day?

Today, a predominantly capitalist economy, whatever its minor deviations from the ideal type, means a private-ownership system marked by great *openness* to the *new commercial ideas* and the *personal knowledge* of private entrepreneurs and, further, by great *pluralism* in the *private knowledge* and *idiosyncratic views* among the wealth-owners and financiers who select the ideas to which to provide capital and incentives for their development.[2]

A corporatist economy today is a private-ownership system with some contrasting features: It is pervaded with most or all of the economic institutions created or built up by the system called *corporatavismo* that arose in interwar Italy: big employer confederations, big labour unions and monopolistic banks – with a large state bureaucracy to monitor, intervene and mediate among them. Yet without some knowledge of the purposes for which the system was constructed it cannot be understood at all adequately.

I think it is fair to say that the core function of the distinctive corporatist institutions is to give voice and levers of power to a variety and range of social interests – "stakeholders" and the "social partners" in post-war terminology – so that they might be able to have a say or even a veto in market decisions that would harm them. The individualism of free enterprise is submerged in favour of these entities and the state representing them. This purpose, or function, expresses what might be called *solidarism/communitarianism* and *consensualism/unanimitarianism*. The very word "corporatism" (*corporatavismo* in Italian) derives from *corporazione*, the Italian word for the medieval gild, which served to empower the artisans in a craft.[3] It is clear on its face that the system operates to *facilitate* the introduction of changes in the direction of the economy sought by the state, following consultations and negotiations with stakeholders and social partners, and to *impede* (thus also to discourage) or *block* changes opposed by some of the stakeholders or partners: relocations of firms, entry of new firms, etc. The system's performance thus depends heavily on the established roles of established companies, helped by local and national banks.[4] (The name "corporatism" fell into disuse after World War II and was replaced by the *social market* in Germany, *concertazione* in Italy and *social democracy* in France. Yet some French politicians and journalists freely speak of *corporatisme*. In any case, the western continental European economies are still importantly corporatist, including those in the big 3 – Germany, France and Italy – both in structure and in intent.[5])

Today economists view capitalism as having evolved into a rousing system for cutting-edge innovation and view corporatism as designed for industrial peace, social consensus and community stability – Mars and Venus, roughly speaking.

The thinking in the second half of the 1920s was more nearly the opposite. In 1927 Italy was suffering the effects of an exchange rate stabilization similar to Britain's crisis over its revaluation of the pound, and it was at that time that Mussolini abandoned the experiment with neoclassical policies and sought the ideas for revamping the economy that would be dubbed corporatist. The redesign was to *go for growth*. Severini's *futurist* paintings came to symbolize the aim of the new economic policy. The economic historian Marcello de Cecco comments on the added purpose, writing about this period, remarks:

The limits and modes of State intervention were to be established not by theory but by necessity, and the only imperative was that of making the country as rich and powerful as was possible, given the constraints that existed at all times.[6]

Yet the Italians did theorize. Many of the corporatist theoreticians thought that the corporatist system beginning to take shape in 1927 would be *more* dynamic than capitalism – maybe not more fertile in little ideas, such as might come to petit bourgeois entrepreneurs, but certainly in big ideas. Not having to fear fluid market conditions, an entrenched company could afford to develop expensive innovations based on current or developable technologies. And with industrial confederations and state mediation available, such companies could arrange to avoid costly duplication of their investments. The state for its part would promote technological advances in cooperation with industry.[7] The state could indicate new economic directions and favour some investments over others through its instrument, the big banks. In the eyes of these theoreticians, then, the system's purpose was a mobilization of the nation's collective knowledge – a view that might be termed *scientism*.

## The corporatism in Keynes

Keynes in the mid-1920s confronted an economic system in Britain that suffered many of the stresses that Mussolini's new economic policy aimed to solve. And Keynes, then in his early 1940s, was not too old to be intrigued by the new arguments against the Smithian economic model coming out of Italy. In fact, Keynes's political economy showed some parallels with corporatist thinking. Some of these parallels are in the area of industrial organization theory and industrial policy.

*Keynes an exponent of top-down growth.* Contrary to American impressions that his microeconomics was neoclassical – more than Marshall's was – Keynes rejected atomistic competition as an efficient market form. The policy he advocated called for the government to assist the ongoing movement towards cartels, holding companies, trade associations, pools and others forms of monopoly power; then the government was to regulate the affected industries.[8] "In the 1920s at least", James Crotty concludes, "Keynes was unabashedly corporatist, supporting a powerful microeconomic as well as macroeconomic role for the state."[9]

Such a wave of consolidation and unionization did occur to varying degrees in the 1930s not only in the United Kingdom, but also on the European continent and in the United States. In the United States by the end of the decade, there were three giant auto makers where there had been tens of companies in the early 1920s. The Temporary National Economic Committee (TNEC) was established by Congress in 1938 to advise on the regulatory and dissolution questions posed by the oligopolistic organization of much of American industry. This was the corporatist-tinged system that prevailed in the United States from the presidential terms of Franklin Roosevelt through those of Richard Nixon, whereupon it began to erode and, in places, to break up with anti-trust break-ups, deregulation initiatives and global competition.

Was this modified system for the good, as Keynes and the corporatists believed? The economies of scale, Chandler's economies of scope, and the dynamic economies of "learning", or practice, on the repetitive assembly line that were achieved over the span of consolidation/rationalization (leaving aside the unionization, which may not have helped) running from 1920 to 1941 must have been extraordinary. The increase in hourly productivity and of total factor productivity over both those decades was unprecedented and has not been matched since (with the possible exception of the past 10-year span). Hitler marvelled at the stunning productivity level at the Ford Motor plant, according to records of his "table talk" in the early 1940s. But was this system better at *innovating* than was the system of the 1920s that it replaced? In the judgement of Joseph Schumpeter in 1944 the answer was yes. That is also the verdict of our own William Baumol in his 2003 book.[10] But the econometric results are not in – not yet, although it is safe to say that they are now not far off. In an excoriating attack on that period, Carl Schramm sees it as having been replaced in successive steps beginning in the 1970s by a more nearly capitalist system that is far more innovative than the semi-corporatist system was.[11]

In the late 1930s and early 1940s, Friedrich Hayek was to initiate a modern theory explaining how a capitalist system, if not too weighed down with imperfections and departures, would possess the greatest dynamism – not socialism and not corporatism.[12] First, virtually everyone right down to the humblest employees has arcane "know-how", some of it what Michael Polanyí called "personal knowledge" and some merely private knowledge, and out of that an idea may come that few others, if any, would have.[13] In its openness to ideas of all or most participants, the economy tends to generate a plethora of new ideas. Second, the pluralism of experience and knowledge that the financiers bring to bear in their decisions gives a wide range of entrepreneurial ideas a chance of an informed, insightful evaluation. And, importantly, the financier and the entrepreneur do not need the approval of the state or of social partners. Nor are they accountable later on to such a social body if the project goes badly, not even to the financier's investors. So projects can be undertaken that would be too opaque and uncertain for the state or social partners to endorse. Third, the pluralism of knowledge and experience that managers and consumers bring to bear in deciding which innovations to try and which of those to adopt is crucial in giving a good chance to the most promising innovations launched. Where the Continental system, acting in the spirit of scientism, convenes experts to set a product standard before any version is launched, capitalism gives market access to all versions – an inconvenience that pays off later.

Keynes writing in the mid-1920s knew nothing of such an argument. Keynes must have reflected upon the theorizing of the Italian corporatists and of Theodore Roosevelt's Progressive Party but could not have encountered the Hayekian argument for the superior innovativeness of capitalism. There is nothing in his writings up to that time that suggests he would have been attuned to it.

*Keynes disdainful of the quest for wealth.* Keynes was blind to almost all of the satisfactions that might come from an economy of real dynamism. He brilliantly grasped the results of Frank Ramsey on the optimality of growing through capital formation until some sort of "bliss" level of satisfaction is reached: After all, he had inspired Ramsey to do the analysis and he provided Ramsey with an intuitive explanation of the algebraic formula for the optimum rate of saving. Keynes's "Economic Possibilities for our Grandchildren" reflects in several passages his clear understanding of the benefit – mainly in the form of rising leisure – that comes from capital accumulation: from piling on more and more machinery until the marginal productivity of it has ceased to justify any more capital deepening. He appeared to see no satisfactions from the growth process.

This attitude of Keynes – unusual for an economist – was emblematic of the intellectual current in Europe at that time called *anti-materialism*. That strain in social thought was the main theme of the "Christian corporatism" that arose on the Continent in the second half of the nineteenth century: an indifference to business life and a devaluation of wealth, its accumulation and its holding. The 1893 Papal Encyclical of Leo XIII, *Rerum Novarum*, is all about the higher value to be placed on life, community and worship compared with the materialist satisfactions of, say, consuming and earning. From this point of view, the commercial economy is no more than a regrettable necessity. That view of the world was yet another strain in twentieth-century economic corporatism, which sees a conflict between employee and shareowner, between one employee and another and between one company and another but did not see know-how, entrepreneurship and innovation as driven by various materialist desires including the pursuit of wealth, know-how and fame.

Keynes and the corporatists did not understand that much of the huge rise of productivity that the world was to see from 1920 onwards would be traceable to new commercial products and new business methods that could only have been developed and launched in the relatively capitalist economies;[14] and that if increased wealth, which successful innovations result in, is denigrated, that would constitute one more "minus" among the pluses and minuses of undertaking innovative projects and that such an effect would put a premature end to economic growth.

*Keynes blind to the intellectual satisfactions in business life.* Corporatism did not comprehend that an economy fired by the new ideas of entrepreneurs serves to transform the workplace – in the firms developing an innovation and also in the firms dealing with the innovations. The challenges that arise in developing a new idea and in gaining its acceptance in the marketplace and the challenges to management and consumers in figuring out how and whether to adopt the latest innovation provide the workforce with high levels of mental stimulation, problem solving and thus employee engagement and personal growth. (Note that an individual working alone cannot easily create the continual arrival of new challenges. It takes a village, better yet the whole society.)

Is there any precedent for thinking that people – virtually all people – value such stimulation, mastery, growth and discovery? The concept that they do originates in Europe: There is the classical Aristotle, who writes of the "development of talents", later the Renaissance figure Cellini, who jubilates in achievement and advancement, and the baroque writer Cervantes, who evokes vitality and challenge. By the early part of the twentieth-century economists Alfred Marshall and Gunnar Myrdal write that engagement in the job is already hugely important in the advanced economies. It may be that this view, sometimes called *vitalism*, is now strongly associated with the pragmatist school founded by the American William James to which Henri Bergson in France and John Dewey in the United States belonged. The American psychologist Abraham Maslow coined "self-actualization" and John Rawls the terms "self-realization" to refer to a person's emerging mastery and unfolding scope. (Amartya Sen has referred to "expanding capabilities to do things".) These two Americans understood that most, if not all, of the attainable self-realization in modern societies can come only from career. We cannot go tilting at windmills, but we can take on the challenges of career. If a challenging career is not the main hope for self-realization, what else could be? Even to be a good mother it helps to have the experience of work outside the home.

The *solidarism* that is a part of corporatist culture militates against a life of such personal development. Although anti-materialism led to a certain devaluation of wealth, and thus also to frowning on any visible efforts at increasing the amount of observable wealth one possessed, the idea of solidarism sees it as unacceptable to move out of one's place in the community. In a solidarist society people who go to great lengths to stand out in their group or to escape their group are hated.

Alas, Keynes conveyed no sense of the role of innovation in imparting excitement and personal development to business careers. Nowhere is this clearer than in his famous passage in "Economic Possibilities of our Grandchildren":

> [I]f we look into the past, we find that the economic problem, the struggle for subsistence, always has been hitherto the primary, most pressing problem of the human race...If the economic is solved, mankind will be deprived of its traditional purpose. Thus for the first time since his creation man will be faced with his real, his permanent problem – how to use his freedom from pressing economic cares, how to occupy the leisure, which and compound interest will have won for him, to live wisely and agreeably and well.
>
> For many ages to come the old Adam will be so strong in us that everybody will need to do *some* work if he is to be contented.... When the accumulation of wealth is no longer of high social importance,...we shall be able to rid ourselves of many of the pseudo-moral principles which have hag-ridden us for two hundred years, by which we have exalted some of the most distasteful of human qualities into the position of the highest virtues.[15]

The most basic of these is that nowhere does Keynes recognize the wisdom of the pragmatist school – from James to Dewey to Rawls and on to Sen – that people need to exercise their minds with novel challenges – new problems to solve, new talents to develop. A mistake like that in the initial premise dooms the essay to misguided conclusions, such as the conclusion that people will learn simply to enjoy things without any effort.

But if Keynes *had* recognized that people *need* a system that throws out problems to challenge the mind and engage the spirit, he would still have gone wrong because he never saw that with the technical progress and capital deepening that he aptly postulates, an ever-increasing share of people can *afford* jobs that are stimulating and engaging; so unless the economic system is prevented from doing so, more and more jobs will be *supplied* that offer stimulation and engagement. So, were working-age people not to work or to work only a few hours a week, a great number of them would find themselves deprived of the fruit that is the special prize of the most advanced economies. The only persuasive position to take is that, with steady technical progress, an increasing number of jobs will offer the change and challenge that only the predominantly capitalist economies, thanks to their dynamism, can generate.

These thoughts point to what might be called the Keynes Puzzle and the likely answer to it. The *puzzle* is that, if we accept Keynes's psychological and economic framework, which is essentially that of Frank Ramsey, we should expect to see the workweek shrinking over the centuries to next to nothing, as Keynes made explicit; and yet we see nothing of the kind. It is a fact – notorious among some social critics – that in the United States the workweek has shrunk little if at all in recent decades. Indeed, as more and more people work in the financial industry and the legal profession, we may see the mean work week begin to reverse field and rise towards some steady-state level higher than it is now. The *answer* to the puzzle is that work is *not everywhere an inferior good*. It is locally inferior at an onerous work level but not at levels so low that they would deprive of us of some of the stimulation, challenge and personal development we can find in our careers. The fact that work has not come to an end in some Ramseyan march towards "bliss" is *strong evidence* of the fallaciousness of the Keynes–Ramsey theory of what people want and where, accordingly, societies are headed – if they haven't already got there.

## The legacy of corporatism

Keynes's thinking nevertheless proved prophetic in a way. Most of the Continental economies, including even the largest ones, though repeatedly able to catch up *technologically* with the world's "lead economies" after one or more of the latter have spurted ahead, continue to exhibit sub-par innovation, job satisfaction and employee engagement. As a result, a range of social and economic indicators, from birth rates and emigration to participation rate and unemployment, continue to signal the stultifying influence of corporatist culture and policy on the Continent.

## Notes

McVickar Professor of Political Economy and Director, Center on Capitalism and Society, Earth Institute, Columbia University. This chapter constitutes the first half of a presentation at the conference *Keynes's General Theory after Seventy Years*, July 3–6, 2006, Santa Colomba (Siena). The thoughts here about Keynes have benefited from conversations with several scholars, including Jean-Paul Fitoussi, Roman Frydman, the late Harry Johnson and Joseph Stiglitz.

1. Many blame the "social model" for the Continent's relatively high unemployment and anaemic participation rates, though perhaps not for the lower hourly productivity. And, empirically, employment does not appear to have suffered in the United Kingdom and Ireland in spite of their large welfare outlays.
2. The term *free enterprise* might convey better this Hayekian conception of capitalism, but I would rather not proliferate terminology.
3. With the rise of the market economy these bodies were criticized as monopolistic and in the French Revolution the D'Allarde Decree abolished them, though many managed to come back.
4. A recent survey of the strains of corporative economic thought in interwar Italy is Marco E. L. Guidi, "Corporative Economics and the Italian Tradition of Economic Thought," in *Storia del Pensiero Economico*, No. 40, 2000/I. The paper is available at www.dse.unifi.it/spe/indici/numero40/guidi.html. I have placed an excerpt in the Appendix.
5. Since World War II, some of them may have become less corporatist with the liberalizations that reduced the monopoly power of firms and banks (as in France). In most of them, however, new corporatist institutions have sprung up: Codetermination (*cogestion* or *Mitbestimmung*) has brought "worker councils" and in Germany a union representative generally sits on the investment committee of the corporation.
6. Marcello de Cecco, "Keynes and Italian Economists," ms., Fiesole, ca. 1983, p. 19. The author emphasizes that some of Mussolini's new economic policy of 1927 had roots in anti-liberal ideology of pre-Fascist times.
7. A presidential decree of February 1919 established a board "aiming at preparing a projected constitution for a National Research Council," the purpose of which was "the planning and promotion of researches for science and industry" along with national defense. The CNR came into being with a decree in November 1923. A similar body in France was formed in 1939. The US National Science Foundation was created only in 1950 "to promote the progress of science; to advance the national health, prosperity, and welfare; to secure the national defense..."

8. Two of these statements are Keynes, "The End of Laissez Faire," reprinted in *Essays in Persuasion*, and the Liberal Party publication, *Britain's Industrial Future* (1928).
9. James Crotty, "Was Keynes a Corporatist? Keynes's Radical Views on Industrial Policy and Macro Policy in the 1920s," *Journal of Economic Ideas*, 33(3), September 1999, 555–78. A reviewer in Amazon.com argues that Keynes's agenda was no different from that of the 1912 Progressive Party of Theodore Roosevelt.
10. J. A. Schumpeter, *Capitalism, Socialism and Democracy*, New York, Harper & Bros., 1944; W. J. Baumol, *The Free-Market Growth Machine*, Princeton, Princeton University Press, 2003.
11. C. J. Schramm, "Entrepreneurial Capitalism and the End of Bureaucracy," Annual Meetings, American Economic Association, Boston, January 2006.
12. F. A. Hayek, *The Economic Order*, London, 1937, and *The Road to Serfdom*, London, 1943.
13. A column in the *Wall Street Journal* told of a deliveryman who was asked whether he found it best to work from the top floor down or the reverse. "It depends on the time of day," he replied. A beautiful Hayekian moment.
14. These include household appliances from vacuum cleaners to refrigerators, sound movies, frozen food, pasteurized orange juice, television, transistors, semi-conductor chips, the internet browser, the redesign of cinemas and the recent retailing methods. (Of course there were often engineering tasks and technical advances required along the way, yet business entrepreneurs were the drivers.)
15. Keynes, "Economic Possibilities for Our Grandchildren," *Atheneum*, 1930, reprinted in *Essays in Persuasion*, London, Macmillan, 1932; New York, Harcourt Brace, 1932.

# 6
# Keynes, Art and Aesthetics

*Gilles Dostaler*

Art occupied a very important place in Keynes's life and thought, more than for any other economist.[1] His wife, Lydia Lopokova, was a ballet dancer. His great friend and once lover, Duncan Grant, was a painter. Vanessa Bell, Virginia Woolf's sister, was one of his main confidents. Most of his closest friends were artists, writers, art and literary critics. The majority of them were part, with him, of the Bloomsbury set. Not an artist, which he regretted, Keynes was an eager consumer of art. The first art into which he was initiated, by his parents, was theatre and he would remain attached to it until the end of his life. In 1896 the New Theatre was founded in Cambridge, where the best companies in England would perform. His mother wrote of him: "he thus acquired that love of drama which developed throughout his life and led to his building the Arts Theater as a gift to the Borough of Cambridge" (Scrase and Croft 1983, p. 7). Keynes later turned to ballet, especially on the arrival of Diaghileff's company in London in 1911. He would rapidly become a passionate amateur of this art bringing together dance, music and painting. He discovered impressionist painting in Paris, where he was travelling with his mother in 1905, and started to buy pictures in 1908. He continued to buy regularly, from his friends and other English painters and, starting from the Degas sale in Paris in 1918, he began acquiring oeuvres from great international masters: Cézanne, Delacroix, Matisse, Picasso, Seurat, Renoir, Derain, Braque and Courbet. These paintings became part of his environment. He often repeated how happy he was to return from a trip to find Cézanne in his bedroom and Sickert over his piano.

Often, if not most of the time, Keynes would be advised when buying by his friends Vanessa Bell, Duncan Grant or Roger Fry. Richard Shone published the following testimony of Duncan Grant:

> To have Maynard and his money there on the spot, to be able to persuade him to buy, was a splendid compensation for relative poverty.... Maynard had, perhaps, little innate feeling and understanding of painting, but his discrimination and knowledge grew over the years and was aided by Lydia's more quickly responsive feelings and definite if somewhat idiosyncratic views.
> 
> (Shone with Grant 1975, p. 284)

Opinions on Keynes's aesthetic sense were divided. Thus Clive Bell wrote:

> He had very little natural feeling for the arts; though he learnt to write admirably lucid prose, and, under the spell of Duncan Grant, cultivated a taste for pictures and made an interesting collection. Said Lytton Strachey once: "What's wrong with Pozzo – a pet name for Maynard which Maynard particularly disliked – is that he has no aesthetic sense".
> 
> (Bell 1956, pp. 134–5)

Keynes played a very important role as patron of the arts in Great Britain. He wrote that "civilized ages have always recognized that a patron of the arts performs for the society he lives in a distinguished and magnanimous function. Without patrons art cannot easily flourish" (Keynes 1921, p. 297). He supported his friends and other English painters such as William Robert, Walter Sickert or Ivon Hitchens by buying their work, but also by direct financial aid. He subscribed in 1909 to an organization launched to buy paintings of contemporary British artists, the Contemporary Arts Society of which he will become a buyer. In 1918, he persuaded his boss, the chancellor of the Exchequer, to allow him to spend £20,000 to buy for the National Gallery at the sale of an important collection of French paintings having belonged to Degas, held in Paris. He founded in 1925, with three other well off mecenes, the London Artists' Association, to manage the artist's financial affairs, take care of selling their work and guarantee them a minimal regular income. After the death, in August 1929, of Diaghileff, the future of ballet in Great Britain became uncertain. Keynes contributed, with his wife, to the founding of the Camargo Society, again with the goal of providing a regular income to all those involved in ballet. He was the treasurer of the organization. In 1933, Keynes embarked on his most ambitious and expensive project, the creation of the Cambridge Arts Theatre. He was actively involved in all aspects of this entreprise, from the building of the theatre to the menu and wine list of the restaurant, the programming of spectacles and of course the financing of all these activities. The Arts Theatre was opened, by a soirée de ballet, with a performance of his wife, the day before the publication of *The General Theory of Employment, Interest and Money*, on 3 February 1936.

As we know, Keynes, then a sick man, was extraordinarily active during the war years, on many different battlefronts. He made six trips to the United States, some of them for many months. At times, he was leading the British delegation, for very difficult and exhausting negotiations. Nevertheless, he accepted, in 1942, the presidency of the Council for the Encouragement of Music and the Arts (CEMA). The objectives of this institution was to help financially artists whose situation had been made precarious by the war and to offer artistic events to a dispersed population cut off from its customary activities during the winter curfew. Despite his other tasks, Keynes followed very closely the CEMA affairs, discussing and approving reports, projects and administrative questions, insisting that all correspondence be sent to him when he was abroad: "He asked that all minutes of meetings be sent to him without delay, wherever he was, and instructed me to write him full reports of everything that happened. These he dissected at once and returned them with comments of devastating frankness" (Glasgow 1975, p. 270). Returning from Bretton Woods, in 1944, Keynes began to think about the creation of a permanent structure to succeed the CEMA, that would place art at the forefront in Great Britain. This would be the Arts Council of Great Britain, the creation of which was approved in January 1945. At a press conference called in June, Keynes declared:

> The purpose of the Arts Council of Great Britain is to create an environment to breed a spirit, to cultivate an opinion, to offer a stimulus to such purpose that the artist and the public can sustain and live on the other in that union which has occasionally existed in the past at the great ages of a communal civilised life.
>
> (Keynes 1945, p. 372)

Trustee of the National Gallery since October 1941, Keynes has been named chairman of the Trustees of the Royal Opera House, Covent Garden, while he was at Bretton Woods in July 1944. He was associated with all aspects of the reopening after the war of Covent Garden, including the hall's decoration. On 20 February 1946, the theatre was inaugurated with a production of Tchaikovsky's *Sleeping Beauty* in the presence of three generations of the royal family. Keynes, who underwent a mild heart attack during the arrival of the royal family, occupied with Lydia neighbouring seats. It would be his last public appearance in his home country. On April 5th, he decided to bequeath £5000 to the Royal Opera Trust. The Arts Council would not see its charter incorporated until 10 July 1946, after the death of its designated president.

## Art, science and society

Keynes's activities in the artistic world are not a kind of side-interest, a recreation from his tasks as an economist, publicist, man of the City and of Whitehall. Nor are there the result of his links with Bloomsbury. They fit in a worldview, a *Weltanschauung* that is fixed very early in his mind. Keynes considered that art is the noblest of human activities, and that it should occupy in a civilized society the first place. This position has been influenced by Moore's *Principia Ethica*, which had such an impact on Keynes and his Apostles friends when it was published 1903:

> its effect on *us*, and the talk which preceded and followed it, dominated, and perhaps still dominate, everything else.... it was exciting, exhilarating, the beginning of a renaissance, the opening of a new heaven on a new earth, we were the forerunners of a new dispensation, we were not afraid of anything.
> (Keynes 1938, p. 435)

This book intends to give an answer to the central question of ethics: What is good? After a detailed criticism of all false answers to this question, Moore affirms that the greatest imaginable goods are states of consciousness associated with aesthetic pleasure, the appreciation of beautiful objects, on the one hand, and with personal affections on the other: "No one, probably, who has asked himself the question, has ever doubted that personal affection and the appreciation of what is beautiful in Art or Nature, are good in themselves" (Moore 1903, p. 237). Commenting on this in 1938, Keynes said to his friends of the Bloomsbury Memoir Club: "The appropriate subjects of passionate contemplation and communion were a beloved person, beauty and truth, and one's prime objects in life were love, the creation and enjoyment of aesthetic experience and the pursuit of knowledge" (Keynes 1938, pp. 436–7). He added that this view was still his religion.

To personal relations and the contemplation of beauty, Keynes thus added, as a third source of good states of mind, the pursuit of truth. But the scientist, who seeks the truth, must recognize that the artist is over him: "This, then, is the first step towards peace, the scientist must admit the artist to be his master". This he wrote in a paper read to the Apostles on 20 February 1909 (Keynes 1909a), at the beginning of his career as an economist. The creative process of an artwork has, on the scale of human activities, a greater intrinsic value than that of the discovery of new knowledge. Keynes himself would have preferred to have been an artist, he told his brothers at the end of his talk. Choosing between Newton, Leibniz and Darwin or Milton, Wordsworth and Velasquez, he would have liked to have been one of the last three. He did not consider himself sufficiently gifted to be an artist. But the gulf between art and science is not as large as we may think. A few years before, he wrote in another chapter, "A Theory of Beauty": "Nothing can be more fatal than the supposed antagonism between the precise and verbal notions of philosophy and the organic, indivisible perceptions of beauty and feeling, between these things that we know piecemeal and those which we may only grasp as wholes, between those who see and those who understand" (Keynes 1905b, p. 2). To understand beauty, but also society, the economy and the world, one must bring together analysis and intuition:

> We require for success at the same time a separation and collaboration of the analytic and intuitive powers. He will be a very singular individual who possesses both in any high degree; but if only the philosopher and the artist lose their mutual feeling of suspicion, and the genius of the one check and direct the genius of the other, then the parts and kinds of beauty will be known at last and knowledge and creation may advance together.
> 
> (Ibid., p. 3)

The artist is unable to translate completely into words the nature of his perceptions. His language must necessarily lack exactitude. But his vision must never be blurred. The artist and the philosopher must both learn to perceive. The philosopher, for his part, may lack an artist's taste and creative capacity, "But he must have enough of the artist in him to know the nature and objects of aesthetic judgment; he must himself be capable of strong and individual impressions on these matters, and he must continually check his analysis by the experience of more subtle and sensitive minds" (ibid., p. 5).

In his 1909 paper, Keynes writes that it is hitherto difficult to excel in the domains of art and science. It is unlikely we will see a new Leonardo da Vinci born in the twentieth century. Moreover, artists and scientists understand each other less and less and at times even look down on each other. It is necessary to overcome these misunderstandings and recognize that the gap between artistic activity and scientific activity is not as wide as one thinks. The scientist, like the artist, is a creator. And both use intuition to develop their works. The greatest scientists, Newton, Einstein and others have insisted on the importance of a theory's elegance, however arid it may be. And to convince their contemporaries of their theory's validity, they must use the art of rhetoric. One of Keynes's last writings deals with Newton, whose manuscripts on alchemy he acquired in 1936. In it he insists on the primordial role of intuition in scientific work, including the field of "hard science". Newton's experiments "were always, I suspect, a means, not of discovering, but always of verifying what he knew already" (Keynes 1947, p. 366). And he concludes that the gap so many others see between Newton's alchemical investigations and his serious scientific work does not exist. For Newton as for Freud, for Darwin so for Keynes, intuition rather than induction is the first step in the process of knowledge.

This view of the relation of art with science has also been developed by Keynes's friend, the oldest member of Bloomsbury, the painter and art critic Roger Fry, who was first trained as a natural scientist.[2] Fry's friend, Charles Mauron, himself chemist and literary critic, wrote "One of the most remarkable traits of his personality was certainly a rare combination of scientific spirit and esthetic sensibility" (Caws and Wright 2000, p. 268). Fry's "An Essay in aesthetics" (1909), alongside Clive Bell *Arts* (1914), define Bloomsbury aesthetic canons. In "Art and science" (1919), Fry explains that one difference between art and science is that emotion is present at all steps in art, while scientific activity can be purely intellectual and mechanical. He borrows from Tolstoy's *What is Art?* the view that aim of art is not the imitation of nature, or the transmission of a message, but a means of communication of emotion between human beings. But he adds:

> None the less, perhaps, the highest pleasure in art is identical with the highest pleasure in scientific theory. The emotion which accompanies the clear recognition of unity in a complex seems to be so similar in art and science that it seems difficult not to suppose that they are psychologically the same.
> 
> (Fry 1919, pp. 57–8)

This points of course in the direction of Freud, an important figure for Bloomsbury, of who Keynes wrote:

> Professor Freud seems to me to be endowed, to the degree of genius, with the scientific imagination which can body forth an abundance of innovating ideas, shattering possibilities, working hypotheses, which have sufficient foundation in intuition and common experience to deserve the most patient and unprejudiced examination, and which contain, in all probability, both theories which will have to be discarded or altered out of recognition and also theories of great and permanent significance.
>
> (Keynes 1925, p. 392)

In his 1909 paper on science and art, Keynes considered a third human activity, the pursuit of wealth, estimating that it stands lower in the scale of human accomplishments:

> I, the moderator, believe that the scientist should take an intermediate position in the world. It is certain that he spends his time much better than the businessman spends his.... But is it not almost as certain that the good artist stands to the scientist very much as the scientist stands to the stockbroker? Putting moneymaker and capacity aside, is there any brother who would not rather be a scientist than a businessman, and an artist than a scientist?
>
> (1909a, p. 1)

Many years later, he gives a psychological explanation to this situation, probably inspired by Freud's theory of sublimation, of which he was surely aware. Businessmen are men with a high libido, but without the intellectual and moral qualities necessary to sublimate these pulsions in the pursuit of knowledge or the creation of beauty:

> Why do practical men find it more amusing to make money than to join in open conspiracy?...That is why, unless they have the luck to be scientists or artists, they fall back on the grand substitute motive, the perfect *ersatz*, the anodyne for those who, in fact, want nothing at all – money.... Clissold and his brother Dickon, the advertising expert, flutter about the world seeking for something to which they can attach their abundant *libido*. But they have not found

it. They would so like to be apostles. But they cannot. They remain business men.

(Keynes 1927a, pp. 319–20)

The problem in modern societies, which manifested itself with the triumph of laissez-faire capitalism, is the debasement of art by money. According to Keynes, statesmen have always been known, both for their own glory and for their people's satisfaction, to spend a considerable part of national income on magnificent buildings, works of art and ceremonies. Of course religion played an important role in these undertakings. Many of the wonders of the world were built in this way. Unfortunately, since the eighteenth Century, a transformation in the vision of State and society has occurred. This reached its zenith in the nineteenth Century, continues to this day and has been catastrophic for civilization:

> This view was the utilitarian and economic – one might almost say financial – ideal, as the sole, respectable purpose of the community as a whole; the most dreadful heresy, perhaps, which has ever gained the ear of a civilized people. Bread and nothing but bread, and not even bread, and bread accumulating at compound interest until it has turned into a stone. Poets and artists have lifted occasional weak voices against the heresy.
>
> (Keynes 1936, p. 342)

In the realm of art as elsewhere, the "vision of the Treasury" has triumphed. Only spending serving exclusively economic ends is acceptable. Solely one form of unprofitable spending has survived from the heroic ages of humanity: war. Three years earlier, in "National Self-Sufficiency", he spoke even more virulently against these effects of capitalism:

> The same rule of self-destructive financial calculation governs every walk of life. We destroy the beauty of the countryside because the unappropriated splendours of nature have no economic value. We are capable of shutting off the sun and the stars because they do not pay a dividend. London is one of the richest cities in the history of civilization, but it cannot "afford" the highest standards of achievement of which its own living citizens are capable, because they do not "pay".

> If I had the power today I should surely set out to endow our capital cities with all the appurtenances of art and civilization on the highest standards of which the citizens of each were individually capable, convinced that what I could create, I could afford – and believing that the money thus spent would not only be better than any dole, but would make unnecessary any dole.
>
> (Keynes 1933, p. 242)

Thus, for Keynes, civilization will thrive only once it has succeeded in liberating itself from the tyranny of financial profitability. As important as monuments and buildings, festivities and ceremonial occasions constitute essential moments in every normal life, which cannot be reduced to often meaningless work. Such events are not generally financially profitable and if they become so, it is most often a sign of decadence: "The exploitation and incidental destruction of the divine gift of the public entertainer by prostituting it to the purposes of financial gain is one of the worser crimes of present-day capitalism" (Keynes 1936, p. 344). The artist today finds himself in such a precarious situation that his "attitude...to his work renders him exceptionally unsuited for financial contacts" (ibid.).

In his article, Keynes proposes a scale of intervention relating to art's more or less public character. Architecture is the most public of the arts, "best suited to give form and body to civic pride and the sense of social unity" (ibid., p. 345). Music comes next, followed by the various performing arts, visual arts, the exception being sculpture, which is a complement to architecture, and finally poetry and literature "by their nature more private and personal" (ibid.). Major spending on the arts is what makes the authoritarian regimes of Germany, Italy and Russia strong. England, France and the United States, perverted by the Treasury vision, lag behind. Beyond maintaining full employment, the State has the responsibility of upholding civilization. This does not mean that artistic activity must be regulated by the State, administered by bureaucrats and politicians, as is the case in totalitarian States. In a broadcast to mark the creation of the Arts Council, Keynes said:

> At last the public exchequer has recognised the support and encouragement of the civilising arts of life as part of their duty. But we do not intend to socialise this side of social endeavour. Whatever views may be held by the lately warring parties, whom you have been hearing every evening at this hour, about socialising industry, everyone,

I fancy, recognises that the work of the artist in all its aspects is, of its nature, individual and free, undisciplined, unregimented, uncontrolled. The artist walks where the breath of the spirit blows him. He cannot be told his direction; he does not know it himself. But he leads the rest of us into fresh pastures and teaches us to love and to enjoy what we often begin by rejecting, enlarging our sensibility and purifying our instincts.

(Keynes 1945, p. 368)

## Reflections on aesthetics

Keynes occasionally published reviews of plays or ballet productions, often anonymously or under a pseudonym, in particular in *The Nation and Athenaeum*. He even once tried his hand at film criticism (1924). He wrote promotion material, which was called "puff", for shows and productions with which he was associated. On several occasions, Keynes appeared within the columns of *Nation and Athenaeum* and elsewhere to give his opinion on the events taking place in the world of visual art. Under the signature of Siela, he intervened in a debate between Sargent and Leonard Woolf on the definition of impressionism (Keynes 1927b). He sometimes composed catalogue introductions.

These again are not peripheral and accidental activities. Friend of artists, consumer and patron of the arts, Keynes also wrote on art and beauty, he had views on aesthetics. This is not as well known as is activities as patron. From the start of his Apostles Society membership, in 1903, to his "taking wings" in 1910, Keynes presented over twenty papers, most of a philosophic nature. Many of them are linked, in one way or another, to Moore's *Principia Ethica*. They deal with ethics, but also with epistemology, leading to *A Treatise on Probability*. About half of them treat also of aesthetic considerations. And, what is more interesting, Keynes develops there certain ideas and themes that will be elaborated independently by other Bloomsbury members, such as Roger Fry, Clive Bell and Virginia Woolf. Thus, if there is an influence of Bloomsbury on Keynes, there is also an influence of Keynes on Bloomsbury.[3]

In "Beauty", presented on 30 April 1904, Keynes engages, as he does with ethics and probability, in a critical development of Moore's arguments. He criticizes Moore's conception of beauty as excessively broad and vague. In *Principia Ethica*, Moore defines the beautiful as "that of which the admiring contemplation is good in itself" (Moore 1903, p. 275). For Keynes, there are things we may contemplate with admiration that are not beautiful: "but I am not so clear that there is one specific thing *beauty* attaching to everything of which the admiring contemplation is good" (Keynes 1904, pp. 3–4). Keynes considers that, excluding natural beauty and perhaps a small number of exceptional art works, there is no beauty in and of itself. We attribute beauty to paintings.

"Miscellenea Ethica", written between July and September 1905, proposes important reflections on aesthetics. It contains a concept which will go on to play a central role in Keynes's aesthetic vision, that of "fitness": " 'Fit' can be completely specified by reference to 'good', but both notions seem to be unique and elementary. Corresponding to every good feeling there is a fit object and we may say that those objects are fit towards which it is possible to have a feeling which is good" (Keynes 1905a, pp. 5–6). Defined in this way, fitness is a mental object that corresponds to an external object. Good states of mind or aesthetic emotions are on the contrary linked to our perception. The beauty of an object comes from its intrinsic characteristics, but also from our organs of perception and from our spatial position relative to it:

> The beauty of some pictures depends a good deal upon the particular method in which we fix them; those in particular which rely for their effect upon distant or elaborate perspective sometimes require that kind of adjustment of the eyes which we must often make in using stereoscopic or opera glasses, if we are to see the object with distinctness.
> 
> (ibid., p. 17)

Furthermore, beauty is an organic unity, in the sense that the beauty of a whole is not the sum of the beauty of its parts, this being the case regardless of whether it is a human being, a painting or any other object likely to provoke an aesthetic emotion.

Between August and October 1905, Keynes wrote "A Theory of Beauty", his most elaborate paper on aesthetics. This text was not written for the Apostles, but for the G. L. Dickinson Society, where it was read on 8 November 1905. The paper was presented before the Apostles on 5 May 1912. He wrote to Lytton Strachey, 12 November 1905: "I forgot to tell you that I read my paper on Beauty at Dickinson's last Wednesday. It was too esoteric and I didn't feel it was much of a success." The text is rather more abstract than esoteric, which is inevitable given the theme it tackles.

Before exposing his own conception of beauty, Keynes criticizes a number of erroneous views. According to Dürer, for example, beauty flows from mathematical proportions between the parts of a whole. For

Burke, a list may be drawn of characteristics enabling one to qualify an object as beautiful. For others, beauty is identified with some other entity external to it, such as the good, the useful or pleasure. Great thinkers such as Socrates and Plato are not spared. Much of the confusion comes from the belief in the fact that beauty is one and indivisible, that there exists but one type of beauty. Having found a criterion to justify our taste in one case, we seek to apply it to all others. Accordingly, we would like Degas for the same reasons we like Botticelli, which, for Keynes, is absurd.

Beauty's value is solely the result of the emotions it arouses within conscious beings: "In the realm of beauty, man is the center of the Universe" (ibid., p. 9). Contrary to Moore, the fact that there are splendours hidden to our eyes in the mountains of the Moon does not increase the beauty of the Universe. It is not beauty in itself that is good, but rather the emotions beauty arouses. The value of these emotions resides in the relation between emotion and the contents of our mind and not in the relation between this content and some cause which is supposed to be the source of the emotion: "There is a further point of a somewhat similar nature, but much more controversial. I maintain that the value of our feelings depends solely on their relation to what we see, and not at all on the relation between what we see and what is there" (ibid., pp. 9–10).

If human beings were to become, like certain animal species, sensitive to ultraviolet or to infrared or able to perceive new types of vibrations, it is probable that the nature of aesthetic emotion would be considerably transformed as a result. Things repellent now might then appear as exquisitely beautiful. Keynes continues to insist on the main idea put forward in his previous chapter, namely that beauty is not an intrinsic characteristic of external objects, that the produced impression varies according to the angle of observation:

> We cannot select one perception and call it and it only the right perception; the beauty of a perceived object is a function not only of the intrinsic characteristics of the object itself, but also of our organs of perception, and of our relative spatial position. Strictly the term beauty ought always to be applied to the *mental* objects which call up aesthetic feelings, and not to the external objects to which these mental objects correspond. For it is impossible to assert dogmatically that to each external object there is only one mental object in true and natural correspondence.
> 
> (Keynes 1905b, p. 12)

That said, there is enough uniformity in the human organs of perception and sensation to attribute beauty to external objects, even if it remains uncertain that all men see the same thing when they examine the same object. The question of our relationship to the external world is a matter for metaphysics, a domain of which Keynes says that it is outside his field of interest at this moment.

Sensitivity to beauty, the capacity to perceive it, are themselves variable qualities among human beings, qualities relating to intelligence, culture and education. Of course, artists possess above average capacities in this domain. But even ordinary men may attain, through education and training, higher "faculties of contemplation". At the bottom of all Keynes's later actions as founder and director of artistic organisations was the explicit objective of "educating the population's taste" so that it may have access to the contemplation of beauty.

Beauty concerns our perceptions of the physical and natural world but it also applies to mental objects, and this despite the fact that aesthetics is mainly concerned with nature or artistic creations. We are not only interested in the physical appearance of our friends, but also in their mind. Of course, analysis becomes more complex in this case, even if fundamentally "the theory of physical and mental beauty is one and embraces the same fundamental notions and ideas" (ibid., p. 27). The concept of fitness, introduced in "Miscellanea Ethica", sheds some light on the matter. Related to goodness though not to be confused with it, fitness also relates to beauty: "The idea of 'fit' is, as it were, a generalized idea of 'beauty'" (ibid., p. 24). The idea of "moral beauty" is better rendered by that of fitness:

> Any object, whose contemplation *ought* to give rise to a state of mind that is good, is fit. A state of mind may, in its turn, become an object of contemplation, and we may, therefore, speak of its fitness as well as of its goodness.... In fact, I distinguish moral excellence and moral beauty; admitting that all moral excellence has some beauty, I deny, though with the utmost hesitation, that the more excellent is necessarily the more beautiful.
>
> (Ibid., pp. 24–5)

It follows from these definitions and considerations that "it is the most beautiful we ought to love, and the most beautiful which ought to fill us with the best and noblest emotions" (ibid. p. 25), it being understood that the beauty in question here is that of the mind as much as the body: "Surely Plato is right in supposing that the peculiar beauty of the opening mind of youth is not only a most natural but a most fit object of affection. I think as men grow older they become less loveable but more excellent" (ibid.).

Keynes ends his chapter by classifying beauty into four types, whose character, he stresses, is relatively arbitrary. "Pure beauty" has a timeless immobility, even if it is that of a storm. It is found in certain Greek statues, Keats, daffodils or glaciers. What he calls the "beauty of interest" is, on the contrary, related to the instability and action of the intellect. It takes on importance, at the expense of the first form of beauty, with the development of humanity: "Pure beauty we can still worship, but it is interest we need for daily food" (ibid., p. 32). "Beauty of consecutive arrangement" flows from perfectly logical arrangements, as with Pythagorean theorems and great works of philosophy. "Tragic beauty" cannot be perceived by the agents of catastrophe, but rather by those who contemplate it from the outside, from the standpoint of the good. Keynes finishes by calling for diversity in matters of art and of beautiful, for cultural diversity:

> Most of us will have our favorite kinds and types; in some particular direction we shall be lovers and judges. Yet we must refrain from narrowing down too far the fit objects of our senses, and, while it is the delight and the duty of all lovers of beauty to dispute and dispute continually concerning tastes, we must not impose on the almost infinite variety of fit and beautiful objects for human emotion tests and criteria which we may think we have established in that corner of the field which is dearest to ourselves; nor must we fail to see beauty in strange places because it has little in common with the kind of beauty we would strive to create, were we artists and not philosophers.
>
> (Ibid., p. 34)

In his subsequent writings, Keynes developed his ideas by branching off into other directions. Lover of theatre, he asked his Apostle brothers, on 5 February 1906, whether writing melodramas was a legitimate activity. His answer was positive, since melodrama justifies itself through its relation to tragic beauty. According to him, the common accusation that melodramas lack realism is unfounded. Realism is not essential. A play does not describe reality, but rather mental events, emotions, feelings: "Mental events compose the essence of the play" (Keynes 1906). It was a matter, as Strachey will do in his biographies and Virginia Woolf in her novels, of exploring a character, of telling the story of its evolution.

By signs and symbols, we show the workings of the mind, and not what our eyes and ears perceive. The artist must bring to perception the smallest vibrations of emotions and feelings. His mission is to undress the soul, not unlike that of psychoanalysis. To do this, one does not turn away from staging violence unheard of in reality, from using conventions and trick effects, from painting characters worse that any found in nature. This theatrical art, Keynes adds, must be available to the masses and not only to the elite.

Two years later, Keynes imagined a dialogue between two princes, Henry and Rupert, the first having an intellectual's rational and reasonable temperament, the other the soul of an artist. It is likely Henry represented the mathematician Henry Norton and the second, the poet Rupert Brooke, the two most recent apostles, and both present at the Society's meeting on 28 November 1908. Prince Rupert's main argument, which is manifestly that of Keynes, is that there is no emotion, aesthetic or not, without bodily sensation: "Emotions, at any rate, are really bodily sensations at bottom" (Keynes 1908, p. 1). Those who no longer feel bodily sensation when reading poetry or contemplating paintings do not derive aesthetic emotions from these activities even if they do derive some pleasure from them: "And the same thing is true of pictures. We often look at them with enjoyment; but we are having no feelings towards them if they leave our bodies unmoved" (ibid., p. 2). We can form a judgment, which would have a certain value, regarding a poem or painting without feeling a real emotion which necessarily manifests itself by a physical sensation. Prince Henry concludes the dialogue by writing: "we must hope for the resurrection of the body" (ibid., p. 5).

In "Can we consume our surplus? Or the influence of furniture on love", Keynes looked into an area of artistic creation that would take on much importance for the Bloomsbury group, through the activities of the Omega Workshops, namely that of furniture and interior design. He states here that the physical environment in which we live, its aesthetic character, has an effect on our activities, type of work, but also on the nature of our romantic activities: "Who could commit sodomy in a boudoir or sapphism in Neville's Court?... One would not easily, for instance, become in love with Cleopatra in the King's Combination Room" (Keynes 1909b, pp. 3–5). It is difficult to work intellectually with ease, to give oneself to flow of ideas, in crowded rooms whose ceilings are very high. Chairs have "an important emotional effect beyond their mere comfort" (ibid., p. 3), which according to Keynes is an important modern discovery: "It is important, therefore, that we should live in rooms and on chairs built to our measure by the most skilled upholsters" (ibid., p. 5). The author of these lines would put these prescriptions into practice by having his London and Cambridge lodgings decorated by his friends Duncan Grant and Vanessa Bell.

***

One cannot help but notice reflections foreshadowing those of Bloomsbury's aesthetic vision, which some described as formalist. They also follow ideas that were developed in the 1890s by Roger Fry, well before his integration in Bloomsbury.[4] In his "Essay in aesthetics", Fry distinguishes, in human life, the actual or biological life, made up of instinctive reactions to sensible objects, and the "imaginative life", linked to man's "peculiar faculty of calling up again in his mind the echo of past experiences of this kind" (Fry 1909, p. 13). Art is part of the imaginative life. Thus work of arts is not copy of the actual world and art "is separated from actual life by the absence of responsive action" (ibid., p. 15). The artists purposively create things possessing order and unity to communicate sensations and emotions. In order to unleash emotions in the spectator, the painter for example combines forms and colours. These ideas will be pursued by Clive Bell in *Art*, where the central idea is that of "significant form", an expression that Fry already used in 1901:

> What quality is common to Sta. Sophia and the windows at Chartres, Mexican sculpture, a Persian bowl, Chinese carpets, Giotto's frescoes at Padua, and the masterpieces of Poussin, Piero della Francesca, and Cézanne? Only one answer seems possible – significant form. In each, lines and colors combined in a particular way, certain forms and relations of forms, stir our aesthetic emotion.
> 
> (Bell 1914, p. 23)

There can be no objective validation of an aesthetic system. Founded on personal experience, it is by nature subjective. Bell does not use the term "beauty" because it might refer to an objective conception. In his memoirs, published more than 40 years later, Bell indicates that "significant form" can be replaced by any other expression, "provided that what you mean by your name is a combination of lines and colors, or of notes, or of words, in itself moving, i.e. moving without reference to the outside world" (Bell 1956, p. 72).

This aesthetic vision also applies to the novelistic art of Virginia Woolf, as it does to Proust, Musil or Joyce. Responding to a question, Virginia Woolf claimed that her writing came more from texture than from structure, and that she handled her pen as others do their paint brush. She ridiculed, in *Mr. Bennett and Mrs. Brown* (1924), the typical Victorian novel which sought to tell a story for the moral elevation of its readers. It was no longer a matter of painting reality as faithfully as possible, but of creating in the reader an aesthetic emotion by describing "streams of consciousness". In this process, time stops flowing regularly towards the future. It dissolves. One goes backwards and takes shortcuts. Such is also the technique Lytton Strachey would use to describe the neuroses of great Victorians in *Eminent Victorians*. Keynes was also a master in the art of psychological biographies, which are found for example in the *Economic Consequence of the Peace* and in his *Essays in Biography*, one of his more remarkable books. Reading these descriptions of characters, we have sometime the impression of looking at paintings. And, even if we are far from aesthetics, one finds in Keynes's approach to economic processes, where "animal spirits", irrational urges, uncertainty and fear of the future play a role, an analogous vision to that which is revealed in the pages of Virginia Woolf or Lytton Strachey. Far from being a rational and calculating *homo oeconomicus*, the human being who evolves on the economic stage has the same characteristics as the tormented characters in Virginia Woolf's novels or the neurotic individuals who inhabit the stories of Lytton Strachey.

Keynes was not an artist, but recalling his gift at explaining simply complicated problems, his friend Clive Bell wrote: "In moments such as these I felt sure that Maynard was the cleverest man I had ever met; also, at such moments, I sometimes felt, unreasonably no doubt, that he was an artist" (Bell 1956, p. 61). In fact, if literature is considered as an art, Keynes was an artist. Virginia Woolf praised his literary talents. Keynes elaborated his own language, which constituted, by its form as much as its content, an instrument in his struggle to transform social and economic reality. The aim of this struggle is to protect a civilization that is threatened by reaction and revolution. In the long run, it is to build a world in which the economic problem, the problem of scarcity and poverty, will be solved and most resources will be devoted to the imaginative life instead of the biological life. This, Keynes claimed in "Economic possibilities for our grandchildren", in 1930, should happen in about one hundred year. We are still very far from it.

## Notes

Unpublished writings of J. M Keynes © The Provost and Scholars of King's College, Cambridge, 2007. Permission to quote from these manuscripts was kindly granted by the Assistant Bursar, on behalf of the Provost and Scholars of King's College, Cambridge.

1. On Keynes and art, see the biographies by Harrod (1951), Moggridge (1992), Skidelsky (1983, 1992, 2000). See also Glasgow (1975), Goodwin (2001, 2006), Heilbrun (1984), Moggridge (2005), O'Donnell (1995) and Shone with Grant (1975). The following draws from Dostaler (2007).
2. See on this Goodwin (1998). Goodwin considers that the influence of Fry's ideas, elaborated in the 1890s, on Bloomsbury, is independent and more important that that of Moore.
3. O'Donnell (1995) is the first paper to present an detailed analysis of these papers.
4. See Goodwin (2006).

# References

Abbreviations:
  JMK: *The Collected Writings of John Maynard Keynes*, London: Macmillan, 1971–1989, 30 volumes.
  KP: Keynes Papers, King's College Library, Cambridge.
Bell, Clive (1914), *Art*, London: Chatto & Windus; London: Arrow Books, 1961.
Bell, Clive (1956), *Old Friends: Personal Recollections*, London: Chatto & Windus.
Caws, Mary Ann and Sarah Bird Wright (2000), *Bloomsbury and France: Art and Friends*, New York: Oxford University Press.
Dostaler, Gilles (2007), *Keynes and His Battles*, Cheltenham, UK and Northampton, USA: Edward Elgar.
Fry, Roger (1909), "An Essay in Aesthetics", *New Quarterly*, 2, April, 171–90; in *Vision and Design*, London: Oxford University Press, 1981, 12–27.
Fry, Roger (1919), "Art and Science", *Athenaeum*, 6 June, 434–5; in *Vision and Design*, London: Oxford University Press, 1981, 55–9.
Glasgow, Mary (1975), "The Concept of the Arts Council", in Milo Keynes (ed.), *Essays on John Maynard Keynes*, Cambridge: Cambridge University Press, 260–71.
Goodwin, Craufurd (ed.) (1998), *Art and the Market: Roger Fry on Commerce in Art. Selected Writings*, Ann Arbor: University of Michigan Press.
Goodwin, Craufurd (2001), "Maynard Keynes and the Creative Arts", in Tony Bradshaw (ed.), *A Bloomsbury Canvas: Reflections on the Bloomsbury Group*, Aldershot, UK: Lund Humphries, 51–3.
Goodwin, Craufurd (2006), "The Art of an Ethical Life: Keynes and Bloomsbury", in Roger E. Backhouse and Bradley Bateman (eds), *The Cambridge Companion to Keynes*, Cambridge: Cambridge University Press, 217–36.
Harrod, Roy F. (1951), *The Life of John Maynard Keynes*, London: Macmillan.
Heilbrun, James (1984), "Keynes and the Economics of the Arts", *Journal of Cultural Economics*, 8(2), 37–49.
Keynes, John Maynard (1904), ["Beauty"], KP, UA/19/3.
Keynes, John Maynard (1905a), "Miscellanea ethica", KP, UA/21.
Keynes, John Maynard (1905b), "A theory of beauty", KP, UA/23/2.
Keynes, John Maynard (1906), "Shall we write melodrama?", KP, UA/25.
Keynes, John Maynard (1908), "Prince Henry or Prince Rupert?", KP, UA/30.

Keynes, John Maynard (1909a), ["Science and art"], KP, UA/32.
Keynes, John Maynard (1909b), "Can we consume our surplus? or The influence of furniture on love", KP, UA/34.
Keynes, John Maynard (1921), "London Group", Catalogue for the London Group Exhibition, Mansard Gallery, October; JMK 28, 296–7.
Keynes, John Maynard (1924), Notice on the movie "Tess of the D'Ubervilles", *Nation and Athenaeum*, vol. 36, 11 October, 53; JMK 28, 316–17. [unsigned]
Keynes, John Maynard (1925), Letter to the Editor [on "Freudian psychoanalysis"], *Nation and the Athenæum*, vol. 35, 29 August, 643–4; JMK 28, 392–3. [signed "Siela"]
Keynes, John Maynard (1927a), "Clissold", *Nation and Athenaeum*, vol. 40, 22 January, 561–2; JMK 9, 315–20.
Keynes, John Maynard (1927b), "Letter to the Editor", *Nation and Athenaeum*, vol. 41, 25 June, 410; JMK 28, 311–12. [signed "Siela"]
Keynes, John Maynard (1933), "National self-sufficiency", *New Statesman and Nation*, vol. 6, 8 July, 36–7, 15 July, 65–7; JMK 21, 233–46.
Keynes, John Maynard (1936), "Art and the State", *Listener*, 26 August; JMK 28, 341–9.
Keynes, John Maynard (1938), "My early beliefs", paper read on 11 September to the Bloomsbury Memoir Club; JMK 10, 433–50.
Keynes, John Maynard (1945), "The Arts Council: Its policy and hopes", *Listener*, 11 May; JMK 28, 367–72.
Keynes, John Maynard (1947), "Newton, the man", in *Newton Tercentenary Celebrations, July 15–19, 1946*, Cambridge, Royal Society of London, 27–34 paper read to the Royal Society, London, 30 November 1942; JMK 10, 363–7.
Moggridge, Donald E. (1992), *Maynard Keynes: An Economist's Biography*, London: Routledge.
Moggridge, Donald E. (2005), "Keynes, the Arts and the State", *History of Political Economy*, 37(3), 535–55.
Moore, George E. (1903), *Principia Ethica*, revised Ed., Cambridge: Cambridge University Press, 1993.
O'Donnell, Rod M. (1995), "Keynes on Aesthetics", in Allin F. Cottrell and Michael S. Lawlor (eds), *New Perspectives on Keynes*, Durham: Duke University Press, 93–121.
Scrase, David and Peter Croft (1983), *Maynard Keynes: Collector of Pictures, Books and Manuscripts*, Cambridge: Provost and Scholars of King's College.
Shone, Richard, with Duncan Grant (1975), "The Picture Collector", in Milo Keynes (ed.) *Essays on John Maynard Keynes*, Cambridge: Cambridge University Press, 280–9.
Skidelsky, Robert (1983, 1992, 2000), *John Maynard Keynes*, London: Macmillan, 3 vols.

# 7
# Keynes and the Social Sciences: Contributions Outside of Economics, with Applications to Economic Anthropology and Comparative Systems

*Mathew Forstater*

Keynes's contributions and influence in the worlds of theoretical and practical economics need no documentation. Clearly, he was the most influential economist of the twentieth century, and clearly his legacy continues into the twenty-first. Well-known also is that Keynes made significant and formal contributions in other fields, in mathematics and statistics (e.g. his *Treatise on Probability*), philosophy, psychology and even historical studies. But Keynes also has had a lesser known and sometimes more indirect and informal influence on the other social sciences, in anthropology, sociology and political science. Following some brief, general comments on these three disciplines, two important case studies will be presented in the areas of economic anthropology and comparative systems.

## Keynes and the social sciences: anthropology, sociology and political science

The selection of these three areas of study has some logic behind it. The goal is to examine Keynes's influence in *social sciences* other than economics, so maths and statistics, philosophy and history, while sometimes having some overlap with social science, are considered here as part of the humanities. The idea is also to highlight areas in which Keynes did not explicitly make formal contributions, as in probability for example (Keynes, 1929). Finally, the goal here is to examine contributions of Keynes that have not been studied already by others. Here again, statistics, psychology and philosophy would be ruled out, as a number of important studies have been made in these areas (see, e.g., Bateman and Davis, 1991; Carabelli, 1988, 2002; Davis, 1994; Parker, 1998).

## Anthropology

Keynes is best-known as an analyst of twentieth-century capitalism, and Keynesian economics is not usually thought to have much to contribute to economic anthropology, a field historically dominated by neoclassical, Institutionalist and Marxist approaches (Gudeman, 1998; Wilk, 1996). Keynes (1982b) studied "Ancient Currencies" in the 1920s, in which he anticipated Bohannan's (1959) notion of "multiples spheres of exchange" (Gregory, 1997, pp. 242, 999, 2000). Keynes used the term "multiple standards of value" to indicate the same idea, which is also related to the notions of "special purpose" and "general purpose" monies. Keynes made clear in his study that "for most important social and economic purposes what matters is the *money of account*; for it is the money of account which is the subject of contract and of customary obligation. The currency reforms that matter are those that change the money of account" (Keynes, 1982b, p. 253) and that the "presumption of many writers that where there were no coins there was barter is far from accordance with the truth" (Keynes, 1982b, p. 255).

Keynes also, "as editor of the *Economic Journal* in the 1920s, actively encourage[d] a dialogue between economists and anthropologists" (Gregory, 2000, p. 999). This included, for example, Keynes's early (1914) review of A. Mitchell Innes's article "What is Money?" (Innes, 1913; see Wray, 2004); the publishing of Malinowski's seminal "The Primitive Economics of the Trobriand Islanders" (1921) and a review of the same author's 1922 book, *Argonauts of the Western Pacific* (Schwiedland, 1923); publication of Cambridge scholar W. E. Armstrong's "Rossel Island Money" (1924), and many other articles and reviews concerning economic anthropology, including reviews of Raymond Firth's *Primitive Economics of the New Zealand Moari* (Marett, 1930) and several books by Richard Thurnwald. A number of the reviews were written by Eugene Schwiedland.

Most importantly for this chapter, Keynes's analysis in the opening pages of his *Treatise on Money* (1930) provides a rich framework for understanding money across cultures and time. It is there that Keynes explicitly adopts Knapp's (1905) chartalist or state theory of money:

"Knapp accepts as "Money" – rightly, I think – anything which the State undertakes to accept at its pay-offices, whether or not it is declared legal-tender between citizens" (1930, pp. 6–7 n1; see Wray, 1998, pp. 29–32 and Goodhart 1998). The development of these insights has resulted recently in the rise of something of a Post Keynesian economic anthropology (Forstater, 2005, 2006; Peacock, 2005; Tymoigne, 2006).

As in the case of sociology and political science, anthropology has employed some of Keynes's contributions originally used to understand capitalist economies. Danby (2002), e.g., takes Keynes's notions of historical time, fundamental uncertainty and "spot" and "forward" transactions to develop a critique of the gift–exchange dichotomy. Both gifting and exchange are time-structured and socially embedded, Danby argues. Earlier, anthropologists such as Hart (1986), Crump (1981), and others have similarly drawn on Keynes's ideas.

## Sociology

Keynes's impact on sociology is at once both greater and more general than in anthropology. Because Keynes was primarily a theorist of contemporary capitalism, and because Keynes was essentially an institutionalist in his approach if not in name, many of his contributions to the economics of capitalism are directly applicable to the sociology of capitalism.

One important area concerns unemployment. Keynes demonstrated the possibility – even the likelihood – of involuntary unemployment, and this opened up an avenue for rich sociological analysis. If unemployment is no longer the fault of the unemployed, the direct and indirect social causes and effects of joblessness become important topics for the sociologist. Thus, the relation of unemployment and crime and unemployment and physical and mental ill health, to cite a couple of examples, come to the fore in sociology following the Keynesian Revolution (see, e.g., Jahoda, 1982; Kelvin and Jarrett, 1985).

Likewise, the development of the modern corporation, especially the separation of ownership and management, is partly inspired by Keynes's analysis in *The General Theory* (1936). Keynes's distinction between speculation and enterprise, and issues related to investor expectations generally, also have been taken up by sociologists (Keynes, 1936, 1937). Less well-known is Keynes's rich, institutional analysis of intra-class competition among workers in Chapter 5 of *The General Theory*. Workers resist cuts in real wages if they are the result of cuts in money wages, but tend to be willing to accept real wages cuts resulting from rises in the price level, not because of "money illusion" but because the former disrupts the *relative* real wage structure while the latter does not.

Of course, the sociology of money bears the imprints of Keynes. From Viviana Zelizer's (1994) analysis of the social meaning of money to Geoffrey Ingham's (2004) work, Keynes thought is in the background, if not in the foreground. Much of this work is interdisciplinary in nature, drawing on not only sociology, but social psychology, political economy and history.

## Political science

As in sociology, Keynes's influence in political science is often broad and general, though just as straightforward, if not more so. Keynes's work framed post-war national economic policy (fiscal and monetary), and his work on Bretton Woods led to the international monetary system, including the World Bank and the IMF. Moreover, Keynes influenced discussions on the proper role of government in a modern capitalist economy (Barnes, 1997).

Even the notion of the modern nation-state itself bears the imprint of Keynes:

> The national economy is privileged in Keynesian theory for the purely practical reason that the nation-state system defines geopolitical space with the necessary features convenient for the theory: a common currency, common laws, and shared institutions.
> (Radice, 1984)

For Keynes, importantly, it also includes national *culture*.

As Martin and Sunley argue, the apparent tension between focus on the nation-state versus the global system is a false one, because the international organizations were designed *"precisely in order to guarantee the stability of each national economy"* (1997, p. 279, emphasis added).

The politics of money and finance also has drawn on the Keynesian legacy. Woodruff (1999, 2005) is but one example recently of a political scientist influenced by Keynes's monetary thought. But Keynes "was also a keen student of comparative economic systems", as we will see below, in this case emphasizing various forms of capitalism and socialism rather than pre-capitalist economies (Gregory, 2000, p. 999). Not only in *Laissez-Faire and Communism* (1926), but throughout his works, as will be seen below, Keynes discussed both actual and imaginary forms of capitalism and socialism.

## Case studies in economic anthropology and comparative systems

### Economic anthropology: the tax-driven cowrie

In the opening pages of the *Treatise on Money*, Keynes explicitly embraces Chartalism, Knapp's State Theory of Money, and specifically the view of money as "tax-driven" – the power of a central political authority to impose tax (and other obligations) and to declare public receivability creates a demand for otherwise valueless tokens, leading to general acceptability. Keynes notes that this has been the case for at least 4000 years.

Chartalism forces a reconsideration of virtually all of the received wisdom coming out of traditional monetary theory and history. The cowrie currency used in parts of Africa and Asia, for example, is often cited as an example of "primitive" money (see, e.g., Friedman, 1972, p. 927). A brief examination of the history of the cowrie, however, shows it to be tax-driven. We would do well to take seriously Polanyi's admonition that "A warning is in order against the ethnocentric bias that so easily takes hold of us on economic subjects that arise outside of our own Western culture" (1966, p. 177):

> We are used to ranging cowrie with the other shells as a sample of primitive money in a supposed evolutionary perspective of the "origins and development of money." Historical research removes this evolutionary bias. Cowrie currencies emerged on the Middle and Upper reaches of the Niger at a time when metal currencies and, indeed, coined money were long established in the Mediterranean heartlands. This is the background against which the emergence of a new nonmetallic currency in Islamic West Africa should be viewed. It will then not be erroneously regarded as part of a general evolution of money, but rather as a feature in the spread both of *centralized government* and of food markets in the early [African] empires which left its imprint on the local history of money.
> 
> (Polanyi, 1966, p. 178, emphasis added)

The use of the cowrie as money in West Africa began between 1290 and 1352, and gold and metallic coin had long been in use prior to that time in the region (Polanyi, 1966, pp. 179–80). According to Polanyi, "Dahomey's cowrie was definitely not primitive money" (1966, p. 189); rather, it is an example of "the launching of a currency as an instrument of taxation" (1966, p. 186). Even the local legend regarding the cowrie's origin supports the thesis that cowrie money is a creature of the state (1966, p. 186).

Cowrie money... appears in the legend as the innovation of an autochthonous king. And the result – "people now found food to eat and no longer exchanged articles" – suggests a close connection between money and markets. Actually, as we know, Dahomean markets were food markets in which – notable fact – cowrie payment was enforced. The acting force that shaped and organized the economy was the state, in the person of the king. Food, money and market are all statemade (Polanyi, 1966, p. 186).

Evidence from other areas and authorities still exists to support the thesis of the tax-driven cowrie. Lovejoy reports that in precolonial Nigeria

> Dependencies of such emirates as Nupe paid their levies in cowries as well, so that the taxation system effectively assured that people participated in the market economy and used the currency, a policy remarkably similar to the one which the later colonial regimes pursued in their efforts to see their own currencies accepted.
> (Lovejoy, 1974, p. 581)

Law confirms the thesis for other areas of West Africa, such as Bornu in the nineteenth century:

> The apparent preference to the payment of taxes in money – cowries or gold – is especially interesting. It must be assumed that the spread of the use of cowry shells as money in West Africa depended upon state initiative – this was certainly the case with the introduction of the cowry currency in Bornu in the 1840s.
> (Law, 1978, p. 49)

One of the factors that sustained the widespread misunderstanding of the origins and nature of the cowrie was the myth that the cowrie was freely available in virtually unlimited quantities. On the contrary, the cowrie was not native to West Africa; the state "guarded against its proliferation by preventing shiploads from being freely imported" (Polanyi, 1966, p. 189); and the *stringing* of cowries "was a monopoly of the palace" (Law, 1978, p. 49; see also Polanyi, 1966). This latter refers to strings of specific numbers of cowries, and specific numbers of strings collected in a "head" (Law, 1977, p. 209).

The cowrie's geographical occurrence in West Africa supports the state money thesis and refutes any evolutionary explanation: "cowrie using areas and areas where it was not accepted for payment were as if their boundaries were drawn by administrative authority" (Polanyi, 1966, p. 190):

> This was a place of multiple currencies, while Dahomey and Ashanti had succeeded in keeping their monetary systems separate in the face of what must appear to the modern mind as insuperable obstacles. Dahomey used cowrie exclusively, in elaborate, never-changing division, maintained at an unvarying exchange rate of 32,000 cowries to one ounce gold – an amazing feat.
> (Polanyi, 1966, p. 29)

The "compulsory monetization of sale-purchase" meant that nothing was available for sale except in cowrie, and there was no barter whatsoever (Polanyi, 1966, p. 84). It now seems likely that the cowrie was also tax-driven in other areas of the world where it served as money. Elwin reported in 1942 that in parts of India, "There are still many of the older generation who remember the days when the cowrie was used as currency and was accepted in the payment of taxes" (Elwin, 1942, p. 121).

The cowrie was clearly tax-driven over most if not all of precolonial West Africa, and elsewhere. This does not mean that all cowrie systems were necessarily money. Much more research is required, of course, but it appears that many more monies in history may have been tax-driven than was previously believed.

## Comparative systems: the nation and the "Middle Way" between *Laissez-Faire* capitalism and "doctrinaire State Socialism"

Keynes believed that the nature of a capitalist economy demanded "much more planning than we have at present", and "that a somewhat comprehensive socialisation of investment will prove the only means of securing an approximation to full employment" (Keynes, 1982a, p. 492; 1936, p. 378).

Keynes saw the solutions to virtually all the ills of the free market to be in some form of state intervention. He fought for such policies throughout his life, often referring to the need for "semi-socialism", "liberal socialism" and "nationalisation". However much he explicitly rejected laissez-faire individualistic capitalism, though, he equally if not more harshly opposed doctrinaire State Socialism.

One objection to State Socialism repeated by Keynes throughout his life was that he saw many of the economic benefits derived therefrom as coming at the expense of individual freedoms. However, the view that this is equivalent to a naïve embrace of nineteenth-century individualism on the part of Keynes would be mistaken, although given his voluminous writings one may find evidence of such a position. Particularly in "The End of Laissez-Faire", Keynes demonstrated a keen understanding of the discursive and historical conditions for the philosophical development of the ideological underpinnings of free-market capitalism. There he analyzes the sources of origins, the sometimes subtle differences between its various manifestations, and the absurdity of many of its assumptions (Keynes, 1926, pp. 5–53). Yet Keynes was morally and philosophically opposed to what he perceived as the restrictions of freedom imposed on the individual by authoritarian regimes of "actually existing" socialism (although he remarked that the Soviet Union was preferable to Czarist Russia because the former had its gaze on "the possibility of things" (1926, p. 144).

Keynes often couched his criticisms in moral or social terms, even when discussing issues that had clear economic implications. He argued that State intervention was not only legitimate, but necessary in some areas, but that in others it is inefficient (Keynes, 1936, pp. 380–1). But Keynes also took care not to send a message that he is "equally opposed both to socialism and private enterprise – to the former because it brings in politics, and to the latter because it depends on speculation and money making. It is much sounder, I think, to believe in them both than to thwart both" (Keynes, 1978, pp. 430–1). As an aside, in his 1941 budget testimony, Keynes told an anecdote that is typical of his position on the moral implications of political and economic debates:

> When I was young I examined in the Cambridge Locals and asked "What is Socialism?" A small girl replied: "The Socialists think it would do the poor good to make them just like the rich. It would not. It would spoil their characters." I am hoping that the Labour Party is still socialist in this sense!
> 
> (Keynes, 1978, p. 272 n 20)

Keynes recognized that one of the tasks facing the modern world was to solve the dilemma characterizing the capitalism/socialism (or the free market/government intervention) debate:

> The true socialism of the future will emerge, I think, from an endless variety of experiments directed toward discovering the respective appropriate spheres of the individual and the social, and the terms of fruitful alliance between these sister instincts.
> (Keynes, 1981, p. 222)

From such experimentation, he hoped, it would become possible to identify those parts of socioeconomic life "which are *technically social* from those which are *technically individual*" (1926, pp. 66–7, original emphasis). It is not only unnecessary, but inefficient to nationalize indiscriminately, while aggregate savings and investment and the banking and credit institutions require socialization.

What Keynes was not arguing for was a complete socialization either of production decisions at the level of the firm or of individual consumption. Such a system would be counter to both individual freedom and the efficiencies of appropriate decentralization.

> Leave individuals to go on doing what they are doing more or less satisfactorily, even though individual action is not perfect – where it exists and is functioning, leave it alone – but do from the centre those things which, if not done from the centre, will not be done at all.
> (Keynes, 1981, 647)

This was a constant theme in Keynes, who in "Can Lloyd George Do It?" had similarly remarked that:

> Thus it is not a question of choosing between private and public enterprise in these matters. The choice has already been made. In many directions – though not in all – it is a question of the state putting its hand to the job or of its not being done at all.
> (1972 [1929], p. 113)

Given his rejection of laissez-faire, Keynes required a more activist economic policy implemented by the state. But given his suspicion of state power and Stalinism, Keynes needed a more benign and less authoritarian institution – the "nation".

Joshua Esty has written that:

> Like many others in the Bloomsbury circle, Keynes distrusted vulgar patriotism, but believed that the English had a particular genius for measured and voluntarist forms of community.
>
> (Esty, 2000, p. 7)

This is what Adolph Lowe called "spontaneous conformity", in his letter to Paul Tillich on the latter's 50th birthday, published by Leonard Woolf's Hogarth Press as *The Price of Liberty* (Lowe, 1937). In a nutshell, spontaneous conformity is the voluntary adherence to social rules or codes of conduct necessary for socioeconomic and political order. The English expression, "It simply isn't done" captures its spirit, and it very much echoes Adam Smith, but not from the *Wealth of Nations*, but rather the *Theory of Moral Sentiments*.

Lowe (1988) made the distinction between removable and irremovable constraints. Removable constraints are those that, if removed, would not threaten social order. Irremovable constraints are those that if removed, would potentially threaten system breakdown, or at least be very disruptive. This all may be fine and well for some types of activity, for example environmental recycling. But if the problem is lack of investment, within the basic framework of capitalist society, can private investors really be asked to invest out of a sense of duty to one's country? If not, the nation-state would have to step in and "do from the centre those things which, if not done from the centre, will not be done at all." This might mean public investment, but it could also mean trying to create an economic environment through national policy that could entice investors to invest, such as lowering the rate of interest relative to the marginal efficiency of capital.

## Conclusion

Keynes was living past that time when "political economy" had become "economics" and separate disciplines of sociology, political science and anthropology had emerged out of what had been discarded from political economy. Yet, in one sense, at least, Keynes – despite his stated distance from "classical economics" – was closer to Classical authors such as Adam Smith, John Stuart Mill and Karl Marx.

Keynes was a political economist, or to use Heilbroner's (1953) term a "worldly philosopher". He took what we would today call a more "interdisciplinary" approach, not because it was a fad, but because, on the one hand, he recognized the dangers of over-specialization in the social sciences and, on the other, he saw this as the only way to approach solving complex, real-world problems.

## References

Armstrong, W. E., 1924, "Rossel Island Money: A Unique Monetary System," *Economic Journal*, Vol. 34, No. 135. (September), pp. 423–9.
Barnes, T., 1997, "Introduction: Theories of Accumulation and Regulation," in R. Lee and J. Wills, eds., *Geographies of Economies*, London: Arnold.
Bateman, B. W. and J. B. Davis, eds., 1991, *Keynes and Philosophy: Essays on the Origin of Keynes's Thought*, Aldershot, Hants, England: Edward Elgar.
Bohannan, P., 1959, "The Impact of Money on an African Subsistence Economy," *Journal of Economic History*, Vol. 19, No. 4. (December), pp. 491–503.
Carabelli, A., 1988, *On Keynes's Method*, New York: St. Martin's Press.
Carabelli, A., 2002, "Keynes on Probability, Uncertainty and Tragic Choices," in S. Nisticò and D. Tosato, eds., *Competing Economic Theories: Essays in Memory of Giovanni Caravale*, London: Routledge.
Crump, T., 1981, *The Phenomenon of Money*, London: Routledge & Kegan Paul.
Crump, T., 1983, "Keynes and Anthropology," *RAIN*, No. 59, p. 2.
Danby, C., 2002, "The Curse of the Modern: A Post Keynesian Critique of the Gift Exchange Dichotomy," *Research in Economic Anthropology*, Vol. 21, pp. 13–42.
Davis, J. B., 1994, *Keynes's Philosophical Development*, Cambridge: Cambridge University Press.
Elwin, V., 1942, "The Use of Cowries in Bastar State, India," *Man*, Vol. 42. (November–December), pp. 121–4.
Esty, J. D., 2000, "National Objects: Keynesian Economics and Modernist Culture in England," *Modernism/Modernity*, Vol. 7, No. 1, pp. 1–24.
Forstater, M., 2005, "Taxation and Primitive Accumulation," *Research in Political Economy*, Vol. 22, pp. 51–64.
Forstater, M., 2006, "Tax-Driven Money: Additional Evidence from the History of Thought, Economic History, and Economic Policy," in M. Setterfield, ed., *Complexity, Endogenous Money, and Exogenous Interest Rates*, Cheltenham, UK: Edward Elgar.
Friedman, M., 1972, "Comments on the Critics," *The Journal of Political Economy*, Vol. 80, No. 5 (September–October), pp. 906–50.
Goodhart, C. A. E., 1998, "The Two Concepts of Money," *European Journal of Political Economy*, Vol. 14, pp. 407–32, reprinted in S. A. Bell and E. J. Nell, eds., 2003, *The State, the Market, and the Euro*, Cheltenham, UK: Edward Elgar.
Gregory, C. A., 1997, *Savage Money: The Anthropology and Politics of Commodity Exchange*, Amsterdam: Harwood.
Gregory, C. A., 2000, "Anthropology, Economics, and Political Economy," *History of Political Economy*, Vol. 32, No. 4, pp. 999–1009.
Gudeman, S., ed., 1998, *Economic Anthropology*, Cheltenham, UK: Edward Elgar.
Hart, K., 1986. Heads or Tails?: Two Sides of the Coin. *Man*, Vol. 21, No. 4, (December), pp. 637–56.
Heilbroner, R. L., 1953, *The Worldly Philosophers*, New York: Simon Schuster.
Ingham, G., 2004, *The Nature of Money*, Cambridge, UK: Polity.

Innes, A. M., 1913, "What is Money?," *Banking Law Journal*, May, pp. 377–408, reprinted in L. R. Wray, ed., *Credit and State Theories of Money*, Cheltenham, UK: Edward Elgar, 2004.
Jahoda, M., 1982, *Employment and Unemployment: A Social-Psychological Analysis*, Cambridge, UK: Cambridge University Press.
Kelvin, P. and Jarrett J. E., 1985, *Unemployment: Its Social Psychological Effects*, Cambridge: Cambridge University Press.
Keynes, J. M., 1914, "Review of 'What is Money?'," *Economic Journal*, Vol. 24, No. 95, pp. 419–21.
Keynes, J. M., 1926, *Laissez-Faire and Communism*, New York: New Republic.
Keynes, J. M., 1929, *A Treatise on Probability*, London: Macmillan.
Keynes, J. M., 1930, *A Treatise on Money*, 2 volumes, London: Macmillan.
Keynes, J. M., 1936, *The General Theory of Employment, Interest, and Money*, London: Harcourt Brace.
Keynes, J. M. (1937) "The General Theory of Employment," *Quarterly Journal of Economics* 51, 209–23.
Keynes, J. M., 1972 [1929], "Can Lloyd George Do It?," in D. Moggridge, ed., *The Collected Writings of John Maynard Keynes, Vol. IX, Essays in Persuasion*, London: Macmillan.
Keynes, J. M., 1978, "A Supplementary Note on the Dimensions of the Budget Problem, Appendix I: Revised Proposal for a War Surcharge," in D. Moggridge, ed., *The Collected Writings of John Maynard Keynes, Vol. XXII, Activities, 1939–1945: Internal War Finance*, London: Macmillan.
Keynes, J. M., 1981, *The Collected Writings of John Maynard Keynes, Vol. XIX, Activities, 1922–1929: The Return to Gold and Industrial Policy, Part 1*, London: Macmillan.
Keynes, J. M., 1982a, *The Collected Writings of John Maynard Keynes, Vol. XXI, Activities, 1931–1939: The World Crisis and Policies in Britain and America*, London: Macmillan.
Keynes, J. M., 1982b, "Keynes and Ancient Currencies," in D. Moggridge, ed., *The Collected Writings of John Maynard Keynes, Vol. XXVIII, Social, Political and Literary Writings*, London: Macmillan.
Knapp, G. F., 1905 [1924], *The State Theory of Money*, New York: Augustus M. Kelley.
Law, R., 1977, *The Oyo Empire, c. 1600–c. 1836: A West African Imperialism in the Era of the Atlantic Slave Trade*, Oxford: Clarendon Press.
Law, R., 1978, "Slaves, Trade, and Taxes: The Material Basis of Political Power in Precolonial West Africa," *Research in Economic Anthropology*, Vol. 1, pp. 37–52.
Lovejoy, P. E., 1974, "Interregional Monetary Flows in the Precolonial Trade of Nigeria," *Journal of African History*, Vol. XV, No. 4, pp. 563–85.
Lowe, A., 1937, *The Price of Liberty*, London: Hogarth Press.
Lowe, A., 1988, *Has Freedom a Future?*, New York: Praeger.
Malinowski, B., 1921, "Primitive Economics of the Trobriand Islanders," *Economic Journal*, Vol. 31, No. 121. (March), pp. 1–16.
Malinowski, B., 1922, *Argonauts of the Western Pacific*, London: Routledge.
Marett, R. R., 1930, "Review of *Primitive Economics of the New Zealand Maori* by Raymond Firth," *Economic Journal*, Vol. 40, No. 157 (March), pp. 137–9.
Martin, R. and P. Sunley, 1997, "The Post Keynesian State and the Space Economy," in R. Lee and J. Wills, eds., *Geographies of Economies*, London: Arnold.

Parker, I., 1998, "On Keynes and Ramsey on Probability," in O. F. Hamouda and B. B. Price, eds., *Keynesianism and the Keynesian Revolution in America: A Memorial Volume in Honour of Lorie Tarshis*, Cheltenham, UK: Edward Elgar.

Peacock, M., 2005, "The Origins of Money in Ancient Greece," *Cambridge Journal of Economics*, Vol. 30, pp. 637–50.

Polanyi, K., 1966, *Dahomey and the Slave Trade; An Analysis of an Archaic Economy*, Seattle: University of Washington Press.

Radice, H., 1984, "The National Economy – A Keynesian Myth?," *Capital & Class*, No. 22 (Spring), pp. 111–40.

Schwiedland, E., 1923, "Review of *Argonauts of the Western Pacific* by B. Malinowski," *Economic Journal*, Vol. 33, No. 132 (December), pp. 558–60.

Tymoigne, E., 2006, "An Inquiry into the Nature of Money," Working Paper No. 481, Levy Economics Institute, November.

Wilk, R. R., 1996, *Economies and Cultures: Foundations of Economic Anthropology*, Boulder, Colorado: Westview Press.

Woodruff, D., 1999, *Money Unmade*, Ithaca, NY: Cornell University Press.

Woodruff, D. M., 2005, "Boom, Gloom, Doom: Balance Sheets, Monetary Fragmentation, and the Politics of Financial Crisis in Argentina and Russia," *Politics & Society*, Vol. 33, No. 1, pp. 3–45.

Wray, L. R., 1998, *Understanding Modern Money*, Cheltenham, UK: Edward Elgar.

Wray, L. R., ed., 2004, *Credit and State Theories of Money*, Cheltenham, UK: Edward Elgar.

Zelizer, V. A., 1994, *The Social Meaning of Money*, New York: Basic Books.

# 8
# Keynes' Enduring Legacy
*Richard N. Cooper*

I feel privileged to have been an eavesdropper in a meeting among specialists on Keynes. Inevitably, as in all meetings of specialists, the discussion focuses on the fine points of his life and his contributions. I cannot contribute usefully to that discourse. Instead, I will suggest what has been Keynes' legacy to the wider world, from the perspective of an economist not specializing on Keynes. I will identify five enduring contributions, four positive and one negative.

First, Keynes' work, even before the *General Theory*, took what we would today call a macroeconomic perspective, a view of a national economy in its entirety. Indeed, the sub-field of macroeconomics arose out of Keynes' work, along with the parallel development of the system of national accounts. These developments were not entirely independent of one another: Keynes was aware of the work of Simon Kuznets, and Richard Stone, I learned here, was a student of Keynes.

I had occasion some years ago to read Alfred Marshall's testimony before the Royal Commission on the Depression in Trade and Industry of 1886. I was impressed by how intelligent and observant Marshall was. But I was also frustrated precisely because he lacked what we economists have come to take for granted, namely an overall view of the interactions among the major components of the economy, such as investment, consumption, and the trade balance. The categories we still use were also emphasized by Keynes, as reflected in the national accounts, even when some of them have become badly dated. Concretely, we continue to count expenditures on consumer durables, and on education, as "consumption" rather than "investment," even though on fundamental grounds they should both be distinguished from current consumption.

Second, Keynes taught that governments should take responsibility for the macroeconomic performance of the national economy, and that they can do so through the appropriate manipulation of monetary and fiscal policies. They were part of Keynes' agenda to save capitalism, in serious crisis during the Great Depression, and under threat from the alternative doctrines of communism, socialism, and corporatist fascism, all of which called for detailed economic intervention or even extensive public ownership of the means of production. Keynes' propositions – both the "should" and the "can" – are now widely accepted. Rearguard developments in the new classical economics have captured the attention of some economists and their graduate students, but not of the general public. Conservative American President Nixon declared that we're all Keynesians now.

Third, the major forecasting models used in the United States – and as far as I know in other countries as well – are "Keynesian" in spirit in that the key concept underlying them is "effective demand." In the short- to medium-run, economic output is assumed to be constrained by demand, not by capacity as in classical economics and its modern variants. To be sure, demand pressing on limited capacity has economic consequences, such as upward pressures on wages and prices. But output is assumed to be responsive to increases in effective demand, even when capacity is limited: work shifts can be added, overtime can be paid, new workers can be drawn into the labor force, etc. To be sure, the models have been modified – and greatly extended – from their simple origins at the hands of such Keynesians as Lawrence Klein (Wharton), Otto Eckstein (Data Resources, now Global Insights), and Franco Modigliani (Federal Reserve). But effective demand remains the core concept in all of them. They remain in extensive use because they have better forecasting records either than most informal forecasters or than formal models that rely on alternative concepts. And predictive capacity is one of the desiderata – some would say the decisive desideratum – of all scientific work.

Fourth, Keynes legacy lives on in the basic rules of the international monetary system, as embodied in the Articles of Agreement of the International Monetary Fund. Keynes of course was one of the architects of the Bretton Woods agreements. They did not emerge exactly as he would have liked, but he vigorously defended them in public debate. It is fashionable to claim that the Bretton Woods system collapsed in the early 1970s, when the United States suspended convertibility into gold of dollars held by monetary authorities, and when fixed exchange rates among major currencies were abandoned. But these were only two features of the Bretton Woods system, and I suspect Keynes would not have been either surprised or displeased by the abandonment of the last remnant of gold in the international monetary system. The core features of the system continued: government responsibility for domestic economic stability (as defined by each government), to be achieved through domestic policy actions, not through beggar-thy-neighbor restrictions on trade or currency manipulation; currency convertibility for current account transactions (i.e. those related to effective demand and the national accounts); permission (but no requirement) for restraint on international capital movements (of which Keynes was suspicious); international financial assistance provided by the IMF for countries in payments difficulty; and even, in its subsequent creation, of an international money in the form of SDRs, reflecting (palely) Keynes proposal for creation of an international money.

Fifth, Keynes unfortunately left an enduring legacy of macroeconomic analysis in terms of a closed economy. As Robert Mundell's chapter reminds us, Keynes spent much of his professional effort on open-economy issues. However, against the backdrop of the 1930s, and probably for ease of exposition, the *General Theory* is cast in a closed economy. Much derivative analysis has retained this analytical convention, and in particular it has pervaded elementary and intermediate textbooks of economics. This convention perhaps was at low cost in the United States of the 1950s; but the American and British textbooks have inappropriately influenced economic thinking around the world, where it was never appropriate; and it has long since ceased to be appropriate for the United States. As Keynes would have observed, the influence of a powerful idea, even a bad (but convenient) one, can be long lasting.

# 9
# The Principle of Effective Demand: The Key to Understanding the *General Theory*

Colin Rogers

## Introduction

It is generally acknowledged that the *General Theory* is enigmatic. On the one hand Keynes's claimed to be presenting a theoretical revolution. Yet on the other hand the majority of Keynes's contemporaries immediately concluded that the *General Theory* was nothing more than a special case of the classical model. The majority of economists have followed Frank Knight's (1937 [1983, p. 157]) advice to, "... simply 'forget' the revolution in economic theory and read the book [the *General Theory*] as a contribution to the theory of business oscillations".

But by abandoning Keynes's revolution in economic theory, Keynesians have abandoned the theoretical foundations of macroeconomics – the study of the behavior of the economy as a whole – and along with it the ability to understand the rationale behind Keynes's policy proposals. Keynesians, old and new, were shunted onto the wrong track when they followed Frank Knight's advice. By taking this first wrong step, Keynesians also paved the way for the repudiation of study of the economy as a whole in favor of a return to microeconomic analysis, the representative agent, and equilibrium real (non-monetary) business cycle theory. Contemporary macroeconomics has more in common with Robertson (1934) than Keynes (1936).

Keynesians, old and new have a theory of the business cycle that rests on the assumption of nominal wage and on price rigidity to produce short-run unemployment. In the long run, flexibility of prices and the price level, through the real balance effect, would restore full employment – at least in theory. In practice this might take a long time. That was the view of old Keynesians.[1] It is still the view today. Consequently, Keynesians embraced the idea that monetary and fiscal policy could speed up the process of adjustment and smooth out the business cycle. But this line of reasoning generates many puzzles.

In this chapter, I briefly outline some of these Keynesian puzzles and explain why the principle of effective demand is the key to understanding both the theoretical claims presented in the *General Theory* and Keynes's post-war policy proposals. The principle of effective demand is the essence of Keynes's aggregate Marshallian monetary theory but Keynesians never adopted this analysis and are therefore unable to "see" the principle of effective demand.

The remainder of this chapter proceeds as follows: Section II clarifies some Keynesian puzzles. Section III outlines the principle of effective demand and illustrates how it replaces Say's Law in a monetary economy. It is also explained how Keynes's concept of long-period equilibrium is consistent with his views on uncertainty and the role of expectations. Section IV considers the impact of wage and price flexibility on the point of effective demand. Section V outlines some of the implications of the principle of effective demand for the role monetary and fiscal policy in a monetary economy. Section VI concludes.

## Clarifying some Keynesian puzzles

It is well known that there are puzzles surrounding the relationship between the economics of Keynes and the Keynesian economics, and I will simply highlight and clarify a few here. The central point is that the *General Theory* is clearly NOT just another theory of business oscillations as claimed by Frank Knight. The *General Theory* contains a theory of the trade cycle as chapter 22 makes clear, but it is much more than that. It presents an analytical framework that explains a structural failure in a *laissez-faire* monetary economy. To make that clear consider the following four points.

First, in the *General Theory* and after, Keynes explicitly states that he is talking about long-period equilibrium and that equilibrium is not unique.[2] In Keynes's opinion, in a *laissez-faire* monetary economy, there is no market mechanism to ensure that the propensity to consume, the rate of interest, and the marginal efficiency of capital should automatically achieve a configuration consistent with full employment. In preparing the *General Theory*, Keynes (CW, XXIX, 1979,

p. 55) was explicit that his new analysis implied multiple long-period equilibria:

> On my view, *there is no unique long-period position* of equilibrium equally valid regardless of the character of the policy of the monetary authority.

Similarly, in the *General Theory*, when discussing the classical theory of interest, Keynes (1936, p. 191) makes the point crystal clear.

> Ricardo and his successors overlook the fact that even in the long period the volume of employment is not necessarily full but is capable of varying, and that to every banking policy there corresponds a different long-period level of employment; so there are a number of long-period equilibrium corresponding to different conceivable interest rate policies on the part of the monetary authority.

Furthermore, Keynes (1936, p. 204, emphasis added) was clear that the normal or "natural" state of a *laissez-faire* economy was likely to be one of unemployment caused by a rate of interest that was too high.

> But it [the rate of interest] may fluctuate for decades about a level which is chronically too high for full employment...

For Keynes the advantages of money come with a macroeconomic coordination cost.

Second, wage rigidity is NOT the cause of unemployment in the *General Theory* – that is the classical explanation. Keynes (1936, p. 257) makes it clear that the rigid wage explanation of unemployment is classical theory.

> For the classical theory has been accustomed to rest the supposedly self-adjusting character of the economic system on an assumed fluidity of money wages; and when there is rigidity, to lay on this rigidity the blame for maladjustment.

Keynes then spends the rest of chapter 19 in the *General Theory* explaining why nominal wage flexibility would not usually restore full employment. It may succeed only under special circumstances. Contra Pigou, Keynes (1936, p. 267) concludes:[3]

There is, therefore, no ground for the belief that a flexible wage policy is capable of maintaining a state of continuous full employment; – any more that for the belief that an open market monetary policy is capable, unaided, of achieving this result. The economic system cannot be made self-adjusting along these lines.

Third, the variability of the marginal efficiency of capital was the major source of fluctuations, and these fluctuations would be too great to be offset by flexibility in interest rates, wages, or prices. For Keynes (1936, p. 313) it is fluctuations in the marginal efficiency of capital, often driven by "animal spirits," that generates the business cycle:

> The trade cycle is best regarded, I think, as being occasioned by cyclical change in the marginal efficiency of capital...

Thus, unlike most Keynesian analysis, it is not the interaction between sticky wages or prices and fluctuations in aggregate demand that generates the business cycle in the *General Theory*.

Hence Keynes's assessment of a *laissez-faire* monetary economy is of an economy that inevitably fluctuates around a relatively stable growth path below its potential because the rate of interest is too high. In a *laissez-faire* economy there is no automatic market mechanism that will produce equality between the marginal efficiency of capital and the rate of interest at full employment. The relationship between the rate of interest and the marginal efficiency of capital is the essence of the principle of effective demand because it is the rate of interest that sets the limit to the profitable production of capital goods. Clearly, the *General Theory* is not primarily about the business cycle. It is a general theory of long-period equilibrium, the growth path about which the economy fluctuates, and includes the classical outcome of the full-employment equilibrium growth path as a special case. This is the central message of the *General Theory* missed by those who took Knight's advice.

Fourth, what has also been overlooked is Keynes's claim to have integrated monetary and value theory. Schumpeter (1954) clearly identified this dimension to Keynes's *General Theory* in his distinction between Monetary and Real Analysis. But this distinction has all but been ignored by Keynesians. The *General Theory* employs Monetary Analysis while virtually all Keynes's contemporaries and followers apply Real Analysis. This has meant that the radical theoretical innovation of the *General Theory*, the principle of effective demand, disappeared from sight. This occurs because *the principle of effective demand does not apply in*

*Real Analysis*. Even those, like Leijonhufvud (1968, 1981) who stressed the distinction between Keynes and the Keynesians, and recognized Keynes's Marshallian heritage, fell under the spell of Real Analysis and the Wicksell connection – the classical or loanable funds theory of the rate of interest.[4] By contrast, the *General Theory* offers the outline for Marshallian macroeconomics in the tradition of Schumpeter's Monetary Analysis where it makes no sense to claim that money is neutral.

## The principle of effective demand

The following discussion draws on Rogers (1989 and 1997b). Put in its most general form, the principle of effective demand is the idea that in a *laissez-faire* monetary economy, producers inevitably encounter a limit to the profitable expansion of output before full employment is reached. For Keynes, the behavior of the rate of interest in a monetary economy is a key element in his analysis. In the *General Theory*, the rate of interest as the key independent variable, as it sets a limit to the profitable expansion of output by setting the standard that the marginal efficiency of a capital asset must achieve if it is to be newly produced. And, contra Say's Law, increasing aggregate supply beyond the point of effective demand will produce losses as it drives demand prices below long-period supply prices. Attempts by firms to increase output beyond the point of effective demand will not create its own profitable aggregate demand as suggested by Say's Law. The propensity to spend of less than unity plays its familiar role in producing a stable equilibrium.[5]

The key to the principle of effective demand is the role of the rate of interest as an independent variable in the sense that there are no forces attracting the market rate of interest to the unique natural rate of interest as in Wicksell's classical vision. Instead, the "natural" rate that emerges in Keynes's long-period equilibrium is not unique and is largely determined by the market or money rate of interest. The principle of effective demand therefore opens up the possibility of multiple long-period equilibria, as opposed to the unique equilibrium of classical theory. To repeat, for Keynes the rate of interest is a key independent variable that sets the standard which the marginal efficiency of capital must exceed to stimulate capital formation and sustain employment in a growing economy. There is no unique Wicksellian natural rate of interest in the *General Theory* contra Leijonhufvud (1968, 1981) and Kohn (1986).[6] Essential to the principle of effective demand is the distinction between the rate of interest and the marginal efficiency of capital. At one point in preparation of the *General Theory* Keynes included both in his functions, Keynes (CW, 1973, XIII, p. 483).

Although Keynes is often accused of obscurity in the *General Theory* I find it difficult to fault the clarity of the message it conveys or the clarifications offered by Keynes in his post *General Theory* publications. A sample of quotes from those publications listed in the *Collected Writings* makes the point.

Keynes (CW, 1973, XIV, p. 103, emphasis added) commitment to what Schumpeter (1954) later labeled Monetary Analysis could hardly be more explicit[7]:

> Put shortly the orthodox theory maintains that the forces which determine the common value of the marginal efficiency of various assets are independent of money, which has, so to speak, no autonomous influence, and that prices move until the marginal efficiency of money, i.e., the rate of interest, falls into line with the common value of the marginal efficiency of other assets as determined by other forces. *My theory, on the other hand, maintains that this is a special case and that over a wide range of possible cases almost the opposite is true, namely, that the marginal efficiency of money is determined by forces partly appropriate to itself, and that prices move until the marginal efficiency of other assets falls into line with the rate of interest.*

Here Keynes is clearly explaining that money is not neutral in his theory, and he has replaced the classical, Wicksellian, theory of interest (and Dennis Robertson's (1934) loanable funds theory) with his own theory and that involves reversing the direction of causation between the rate of interest and the marginal efficiency of capital. He goes on to stress the latter point, Keynes (CW, XIV, 1973, p. 123):

> Thus instead of the marginal efficiency of capital determining the rate of interest, it is truer (though not a full statement of the case) to say that it is the rate of interest which determines the marginal efficiency of capital.

Hence the principle of effective demand is a property of Monetary Analysis and has three key elements: (1) a propensity to consume less that unity, (2) the marginal efficiency of capital, and (3) the rate of interest. Keynes (1936, p. 245, emphasis added) stresses the key role of the rate of interest in his restatement of the *General Theory* in chapter 18, where he clearly identifies the rate of interest as one of three key independent variables in his scheme:[8]

> Our independent variables are, in the first instance, *the propensity to consume, the schedule of the marginal efficiency of capital and the rate of interest*, though as we have seen these are capable of further analysis.

It is the relationship between the last two that is Keynes's revolutionary theoretical proposal underpinning the principle of effective demand which he employs to explain why a *laissez-faire* monetary economy may fluctuate for decades about a level of economic activity that is too low for full employment. They key to this outcome is the high level of the rate of interest relative to an uncertain and potentially volatile marginal efficiency of capital. Keynes (1936, p. 204) sums up the situation as follows:

> But it [the rate of interest] *may fluctuate for decades* about *a level which is chronically too high for full employment*; – particularly if it is the prevailing opinion that the rate of interest is self-adjusting so that the level established by convention is thought to be rooted in objective grounds much stronger than convention, the failure of employment to attain an optimum level being in no way associated in the minds of either the public or of the authority, with the prevalence of an inappropriate range of rates of interest.

In the *General Theory* there are also numerous references to the implications of the principle of effective demand.[9] For example, Keynes (1936, p. 261) also gives a clear description of the point effective demand:

> For if entrepreneurs offer employment on a scale which if they could sell their output at the expected price, would provide the public with incomes out of which they would save more than the amount of current investment, entrepreneurs are bound to make a loss equal to the difference; and this will be the case irrespective of the level of money wages.

Thus if firms attempt to expand output beyond the point of effective demand they will incur losses (recall the *Treatise*). The behavior of the rate of interest is crucial because it sets the standard that the marginal efficiency of capital must reach if capital is to be newly produced, i.e. it determines the rate of investment, economic activity, and employment. As Keynes (1936, p. 222) observes in the opening to chapter 17:

> It seems then, that the rate of interest on money plays a peculiar part in setting a limit to the level of employment, since it sets a standard to which the marginal efficiency of a capital asset must attain to be newly produced.

The liquidity preference theory of the rate of interest is therefore central to Keynes's principle of effective demand. In short, it explains why, given inappropriate monetary and fiscal arrangements, the rate of interest may be too high to ensure full employment. In Marshallian terms, at the point of effective demand, demand prices have been driven to equality with long-period supply prices. A unilateral attempt by entrepreneurs to increase production, without an associated fall in the rate of interest or increase in the marginal efficiency of capital will result only in losses. Supply does not create its own demand in a monetary economy, contra Say's Law.

Keynes (1936, p. 145) also points out that the marginal efficiency of capital depends on both technical factors and the prospective yield of capital assets. The marginal efficiency of capital is a forward-looking expectational variable.

> The schedule of the marginal efficiency of capital is of fundamental importance because it is mainly through this factor (much more than through the rate of interest) that the expectation of the future influences the present.

As suggested in Rogers (1989, chapter 9), the marginal efficiency of capital is a generalization of the concept of Wicksell's natural rate to a monetary economy and incorporates a version of Wicksell's concept of the natural rate.

Finally, what is also of central importance is that Keynes realized that in a *laissez-faire* monetary economy, the direction of causation between the market rate of interest and the marginal efficiency of capital ran predominantly from the market rate to the marginal efficiency of capital, contrary to what classical economists believed. As Kregel (1976) and Rogers (1989, 1997b) have suggested, in Keynes's long-run equilibrium the marginal efficiency of capital adjusts to the rate of interest so the direction of causation of classical theory is reversed. There are many "natural" rates of interest in the *General Theory*.

In the *General Theory* Keynes's (1936, p. 242, emphasis added) drew attention to these key changes in his theory between the *Treatise* and the *General Theory* when he explained:

> In my *Treatise on Money* I defined what purported to be a unique rate of interest which I labeled the natural rate of interest.... I had, however overlooked the fact that in any given society *there is, on this definition, a different natural rate of interest for each hypothetical level of employment.*

Furthermore, as pointed out in Rogers (1989, 1997b) several of Keynes's contemporaries accurately described the properties of his analysis I have sketched above. For example, Joan Robinson (1947, 55–6, emphasis added) clearly understood where Keynes's analysis of the Fundamental Equations in the *Treatise* was leading.

> ... it was only with disequilibrium positions that Mr. Keynes was consciously concerned when he wrote the Treatise – *he failed to notice that he had incidentally evolved a new theory of the long-period analysis of output.*

In his assessment of the *General Theory*, Harrod (1947, 69, emphasis added) correctly summarized Keynes's intentions as follows:[10]

> *The theory of interest is, I think, the central point in his scheme.* He departs from old orthodoxy in holding that the failure of the system to move to a position of full activity is not primarily due to friction, rigidity, immobility or to phenomena essentially connected with the trade cycle. *If a certain level of interest is established, which is inconsistent with full activity, no flexibility or immobility in other parts of the system will get the system to move to full activity.* But this wrong rate of interest, as we may call it, is not in itself a rigidity or inflexibility. It is natural, durable, and in certain sense, in a free system, inevitable.

Of other post *General Theory* writers, Kregel (1976) and Meltzer (1988) also present clear statements of Keynes's intentions. On the other hand, as discussed in Rogers (1997a,b) it seems that too many mainstream

Keynesian interpretations of effective demand have placed it in the context of short-run Real Analysis thereby reducing the *General Theory* to another theory of the trade cycle.

To sum up the argument so far, Keynes's principle of effective demand replaces Say's Law in a monetary economy. The key to the principle of effective demand is the replacement of the loanable funds theory by the liquidity preference theory. The latter is a theory in the tradition of Monetary Analysis with the key feature that the level of "the" rate of interest cannot be determined independently of existing monetary and fiscal institutions. As suggested by Pasinetti (1974, p. 47), "the" rate of interest is exogenous to the income generation process. Once the rate of interest is "set" the level of activity expands up to the point of effective demand, where demand prices equal long-period supply prices, and entrepreneurs earn normal profits in long-period equilibrium. The *General Theory* contains a model of the long-period equilibrium achieved by a *laissez-faire* monetary economy.

Finally, the principle of effective demand is consistent with Keynes's treatment of expectations and uncertainty. This is most obvious from his treatment of all three independent variables as psychological and expectational variables.[11] The latter characteristic is most apparent in the case of the marginal efficiency of capital as a forward-looking variable and the "bootstraps" property of the rate of interest. The key variables that define the point of effective demand are variables that cannot be defined in purely real terms.

Shackle (1967, 247) summed it up best:

> The interest rate in a monetary economy. This was the enigma that led Keynes to the nihilism of his final position...... *The interest rate depends on expectations of its own future. It is expectational, subjective, psychic, and indeterminate.* And so is the rest of the economic system. The stability, once doubted, is destroyed, and cascading disorder must intervene before the landslide grounds in a new fortuitous position. Such is the last phase of Keynesian economics. *But Keynes showed governments how to prolong the suspension of doubt.*

There is simply no way in which the *General Theory* can be understood without reference to expectations and uncertainty as many have stressed. However, these features of his analysis are not inconsistent with his use of the concept of long-period equilibrium, as some have claimed (See Rogers 1989, pp. 266–9). What this means is that although the theorist can conceive of a long-period equilibrium in a *laissez-faire* economy, that equilibrium will have a "bootstraps" or self-fulfilling prophecy property that once disturbed may result in a sub-optimal outcome.[12] Here, Shackle's notion of Keynesian Kaleidics and Kregel's (1976) notion of "shifting equilibrium" come into view. However, although there is an element of unpredictability when shifting between long-period equilibria it should be stressed that Keynes's did not believe that the *laissez-faire* economy was chronically unstable but that it was prone to oscillate around a sub-optimal level of activity. Also, as Shackle stressed, Keynes put forward policy proposals to harness the "animal spirits" of entrepreneurs and quell the bearish tendencies of liquidity preference and thereby banish the nihilistic implications of Keynesian Kaleidics.

On the basis of the argument presented here we should certainly doubt Blinder's (1988, p. 132) opinion that Keynes's claim about the existence of long-period unemployment equilibrium is just loose talk. To assess Keynes's theory in the context of Real Analysis is to miss the point entirely as the principle of effective demand has no role to play in that context. Real Analysis is the world of Say's Law and long-run monetary neutrality. Unfortunately, this is the classical world embraced by many Keynesians.

But to assess Keynes's claims it is necessary to examine them in the context of his Monetary Analysis and the principle of effective demand. In that context the question to be answered is unsurprising: will deflation automatically produce a return to full employment? As Harrod stressed, Keynes argued that once long-period equilibrium was established by equality of the rate of interest and the marginal efficiency of capital, flexibility in the rest of the system would generally not shift it to automatically achieve full employment. What is the basis of this argument and is it overturned by the real balance effect?

## The point of effective demand and flexibility of wages and prices

The following discussion builds on Rogers (1997a). Given that the point of effective demand depends on the three factors, the propensity to consume, the rate of interest and the marginal efficiency of capital, Keynes (1936, p. 262) argues that it is only in terms of these three elements that it is possible to examine the consequences of wage and price flexibility on the point of effective demand. Also, he claims that the classical economists, without the principle of effective demand, have no way of analyzing the issue. Nevertheless, he concedes, Keynes (1936, p. 257), that a reduction in money wages and prices is capable under some circumstances of stimulating output as the classical economists claim but not for the theoretical reasons they give. This is probably the source of the view that Keynes simply offers an alternative analysis of the classical story. But that is not the case. What he argues is that there is no automatic market mechanism that will allow flexible wages, prices, and market interest rates to guide the *laissez-faire* economy into equilibrium at full employment determined, in his scheme, by a unique marginal efficiency of capital. The optimal configuration of the three determinants of the point of effective demand would, in a *laissez-faire* monetary economy, be a matter of luck. Further, given the durability of his 'bootstraps' equilibrium it was possible for a *laissez-faire* economy to languish for decades at a sub-optimal or less than full-employment equilibrium.

In chapter 19 of the *General Theory*, Keynes examines the numerous ways in which falling wages and prices may act on the rate of interest and the marginal efficiency of capital and identifies several circumstances through which they may, in principle, shift the point of effective demand in a favorable direction. His general conclusion is that these circumstances do not apply in a *laissez-faire* economy (but might be feasible in an economy with centralized wage fixing), and the flexibility of wages and prices may have a negative impact on the point of effective demand – the rate of interest may rise, if liquidity preference increases sufficiently relative to the increase in the real quantity of money and the marginal efficiency of capital may fall, if demand prices fall faster than supply prices, with the consequence that the real wage rises rather than falls. In particular see Keynes (1936, p. 264) and Meltzer (1988).

All this also presupposes that falling wages and prices can produce an orderly reassessment of the normal or durable rate of interest and normal long period supply prices that underpin the "bootstraps" equilibrium in a monetary economy. In terms of Kregel's (1976) terminology, what market mechanisms exist to guide the system to full-employment equilibrium in the case of Keynes's model of "shifting equilibrium"? If the state of long-term expectations begins to shift there is no market mechanism, no classical capital market outside of a corn economy, where the forces of productivity and thrift produce a unique natural rate of interest consistent with full employment. In Keynes's Monetary Analysis his monetary equilibrium has a "self-fulfilling prophecy" property, as outlined in Rogers (1996) and there is no market in which expectations can be coordinated (a missing markets type problem). If the "bootstraps" equilibrium is disturbed, cascading disorder may result before a new equilibrium is established. Recall Shackle (1967). However, Keynes argued that the stability of the system was improved by inertia in expectations and the stickiness of money prices and wages. Stable wages and prices are desirable because excessive flexibility of the wage and price level is potentially destabilizing.

Thus at one level, Keynes presents an argument against reliance on wage and price flexibility on the grounds that in a *laissez-faire* economy, the impact on the point of effective demand is ambiguous. At another level he suggests that wage flexibility is potentially destabilizing and is not a mechanism to be relied on to shift between long-period equilibria. Furthermore, a flexible monetary policy was superior to a flexible wage policy, but in any event a flexible monetary policy alone would be incapable, in a *laissez-faire* economy, of stabilizing the system at full employment given the high degree of uncertainty and variability in the marginal efficiency of capital. A flexible wage policy is subject to the same limitations as a flexible money policy.

In all this Keynes does not explicitly consider, in the *General Theory*, what has become known as the real balance effect on consumption and this is the source of the claim that, as a matter of pure theory, Keynes failed to make his case for the persistence of long period unemployment equilibrium. But does this real balance effect make any difference? Was Keynes quite right to simply ignore it in the *General Theory*?[13] Consider the real balance analysis presented by Friedman (1976, pp. 319–22), who argues as follows:

> There always exists, with a fixed nominal quantity of money, *a rate of price decline sufficiently great* to reconcile at full employment the desires of producing enterprises to invest and of wealth-holders to save, no matter how stubborn both are.

The argument is that increasing wealth from the rising purchasing power of cash balances will stimulate consumption spending directly and shift the consumption function until full employment is reached. In terms of Keynes's scheme it is through the propensity to consume that Friedman's real balance effect has its impact. But to shift the point of effective demand the increase in spending must induce entrepreneurs to increase employment. This they would do if the marginal efficiency of capital increased relative to the rate of interest. For this to happen, demand prices must lie above supply prices. In the case of deflation, demand prices must fall more slowly than supply prices – prices must be stickier than wages. Friedman's analysis makes no such distinction and asserts only that a sufficiently rapid price decline will do the trick. But a rapid decline in demand prices, relative to supply prices, will depress the marginal efficiency of capital. And even if wages decline more rapidly than prices Friedman ignores the possibility that the income effect (or bankruptcy) will swamp the real balance effect. So even if the rate of interest declines, as a result of an increase in the real quantity of money (with the nominal quantity fixed by the monetary authority) there is no *a priori* reason why the point of effective demand should shift in a favorable direction as a result of a real balance effect.

Another issue concerns the fixity of the money supply for, as Keynes (1936, p. 266) notes, if the quantity of money contracts when prices fall there is no leverage for the real balance effect. Some Post Keynesians, e.g., Moore (1988), use this argument to dismiss the real balance effect. But most argue that Keynes clearly assumed that the quantity of money was fixed. However, as Tily (2007) points out, Keynes consistently argued the case for managed money against the argument for fixing the quantity of money, as was the case with the gold or gold exchange standards. In other words, Keynes was against attempts to make the bank money system behave as if it were a commodity money system. Fixing the quantity of money leaves the rate of interest hostage to the liquidity preference of the public and the private banks. With no unique full-employment natural rate to guide it, the market rate that results would inevitably be set too high to ensure full employment in a *laissez-faire* economy. The liquidity preference of the public would interact with the "animal" spirits of entrepreneurs to produce a point of effective demand that was consistent with full employment only by chance. Hence Keynes was an advocate of managed money where the latter meant that the authorities, both fiscal and monetary, operated to keep the structure of interest rates low (Keynes's "cheap money" policy) and immune from the whims of the liquidity preferences of the public and the private banks.

Control of "the" interest rate was thus a key element in Keynes's monetary policy which in turn means that for Keynes money is an inside money in which the central bank controls the bank rate and allows the money supply to adjust to demand. This does not mean that there is no way for monetary policy to influence macroeconomic performance. As the monopoly suppliers of clearing balances, central banks can impose losses on the banks and this gives them effective control over short-term interest rates but perhaps only indirect control over long-rates, unless they are prepared to deal in longer dated securities (or the Treasury so acts in management of the national debt). In this context the important point is that although Keynes considers the case of a fixed money supply, he would regard a policy that attempted to produce such a result as counterproductive. For Keynes, bank money should be endogenous. In such a monetary economy there is no leverage for real balance effects *a la* Pigou or Friedman. Also, in such a monetary economy the elasticity of expectations, distributional, real debt burden and bankruptcy effects also come to dominate any purely logical real balance effects as Fisher (1930) realized and Keynes (1936, p. 264) acknowledged. All this was neatly summarized by Dimand (1991).

To sum up, Keynes's presents theoretical arguments to explain why, in a *laissez-faire* monetary economy, flexibility of wages and price cannot be relied on to shift the economy between long-period equilibria in an orderly fashion. Encouraging greater flexibility of wages and prices is a risky strategy because it may undermine the norms and conventions that sustain a long-period "bootstraps" equilibrium. The consequence of such action is unpredictable. As a matter of policy his theory also suggests why it would be counterproductive for the monetary authority to fix the quantity of money. Control of the interest rate is important for the implementation of low and stable interest rates as the contribution of monetary policy to sustaining a point of effective demand close to full employment. In such a world real balance effects have no leverage and monetary policy must complement the socialization of investment, which is intended to stabilize and increase the marginal efficiency of capital.

## Implications for modern macroeconomic policy

From Keynes's perspective the last 70 years of macroeconomic policy are largely a vindication of the *General Theory*. The principle of effective demand suggests that macroeconomic policy be directed to achieve several key objectives to sustain the point of effective at a level consistent with full employment. To obtain these objectives a structural change in the role of government is required. The irony is that the structural change to the role of government has occurred but without an understanding of the theoretical analysis on which it is based. Academic Keynesians old and new, continue to base their analysis on the pre-*General Theory* Real Analysis of Pigou and Robertson. There is no sign of the principle of effective demand in new Keynesian theory.

The principle of effective demand suggests what structural change is required to stabilize a *laissez-faire* economy and what macroeconomic policy – monetary and fiscal – should aim to achieve. First, government needs to be in a position to increase the marginal efficiency of capital and reduce its variance. Second, monetary policy should aim to keep interest rates low relative to the marginal efficiency of capital until full employment has been achieved. To assist in the latter an international system of exchange rate management is needed so that domestic policy could be aimed at achieving full employment rather than held hostage to an overvalued exchange rate.

In the absence of a unique natural rate of interest, macroeconomic policy requires a role for government to stabilize and raise entrepreneurs' assessment of the expected "normal" rate of return on capital. Keynes's proposal for the "socialization" of investment is a proposal to achieve this result and thereby stabilize aggregate demand and "crowd-in" private sector investment. In other words, Keynes's policy proposals are intended to shift the growth path of the economy closer to its full-employment potential path. This would require a structural change to the role of government in the economy relative to its *laissez-faire* state. Keynes (1936, p. 164) argues as follows:

> I expect to see the State, which is in a position to calculate the marginal efficiency of capital goods on long views and on the basis of the general social advantage, taking an ever greater responsibility for directly organising investment.

Kregel (1985) provides a comprehensive assessment of Keynes's policy proposals along these lines and highlights how they differ from the deficit financing and fine-tuning often proposed by Keynesians. From this perspective, it could be argued that although imperfect, government implementation of economic policy in the post-war period is a vindication of Keynes's analysis. The last 70 years have seen the most dramatic "crowding-in" of private sector investment in the history of the world economy, yet Keynesians are happy to use a *laissez-faire* model that is self-adjusting to full employment in the long run. What is worse, many modern macroeconomic models have no role for money or government and therefore no basis for macroeconomic policy.

Like the role of fiscal policy Keynes also called for a structural change to the monetary system. In particular Keynes advocated managed money as opposed to the "automatic" mechanism of the gold standard. Although somewhat enigmatic the following assessment from chapter 17 of the *General Theory* (1936, p. 235) makes the point.

Unemployment develops, that is to say, because people want the moon; – men cannot be employed when the object they desire (i.e. money) is something which cannot be produced and the demand for which cannot be readily chocked off. There is no remedy but to persuade the public that green cheese is practically the same thing and to have a green cheese factory [i.e. a central bank] under public control.

In other words paper money (green cheese) is to replace gold, and the central bank should take responsibility for managing the monetary system and setting the level of interest rates. There is no natural rate of interest as claimed by the classical theory. Keynes (1936, p. 204) also argued that the normal rate of interest was determined by conventions and psychological factors that could be manipulated by the central bank.

...the convention is not rooted in secure knowledge, it will not be always unduly resistant to a modest measure of persistence and consistency of purpose by the monetary authority.

Today, it is taken for granted that central banks manage the monetary system and that the cash or overnight rate is the instrument of monetary policy. See, for example DeLong (2000) and Romer (2000) but note that their theory remains rooted in Real Analysis.

Thus for both monetary and fiscal policy it could be argued that the structural policy changes advocated by Keynes have been implemented. However, it is equally apparent that the theoretical analysis from which those policies were derived has been rejected.

## Concluding remarks

Looking back over the last 70 years it is an inescapable fact that the theoretical arm of the Keynesian Revolution never got off the ground. Immediately after the war the work of Hicks and Robertson reinstated the loanable funds theory of the rate of interest and the classical interpretation of the IS–LM model soon dominated the teaching of Keynesian economics. Real Analysis was reasserted and continues to rule to this day in various forms. The principle of effective demand, as a key insight of Keynes's Monetary Analysis, finds no home in any form of Keynesian Real Analysis.

On the policy front, it could be argued that Keynes's policy revolution has been an amazing success. Today the legacy of Keynes is that governments and central banks do act to manage the economy in a way that was unthinkable before the *General Theory*. In western democracies, voters have come to expect that and punish governments who under-perform. Despite this dramatic change in the role and scope of government in economic management many academic economists continue to view the world through a model where the issues raised by Keynes are simply assumed away. Perhaps a true test of the view that the *General Theory* is nothing more than another theory of the business cycle, as Knight suggested, would be to advocate a return to the policy of *laissez faire*. Political leaders sometimes threaten to implement such an experiment, but the record speaks for itself.

## Notes

1. For example, Tobin (1975, pp. 195–6) concluded: '[t]he predominant verdict of history is that, as a matter of pure theory, Keynes failed to make his case. The real issue is not the existence of a long-run equilibrium with unemployment, but the possibility of protracted unemployment which the natural adjustments of the market economy remedy slowly if at all.... The phenomena he described are better regarded as *disequilibrium dynamics*.' Patinkin's (1965, 1976) disequilibrium interpretation of Keynes is also well known.
2. Uniqueness of equilibrium is a special case unattainable even by an aggregate version of the Arrow-Debreu model. See Kirman (1989).
3. Keynes goes on to note that if the intention is for flexible wages and prices to reduce the rate of interest then a flexible wages policy is effectively placing monetary policy in the hands of the trade unions.
4. Keynes accused the classical theory of logical error. In this respect, it is now recognized that Wicksell's concept of the natural rate is restricted to the corn economy (Rogers 1989, Chapter 2) and the sequence analysis of the loanable funds theory is flawed. Bibow (2001, p. 598) argues: "The loanable funds fallacy consists of the following fatal oversight: loanable funds theory completely overlooks the fact that-in one way or another-the firms facing the unexpected rise in thrift will be 'in the loanable funds market' to cover their unexpected cash-flow shortfall. Indeed, what loanable funds theorists see as an additional supply of loanable funds is exactly matched in size, but possibly not in composition, by the additional demand for loanable funds due to distress borrowing – of one form or another-on the part of those having to cope with the unexpected rise in thrift". The fundamental problem for loanable funds theorists is that they confuse saving with money.
5. Bibow (2001, p. 603, fn1) suggests that the fundamental psychological law underpinning the consumption function in the *General Theory* provided the insight for Keynes's adoption of multiple *stable* equilibria as opposed to the *Treatise* analysis with either the unique equilibrium at full employment or the complete collapse of output in the banana republic parable.

6. Rogers (1988) argues that Kohn (1986) does not apply Schumpeter's definition of Monetary Analysis despite his reference to Schumpeter. Consequently he erroneously concludes that Monetary Analysis is incompatible with the equilibrium method.
7. Earlier work on the monetary theory of production that was excluded from the published version of the *General Theory* also makes this clear, Keynes (CW, XXIX, 1979).
8. Traditional interpretations of Keynes put more weight on his following statement that *sometimes* the quantity of money as determined by the central bank and the liquidity preferences of the public can determine the rate of interest. That would indeed be the case if the central bank sought to restrict the quantity of money but that is a particular form of monetary policy and one that attempts to make a bank money system mimic the properties of commodity money; something that Keynes rejected on the grounds that it left the rate of interest to be determined by the liquidity preference of the public and the banks.
9. Pasinetti (1997) notes that, despite the title to Chapter 3, Keynes never explicitly set out what he meant by the principle of effective demand. Keynes seems to take it for granted that the reader knows what it is! I drew my insight into the principle of effective demand from Chick (1983).
10. Harrod thought that Keynes was too controversial and persuaded him to tone down his critique of classical theory.
11. Keynes (CW, 1973, XIII, p. 441) included the state of long-term expectations in the investment and consumption functions in an early draft of the *General Theory*.
12. See Kregel (1976) and Rogers (1989, 1997b) for a discussion of Keynes's application of the Marshallian method to the analysis of long-period equilibrium and expectations. As Keynes (1936, p. 245) explained in the *General Theory*, treating factors as given is not the same as assuming they are constant: "This does not mean that we assume these factors to be constant; but merely that, in this place and context, we are not considering or taking into account the effects and consequences of changes in them." Here Keynes is simply applying Marshall's method of treating "variables as constants" and statics is part of dynamics.
13. Bibow (2001, p. 607, fn1) considers the real balance effect to be empirically irrelevant. Although true that does not address the theoretical question posed by the conventional interpretation of Keynes.

## References

J. Bibow, "The loanable funds fallacy: exercises in the analysis of disequilibrium", *Cambridge Journal of Economics* (2001), 25, 591–616.
A. Blinder, "The Fall and Rise of Keynesian Economics", *Economic Record* (1988), 64, 278–84.
V. Chick, *Macroeconomics After Keynes* (London: Philip Allan, 1983).
R. W. Dimand, "Keynes, Kalecki, Ricardian equivalence, and the real balance effect", *Bulletin of Economic Research* (1991), 43(3), 289–92.

J. B. DeLong, "How to Teach Monetary Policy: Do Central Banks Set the Interest rate, or Do They Target the Money Stock?", (2000), http://www.j-bradford-delong.net/

I. Fisher, "The debt-deflation of great depressions", *Econometrica* (1930), 1, 337–57.

M. Friedman, *Price Theory*, 2nd edition (Chicago: Aldine, 1976).

R. F. Harrod, "Keynes the Economist", in *The New Economics: Keynes's Influence on Theory and Policy*, ed. S. E. Harris, 65–72 (New York: Alfred A. Knopf, 1947).

J. M. Keynes, *The General Theory of Employment, Interest and Money* (London: Macmillan, 1936).

J. M. Keynes, *The Collected Writings of John Maynard Keynes, The General Theory and After, Part I: Preparation*, Vol XIII, ed. Donald Moggridge (London: Macmillan, 1973).

J. M. Keynes, *The Collected Writings of John Maynard Keynes, The General Theory and After, Part II: Defence and Development*, Vol XIV, ed. Donald Moggridge (London: Macmillan, 1973).

J. M. Keynes, *The Collected Writings of John Maynard Keynes, A Supplement*, Vol XXIX, ed. Donald Moggridge (London: Macmillan, 1979).

F. Knight, "Unemployment and Mr Keynes" revolution in economic theory', 1937, reprinted in *John Maynard Keynes: Critical Assessments*, Vol II, ed. J. C. Wood (London: Croom Helm, 1983).

M. Kohn, "Monetary analysis, the equilibrium method and Keynes's *General Theory*", *Journal of Political Economy* (1986), 94, 1191–224.

J. A. Kregel, "Economic methodology in the face of uncertainty: The modelling methods of Keynes and the post keynesians", *Economic Journal* (1976), 86, 209–25.

J. A. Kregel, "Budget deficits, stabilization policy and liquidity preference: Keynes's post-war policy proposals", in *Keynes Relevance Today*, ed. Fausto Vicarelli (London: Macmillan, 1985).

Alan P. Kirman, "Intrinsic limits of modern economic theory: The emperor has no clothes", *Economic Journal* (1989), 99, Conference Supplement, p. 137.

A. Leijonhufvud, *On Keynesian Economics and the Economics of Keynes*, (London: Oxford University Press, 1968).

A. Leijonhufvud, "The Wicksell connection: Variations on a theme", in *Information and Coordination: Essays in Macroeconomic Theory*, 131–202 (Oxford: Oxford University Press, 1981).

A. H. Meltzer, *Keynes's General Theory: A Different Perspective* (Cambridge: Cambridge University Press, 1988).

B. Moore, *Horizontalists and Verticalists* (Cambridge: Cambridge University Press, 1988).

D. Patinkin, *Money Interest and Prices*, 2nd edition (New York: Harper and Row, 1965).

D. Patinkin, *Keynes' Monetary Thought: A Study in its Development* (Durham: Duke University Press, 1976).

Lugi, L. Pasinetti, *Growth and Income Distribution: Essays in Economic Theory*, (Cambridge: Cambridge University Press, 1974).

Lugi, L. Pasinetti, "The principle of Effective Demand", in *A "Second Edition" of the General Theory*, eds. G. C. Harcourt and R. Riach (London: Routledge, 1997).

D. Robertson, "Industrial fluctuations and the natural rate of interest", *Economic Journal* (1934), 44, 650–6.

J. Robinson, "The long-period theory of employment", in *Essays in the Theory of Employment*, 75–100 (Oxford: Blackwell, 1947).

D. Romer, "Keynesian macroeconomics without the LM curve", *Journal of Economic Perspectives* (2000) 14, 2, Spring.

C. Rogers, "Monetary Analysis, the Equilibrium Method, and Keynes's General Theory: An alternative perspective". Unpublished working paper, University of Adelaide (1988).

C. Rogers, *Money, Interest and Capital: A Study in the Foundations of Monetary Theory* (Cambridge: Cambridge University Press, 1989).

C. Rogers, "Self-fulfilling expectations and the *General Theory*", *History of Economics Review* (1996), 25, 172–83.

C. Rogers, "Post-Keynesian monetary theory and the principle of effective demand", in *Money, Financial Institutions and Macroeconomics*, eds. Avi J. Cohen, Harald Hagemann and John Smithin (Boston: Kluwer, 1997a).

C. Rogers, "The general theory: Existence of a monetary long-period unemployment equilibrium" in G. C. Harcourt and R. Riach (eds.) *A "Second Edition" of the General Theory* (London: Routledge, 1997b).

G. L. S. Shackle, *The Years of High Theory: Innovation and Tradition in Economic Thought 1926–1939* (Cambridge: Cambridge University Press, 1967).

J. A. Schumpeter, *History of Economic Analysis* (New York: Oxford University Press, 1954).

G. Tily, *Keynes's General Theory, the Rate of Interest and Keynesian Economics; Keynes Betrayed* (London: Palgrave Macmillan, 2007).

J. Tobin, "Keynesian Models of recession and Depression", *American Economic Review, Papers and Proceedings* (1975), 65, 195–202.

# 10
## Getting Rid of Keynes? A Reflection on the Recent History of Macroeconomics

*Michel De Vroey*

### Introduction

The title of this chapter springs from the obvious observation that the days when macroeconomics and Keynesianism were part and parcel of each other are gone. My aim in this chapter is to reflect on this process of de-Keynesianisation.

Several papers dealing with the history of macroeconomics have been published in the recent years, the most renowned ones being those of Blanchard (2000) and Woodford (1999).[1] The originality of this chapter lies in my claim that in order to make sense of the evolution of macroeconomics it is both possible and fruitful to do more than just describe the different stages the discipline has passed through. It would be too pretentious to say that this chapter provides a theory of the history of macroeconomics, but it does aim at analysing it in a theoretical framework. This framework combines two distinctions. The first I will call the Marshall–Walras divide, the second is the distinction between Keynesianism viewed as a conceptual apparatus and Keynesianism viewed as a policy cause. To mention just one conclusion that will be reached using these distinctions, the emergence of new classical macroeconomics can be encapsulated as the replacement of Marshallian by Walrasian macroeconomics, on the one hand, and, on the other hand, as the appearance of models that are anti-Keynesian on the score of both their analytical apparatus and their view of policy.

The next three sections are concerned with preliminary matters, defining macroeconomics and explaining the two distinctions outlined above. In the subsequent sections, I reflect on the most salient episodes in the history of macroeconomics and locate them within the taxonomy that can be constructed on the basis of these two distinctions. I comment in turn on the IS–LM model, monetarism, so-called disequilibrium theory, new classical macroeconomics, the real business cycle approach, new Keynesian models and the new neoclassical synthesis.

To conclude this introduction, a few remarks are worth making. First, this chapter spans half a century and covers a wide range of models. This compels me to concentrate on the essential elements of each theory. I shall also presume that the reader is knowledgeable about the models that are being discussed. Not all the episodes discussed will be dealt with equally, IS–LM and dynamic stochastic macroeconomics receiving more attention than the others. Second, my purpose in this chapter is to assess the aim pursued in different macroeconomic models, and not to evaluate whether these aims have been achieved. Third and finally, my chapter proposes a classification scheme. Constructing taxonomies implies making choices, which can always be contested for one reason or the other. Hence, this chapter ought to be judged on whether it allows making some order in a disordered world beyond the possible objections that can be addressed to my classification of any of the models considered.

## Defining macroeconomics

Macroeconomists have never paid much attention to the definition of macroeconomics. When in need of a definition, they content themselves with short straightforward statements. For example, both Woodford (1999) and Blanchard (2000) define it as the study of fluctuations. To me, such a definition is too limited. It may well fit the current practice of macroeconomists but it amounts to claiming that everything that was considered to be macroeconomics label before the development of real business cycle models does not belong in the field of macroeconomics, a rather weird point of view. A more elaborate definition is thus needed. Mine is based on the following five criteria:

1. Macroeconomics studies an economy as a whole; therefore it belongs to general equilibrium theory;
2. It is concerned with simplified general equilibrium models;
3. It is formalised, and it consists of mathematical models;
4. It is concerned with policy issues and aims at providing practical macroeconomic policy advice;
5. It pursues an applied purpose and its models are geared towards a confrontation with the data.

Several comments are in order. First, by general equilibrium theory I mean any theory that is concerned with the economy as a whole rather than just with parts of it. The usual view to the contrary notwithstanding, general equilibrium theory should not be equated with the Walrasian research programme. General equilibrium models belonging to other traditions (e.g. Sraffian theory) cannot be excluded. So, it is not because macroeconomics is a subset of general equilibrium theory, that it is necessarily Walrasian. On the contrary, I shall argue that during the first decades of its existence macroeconomics was not so. Of course, it would be preposterous to claim that the Marshallian and the Walrasian general equilibrium traditions have the same status. Only the second has a fully fledged existence to the point of having become the cuckoo in the nest. Marshallian general equilibrium theory, although stoutly defended by authors such as Clower and Leijonhufvud ([1975] 1984) or, more recently, Colander and associates (Colander 1996, 2006), has hardly taken the forefront. However, it exists in a more or less hidden way. By this, I mean that some models exist, which are presented simply as non-Walrasian but emerge as Marshallian once the criteria for differentiating the Walrasian and the Marshallian approaches have been set out. This claim will be justified below.

Second, two types of general equilibrium models can be distinguished which, for lack of a better appellation, I shall brand as "complex" and "simple" (and for that matter extra-simple!). Walras's model in his *Elements of Pure Economics* (1954) and the Arrow–Debreu model (1954) constitute the pillars of the complex type. Macroeconomic models constitute the second type. They comprise a small number of variables. They study a few markets, possibly named after those markets that are deemed to be the most important in the real world. They deal with aggregates by reasoning in terms of representative firms or agents. They may include a few institutions, such as the government and the central bank. The rationale behind these simplifications lies in items four and five of my definition: these models are geared towards addressing policy issues, such as the level of employment, national output, inflation, government deficit, the effects of changes in the money supply, etc. They claim to be empirically relevant and to give results, which can be tested against reality.

I admit that my view that macroeconomics is a sub-category of general equilibrium analysis may look odd at first sight. In so far as general equilibrium analysis is considered part of microeconomics, as it is usually the case, it follows that macroeconomics ought to be considered a branch of microeconomics! This confusing assessment could have been avoided had the terminology suggested by Frisch (Frisch 1933) when he introduced the term of macroeconomics been adopted. According to Frisch, the subject matter of macroeconomics is "the whole economic system in its entirety" while microeconomics is defined as concerned with individual optimising planning. In this conception, general equilibrium theory is definitely macro and not micro. Unfortunately, Frisch has not been followed. The scope of microeconomics has become wider as it grew to cover models of both particular markets and of the economy as a whole. By the same token, the term macroeconomics has received a narrower meaning.

As to my third criterion, I do not want it to be a bone of contention. It is introduced just as a matter of convenience to separate non-formalised studies of the economy as whole (as in, for example, the writings of classical political economists) from the later formalised approach to this topic, which is the sole object of my analysis. Adopting it permits me to avoid having to make clear that I am referring to "modern" as opposed to "old" macroeconomics.

Fourth and finally, my definition is not concerned with substance. Consideration of the privileged object of analysis is useful for separating different phases in the development of macroeconomics, but it should not be taken as a criterion for defining the discipline. It is, however, worth looking at the type of issues with which macroeconomists are primarily concerned. It then appears that the field started with one overriding preoccupation, to explain the phenomenon of mass unemployment. In contrast, the new classical revolution has replaced this object of analysis with the study of the business cycle.

## The Marshall–Walras divide

It is widely admitted that Marshall and Walras differed sharply in terms of methodology.[2] Yet, co-existing with such a judgement is the view that when it comes to contents the two authors are very close.[3] Marshall's partial equilibrium analysis and Walras' general equilibrium analysis are considered complementary approaches. In contrast, I want to claim that the Marshallian and the Walrasian approaches constitute two alternative research programmes within the neoclassical school of thought. It is beyond the scope of this chapter to present a full analysis of their differences.[4] For my purpose what matters is the account of the working of the economy underpinning each of them.

In the general equilibrium literature, the notion of an economy is usually understood in a narrow sense as referring to a list of agents (with their endowments, preferences and objectives), a list of commodities and a list of firms (with their ownership structure and technical constraints). This account is, however, incomplete due to its silence on the subject of the functioning of the economy. Such a neglect is due to the fact that the task usually assigned to general equilibrium theory is to analyse the existence, uniqueness, stability and welfare characteristics of the equilibrium of a given economy at one point in time and over time. However, the theoretical investigation should not be stopped at this stage. The economy whose equilibrium is discussed ought also to be depicted as a social system, comprising a minimal set of institutions, trade arrangements, rules of the game and means of communication between agents. I propose to use the notion of an economy in a broader than usual sense to include these institutional features. My claim is then that the Marshallian and the Walrasian economy are two distinct objects.

## The Walrasian economy

One of Walras's strokes of genius was to have started his analysis by studying an entire economy at once, rather than a section of it. Take his two-good model. It bears on a full economy, albeit the simplest one that can be conceived of, rather than on a market understood as a fraction of an economy. This was a counter-intuitive methodological decision. Intuitively, most people would rather take a stepwise approach consisting of first studying the functioning of an isolated, typical market, while relegating the study of the interrelationship of markets, the piecing together of the results of partial analysis, to the second stage of the enterprise.

The distinctive feature of the Walrasian economy is the presence of the auctioneer, a fictive agent announcing prices and changing them until a state of equilibrium is obtained. While most Walrasian economists accept this fiction only grudgingly, for my part I am willing to go as far as identifying the Walrasian approach with the presence of the auctioneer.

Let me now evoke the implications of adopting the auctioneer hypothesis. First, in an auctioneer-led economy, agents do not need to hold information about excess demand functions and their underpinnings. As stated by Kirman, "assuming the Walrasian auctioneer, little information is needed by individual agents; the information has all been processed for them" (Kirman 2006: XV). Second, adopting the auctioneer hypothesis amounts to considering that at each trading round the equilibrium is arrived at in logical time, i.e. instantaneously. Third, whenever the auctioneer assumption is made, price flexibility is compelling. As Lucas points out, once it is admitted that the auctioneer is an artefact introduced to dodge the thorny problem of price formation, it makes little sense to impede it from doing the job of bringing prices to their equilibrium values (Lucas 1987: 52). Fourth and finally, the auctioneer hypothesis and imperfect competition run counter each other. This follows from reflecting on the communication structure of an auctioneer-led system. The auctioneer economy is a set of bilateral relationships between the auctioneer and isolated individual agents. Before the attainment of equilibrium, agents' exclusive social link is with the auctioneer. They do not interact and communicate between themselves. As a result, whenever a given agent makes a trading offer by responding to the prices announced by the auctioneer, he or she does not know how many other agents are making a similar offer. An agent can be in a monopolistic position whilst being unaware of this state of affairs and hence incapable of taking advantage of it! The same point can be made by looking at things from the information point of view. In an auctioneer economy, agents are supposed to hold no knowledge about market excess demand functions. This feature runs counter to the central trait of monopoly or oligopoly theory that the agent holding market power is supposed to know the objective demand function for the good it sells. Hence the tâtonnement set-up itself guarantees the "perfectness" of competition, whatever the possible monopolistic factors that may be present in the economy. To conclude this point, Walrasian theory and price rigidity, on the one hand, and Walrasian theory and imperfect competition, on the other, are incompatible bedfellows. This is a direct result of the adoption of the auctioneer assumption.[5]

A final aspect to be considered is whether a Walrasian economy is monetary. For the sake of differentiating the Walrasian and Marshallian approaches, it suffices to note that the presence of money in Walrasian theory is at best problematic while, as will be seen, it is compelling presence in the Marshallian approach.[6]

## The Marshallian economy

By extrapolating from the institutional set-up on which Marshall's partial equilibrium analysis is based, we can reconstruct the trade technology that would have underpinned his general equilibrium analysis had he been able to construct one.

The central feature of a Marshallian economy is that it comprises separate markets, each of which is a separate locus for the formation of market equilibrium. Unlike Walras, Marshall assumes that production occurs in advance of trade. Thus we have a sequence economy with input markets taking place in advance of goods markets. Households enter the goods markets with an income originating from the sale of services in the factors markets and the distribution of profits from earlier market days.

Another feature of the Marshallian economy lies in is its monetary character. Money is present from the beginning of Marshall's analysis of the market. In fact, it forms part of the definition of a market, since this is defined as an institutional arrangement whereby a given good is exchanged for money.

The price formation process occurs without auctioneer. As a result, the above-mentioned implications are absent as well. The banning of rigidity and imperfect competition proper for the Walrasian economy is absent from the Marshallian. As to an alternative price formation process, two distinct scenarios are to be found in Marshall's writings. The first, which is conditional on the assumption of a constant marginal utility of money, permitted him to represent the attainment of equilibrium as the result of a bargaining process between agents. It involves trial and error, and exchanges at "false prices", which makes the scenario relatively realistic. However, since this assumption cannot be generalised, Marshall had to fall back on the assumption that agents are so well-informed about market conditions that they are able to mentally reconstruct market supply and demand functions.

## The two meanings of the "non-Walrasian" modifier

Finally, I need to introduce one further distinction concerning the Walrasian approach. Walrasian models departing from the Walrasian canonical model (as set out in Walras's *Elements* or in the Arrow–Debreu model), for example because they introduce price rigidity or imperfect information, have been branded "non-Walrasian". Such terminology is unfortunate because these models are part of the Walrasian approach as far as all their other traits are concerned. In other words, they should be considered "quasi-Walrasian". It would have been preferable to reserve the "non-Walrasian" modifier for characterising models that differ radically from the Walrasian approach. Since changing an established terminology is difficult, my way out is to draw a distinction between a weak and a strong understanding of this modifier. A model will be called non-Walrasian in the weak sense if it features an equilibrium outcome different from Walrasian equilibrium while still resting on the Walrasian institutional set-up as described above and centred on

*Table 10.1*

|  |  | Two types of general equilibrium models | |
|---|---|---|---|
|  |  | Complex models | Simplified models |
| Two distinct neoclassical approaches | The Marshallian approach |  |  |
|  | The Walrasian approach |  | *Walras*'s Elements of Pure Economics |

the auctioneer artefact. In a model that is weakly non-Walrasian, the departure from the canonical Walrasian model is well circumscribed; it pertains to a single element while the others remain as they are in the canonical model. For example, in some general equilibrium search models, it is assumed that the auctioneer continues to fix the equilibrium price vector while the search for partners is left to the agents. In contrast, a non-Walrasian model in the strong sense is a model where the equilibrium can be non-Walrasian and, on top of this, the institutional set-up is radically different from the Walrasian set-up. If my above distinction between the Walrasian and the Marshallian economy is accepted, imperfect competition models ought to be branded as non-Walrasian in the strong sense.

The distinctions between the two ways of engaging in general equilibrium theory and between the Marshallian and the Walrasian approaches are combined in a box diagram in Table 10.1.[7]

## The meaning of the Keynesian modifier

What exactly should be understood by the widely used modifier "Keynesian"? This is a question that is seldom addressed. In my opinion, the basic distinction that needs to be made here is between Keynesianism as an analytical apparatus and Keynesianism as a policy cause.[8]

Let me start with the policy dimension. Here, the "Keynesian" modifier is used with reference to Keynes's motivation to write the *General Theory*, bringing out market failures that state interventions would be able to remedy.[9] The opposite standpoint or the anti-Keynesian policy cause is the view that the unfettered working of competition will lead the economy to the best attainable position. The existence of such a divide is for example acknowledged by Lucas: "In economic policy, the frontier never changes. The issue is always mercantilism and government intervention vs. laissez faire and free market" (Lucas 1993: 3). More narrowly, the Keynesian standpoint can be equated with a trust in the efficiency of stabilisation policies and the anti-Keynesian standpoint with a belief in the inefficiency of such policies.

I now turn to the methodological dimension. I take it that the IS–LM model gives a fair rendition of Keynes's reasoning in the *General Theory*. Therefore, by a "Keynesian methodology", I mean the use of the IS–LM model. The latter, I will argue below, has a definite Marshallian lineage. So, we have a Marshall–Keynes–Hicks conceptual apparatus. Turning now to the non-Keynesian method of studying an economy, two possibilities will have to be considered. First, we will encounter models that are not "Keynesian–Hicksian" but are nonetheless part of the Marshallian approach. One type of such models, which will be subsumed under the name of the "Marshall-Chamberlin lineage", will play an important role in my account of the unfolding of macroeconomics. The second possibility of an alternative to the Keynesian way of positing issues is of course the Walrasian methodology.

By combining the policy and the methodological dimensions we get a second box diagram, comprising eight slots (see Table 10.2). First, authors and models can be Keynesian on both the policy and the methodology score (Table 10.1). In this case, the Keynesian modifier is unambiguous.[10] Symmetrically, we might conceive of models that are completely anti-Keynesian (Tables 10.4, 10.6, and 10.8). Next, there are

*Table 10.2*

|  |  | Policy cause standpoint | |
|---|---|---|---|
|  |  | Justifying demand activation | Defending laissez-faire |
| Conceptual apparatus | Marshallian macroeconomics | | |
|  | The Marshall–Keynes–Hicks lineage | 1 | 2 |
|  | The Marshall-Chamberlin lineage | 3 | 4 |
|  | Walrasian macroeconomics | | |
|  | Walrasian models | 5 | 6 |
|  | Non-Walrasian models | 7 | 8 |

intermediate cases, where the two dimensions split. Models to be placed in box 2 are Keynesian in the methodological sense yet anti-Keynesian in the policy sense. Models in boxes 3, 5 and 7 are Keynesian in the policy sense but non-Keynesian in the methodological sense.

## The emergence of macroeconomics

As the result of my narrow definition of macroeconomics, I view its rise as the result of a three-stage process. Keynes's *General Theory* constitutes the first stage, Hicks's IS–LM model the second, the emergence of econometric models the third step.

That Keynes's *General Theory* was the foundation stone for the emergence of macroeconomics is of course undeniable. Its aim was to elucidate the causes of the phenomenon of mass unemployment that affected all economies during the Great Depression. This was a time of great disarray with no remedy at hand to fix the ailing economic system. The general confusion did not spare academic economists, who were torn between their expertise and their guts. According to economic theory, unemployment must have been caused by too high real wages and decreasing them was the remedy. Yet their instinct told them that this was untrue and that the remedy lay in state-induced demand activation. Keynes's book, which was mainly addressed to his fellow economists, aimed at solving this contradiction by providing a theoretical basis for economists' gut feelings. The path to be taken to this end was to generalise Marshallian theory, which was exclusively concerned with partial equilibrium analysis, as to enable it to address issues related to interdependency across markets.[11] Keynes's hunch was that unemployment, though a labour market manifestation, had its roots in other sectors of the economy, specifically the money market or finance. Therefore, the study of the interdependency across markets became crucial. Of course, a theory geared to such a purpose, Walrasian general equilibrium theory, existed. Yet Keynes had a poor opinion of it, and viewed it as lacking any merit.[12]

Keynes ended up proposing a theory where involuntary unemployment – a state of affairs where some people are willing to participate in the labour market at the given wage or even at a lower wage yet are unable to follow through on this plan – is due to a deficiency in aggregate demand. While his central aim was to demonstrate the logical existence of involuntary unemployment, his book was kaleidoscopic, mingling several threads of reasoning, which were barely reconcilable. In spite of its obscurity, the book received a positive reception, especially from young scholars who were craving for theoretical novelty. At the time of its publication, the pressure to produce a new theoretical framework that might account for the obvious dysfunctions in the market system was such that dissenting voices had little impact. Nevertheless, the perplexity as to the central message of Keynes's book was great, even amongst his admirers. Its central message was clarified when a session of the Econometric Society Conference was devoted to the book. Meade ([1937] 1947), Harrod (1937) and Hicks ([1937] 1967) gave three distinct papers about it (see Young 1987). All three saw it as their first task to reconstruct the classical model in order to assess whether Keynes's claim that his model was more general than the classical was right. They all concluded against Keynes's claim. Their interpretations were also rather similar. However, one of the three papers came to prominence, Hicks's piece, containing the first version of what was to become the IS–LM model. The reason for its success surely lay in its ingenious graph, allowing the joined outcome of three different markets to be represented in a single graph. This allowed Keynes's reasoning using "models in prose" to be transformed into a simple system of simultaneous equations, so that it became comprehensible to working economists.[13]

The third and final stage in the emergence of macroeconomics consisted of transforming qualitative models into empirically testable ones. An author who played a decisive role in this respect is Jan Tinbergen. Like Keynes, he was a reformer, motivated by the will to understand the Great Depression and to develop policies that would impede its return. Tinbergen's (1939) League of Nations study of business fluctuations in the United States from 1919 to 1932 can be pinpointed as the first econometric model bearing on a whole economy. The second pioneer piece of macroeconomics econometrics was Larry Klein's *Economic Fluctuations in the United States 1921–1941*, published in 1950 for the Cowles Commission. In his celebrated book, *The Keynesian Revolution*, Klein (1948) had commented that Keynes's concepts were crying out for a confrontation to the data. With other colleagues, he played a decisive role in implementing this insight.

In this way, the three constitutive elements of macroeconomics came into existence. Very soon macroeconomics became a new and thriving sub-discipline of economics. Its hallmark is that it emerged as the daughter of the Great Depression. Without the Great Depression, macroeconomics would not have seen the light of day, at least not with its specific features. Its overarching aim was to highlight market failures that could be remedied upon by state action. So, from the onset, it had a reformist flavour. It was more to the left – albeit centre-left rather than hard-left – than microeconomics. Unemployment – and in particular involuntary unemployment – was its defining element. Macroeconomists had, as it were, stolen the theme of unemployment from labour economists.

## IS–LM macroeconomics

With the IS–LM model needing no introduction, let me examine at once how it fits within my taxonomy. I start with the policy dimension. The IS–LM model allows a confrontation between two regimes, the classical regime, where wages are flexible and the Keynesian regime, where nominal wages are rigid. Therefore it could be argued that the IS–LM model can be used in support of both the Keynesian and the anti-Keynesian stance. This is true in principle. However, during the heydays of the IS–LM model in the 1950s and 1960s, most of its users were firmly convinced that the Keynesian sub-model was the right one (i.e. was descriptively true), while the classical model served as a foil. Hence my claim that at the time the IS–LM model was subservient to the Keynesian policy cause.

Turning to the methodological aspect, the issue to be addressed is "Is the IS-LM model Walrasian or Marshallian from a methodological point of view"? My answer is that it is Marshallian, its frequent characterisation to the contrary notwithstanding.[14] Let me start by asking why it is that the IS–LM is often characterised as Walrasian. A first reason is the lack of awareness of the existence of the Marshall–Walras divide. As a result, general equilibrium is equated with Walrasian or neo-Walrasian theory. Such a stance is inappropriate as soon as it is admitted that the Walrasian approach is not the only way of doing general equilibrium analysis.

A second reason is that Hicks, the initiator of the IS–LM tradition ([1937] 1967), is often considered a Walrasian economist – at least, he supposedly was at the time he wrote "Mr. Keynes and the 'Classics'". This was also the period during which he was working on *Value and Capital* ([1939] 1946), which is often and rightly credited with having revived Walrasian theory. Hence the conclusion that IS–LM must be Walrasian. The snag, however, is that *Value and Capital* mixes Walrasian and Marshallian elements (actually it started the obscuration of the Marshall–Walras divide). In my opinion, Hicks was never more than a half-hearted Walrasian. He may well have considered that Walrasian theory opened a window on new horizons ([1979] 1983: 358), yet he always read Walras through Marshallian glasses.

So there is no a priori reason for considering that the IS–LM model is Walrasian. In fact, I have never seen any justification of such an assertion. On the contrary, whenever the issue of its characterisation is taken in earnest, it turns out that it definitely leans towards the Marshallian approach. The following factors explain why.

### The structure of the economy

A Walrasian economy constitutes a single market encompassing every commodity and all agents, with the equilibrium contract bearing on all commodities, and reached in one stroke. In contrast, a Marshallian economy is composed of markets that function separately, each of them being an autonomous locus of equilibrium. Against this divide, it is clear that the IS–LM model belongs to the Marshallian approach.

### Walras's law

When looking at whether Walras's Law is verified in IS–LM models, it turns out that it is in some models (e.g. Modigliani 1944) but not in others (Klein 1948). A model that allows Walras's Law to be contradicted cannot be Walrasian. In contrast, in a Marshallian economy it is conceivable to have one market in disequilibrium for reasons linked with the sequential character of its functioning (see De Vroey 1999b).

### Expectations

Since Hicks's recasting of Walrasian theory in an intertemporal framework, expectations have received pride of place in the Walrasian approach. In contrast, as often noted (e.g. King 1993), a defect of the IS–LM model is that it has little room for expectations. To me, this lack is due to the stationary equilibrium concept underpinning the Marshallian approach (cf. De Vroey 2006). This conception of equilibrium assumes that the economic data remain constant over the period of analysis, except for shocks that are scarce and reversible. For, if shocks come as a total surprise, if their impact is well circumscribed (so that all the other data of economy remain unchanged), and transitory, why on earth should expectations play any central role in the analysis?

### Dynamic analysis

Expectations and dynamics go hand in hand. The first generation of IS–LM models was totally static. As noted by Blanchard (2000), progress was made in this respect by authors such as Modigliani as far as consumption and saving are concerned, Jorgenson for investment, and

Tobin for financial decisions. Lucas and Rapping when developing their 1969 model had in mind to make progress in the same direction by dynamising the production/employment sector. What makes these developments Marshallian is their partial equilibrium framework. They break the economy up into separate sectors to which dynamics is applied in isolation. Walrasian dynamic analysis, by contrast, is concerned with the economy as a whole.

## Microfoundations

The IS–LM model has often been criticised for its ill-specified microfoundations. But then the attention given to micro-foundation is typical of the difference in method between Walras and Marshall. While the former insisted on constructing them, Marshall found it unnecessary to develop them rigorously. The IS–LM model is typically Marshallian in this respect.

## Time

The IS–LM model is always presented as a short-period model. This raises the semantic issue of whether it pertains to a given market day or to a short span of successive markets. Be this as it may, the distinctive feature of the IS–LM model with respect to the time dimension is the methodological decision to analyse the short period in isolation from the long period. This, again, is a typically Marshallian point of view; the Walrasian standpoint is quite different. Here, a specific point in time equilibrium is associated with a precise trade round. With some twist in language, this point in time outcome can be called a short-period equilibrium and the intertemporal equilibrium a long-period equilibrium. Still, in the Walrasian approach the short-period equilibrium will never be severed from the long period.

## Price formation

In the Walrasian set-up, a single price-formation process is at work with prices being announced by the outside auctioneer and changed until equilibrium is reached. This scenario is wanting although it has the merit of existing. However, I have never seen authors claim that in the IS–LM model prices are formed under the auspice of an auctioneer. This is another sign of the Marshallian character of the IS–LM model.

Taken separately, each of the above arguments might fail to win the day. Collectively, in my opinion, they surely do so. This conclusion is in accordance with the implicit view taken by most defenders of IS–LM macroeconomics (e.g. Lipsey 2000: 69), who firmly believe that their approach is poles apart from Walrasian microeconomics.

To conclude, I view the IS–LM model as a simplified Marshallian general equilibrium theory. Admittedly, it is a messy model compared to the standards of rigour witnessed in Walrasian theory. This can be related to an anomaly in its origin. Logic would have it that the simple model would come to emerge as the simplification of a pre-existing complex model (as happened in the emergence of Walrasian macroeconomics). However, no complex Marshall's general equilibrium model existed that could be simplified.

If this conclusion is accepted, locating the IS–LM model within my taxonomy is an easy task. As far as box diagram No. 1 is concerned, it marks the rise of Marshallian macroeconomics (see Table 10.3, where

*Table 10.3*

|  |  | Two types of general equilibrium models | |
|---|---|---|---|
|  |  | Complex models | Simplified models |
| Two distinct neoclassical approaches | The Marshallian approach |  | The IS–LM model |
|  | The Walrasian approach | Walras's Elements of Pure Economics The Arrow–Debreu model |  |

*Table 10.4*

|  |  | Policy cause standpoint | |
|---|---|---|---|
|  |  | Justifying demand activation | Defending laissez faire |
| Conceptual apparatus | Marshallian macroeconomics | The IS–LM model |  |
|  | The Marshall–Keynes–Hicks lineage |  |  |
|  | The Marshall–Chamberlin lineage |  |  |
|  | Walrasian macroeconomics |  |  |
|  | Walrasian models Non-Walrasian models |  |  |

I also introduce the Arrow–Debreu model, the emblematic neo-Walrasian model). As far as box diagram No. 2 is concerned, the IS–LM model marks the heydays of Keynesian macroeconomics, the period where the Keynesian modifier meant both an analytical apparatus and the defence of an activist policy view (and hence was unambiguous). It is firmly located in the top left row (see Table 10.4).

## Monetarism

Monetarism is associated with the work of Milton Friedman and his criticism of Keynesian activist policy. At a certain juncture, it was believed that it might become a new paradigm, rival to the Keynesian (see Johnson 1971). At present, a different view prevails. For example, Woodford thinks that monetarism has won the day by bringing monetary policy and expectations to the forefront, yet he considers that, from a methodological viewpoint, it has been absorbed within the Keynesian paradigm (Woodford 1999: 18).[15]

Friedman's contribution should not be viewed as a rejection of Keynes's methodology. Let me just evoke three elements of justification. First, Keynes and Friedman shared the same style of theorising and a common connection to the Marshallian tradition.[16] Friedman praised Keynes for being "a true Marshallian in method" and for adopting the Marshallian rather than the Walrasian framework (1974: 18). Second, when requested to put his claim in a broader theoretical perspective the model on which Friedman fell back was the IS–LM model (Friedman 1974). Third, as argued in De Vroey (2001), Friedman's conception of expectation in his expectations-augmented Phillips Curve model must be characterised as Marshallian rather than as Walrasian.

Monetarist models ought to be viewed as Marshallian simplified general equilibrium models.[17] Hence they should be place alongside the IS–LM model in my box diagram No. 1 (see Table 10.5). As far as box diagram No. 2 is concerned, Friedman's aim was to reverse Keynesian policy conclusions. Yet he hardly felt it necessary to overthrow the Keynesian theoretical apparatus, contrary to what Lucas and Sargent would be pleading ten years later (Lucas and Sargent [1979] 1994). In short, Friedman should be considered as Keynesian from the methodological viewpoint and as anti-Keynesian from the policy viewpoint.[18] The so-called monetarist counter-revolution should thus be ranked in the upper right box of my second diagram (see Table 10.6).

*Table 10.5*

|  |  | Two types of general equilibrium models | |
|---|---|---|---|
|  |  | Complex models | Simplified models |
| Two distinct neoclassical approaches | The Marshallian approach | | The IS–LM model Monetarist models |
|  | The Walrasian approach | Walras's Elements of Pure Economics The Arrow–Debreu model | |

*Table 10.6*

|  |  | Policy cause standpoint | |
|---|---|---|---|
|  |  | Justifying demand activation | Defending laissez faire |
| Conceptual apparatus | Marshallian macroeconomics | The IS–LM model | Monetarist models |
|  | The Marshall–Keynes–Hicks lineage | | |
|  | The Marshall–Chamberlin lineage | | |
|  | Walrasian macroeconomics | | |
|  | Walrasian models Non-Walrasian models | | |

## Disequilibrium theory

Here I have in mind the series of models, which were initially called disequilibrium' models and later "non-Walrasian equilibrium" models.[19] They are associated with the names of Benassy, Barro and Grossman, Drèze, Malinvaud and others.[20] The aim of these models was to introduce price and/or wage rigidity into Walrasian theory on the grounds that price and wages stickiness, if not rigidity, was a compelling feature of the real world.[21] What needs to be stressed is that they belong to the Walrasian tradition. In particular, these authors were attentive to the micro-foundations aspects. Some of these models (e.g. Drèze (1975)) were at too a high level of abstraction to accord with my criterion that a macroeconomic model should be a simplified general equilibrium model. Yet this was not the case for others. Barro and Grossman's (1971) model is the emblematic simplified non-Walrasian model. That these models were geared to policy advice is also obvious. The contrast drawn by Malinvaud (1977) between Keynesian unemployment and classical unemployment points to two distinct types of policy options according to the diagnosis made about the sort of non-Walrasian equilibrium the economy is stuck in. The policy aim consists in bringing it from the non-Walrasian equilibrium to the Walrasian equilibrium.

So, these models ought to be hailed for being the first Walrasian macroeconomic model (see Table 10.7).[22] However, while this approach got off to a quick start, it was soon criticised for its rigidity assumption. Rigidity might well a real-world feature yet, according to the detractors of the approach, this was not a sufficient condition for introducing it into the Walrasian construct. This was the gist of Lucas's criticism (Lucas 1987: 52–3). The defenders of the new school admitted that a foundation needed to be provided for rigidity, yet to them this lack did not justify discarding their approach.[23] Be that as it may, most of its proponents, beginning with Barro and Grossman themselves, changed their minds and abandoned this line of research. As far as box diagram No. 2 is concerned, disequilibrium models are non-Keynesian from the conceptual apparatus point of view but Keynesian from the policy viewpoint (see Table 10.8). As a result, the meaning of the Keynesian modifier now becomes ambiguous.

*Table 10.7*

|  |  | Two types of general equilibrium models | |
|---|---|---|---|
|  |  | Complex models | Simplified models |
| Two distinct neoclassical approaches | The Marshallian approach  The Walrasian approach | Walras's Elements of Pure Economics  The Arrow–Debreu model | The IS–LM model  Monetarist models  Disequilibrium models |

*Table 10.8*

|  |  | Policy cause standpoint | |
|---|---|---|---|
|  |  | Justifying demand activation | Defending laissez faire |
| Conceptual apparatus | Marshallian macroeconomics | The IS–LM model | Monetarist models |
|  | The Marshall–Keynes–Hicks lineage |  |  |
|  | The Marshall–Chamberlin lineage |  |  |
|  | Walrasian macroeconomics |  |  |
|  | Walrasian models |  |  |
|  | Non-Walrasian models | Disequilibrium models |  |

## The new classical revolution

Friedman's anti-Keynesian offensive dealt exclusively with policy. His was an internal criticism led from within the Marshallian–Keynesian conceptual apparatus. This is no longer true for the attack against Keynesian theory led by Lucas and his associates. As an external criticism, Lucas's attack led to a change that had all the hallmarks of a Kuhnian scientific revolution: a shift in the type of issues that are addressed, a new conceptual toolbox, new mathematical methods, the coming into power of a new generation of scholars, etc.[24]

In the beginning, Lucas's work was branded as "monetarism mark II", an inappropriate terminology in view of the deep methodological breach separating Lucas from Friedman (see Hoover 1984). This terminology was rightly soon abandoned in favour of the "new classical" label, meant to honour Keynes's predecessors (such as Hayek) who claimed that the way forward was to dynamise Walrasian static equilibrium theory. The DSGE acronym (dynamic stochastic general equilibrium) has recently been proposed to characterise modern macroeconomics. What ought, however, to be noted is that successive phases have evolved within the new approach, Lucas's models being the first of them. It was followed by another class of models, real business models, associated with the work of Kydland and Prescott (1982). Now, we are witnessing the emergence of a third phase where the canonical real business cycle model is transformed through the integration of non-Walrasian elements. I shall deal with these three phases in turn (with an interruption between the first and the second to discuss new Keynesian models).

As in all scientific revolutions, the new approach combined a criticism of the previous and the emergence of a new direction of research. I will not go into details on the former, contenting myself with mentioning a few of the main criticisms. One type of criticism, mainly made by Lucas, bore on the methodological flaws in Keynes's approach. For example, Lucas wrote a clever article criticising the notion of involuntary unemployment (Lucas [1978] 1981). Another attack, which became known as the "Lucas critique", pertained to the inability of Keynesian models to provide a robust basis on which to assess alternative economic policies (Lucas [1976] 1981). Finally, another influential critical piece was Kydland and Prescott's (1977) time inconsistency article, aiming at clinching the case for rules against discretion in monetary policy as well as more generally.

Turning to the positive side, the most salient traits of the new approach are as follows.[25]

### The equilibrium discipline

A first trait is what Lucas called the equilibrium discipline, the fact that postulating optimising behaviour and market clearing is considered the *sine qua non* of sound economic reasoning. It is a discipline in the moral sense of the term, a rule that one imposes on oneself in order to attain a given aim.

Clearly, this standpoint amounts to sweeping under the rug the issue of the working or failure of the invisible hand. The underlying rationale is that interesting economic models can be constructed while neglecting this issue. In defence of this standpoint, it can be claimed that Lucas did nothing more than make explicit the dominant practice of neoclassical economists (with the exception of the Austrians, on the one hand, and Keynes, on the other). New classical economists did not invent market clearing; they have merely given it a higher, more visible, status (see De Vroey 2007).

The new perspective was accompanied with an important shift in the meaning of the concept of equilibrium. In earlier times, from Adam Smith to Marshall and Keynes, the notion of equilibrium was little different from its common-sense understanding. It was viewed as a standstill position, a centre of gravity. The hallmark of equilibrium was the persistence of the same outcomes over time. The question raised about equilibrium was whether a given market or a given economy was in a state of equilibrium at a given point in time. Lucas's originality was to depart from this traditional conception by adhering to a conception of equilibrium where the economy could be stated to be in equilibrium while evincing ever-changing outcomes over time. Moreover, for Lucas, equilibrium was no longer a feature of reality. The following quotation, drawn from an interview with Snowdon and Vane, illustrates his viewpoint:

> I think general discussions, especially by non-economists, of whether the system is in equilibrium or not are almost entirely nonsense. You can't look out of this window and ask whether New Orleans is in equilibrium. What does that mean? Equilibrium is a property of the way we look at things, not a property of reality.
> (Snowdon and Vane, 1998: 127)

*The take-over bid for business cycle theory by value theory*

A distinctive feature of the new approach lies in its having extended the scope of relevance of value theory to a domain, the business cycle, which previously was believed to be beyond its grasp. Thereby a gulf, which had marked economic theory for more than a century – its split in two distinct branches, value or price theory, on the one hand, and business cycle theory, on the other – was bridged. With the development of an equilibrium theory of the business cycle, the two fields merged.

Several implications follow. Let me mention two of them. The idea that one might construct a theory of the business cycle without resorting to the unemployment notion was previously deemed inconceivable. Now it turns out that the decisive factor to be considered in the study of the business cycle is the total numbers of hours worked rather than the rate of unemployment. Whether this total number is equally or unequally divided among the labour force is deemed to be of secondary importance. A second implication is that the earlier judgements made about the harmful character of business cycles vanishes. Business cycles are no longer considered the manifestation of some malfunctioning to be corrected by the state.

## The rise of Walrasian macroeconomics

I claimed above that the disequilibrium approach constituted the first attempt at developing Walrasian macroeconomics, yet, for better or worse, it failed to be met with lasting success. Lucas, Kydland and

Prescott were more successful. In the wake of their work, macroeconomics became predominantly Walrasian.[26] The new approach abides by my definition according to which macroeconomics consists of a simplification of complex general equilibrium models as it marks a return a return to square one of Walras' construction, the two-good exchange economy. This is topped with the introduction of a few additional elements borrowed from the Arrow–Debreu model, such as intertemporal substitution and a more complex notion of commodity. Still, the Walrasian lineage is undeniable. On the other hand, the drawback besetting the birth of Keynesian macroeconomics, that there existed no well-established Marshallian general equilibrium model of the complex type from which to start in order to construct simplified models, is of course now absent.

An important methodological difference from earlier Walrasian authors ought, however, to be noticed. Authors like Arrow, Debreu, Mackenzie, Hahn and their followers have repeatedly insisted that neo-Walrasian general equilibrium theory is an abstract construction, the strength of which lies in its ability to posit issues in a rigorous way. Its main interest with respect to reality, they argue, it to provide a negative benchmark. In short, theses authors admit to a no bridge between their theoretical constructs and real-world market economies.[27] Real business cycle models mark a radical change in this respect by claiming that the validity of their models rests on their capacity to mimic real-world time-series. Neither Walras nor earlier neo-Walrasian authors would ever have made such a claim.

## A change in research priorities

The main change has concerned the research agenda. In 1971, in his Presidential Address to the American Economic Association, Tobin wrote that macroeconomics deprived of the full employment concept was unimaginable (1972: 1). But this is exactly what happened to macroeconomics. The unemployment theme – and in a wider sense the search for the malfunctioning of markets – has ceased to be an important preoccupation of macroeconomists.[28] It has fallen out of fashion, macroeconomists being glad to send it back to labour economists. At the top of the agenda, we now have issues related to the business cycle and a wider and wider spectrum of themes related to growth and development.

After these general considerations, I now return to the narrower new classical or Lucasian type of model (Lucas [1972] 1981, [1975] 1981,

Table 10.9

|  |  | Two types of general equilibrium models | |
|---|---|---|---|
|  |  | Complex models | Simplified models |
| Two distinct neoclassical approaches | The Marshallian approach | | The IS–LM model Monetarist models |
|  | The Walrasian approach | Walras's Elements of Pure Economics The Arrow–Debreu model | Disequilibrium models New Classical models à la Lucas |

[1976] 1981) with the aim of positioning it in my taxonomy. As far as box diagram No. 1 is concerned, Lucas's contribution allows me to fill in a new slot corresponding to the full establishing of Walrasian macroeconomics, after the initial disequilibrium attempt (see Table 10.9).

Turning to my box diagram No. 2, Lucas's model is definitely anti-Keynesian both from the policy cause and the conceptual apparatus points of view. It marks a break between macroeconomics and Keynesianism since it is anti-Keynesian in both senses of the term. On the other hand, it belongs to the Walrasian tradition yet features a

Table 10.10

|  |  | Policy cause standpoint | |
|---|---|---|---|
|  |  | Justifying demand activation | Defending laissez faire |
| Conceptual apparatus | Marshallian macroeconomics | The IS–LM model | Monetarist models |
|  | The Marshall–Keynes–Hicks lineage The Marshall–Chamberlin lineage | | |
|  | Walrasian macroeconomics | | |
|  | Walrasian models Non-Walrasian models | Disequilibrium models | New classical models à la Lucas |

non-Walrasian result (in the weak sense of the modifier) since the outcomes are different from those that would have arisen in a perfect information context. Its positioning in the bottom right-hand box is shown in Table 10.10.

## New Keynesian models

Before continuing my study of DSGE macroeconomics, I need to consider the reactions of Keynesian economists to the Lucasian anti-Keynesian offensive. There were two distinct types of reactions. One was total rejection.[29] The other amounted to admitting that Lucas's criticisms were well founded and could not be dismissed with a sweep of hand. This attitude was the hallmark of "new Keynesian" economists.[30] While wanting to re-habilitate Keynes's insights, they agreed to wage the war on Lucas's turf, i.e. to respect the micro-foundations requirement. However, new Keynesian economics was far from being a unified approach. Let me just mention a few of the lines of research taken. Some new Keynesian models – such as efficiency wage models (e.g. Shapiro and Stiglitz (1984)) – made it their priority to demonstrate the equilibrium existence of involuntary unemployment. Others – in particular coordination failures models (e.g. Diamond ([1982] 1991) – forewent the aim of demonstrating involuntary unemployment in a strict sense, instead concerning themselves with the less ambitious aim of demonstrating underemployment in a multiple equilibria framework. Thereby, they were able to exonerate wage rigidity as a cause of the phenomenon and to vindicate demand activation. Still other authors (e.g. Hart ([1982] 1991), Blanchard and Kiyotaki ([1987] 1991)), also concerned with underemployment, adopted an imperfectly competitive framework. This enabled them to give a foundation to the non-neutrality of money and thus to offer a rebuttal of the claims made by Friedman and Lucas.[31]

Locating the new Keynesian models in my taxonomy is more complicated than locating the earlier models, if only because they are too varied to be placed in the same slot. Some of them should actually be considered as falling outside of the scope of macroeconomics as I have defined it because they do not deal with the economy as a whole. This is the case for early efficiency wages models. If they are considered as having a place within macroeconomics, it is simply because of their concern with involuntary unemployment, and to me this is the wrong criterion. Hence their exclusion from box diagram No. 1 (see Table 10.11) and the need for a new row in my box diagram No. 2 (see Table 10.12). As to the other New Keynesian models, which

*Table 10.11*

|  |  | Two types of general equilibrium models | |
|---|---|---|---|
|  |  | Complex models | Simplified models |
| Two distinct neoclassical approaches | The Marshallian approach |  | The IS–LM model Monetarist models Imperfect competition models |
|  | The Walrasian approach | Walras's Elements of Pure Economics The Arrow–Debreu model | Disequilibrium models Coordination failures models |

*Table 10.12*

|  |  | Policy cause standpoint | |
|---|---|---|---|
|  |  | Justifying demand activation | Defending laissez faire |
| General equilibrium definition of Macroeconomics | Marshallian macroeconomics The Marshall–Keynes-Hicks lineage | The IS–LM model | Monetarist models |
|  | The Marshall–Chamberlin lineage | Imperfect competition models |  |
|  | Walrasian macroeconomics Walrasian models |  |  |
|  | Non-Walrasian models | Disequilibrium models Coordination failures models | New Classical models Lucas |
| Macroeconomics as the study of unemployment |  | Efficiency wage models |  |

do adopt a general equilibrium perspective, coordination failures models ought to be placed alongside disequilibrium models in box diagram No. 1 (see Table 10.11). As far as box diagram No. 2 is concerned, they can be ranked within the non-Walrasian branch of the Walrasian tradition on the one hand, and within the Keynesian policy cause, on the other hand (see Table 10.12).

More attention ought to be paid to imperfectly competitive general-equilibrium models because of their resurgence in the third phase of DSGE macroeconomics. The question to be raised is how they fare with the Marshall–Walras divide evoked in Section 3. My claim here is that, when gauged against this divide, they must be viewed as sub-types of the Marshallian economy rather than of the Walrasian economy universe. Several factors explain: the economy is divided into isolated markets, which are autonomous loci for formation of equilibrium; money is present; imperfect competition prevails; no auctioneer is present, a fraction of the agents are price-makers, the others being price-takers; price-making agents have perfect information about market conditions. So, imperfect competition models must be considered as being non-Walrasian in the strong sense of the term.

In Table 10.11, I locate imperfect competition models in the upper right box as a new type of Marshallian simplified general equilibrium models. As far as box diagram No. 2 is concerned, I am reluctant to place imperfect competition in the same box as the Marshallian models examined earlier (the Marshall–Keynes–Hicks lineage). Their abode is rather the "Marshall–Chamberlin line". Turning to the policy cause defended, it is clear that they should be located in the left column (see Table 10.12).

Returning to new Keynesian economics in general, the judgment to be made about their success is mixed. In my opinion, in so far as the battle waged by these economists was geared to demonstrating the existence of involuntary unemployment or underemployment, it has been lost. Not so much because clever models achieving this aim have failed to emerge, but rather because the change in paradigm meant that unemployment ceased to be an exciting topic. The game in town had changed; the Lucas–Kydland and Prescott bandwagon was rolling too fast to be stopped.

### Real business cycle models

Real business cycle models are an outcrop from Lucas's initial models. The two seminal papers that triggered it off are Kydland and Prescott's

(1982) article, "Time to Build and Aggregate Fluctuations" and Long and Plosser's (1983) paper, "Real Business Cycles". It was the first of these that set the pace. The main differences between this and Lucas's model are: (a) shocks are now real, having a technological origin, (b) information is perfect and (c) The Kydland–Prescott model pursues a quantitative rather than a qualitative aim.

I shall not delve in the contents of real business cycle models, contenting myself with making three remarks. First, Kydland and Prescott's feat is to have been able to mimic real-world data on the fluctuations of the US economy over 25 years fairly well, with the most parsimonious conceivable type of model. Second, their model has developed into a canonical model, which has become the base-camp for the construction of models addressing a wide range of stylised facts. Third, their model provided a unified approach to two phenomena that had always been considered as needing different theoretical frameworks, the business cycle and economic growth.

Turning to the task of locating Kydland and Prescott's model in my taxonomy, unsurprisingly, it is placed close to the classification of Lucas's model (see Tables 10.13 and 10.14). The only slight difference is present in Table 10.14 and bears on the fact that Kydland and Prescott's model is Walrasian while Lucas's is non-Walrasian.

*Table 10.13*

|  |  | Two types of general equilibrium models | |
|---|---|---|---|
|  |  | Complex models | Simplified models |
| Two distinct neoclassical approaches | The Marshallian approach |  | The IS–LM model Monetarist models Imperfect competition models |
|  | The Walrasian approach | Walras's Elements of Pure Economics The Arrow–Debreu model | Disequilibrium models Coordination failures models New Classical models à la Lucas Real Business cycle models |

Table 10.14

|  |  | Policy cause standpoint | |
|---|---|---|---|
|  |  | Justifying demand activation | Defending laissez-faire |
| General equilibrium definition of macroeconomics | Marshallian macroeconomics The Marshall–Keynes–Hicks lineage | IS–LM model | Monetarist models |
|  | The Marshall–Chamberlin lineage | Imperfect competiton models |  |
|  | Walrasian macroeconomics Walrasian models |  | Real business cycle models |
|  | Non-Walrasian models | Disequilibrium models Coordination failures models | New Classical models Lucas |
| Macroeconomics as the study of unemployment |  | Efficiency wage models |  |

## The new neoclassical synthesis

If time were to stop at this point in my story, the answer to the question in the title of my article would be positive. Macroeconomics has become fully divorced from its Keynesian origin. As long as real business cycle models are the prevailing way of practising macroeconomics, not the least reference to Keynes is necessary.

However, economic theory is an ongoing process, models are there to be criticised and superseded. While no radical dethroning of the DSGE approach has taken place, several endogenous transformations have occurred. Here I will limit myself to one of them, namely models re-addressing the issue of the efficiency of monetary policy that Friedman and Lucas seemed to have written off.[32] Theoretical considerations might well have concluded that monetary policy was indeed inefficient but the stylised facts indicated that changes in the money supply have persistent effects. The models that were constructed to tackle this issue have been labelled as either "new neoclassical synthesis" models (Goodfriend and King 1997) or "new Keynesian Phillips curve" models (Clarida et al. 1999). Whatever the tag, what is involved is a shift from a Walrasian to a non-Walrasian perspective, which merges "Keynesian" (money, imperfect competition and sticky prices) and real business cycle elements (intertemporal optimisation, rational expectations, market clearing and their integration into a stochastic dynamic model).[33]

The main approach has been to enrich the Dixit–Stiglitz model (Dixit and Stiglitz 1977) by making it doubly imperfect, i.e. by combining a real imperfection (imperfect competition) with a nominal imperfection (sticky prices). Sticky prices are obtained either by resorting to staggered wage-setting *à la* Taylor (1979) or to price-setting *à la* Calvo (1983) (where it is assumed that only a given proportion of all firms are able change their prices at each period). An unanticipated nominal shock (central banks following the Taylor rule) occurs, typically taking the form of a decrease in the interest rate. The ensuing increase in the demand for goods will be met by an increase in the level of activity. As a result, the gap between the Walrasian and the non-Walrasian output will be reduced. All in all, monetary expansion can be considered to be efficient.

Strikingly, all participants in the debate agree on the rules of the games, the principles that sane modelling ought to respect. Does this mean that ideology has vanished from the scene? This is Blanchard's opinion:

> Most macroeconomic research today focuses on the macroeconomic implications of some imperfection or another. At the frontier of macro-economic research, the field is surprisingly a-ideological.
> (Blanchard 2000: 39)

If ideology means the policy cause espoused by economists, Blanchard's view can be questioned since perfect agreement on the conceptual apparatus can accompany opposed policy views. So, I would rather stick with Lucas's opinion as expressed on p. 8.

Back now to my typology. All the authors involved agree that the new models are non-Walrasian as far as their conceptual apparatus is concerned. But they leave the matter there since they are unaware of the distinction that I have proposed above between the two meanings of the term "non-Walrasian". Taking this distinction into account leads me to claim that these models are non-Walrasian in the strong sense of the term in the same way as the first generation of imperfect competition models were. Therefore they ought to be located likewise (see Tables 10.15 and 10.16). Admittedly, this cannot be the last word about them. In these models the analysis actually goes back and forth

*Table 10.15*

|  |  | Two types of general equilibrium models | |
|---|---|---|---|
|  |  | Complex models | Simplified models |
| Two distinct neoclassical approaches | The Marshallian approach | | The IS–LM model<br>Monetarist models<br>Imperfect competition models<br>New neoclassical synthesis models |
|  | The Walrasian approach | Walras's Elements of Pure Economics<br>The Arrow–Debreu model | Disequilibrium models<br>Coordination failures models<br>New classical models à la Lucas<br>Real business cycle models |

between the Marshallian and the Walrasian approach. The account of the economy underlying them is Marshallian, its equilibrium result is non-Walrasian yet the whole point of building them is to compare their equilibrium outcome with the result that would have prevailed if the economy had been Walrasian.

Authors such as Clarida *et al.* are able to bring out a link between their model and the IS–LM model. It may then be wondered whether new neoclassical synthesis models bear witness to a Keynesian recovery. It is too early to know how or indeed whether they will continue to develop. Be that as it may, it ought to be realised that the type of Keynesianism, which they embody, is significantly different from any previous variety. First of all, they are not concerned with unemployment but only with underemployment.[34] Moreover, they are hardly Keynesian from the conceptual apparatus standpoint (but Marshallian nevertheless). Their target (demonstrating the existence of market imperfections) is also milder than that of earlier Keynesians (demonstrating the existence of market failures). On the other hand, if the debate between Keynesians and anti-Keynesians is viewed as boiling down to a confrontation over the issue of the efficiency of monetary policy (with Keynesians being on the side of efficiency and anti-Keynesians on that of inefficiency), then these models do indeed mark a re-birth of the Keynesian cause.

Table 10.16

|  |  | Policy cause standpoint | |
|---|---|---|---|
|  |  | Justifying demand activation | Defending laissez faire |
| General equilibrium definition of macroeconomics | Marshallian macroeconomics<br>The Marshall–Keynes–Hicks lineage | The IS–LM model | Monetarist models |
|  | The Marshall–Chamberlin lineage | (Static) imperfect competition models<br>New neoclassical synthesis models |  |
|  | Walrasian macroeconomics<br>Walrasian models |  | Real business cycle models |
|  | Non-Walrasian models | Disequilibrium Models<br>Coordination failures models | New classical models à la Lucas |
| Macroeconomics as the study of unemployment |  | Efficiency wage models |  |

## Concluding remarks

The aim of this chapter was to give an account of the history of macroeconomics from Keynes to the present day using a grid formed by the combination of two distinctions, the distinction between the Marshallian and the Walrasian approach, on the one hand, and the distinction between Keynesianism as a theoretical apparatus and Keynesianism as a policy cause, on the other. This has led me to recount this history as if it were a matter of filling in, step by step, the different slots in my two box diagrams.

I have characterised the evolution of macroeconomics in a twofold way. The first is a shift from a Marshallian to a Walrasian perspective, with a return to the former taking shape. The second is a shift from macroeconomic models that are fully Keynesian (as determined by my two criteria) to models that are fully anti-Keynesian, with a mild reversal also beginning to occur here. My claim is that this way of positing issues sheds an original and more complete light on the history of macroeconomics.

I have also brought out that, to date, the history of macroeconomics has witnessed to two defining moments. The emergence of macroeconomics – narrowly defined, as the conjunction of three distinct episodes (Keynes's *General Theory*, the recasting of this by Hicks in his IS–LM model, and the rise of econometric models) – is the first of them. The second is the scientific revolution that dethroned Keynesian macroeconomics and replaced it by DSGE models.

Have macroeconomists really got rid of Keynes? No straightforward answer can be given to this question. As far as the conceptual apparatus is concerned, the answer is yes (but if Keynes is out, Marshall is still in!). This is no wonder. The fact that the IS–LM model would still be the overarching model would mean that little progress has occurred in macroeconomics over the years. As far as the other dimension is concerned, two observations are worth making. The first is that some Keynesian cause always seems to crop back up again after a phase where the opposite camp has been winning (and vice versa). The second is that a mellowing of the Keynesian cause has occurred over the years, a shift away from the aim of demonstrating market failures, in particular involuntary unemployment, to the less ambitious goal of bringing imperfections to the forefront.

So, the final word is that the Keynesian modifier as it is used at present has only a remote relation to the concepts used by John Maynard Keynes. Nonetheless it has little chances of disappearing from the scene because it has become a banner under which economists having doubts about unfettered laissez faire like to rally.

## Acknowledgements

This work was supported by the Belgian French-speaking Community (Grant ARC 03/08-302) and the Belgian Federal Government (Grant PAI P5/10). I am grateful to Anna Batyra and David de la Croix for their comments on an earlier version of this chapter.

## Notes

1. Other articles are: Blinder ([1988] 1997), Danthine (1997), Drèze (2001), Hairault (1999), Leijonhufvud (2006a), Lipsey (2000), Mankiw (1990, 2006), Snowdon and Vane (1996), Van der Ploeg (2005).

2. As noted for example by Negishi, "Marshallian models are practically useful to apply to what Hicks called particular problems of history or experience. On the other hand, Walrasian models are in general not useful for such practical purposes.... Walras' theoretical interest was not in the solution of practical problems but in what Hicks called the pursuit of general principles which underlie the working of a market economy" (Negishi 1987, 590).
3. This is the view put forward by Hicks. See Hicks ([1934] 1983: 86).
4. For a more in-depth examination, see (De Vroey 1999a, 2006). For alternative accounts of the opposition between the Marshallian and the Walrasian approaches, see Hoover (2006a, 2006b) and Leijonhufvud (2006b).
5. A full realization of the incompatibility between the auctioneer and the existence of rigidities had to wait until models introducing rigidity into a Walrasian economy (a line of research that will be discussed in Section 8 below) were proposed.
6. Ostroy states, "By introducing money after he had completed his theory of exchange, Walras clearly made monetary phenomena an optional ad-on rather than an integral component of the mechanism of exchange" (1992 784). The same point has been made repeatedly by Hahn. "There is nothing we can say about the equilibrium of an economy with money which we cannot also say about the equilibrium of a non-monetary economy, [that is] the money of this construction is only a contingent store of value and has no other role" (Hahn 1973: 160).
7. At the outset of my story, the only slot filled is the lower left one, occupied by Walras's theory.
8. A similar distinction is proposed by Blinder when claiming, "the division of Keynesian economics into positive and normative component is central to understanding both the academic debate and its relevance to policy". (Blinder ([1988] 1997: 112).
9. Market failures are defects in the supposedly self-adjusting market forces. They ought to be viewed as more serious flaws than imperfections. I surmise that Keynes refrained from adopting the imperfect competition line that was developing in Cambridge at the time he was writing because he wanted to discuss system failures deeper that were deeper than imperfections.
10. Whenever I use the Keynesian modifier *tout court*, it refers to this case.
11. As noted by Friedman, "In one sense, his [Keynes's] approach was strictly Marshallian: in terms of demand and supply. However, whereas Marshall strictly dealt with specific commodities and 'partial equilibrium', Keynes proposed to deal with what he called 'aggregate demand' and the 'aggregate supply function' and with general not partial equilibrium" (Friedman [1989] 1997: 8).
12. Clower quotes an extract of a letter from Keynes to Georgescu-Rodan, dated December 1934 and running as follows: "All the same, I shall hope to convince you some day that Walras' theory and all the others along those lines are little better than nonsense!"(Clower [1975] 1984: 190).
13. In his book, *Fabricating the Keynesian Revolution*, the main gist of which is that Keynes and his predecessors stand in a relationship of continuity, Laidler implicitly makes the same claim when he acknowledges that a break occurred shortly after the publication of the *General Theory*: "IS-LM itself represented a synthesis, albeit a very selective synthesis, of theoretical ideas

which long antedated its appearance, and which had underpinned the policy attitude in question. The model was, nevertheless, logically self-contained; it could be, and soon was, taught independently of the literature in which it had its roots. IS–LM thus seemed to embody a revolution in economics, in the sense that an old order had been swept away and replaced by something brand-new" (Laidler 1999: 324).
14. See e.g. Vercelli (2000). This view that the IS–LM model is Walrasian is also taken for granted in several of the contributions to the Young and Zilberfarb (2000) volume on IS–LM.
15. The same point is made by Snowdon and Vane (1996: 386). See also Lipsey (2000), Laidler (1981), De Long (2000).
16. On this, see Hirsch and de Marchi (1990), Dostaler (1998) and Hammond (1992).
17. Brunner and Meltzer (1993) is emblematic in this respect.
18. This is also Blinder's conclusion: "The long and to some extent continuing battle between Keynesians and monetarists, you will note, has been primarily fought over the *normative issues*.... Thus, by my definition, most monetarists are positive Keynesians, but not normative Keynesians" (Blinder [1988] 1997: 113).
19. Backhouse and Boianovsky (2005) is a fine account of the arising of the disequilibrium school.
20. With hindsight, the disequilibrium label has been deemed inappropriate for most of these models, and they were soon re-labelled as non-Walrasian models (my own further qualification being that they are non-Walrasian in the weak sense of the term). In view of the purpose of my paper, the case of Benassy is worth retaining the attention. While most of Benassy's models were part of the Walrasian programme, he also proposed an imperfect competition model (Benassy 1976), anticipating the type of models to be developed by some new Keynesian economists. According to my taxonomy, as will be claimed below, such models are Marshallian – i.e. they are non-Walrasian in the strong sense of the term. The lesson to be drawn is that the Marshallian or Walrasian label ought to be attached to models rather than to authors.
21. For a justification of this view, see Tobin ([1993] 1997).
22. An earlier attempt to the same effect is of course Patinkin ([1956] 1965).
23. As stated by Malinvaud, "Economics is therefore not at fault in considering the consequences of wage rigidity if this rigidity has been proved to exist. Of course, explanations of it are (or would be) useful for subsequent scientific progress, but even if they are (or were) lacking, it would still be wrong to overlook the observed facts" (Malinvaud 1984: 21).
24. An early assessment of Lucas's contribution, which is still worth consulting, is Hoover (1988).
25. The rational expectations hypothesis is probably the most outstanding feature of the new approach, but I shall not expand on it because it is too well known.
26. This characterization is valid for the first two phases of the DSGE approach but not for the third one, which evinces the emergence of non-Walrasian models.

27. As stated by Weintraub, "the [Walrasian] 'equilibrium' story is one in which empirical work, ideas of fact and falsifications, played no role at all" (1983: 37).
28. The following comment by Hahn and Solow captures the outrage of earlier authors faced with this dismissal: "The irony is that macroeconomics began as the study of large-scale economic pathologies: prolonged depressions, mass unemployment, persistent inflation, etc. This focus was not invented by Keynes (although the depression of the 1930s did not pass without notice). After all, most of Haberler's classic *Prosperity and Depression* is about ideas that were in circulation before *The General Theory*. Now, at last, macroeconomic theory has as its central conception a model in which such pathologies are, strictly speaking, unmentionable. There is no legal way to talk about them" (Hahn and Solow 1995: 2–3).
29. The following two excerpts illustrate this strand. "I argue... that there was no anomaly, that the ascendancy of new classicism in academia was instead a triumph of *a priori* theorizing over empiricism, of intellectual aesthetics over observation and, in some measure, of conservative ideology over liberalism" (Blinder [1988] 1997: 110). "To many Keynesians, the new classical programme replaced messy truth by precise error" (Lipsey 2000: 76).
30. See Mankiw and Romer (1991) and Howitt (1990).
31. In my book (De Vroey 2004), I have assessed several of these models against what I called the "Keynes's programme", i.e. the simultaneous achievement of four objectives – (a) demonstrating involuntary unemployment in an individual disequilibrium sense; (b) exonerating wage rigidity from causing it; (c) bringing out a system failure; (d) vindicating demand activation.
32. Another thriving line of research is search theory. See Rogerson et al. (2005).
33. "New" imperfect competition models differ from earlier ones because of their dynamic stochastic character.
34. Amongst the new types of models that are emerging, Cole and Ohanian (2005) model of slow recovery from the Great Depression is worth mentioning here. It constitutes yet another new combination of factors, since it intertwines real shocks with imperfect competition. Its interest for my purpose lies in the following contrast. While the Keynesian models rest on the market clearing assumption (their object of study being underemployment), Cole and Ohanian's model, which is definitely non-Keynesian in its policy dimension, yields an involuntary unemployment result. However, the latter expresses a government rather than a market failure, the allegedly inept New Deal policies. In other words, the initially Keynesian notion of involuntary unemployment has now changed camp!

# References

Arrow, K. and G. Debreu (1954), "Existence of Equilibrium for a Competitive Economy", *Econometrica*, vol. 22, pp. 265–90.
Backhouse, R. and M. Boianovsky (2005), "Disequilibrium Macroeconomics. An episode in the Transformation of Modern Macroeconomics", Anais do XXXIII Encontro Nacional de Economia [Proceedings of the 33th Brazilian Economics Meeting].

Barro, R. and H. Grossman (1971), "A General Disequilibrium Model of Income and Employment", *American Economic Review*, vol. 61, pp. 82–93.

Benassy, J.-P. (1976), "The Disequilibrium Approach to Monopolistic Price Setting and General Monopolistic Equilibrium", *Review of Economic Studies*, vol. 43, pp. 69–81.

Blanchard, O. (2000), "What do We Know about Macroeconomics that Fisher and Wicksell did not?", *Quarterly Journal of Economics*, vol. 115, pp. 1375–409.

Blanchard, O. and N. Kiyotaki ([1987] 1991), "Monopolistic Competition and the Effects of Aggregate Demand", in Mankiw, G. and D. Romer (eds.), *New Keynesian Economics*, vol. 1, *Imperfect Competition and Sticky Prices*, Cambridge (Mass.): The M.I.T. Press, pp. 345–75.

Blinder, A. ([1988] 1997), "The Fall and Rise of Keynesian Economics", in Snowdon, B. and H. Vane (eds.), *A Macroeconomics Reader*, London: Routledge, pp. 109–34.

Brunner, K. and A. Meltzer (1993), *Money and the Economy. Issues in Monetary Analysis*, Raffaele Mattioli Foundation lectures, Cambridge: Cambridge University press.

Calvo, G. (1983), "Staggered Price Setting in a Utility-Maximizing Framework", *Journal of Monetary Economics*, vol. 12, pp. 383–98.

Clarida, R., J. Gali and M. Gertler (1999), "The Science of Monetary Policy: A New Keynesian Perspective", *Journal of Economic Literature*, vol. 37, pp. 1661–707.

Clower, R. ([1965] 1984), "The Keynesian Counterrevolution: A Theoretical Appraisal", in Walker D. (ed.), *Money and Markets. Essays by Robert Clower*, Cambridge: Cambridge University Press, pp. 34–58.

Clower R. and A. Leijonhufvud ([1975] 1984), "The Coordination of Economic Activities: a Keynesian Perspective" in Walker D. (1984) (ed.), *Money and Markets. Essays by Robert Clower*, Cambridge: Cambridge University Press, pp. 209–17.

Colander, D. (1996) (ed.), *Beyond Microfoundations: Post-Walrasian Macroeconomics*, Cambridge: Cambridge University Press.

Colander, D. (2006) (ed.), *Post-Walrasian Macroeconomics: Beyond the Dynamic Stochastic General Equilibrium Model*, Cambridge: Cambridge University Press.

Cole, H. and L. Ohanian (2004), "New Deal Policies and the Persistence of the Great Depression: A General Equilibrium Analysis", *Journal of Political Economy*, vol. 112, pp. 779–816.

Danthine, J.-P. (1997), "In Search of a Successor to IS-LM", *Oxford Review of Economic Policy*, vol. 13, no. 13, pp. 135–44.

De Long, B. (2000), "The Triumph of Monetarism", *Journal of Economic Perspectives*, vol. 14, pp. 83–94.

De Vroey, M. (1999a), "The Marshallian Market and the Walrasian Economy. Two Incompatible Bedfellows", *The Scottish Journal of Political Economy*, vol. 46, pp. 319–38.

De Vroey, M. (1999b), "Keynes and the Marshall-Walras Divide", *Journal of the History of Economic Thought*, vol. 21, no. 2, pp. 117–36.

De Vroey, M. (2001) "Friedman and Lucas on the Phillips Curve: From a Disequilibrium to an Equilibrium Approach", *Eastern Economic Journal*, vol. 27, pp. 127–48.

De Vroey, M. (2004), *Involuntary Unemployment: The Elusive Quest for A Theory*, London: Routledge.

De Vroey, M. (2006), "Marshall versus Walras on Equilibrium", in Becattini, G., M. Dardi and T. Raffaelli (eds.), *The Elgar Companion to Marshall*, Cheltenham: Edward Elgar, pp. 237–48.
De Vroey, M. (2007), "Did the Market-clearing Postulate Pre-exist New Classical Economics? The Case of Marshallian Theory", *The Manchester School*, vol. 75, pp. 3–38.
Diamond, P. ([1982] 1991), "Aggregate Demand Management in Search Equilibrium", in Mankiw, N. G. and D. Romer (eds.), *New Keynesian Economics, Volume 2, Coordination Failures and Real Rigidities*, Cambridge (Mass.): The M.I.T. Press, pp. 31–46.
Dixit, A. and J. Stiglitz (1977), "Monopolistic Competition and Optimum Product Diversity", *American Economic Review*, vol. 67, pp. 297–308.
Dostaler, G. (1998), "Friedman and Keynes: Divergences and Convergences", *European Journal of the History of Economic Thought*, vol. 5, pp. 317–47.
Drèze, J. H. (1975), "Existence of Equilibrium Under Price Rigidities", *International Economic Review*, vol. 16, pp. 301–20.
Drèze, J. H. (2001), *Advances in Macroeconomic Theory*, Basingstoke: Palgrave-Macmillan in Association with International Economic Association.
Friedman, M. (1974), "A Theoretical Framework for Monetary Analysis", in R. J. Gordon (ed.), *Milton Friedman's monetary Framework*, Chicago: Chicago University press, pp. 1–62, 132–77.
Friedman, M. ([1989]1997), "John Maynard Keynes", Federal Reserve Bank of Richmond, *Economic Quarterly*, vol. 83, pp. 1–23.
Frisch, R. (1933) Propagation Problems and Impulse Problems in Dynamic Economics, in *Economic Essays in Honour of Gustav Cassel*, London: George Allen & Unwin, as reprinted in R. A. Gordon and L. R. Klein, eds. (1965). *Readings in Business Cycles*, Homewood, IL: Richard D. Irwin, 155–185.
Goodfriend, M. and R. King (1997), "The New Neoclassical Synthesis and the Role of Monetary Policy", in B. Bernanke and J. Rotenberg (eds.), *NBER Macroeconomics Annual 1997*, Cambridge (Mass.): The M.I.T. Press, pp. 231–83.
Hahn, F. (1973), "On the Foundations of Monetary Theory", in M. Parkins and A. R. Nobay (eds.), *Essays in Modern Economics*, London: Longman, pp. 230–42.
Hahn F. and R. Solow (1995), *A Critical Essay on Modern Macroeconomic Theory*, Oxford: Basil Blackwell.
Hairault, J.-O., (1999), "Vers une nouvelle synthèse néoclassique?", *Revue d'Économie Politique*, vol. 109, pp. 613–69.
Hammond, J. D. (1992), "An Interview with Milton Friedman on Methodology", in B. Caldwell (ed.), *The Philosophy and Methodology of Economics*, vol. I. Edgar Elgar, pp. 216–38.
Harrod, R. F. ([1937] 1947), "Mr Keynes and Traditional Theory", in S. Harris (ed.) *The New Economics. Keynes Influence on Theory and Public Policy*, New York: A. A. Knopf, pp. 591–605.
Hart, O. ([1982] 1991), "A Model of Imperfect Competition with Keynesian Features", in Mankiw, G. and D. Romer (eds.), *New Keynesian Economics*, vol. 1, *Imperfect Competition and Sticky Prices*, Cambridge (Mass.): The M.I.T. Press, pp. 313–44.
Hicks, J. R. ([1946] 1939), *Value and Capital*, (second edition) Oxford: Clarendon Press.

Hicks, J. R., ([1934] 1983), "Léon Walras", in *Classics and Moderns. Collected essays on Economic Theory*, vol. III, Oxford: Basil Blackwell, pp. 85–95.

Hicks, J. R. ([1937] 1967), "Mr Keynes and the 'Classics'", reprinted in *Critical Essays in Monetary Theory*, pp. 126–42.

Hicks, J. R. ([1979] 1983), "The Formation of an Economist", in *Classics and Moderns. Collected essays on Economic Theory*, vol. III, Oxford: Basil Blackwell, pp. 355–64.

Hirsch, A. and de Marchi, N. (1990), *Milton Friedman, Economics in Theory and Practice*, New York: Harvester Wheatsheaf.

Hoover, K. (1984), "Two Types of Monetarism", *Journal of Economic Literature*, vol. XXII, pp. 58–76.

Hoover, K. (1988), *The New Classical Macroeconomics: A Sceptical Inquiry*, Oxford: Basil Blackwell.

Hoover, K. (2006a), "Doctor Keynes: Economic Theory in a Diagnostic Science", in Backhouse, R. and B. Bateman (eds.), *The Cambridge Companion to Keynes*, Cambridge: Cambridge University Press, pp. 78–97.

Hoover, K. (2006b), "The Past as Future: The Marshallian Approach to Post Walrasian Econometrics", in Colander, D. (ed.), *Post-Walrasian Macroeconomics. Beyond the Dynamic Stochastic General Equilibrium Model*, Cambridge: Cambridge University Press, pp. 239–57.

Howitt, P. (1990), *The Keynesian Revolution and Other Essays*, Hertfordshire: Philip Allan.

Johnson, H. (1971), "The Keynesian Revolution and the Monetarist Counterrevolution", *American Economic Review*, vol. 61, pp. 91–106.

Keynes, J. M. (1936), *The General Theory of Employment, Interest, and Money*, London: Macmillan.

King, R. (1993), "Will the New Keynesian Macroeconomics Resurrect the IS-LM Model?", *Journal of Economic Perspectives*, vol. 7, pp. 67–82.

Klein, L. ([1956] 1964), *Economic Fluctuations in the United States, 1921–1941* (fourth edition), New York: Wiley.

Klein, L. (1948), *The Keynesian Revolution*, New York: Macmillan.

Kirman, A. (2006), "Foreword", in D. Colander (ed.), *Post-Walrasian Macroeconomics. Beyond the Dynamic Stochastic General Equilibrium Model*, Cambridge: Cambridge University Press, pp. XIII–XXI.

Kydland, F. and E. Prescott (1977), "Rules rather than Discretion: the Inconsistency of Optimal Planes", *Journal of Political Economy*, vol. 85, pp. 473–91.

Kydland, F. and E. Prescott (1982) "Time to Build and Aggregate Fluctuations", *Econometrica*, vol. 50, pp. 1345–70.

Laidler, D. (1981), "Monetarism: An Interpretation and An Assessment", *The Economic Journal*, vol. 91, pp. 1–28.

Laidler, D. (1999), *Fabricating the Keynesian Revolution. Studies of the Inter-War Literature on Money, the Cycle, and Unemployment*, Cambridge: Cambridge University Press.

Leijonhufvud, A. (2006a), "Episodes in a Century of Macroeconomics", in Colander, D. (ed.), *Post-Walrasian Macroeconomics. Beyond the Dynamic Stochastic General Equilibrium Model*, Cambridge: Cambridge University Press, pp. 27–45.

Leijonhufvud, A. (2006b), "Keynes as a Marshallian", in Backhouse, R. and B. Bateman (eds.), *The Cambridge Companion to Keynes*, Cambridge: Cambridge University Press, pp. 58–77.

Lipsey, R. (2000), "IS-LM, Keynesianism, and the New Classicism", in Backhouse, R. and A. Salanti (eds.), *Macroeconomics and the Real World*, vol. 2 *Keynesian Economics, Unemployment and Policy*, Oxford: Oxford University Press, pp. 57–82.

Long, J. and C. Plosser (1983), "Real Business Cycles", *Journal of Political Economy*, vol. 91, pp. 39–69.

Lucas, R. E. Jr. ([1972] 1981), "Expectations and the Neutrality of Money", in *Studies in the Business-Cycle Theory*, Cambridge (Mass.): The M.I.T. Press, pp. 66–89.

Lucas, R. E. Jr. ([1975] 1981), An Equilibrium Model of the Business Cycle", in *Studies in the Business-Cycle Theory*, Cambridge (Mass.): The M.I.T. Press, pp. 179–214.

Lucas, R. E. Jr. ([1976] 1981), "Econometric Policy Evaluation: a Critique", in *Studies in the Business-Cycle Theory*, Cambridge (Mass.): The M.I.T. Press, pp. 104–30.

Lucas, R. E. Jr. ([1978] 1981), "Unemployment Policy", in *Studies in Business Cycle Theory*, Cambridge (Mass.): The M.I.T. Press, pp. 240–7.

Lucas, R. E. Jr. (1987), *Models of Business Cycle*, Oxford: Basil Blackwell.

Lucas, R. E. Jr. (1993), "Interview with Robert E. Lucas Jr.", Federal Reserve Bank of Minneapolis, *The Region*, pp. 2–7.

Lucas R. E. Jr. and T. Sargent ([1979] 1994), "After Keynesian Macroeconomics" in Preston. R. Miller (ed.), *The Rational Expectations Revolution. Readings from the Front Line*, Cambridge (Mass.): The M.I.T. Press, pp. 5–30.

Malinvaud, E. (1977), *The Theory of Unemployment Reconsidered*, Oxford: Basil Blackwell.

Malinvaud, E. (1984), *Mass Unemployment*, Oxford: Basil Blackwell.

Mankiw, G. (1990), "A Quick Refreshing Course in Macroeconomics", *Journal of Economic Literature*, vol. 28, pp. 1645–60.

Mankiw, G. (2006), "The Macroeconomist as Scientist and Engineer", *NBER, Working Paper* 12349.

Mankiw, G. and D. Romer (1991), *New Keynesian Economics, Vol. I, Imperfect Competition and Sticky Prices, Vol. II, Coordination Failures and Rigidites*, Cambridge (Maas.): The M.I.T. Press.

Meade J. ([1937] 1947), "A Simplified Model of Keynes's System", in Harris, S. (1947), (ed.), *The New Economics. Keynes Influence on Theory and Public Policy*, New York: A. A. Knopf, pp. 606–18.

Modigliani, F. (1944), "Liquidity Preference and the Theory of Interest and Money", *Econometrica*, vol. 12, pp. 44–88.

Negishi, T. (1987), "Tâtonnement and Recontracting" in Eatwell, J., M. Milgate and P. Newman (eds.), *The New Palgrave. A Dictionary of Economics*, vol. II, London: Macmillan, pp. 589–95.

Ostroy, J. (1992), "Money and General Equilibrium Theory", in J. Eatwell, M. Milgate and P. Newman (eds.), *The New Palgrave Dictionary of Money and Finance*, London: Macmillan, vol. II, pp. 783–6.

Patinkin, D. (1965), *Money, Interest and Prices*, (second edition), New York: Harper and Row.

Rogerson, R., R. Shimer, and R. Wright (2005), "Search-Theoretic Models of the Labor Market: a Survey", *Journal of Economic Literature*, vol. XLIII, pp. 959–88.

Shapiro, C. and J. E. Stiglitz (1984), "Equilibrium Unemployment as Worker Discipline Device", *American Economic Review*, vol. 74, pp. 433–44.

Snowdon, B. and H. Vane (1996), "The Development of Modern Macroeconomics: Reflections in the Light of Johnson's Analysis After Twenty-Five years", *Journal of Macroeconomics*, vol. 18, pp. 381–401.

Snowdon, B. and H. R. Vane (1998), "Transforming Macroeconomics: an Interview with Robert E Lucas Jr.", *Journal of Economic Methodology*, vol. 5, pp. 115–45.

Taylor, J. B. (1979), "Staggered Wage Setting in a Macro Model", *American Economic Review*, vol. 69, pp. 108–13.

Tinbergen, J. (1939), *Statistical Testing of Business Cycle Theories*, Geneva: League of Nations.

Tobin, J. ([1993] 1997), "Price Flexibility and Output Stability. An Old Keynesian View" in Snowdon, B. and H. Vane (eds.), *A Macroeconomics Reader*, London: Routledge, pp. 135–55.

Vercelli, A. (2000), "The Evolution of IS-LM Models: Empirical Evidence and Theoretical Presuppositions", in R. Backhouse and A. Salanti (eds.), *Macroeconomics and the Real World, vol. 2 Keynesian Economics, Unemployment and Policy*, Oxford: Oxford University Press, pp. 25–42.

Van der Ploeg, F. (2005), "Back to Keynes?", *CESifo Working Paper*, No. 1424.

Walras, L. (1954), *Elements of Pure Economics*, translated by Jaffé W., London: Allen and Unwin.

Weintraub, R. (1983), "On the Existence of Competitive Equilibrium: 1930–1954", *Journal of Economic Literature*, vol. 21, pp. 1–39.

Woodford, M. (1999), "Revolution and Evolution in Twentieth-Century Macroeconomics", in P. Gifford (ed.), *Frontiers of the Mind in the Twenty-First Century*, Cambridge (Mass.): Harvard University Press.

Young, W. (1987), *Interpreting Mr Keynes. The IS-LM Enigma*, London: Polity Press.

Young, W. and B. Z. Zilberfarb (2000) (eds.), *IS-LM and Modern Macroeconomics*, Boston, Dordrecht, London: Kluwer Academic Publishers.

# 11
## Aggregate Demand, Employment and Equilibrium with Marginal Productivity: Keynesian Adjustment in the Craft Economy

*Edward J. Nell*

Most Post Keynesians have approached the idea that marginal productivity accounted for the demand for labor with caution and skepticism; some, like Paul Davidson and Victoria Chick, have accepted it with reservations. None of them, however, have thought that the account was illuminating or that supply and demand for labor determined employment and real wages. Ingrid Rima, for example, insists that the behavior of the labor market is chiefly determined by institutions, while Davidson and Chick have tried to accommodate Keynes's insistence that the real wage did equal the marginal product of labor, even in less than full-employment equilibrium. All agree that Keynes's approach recast the argument in money rather than real terms, rejecting the Classical Dichotomy. But if the market operates with money wages, how exactly does the real wage adjust to the marginal product? If the real wage adjusts in the labor market, why is full employment not established? And when there is unemployment in "equilibrium," why is it so deep and persistent?

Keynes repeatedly insisted that his argument proceeded to establish less-than-full-employment equilibrium "...without disputing the vital fact which classical economist have rightly asserted...that the real wage has a unique inverse correlation with the volume of employment.... This is simply the obverse of the familiar proposition that industry is normally working subject to decreasing returns" *General Theory*, p. 17. Post-Keynesian interpreters contend that this implies that the marginal product curve shows positions of market equilibrium.[1] This could be argued if prices generally were equal to marginal costs, as Keynes seems to have supposed (with marginal costs rising). A suggestion can be found in Keynes's *Lectures*. On p. 137, starting from the expression giving employment as a function of expected sales proceeds, Keynes proceeds to derive an equation showing price equal to the wage-bill times a markup expression divided by output. Under competitive conditions (with appropriate further assumptions) this would show price equal to or proportional to marginal cost, which would imply a corresponding relationship between the real wage and the marginal product of labor. But while a discrepancy between the real wage and the marginal product, under competitive conditions, can be considered a disequilibrium, how the market moves to correct this is not spelled out. It is necessary to show how the equilibrium can be reached by market processes, given that labor will respond only to money wages. This is not easy to find in the literature.

However, a simple diagram can help, though it will take some explanation. To develop it, we will start from the assumption of given plant and equipment, operating under diminishing returns to additional employment of labor (what Joan Robinson called a "utilization function"). Initially we will take the money wage as given ... But to explain in what sense, we will have to explore Keynes's conception of the labor market.

### The Marginalist account of the labor market

When the General Theory was first published, many commentators, for example, Modigliani and Klein, simply assumed that the marginalist account of the labor market was broadly accurate, provided wages and prices were flexible. But Keynes was correct, they argued, to note that, as a matter of fact, money wages (and prices) are often not flexible – for reasons which the early Keynesians did not explore very deeply. "New Keynesians" have since advanced an array of carefully developed theories to account for this – acknowledging and modeling imperfect markets and coordination failures (monopolies, oligopolies, unions, menu and transaction costs, bounded rationality), examining explicit and implicit labor market contracts, "insider" markets and "efficiency wage" systems, and exploring the effects of asymmetric risk aversion and asymmetric information in credit (and other) markets. Starting from utility maximizing households and profit-maximizing firms, with Walrasian markets and the usual forms of rational economic calculation, New Keynesians have shown that introducing these plausible and largely realistic imperfections and limitations will result in price and wage rigidities that yield involuntary unemployment and other Keynesian conclusions.

In the light of history there is something very odd about this. In the late nineteenth and early twentieth century, both prices and money wages *were* flexible. That is, in response to variations in demand they both rose and fell, although prices were markedly *more* flexible in both directions than wages. (And both were more flexible than output and especially employment – with the result that higher levels of output and employment were statistically associated with lower real wages (Dunlop, 1938; Tarshis, 1938, 1939; for recent studies, Nell, 1998, and Nell, ed., 1998)). Yet during this period, when prices and wages were flexible, virtually *all* the imperfections developed by New Keynesians and canvassed above were substantially more widespread and more severe, than in later periods when they are supposed to account for rigidity!

The standard Keynesian models take the money wage to be fixed, so that the system is in a kind of institutional disequilibrium – the labor market cannot do its job, because there will be no proper labor supply function. Supply and demand do not operate as they normally would. Yet if that is so it may seem unclear why the real wage should end up being equal to the marginal product of labor. All parts of the model interact, but what exactly brings the real wage and the marginal product to this position if the money wage cannot move? If the money wage is allowed to be flexible, will that affect how marginal productivity adjusts? If wages are flexible there will be a labor supply function, so the market will work as it "should." This is the position taken for example by Modigliani.[2]

By contrast Keynes's position – and that of most post-Keynesians – is that the starting point, the marginalist labor market, is simply not a correct account of wages and employment. The employment of labor and the setting of wages are not brought about through the functioning of a market in the marginalist sense – that is, a market in which the wage reflects productivity at the margin on the one hand, and the disutility of additional effort on the other. In such a market, in which behavior is governed by costs on both sides, we might expect effort to be allocated optimally, if other appropriate conditions are met; to define such a market, to serve as the norm or standard, is presumably the neo-Classical project. But, according to Keynes, the labor market does not and cannot function that way. The wage, he argues, does indeed reflect the marginal productivity of labor, but it does not and cannot reflect its marginal disutility. There is no adjustment mechanism, no way that the real wage could be brought into alignment with the marginal disutility of labor. Labor could accept or reject a money wage; but they could do nothing about prices, nor could they reliably know whether prices would be stable or changing in the near future.[3]

Keynes objected not only to the marginalist labor supply function, but most importantly to the idea that employment and real wages (and so output) were determined in the labor market. Labor supply depends on people needing jobs, and can be taken, in the short run, as an institutional datum, influenced to changing degrees by many factors. Money wages may have an influence; so may prices. So may the availability of jobs. These factors may be affected in unpredictable ways by non-economic matters. The labor market will influence only *money* wages, while the product market will affect prices, and adjustment will take place through the interaction of all parts.

In short, he argues that a marginal product curve can be defined, but not a supply curve based on relating disutility of labor to the real wage. Yet he does not explain how the real wage is brought and kept equal to the marginal product. Nevertheless, he argues that the economy will tend to equilibrium, in the sense that the real wage will equal the marginal product of labor, thus maximizing profits, even though the economy typically reaches a position of less than full employment. Most significantly, he argues that fluctuations due to changes in investment spending will be *amplified* – consumption will move in the same direction as investment. How can these points all be brought together? To what extent do they depend on relating behavior and choice to *money variables*, rejecting the Classical Dichotomy?

The argument here will be an extension of the Keynesian position, starting from the idea that the labor market works differently under different technologies, because costs are different. The suggestion here is that technology governs the behavior of costs, and that the behavior of costs determines whether and to what extent prices and wages are flexible – and, indeed, may generate market incentives to change that flexibility. A brief sketch outlining this view might help.

Two technologies will be considered, one which can be labeled "Craft-based" or "Marshallian," in which small enterprises employ skilled work teams, and in which it is difficult and costly to vary output or employment. The other is Mass Production, in which output and employment are easily and rapidly adjusted to variations in sales, and variable costs tend to be constant over a wide range of output levels. We will argue that neither allows for a labor market in which there will be an adjustment process that would tend to move the system toward a position in which all labor seeking jobs will find employment at a determinate wage.

In what follows, we will first explore the adjustment of employment and wages in the Craft or Marshallian economy, and then consider adjustment in a Mass Production system.

We start with a Marshallian technology showing clear diminishing returns to employing additional labor with given plant and equipment. But this is an unsatisfactory technology, and firms will try to gain greater control over costs, leading eventually to a "flattening" of the employment-output function, until it becomes a straight line, indicating constant returns. In the Marshallian economy both wages and prices are flexible, but prices are more flexible than wages – the proportional deviations are greater – and both fluctuate more than employment. This is because production is based on a technology of skilled craft workers; production teams must work together; their ability to function together is part of the "embodied" capital of the firm – breaking them up will be a capital loss. Plus start-up and shutdown costs are high. Hence only inessential workers can be laid off. Thus demand fluctuations will be met by slowing down production somewhat, but not reducing employment much. Profits will bear much of the burden of slower sales, providing an incentive to firms to gain better control over their costs. This they will do by increasing their capital investment and mechanizing. This will make it possible to vary output and employment together over a range, with unit running costs staying constant.

## A model with Marshallian technology and Keynesian wages

We can write a set of equations related to traditional interpretations, e.g. Modigliani's system, but which, arguably, will be closer to Keynes. (See GTTG, Chapter 12, part I.) In this interpretation of Keynes the behavioral equations are written in real terms, so there is no possibility of money illusion. Furthermore, while the real wage is equal to the marginal product of labor in general, the real wage and employment are *not* determined in the labor market. They emerge from the entire system (Keynes, GT, Chapter 2; Rymes, *Keynes's Lectures, 1932–5*, 4, 6). Instead prices and demand are determined in the product markets, and employment adjusts to demand. Two cases are considered: in the first, money wages are given, in the second they are influenced by the level of employment in relation to full employment.

$$Y = Y(N, K^*) \tag{1}$$

$$\frac{w}{\pi} = \frac{\delta Y}{\delta N} = Y'(N) \tag{2}$$

$$C = w/\pi N \tag{3}$$

$$I = I(i, C), \quad I_i < 0, I_C > 0 \tag{4}$$

$$\frac{M}{\pi} = L(I, Y), \quad L_i < 0, L_Y > 0 \tag{5}$$

$$Y = C + I \tag{6}$$

$$Y = \frac{w}{N + P} \tag{7}$$

$$w = w^* \quad w^* \text{ is rigid or fixed} \tag{8a}$$

$$w = w - w^* = F(N - N^*), \tag{8b}$$

where $w^*$ is the normal or initial level, and $N^*$ is full employment

[Neither Modigliani nor Hicks even consider the possibility of an equation like 8b, yet it seems to be suggested by Keynes's discussion of money wages and prices.]

A thought experiment will shed some light on the idea of flexible money wages and prices: substitute the above equation 8b for the equation 8a in this model. The lower money wage will require a lower price level to sustain the same real wage. But $M$ is fixed; with lower prices, there will be lower transactions demand, requiring a lower rate of interest to absorb the money supply. The lower rate of interest will mean higher investment demand, implying higher $N$, and a lower real wage, with the effect on consumption depending (as we shall see) on the elasticity of the marginal product curve. This is to some extent offsetting – there is no reason to think that a decline in money wages proportional to unemployment would lower transactions demand, and so the interest rate, enough to generate the investment demand needed to move to full employment, especially if it has to offset reduced consumption spending.

*Perfectly flexible money wages*, on the other hand, would be different. In that case, a small amount of unemployment would bring about an indefinitely large decline in money wages. In that purely artificial case – if prices followed suit immediately so that the real wage is unchanged – then the transactions demand would fall toward zero, bringing the rate of interest down to the liquidity trap level. Then, depending on the elasticity of $I$ with respect to interest, the economy might tend toward full employment. But the idea of perfect price/wage flexibility is not just unrealistic; it is evidently inconsistent with the widespread use of forward money contracts. Such contracts, designed to reduce uncertainty, are a fundamental aspect of a monetary economy – a point Keynes emphasized, as Davidson reminds us. But *moderately* flexible money wages will not necessarily move the economy toward full employment, as we shall see.

To show this, we need a reasonable account of how market pressures drive the adjustment to the point where the real wage equals the marginal product of labor. Keynes does not provide this, but we will construct an argument that is consistent with his assumptions and approach. On this basis we can justify his claim that there may be many possible equilibrium positions, that all but one of these will be at less than full employment, and that flexible money wages will not move the system to full employment. Keynes assumed aggregate diminishing returns; accordingly we assume that the technology is "Marshallian," that is, that craft labor can be applied to given equipment in the short run, resulting in diminishing returns, as in Marshall's account.

## The price mechanism and Marshallian technology[4]

The principles underlying the Craft economy center on the short-run employment–output relationship.[5] In the Craft Economy (Nell, 1998; Nell, ed., 1998), we can reasonably assume diminishing returns to the employment of labor, in relation to a normal position. Adding extra workers to work teams operating given equipment brings progressively lower rewards, while removing workers leads to progressively larger losses of output. In general, it will be difficult to adjust levels of employment. Workers cooperate in teams that cannot be lightly broken apart or added to; all workers have to be present and working for a process to be operated at all; processes cannot easily be started up and shut down. So the Craft Economy not only has diminishing returns, it also has inflexible employment (Nell, 1998, Ch. 9).[6]

Our model is based on such an aggregate function, given as Equation 1 above, where we have assumed a conventional shape and properties. This is appropriate for a Craft Economy[7] where output increases with labor according to a curved line that rises from the origin with a diminishing slope (by contrast, Mass Production will be characterized by a straight line rising from the origin[8]). As a first approximation Consumption can be identified with wages and salaries[9], while for the purpose of drawing the diagram Investment can be taken as exogenous. As employment rises, the wage bill – and so Consumption spending – will rise at a constant rate, namely the normal wage rate. Total expenditure will then be shown by adding Investment to the wage-consumption line.

The diagram presents the aggregate utilization function, with output on the vertical axis and labor employed on the horizontal. The function of the Craft economy is curved, its slope falling as $N$ increases (the Mass production line would rise to the right with a constant slope). The wage bill (including salaries) will be assumed to be equal to Consumption spending (transfer payments could be included also). No household saving and no consumption out of profits – but both assumptions are easily modified.[10] So the wage bill, also representing consumption spending, is shown by a straight line rising to the right from the origin; its angle is the wage rate. Investment spending will be treated as exogenous in the short run, so will be marked off on the vertical axis. Aggregate demand will then be the line $C+I$, rising to the right from the $I$ point on the vertical axis; its slope is the wage rate.

## Adjustment to demand fluctuations in the craft economy

Suppose Investment is unusually low, below normal, so that this line cuts the utilization function at a point below the normal level of output and employment, $N'_1$ (Figure 11.1). Since it is difficult to adjust employment and output, there will tend to be overproduction, and prices will fall. Since it is even harder to adjust employment than output, prices will fall more readily than money wages. Hence the real wage will rise, from $w_0$ to $w_1$. As a result the $C+I$ line will swing upward, until it is *tangent* to the utilization function; employment thus settles not at $N'_1$ but at $N_1$. Notice that this point of tangency will tend to be close to the normal level of employment and output, and will be closer the more concave the function. In short, when Investment is abnormally low, the real wage will rise; if the rise in real wages is proportionally greater than the decline in employment, Consumption will increase. This is the case illustrated in the diagram; investment falls from $I_0$ to $I_1$, prices fall and the real wage rises. Clearly the wage bill, and so consumption, is higher at $N_1$ than at $N_0$.

Conversely, suppose Investment were exceptionally high, or that the $C+I$ line had too steep a slope, indicating too high a real wage. In either case, expenditure would lie above output at any feasible level of employment. Under these conditions prices would be bid up relative to money wages, and the $C+I$ line would swing down, until it came to rest on the utilization function in a point of tangency (Nell, 1998, pp. 455–7). Again this point would tend to lie close to the normal level, being closer the more concave the function. When Investment is unusually high, Consumption will tend to adjust downward.

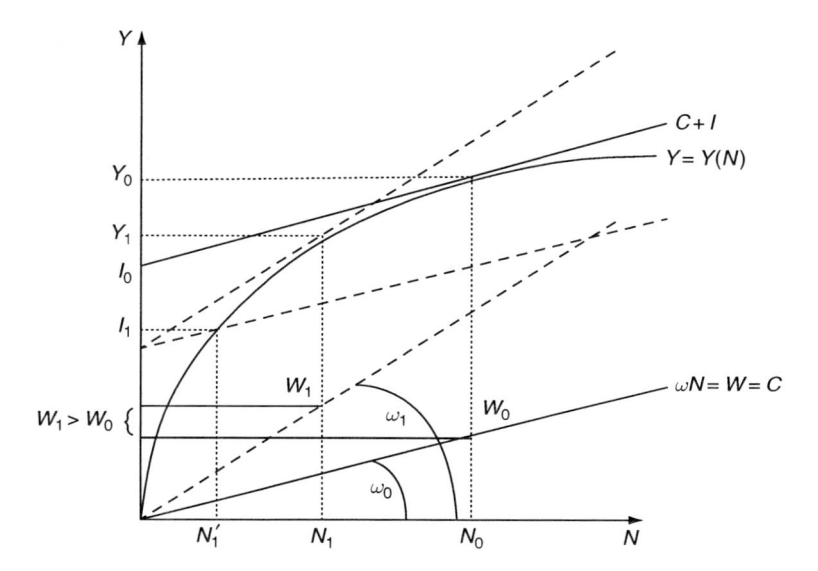

*Figure 11.1* Adjustment in the craft economy.

Notice that adjusting the real wage to equal the marginal product of labor both assures a unique equilibrium and maximizes profit.[11] When the $C+I$ line is tangent to the utilization curve the distance to the wage line is at a maximum; if $C+I$ cuts the utilization curve, there will be two equilibria and the distance between the intersection points and the wage line will be less than that at the tangency. (Given the real wage, profit rises with employment at a diminishing rate from the origin to the tangency point; it then falls at an increasing rate until it reaches zero at the point where the production function intersects the wage line.)

We need to define the point of full employment – at which the entire labor force has jobs (Figure 11.2). An appropriate concept of full employment would be "no vacancies" or, rather, "no vacancies except turnover vacancies." Employment is full when all farms, factories, offices and shops have hired the employees they need to operate at their optimal level. Output at the point of full employment will be associated with a marginal product; that marginal product will become a real wage, which multiplied by the level of full employment defines the wage bill, equal, *ex hypothesi*, to consumption. The difference between full employment output and consumption must be filled by investment. Now let investment fall below this full employment level. As it does, it will trace out

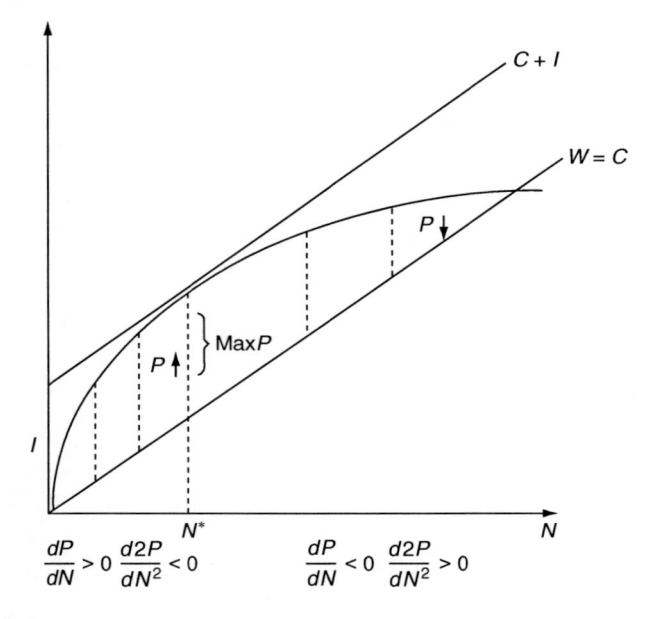

*Figure 11.2* Behavior of profits.

Figure labels: $C+I$; $W=C$; $P\downarrow$; MaxP; $P\uparrow$; $I$; $N^*$; $N$; $\frac{dP}{dN}>0$, $\frac{d^2P}{dN^2}<0$; $\frac{dP}{dN}<0$, $\frac{d^2P}{dN^2}>0$.

the marginal product curve; at each lower level of investment, prices will fall, and the real wage rise, while employment falls; the overall effect on consumption will depend on the elasticity of the marginal product curve. But each point on the curve will be an equilibrium, in the sense that money wages and prices have adjusted to produce the profit maximizing position.

That this pattern of price flexibility dampens fluctuations by partially offsetting them, in conditions of strongly diminishing returns, can be shown very simply. Recalling our equations: $Y$ is real output, $N$ employment, $w/\pi$ the real wage, and $I$ investment. All wages are consumed. As above,

$$Y = Y(N), \quad Y' > 0, \; Y'' < 0$$
$$Y = C + I$$
$$\frac{w}{\pi} = Y'(N)$$
$$C = \left(\frac{w}{\pi}\right)N$$

Clearly

$$Y = I + (w/\pi)N,$$

so

$$dY/dI = \delta I/\delta I + N[\delta(w/\pi)/\delta I] + (w/\pi)/[\delta N/\delta I]$$
$$= 1 + N[\delta(w/\pi)/\delta I] + (w/\pi)[\delta N/\delta I]$$

where $N[\delta(w/\pi)/\delta I] < 0$ and $(w/\pi)[\delta N/\delta I] > 0$. So $dY/dI >$ or $< 1$ according to whether $N[\delta(w/\pi)/\delta I] >$ or $< (w/\pi)[\delta N/\delta I]$.[12] So long as returns diminish sufficiently $dY/dI < 1$; price changes due to variations in investment demand will lead to a partial offset.[13]

In short, so long as diminishing returns are significant the price mechanism will lead Consumption to adjust so that it will tend to make up for a shortfall or offset an excess of Investment. It thus tends to stabilize demand around the normal level of output and employment.

This form of adjustment brings to mind the doctrine of "forced saving" (Thornton, 1802; Hayek, 1932; Robertson, 1931). Here, however, the price changes are assumed to reflect changes in demand pressure – not necessarily connected to changes in the quantity of money – and are shown to result in a Marshallian "marginal productivity" equilibrium.[14] The traditional "forced saving" discussion usually started from an assumed increase in the money issue or in an exceptional extension of credit, and, indeed, a rise in demand of the kind considered here would require just such additional finance – which the resulting rise in prices relative to money wages would tend to support. (The higher profits will allow banks to charge higher interest rates, enabling them to attract additional reserves. The higher interest rates, however, should tend to dampen further expansion.)[15]

This shows that there is good reason to expect adjustment to bring about a real wage and a level of employment, such that the real wage will be equal to the marginal product of that level of employment – which need not be full employment. So let's return to model and work through it – starting with the solution when we have a fixed money wage. An instructive informal approach: set the Investment function equal to profits, in effect setting out an analogue to the conventional IS curve. This combines equations 4, 6 and 7 with 1, 2 and 3, yielding a relationship between $i$ and $N$, based on the equality of $I$ and $P$. Then equation 5 can be combined with 1 and 2, to form another function relating $i$ and $N$, based on the equality of $M$ and liquidity demand. But since equation 2 is drawn on in constructing both, equation 8a must be used to set the money wage at the fixed level. Then these two relationships can be solved for $i$ and $N$, and the results (which will depend on the form of the functions[16]) substituted back to establish the equilibrium values of the other variables. All the markets interact, but there is no reason to expect full employment.

Now let's turn to the second case, replacing the fixed wage equation with flexible money wages, equation 8b. This states that when there is unemployment money wages will fall, with the decline proportional to the rate of unemployment. Given that unemployment reflects lower demand, we can expect that prices will also fall, but prices will have to fall further, in order for the wage bill to rise enough for there to be an offset to the lower demand. If there is no offset then the fall in money wages could reduce the real wage, and make unemployment worse than if money wages had been rigid.

Next we propose to deal more fully with the financial market by allowing for arbitrage between equity and bonds. (The Modigliani–Miller Theorem argues that arbitrage ensures that bonds and equity are perfect substitutes. The proposal here is much less extreme; it just asserts that there will be market pressures to pull the current rate of profit and the rate of interest together, in circumstances where the Central Bank is not pegging.)

$$P/K = [Y - (w/\pi)N]/K = \varepsilon i, \qquad (8c)$$

where $\varepsilon$ is a parameter representing risk and the "equity premium."

This has the effect of fixing the interest rate, but because we have dropped 8a, it leaves the money wage as a variable, although we have not specified an equation to govern it. It will simply be determined as a residual – for the moment. The result is quite striking: a version of the Classical Dichotomy reappears – but there is no reason to expect full employment.

An informal argument can support this as follows: Start with 4, the investment equation,

$$I = I(i, C)$$

and eliminate $i$ and $C$ on the RHS, by substituting into it, using the production function, 1, the real wage equation, 2, consumption, 3, and the income equation, 7. In this way eliminate the other variables until only $N$ and coefficients remain. Note that to remove the interest rate, $i$, equation 8c will have to be used. (When the model rested on 8a, fixed wages, the interest rate could not be removed from the investment equation, 4, without drawing on the monetary equation, 5; monetary and real parts of the economy interact.) Next use equation $Y = C + I$ to replace $I$ on the LHS, and then draw on equations 1, 2, and 3 to reduce every expression to a function of $N$. Then solve for $N$, and substitute back. From equation 1, we find $Y$; from 2, $w/\pi$; from 3, $C$; from 6, $I$. Then with $I$ and $C$, the interest rate, $i$, will follow from equation 4. Finally, equation 8c yields $P$, profits. Thus the seven equations pertaining to Savings-Investment and Output-Employment determine the seven *real* variables:

$$N, Y, C, I, P, i, \text{ and } w/\pi.$$

Equation 5, for the money market, is left to determine $\pi$, the price level, which will then give us the money wage from equation 2. So real relationships determine real variables and monetary forces affect only nominal variables!

But to leave the money wage simply drifting, determined residually, cannot be allowed, given the intense market (and non-market!) pressures on money wages. However, we can turn to equation 8b which models the pressures on the money wage. Yet adding this equation, too, would appear to overdetermine the model. The natural response would be to allow for a flexible money supply – so that $M$ becomes a variable that will adapt to the pressures of the market. This can be allowed to drift, for that simply says that the authorities will accommodate. Thus a version of the Classical Dichotomy can be derived, with the real wage equal to the marginal product of labor, although the model is demand-driven, and need not reach equilibrium at full employment.[17]

The importance of money here lies in the fact that wages are paid in money, and prices charged in money. Labor never faces real wages in the market; it can only react to the money wage, which means that supply and demand in the labor market cannot determine employment and the real wage, as mainstream economics has held. The mainstream system pretended that markets adjusted in response to real variables, whereas in fact adjustments necessarily take place in response to money variables. Worse, the traditional approach assumed that the economy always operated at full employment. This was unjustified.

But rejecting the Classical Dichotomy by itself did not explain either unemployment or why the Depression was so severe. Equilibrium was possible at less than full employment because employment was determined by aggregate demand, not in the labor market. But this still did not explain why the depression was so deep. That became clear with the understanding that changes in investment led to changes in consumption *in the same direction* – the idea behind the multiplier. When investment fell, consumption *also* fell. This was why the fluctuations were so serious. And this is consistent with the real wage adjusting to equal the marginal product of labor – so there is a profit-maximizing equilibrium, one among many possible, even though full employment may not be reached and the swings may be severe.

When the curvature of the production function is considerable, the elasticity of the marginal product curve will be greater than $-1$, so a fall in investment will lead to a rise in the wage bill and therefore in consumption spending, as shown in the diagram. But when the production function is rather flat, the elasticity of the marginal product curve will be less than $-1$, so that a fall in investment will lead to a decrease in the wage bill and consumption spending, as indicated. In this case there is not only no offset to the drop in investment – the effects are actually made worse. And that is the conclusion Keynes reached and tried to explain in the lectures he gave in Cambridge.

1. The variability of profits provides an incentive to change the technology so as to control current costs; the innovations must change current costs from fixed to variable; this will be done by increasing capital costs. Consider a Samuelson surrogate production function, with pressures for $W$ to increase – at the higher wage it is worthwhile to mechanize, so in current prices capital per worker rises, and the scale effects allow for greater flexibility in adjusting employment to changes in the level of demand

## The multiplier replaces the price mechanism

Fluctuations in $I$ will normally have some impact on $N$ even in a Craft economy. But there will be an offsetting movement in $C$ so long as the curvature of the employment function is large. The price mechanism is stabilizing for the system as whole, but the effect is that profits fluctuate sharply for individual businesses. So firms will be motivated to redesign their production systems to allow greater flexibility in adapting to demand fluctuations. This means being able to add on or layoff workers, without greatly disturbing unit costs. As such redesigning takes place, it will reduce the curvature of the employment function; that is, diminishing returns will be lessened. We can think of this as a progressive "flattening" of the employment function. When this has reached the point where the marginal product curve has unitary elasticity, so that the proportional change in the real wage is just matched by that in employment, then the total wage bill is unaffected by the price changes following the change in $I$. If the total wage bill is unaffected, then, on the assumptions made earlier, total $C$ will be unchanged.

This will be the case, for example, when the employment function takes the form: $Y = A(\ln N)$. Hence $I$ may fall, for example, but $C$ will not change. There will be no offset. So $dY/dI = 1$. Any *further* reduction in the rate at which returns diminish will mean that the *change in employment will outweigh the change in the wage bill*, so that $C$ will move in the same direction as $I$. In this event $dY/dI > 1$ will always hold (Nell 1998, 1992).

It can be argued that this was the conclusion that Keynes seems to have been seeking (Figure 11.3). In his Second Lecture in the Easter Term, 1932, Keynes reached "...the remarkable generalization that, in all ordinary circumstances, the volume of employment depends on the volume of investment, and that anything which increases or decreases the latter will increase or decrease the former" Vol XXIX, p. 40. See also T. K. Rymes, *Keynes's Lectures, 1932–1935*, pp. 30–44. The "Manifesto" written by Joan Robinson and Richard Kahn, with the concurrence of Austin Robinson, challenged not the result, but the reasoning used

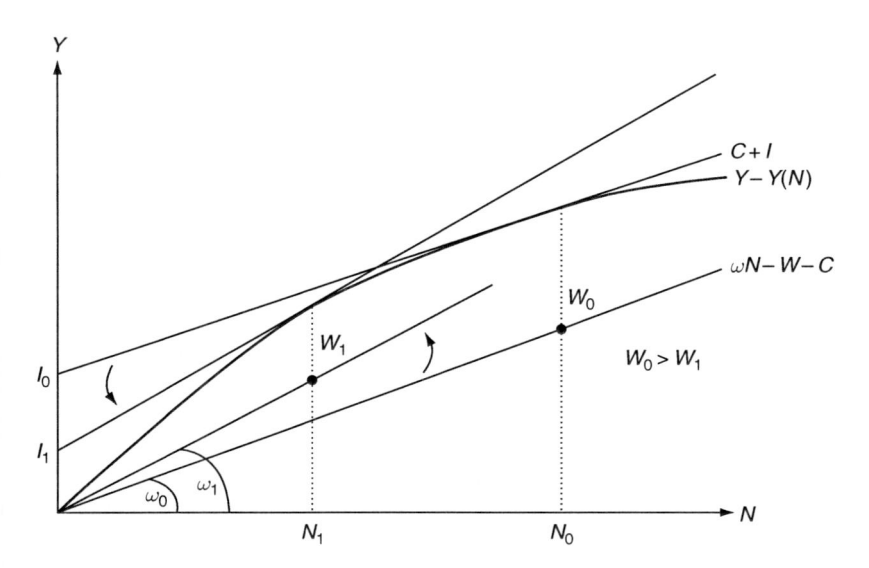

*Figure 11.3* Consumption moves with Investment.

in reaching it. As noted above, part of their discussion concerned the effects of price changes on demand. Rymes notes, "The "manifesto" claimed that the case of no increase in the demand for consumption goods [following an increase in investment spending] was the one exceptional case Keynes had dealt with...It is...an obviously special case." On the assumptions here it is the case where the elasticity of the marginal product curve is unitary. Both Keynes and the "manifesto" authors considered the "elasticity of supply" to be a determining factor, but neither presents a precise analysis.

## Adjustment to Demand Fluctuations in the Mass Production economy

Modern economies appear to be subject to strong fluctuations in demand. Indeed, examples of market instability can be found everywhere, although the instability is usually bounded in some way. But there do not appear to be, in the modern world, strong and reliable market-based forces ensuring stability. Investment spending appears to be a major source of demand variation. Yet if the purpose of investment were simply a corrective, moving the actual capital/labor ratio to its optimal level, stabilization would hardly be needed. Such a long-run position would be stationary, or, if the labor force were growing, the economy would expand uniformly. This is the picture presented by neo-Classical theory, articulated, for example, by Hayek (1941).

But both Keynes and the older Classicals, especially Ricardo and Marx, offer a different view: investment is the accumulation of capital, a process by which productive power is created, organized and managed. It is driven by the desire for power and wealth, and there is no definable "optimum." Investment expands productive power, but does not move the economy toward any definite destination. Given such motivation and the important role of technological innovation, the urge to invest will sometimes be strong and widespread, but at other times weak and uncertain. This may help to explain the need for stabilizing policies, arising from the demand side.

In post-War Mass Production economies (Nell, 1998), prices do not play an important role in adjustment to changing demand. Employment is much more flexible, and constant returns appear to prevail in the short run; to put it differently, unit costs are broadly constant as employment and output vary over a wide but normal range. Workers need only be semi-skilled and teams can easily be broken up and re-formed; processes can be operated at varying levels of intensity in response to variations in demand, and they can easily be shut down and started up. It is likewise easy to layoff and recall workers.

As before, we have an aggregate utilization function: here the Mass Production economy will be characterized by a straight line rising from the origin, showing constant marginal returns. As a first approximation, Consumption can be identified with wages and salaries, while Investment can be taken as exogenous. As employment rises, the wage bill – and so Consumption spending – will rise at a constant rate, namely the normal wage rate. The wage bill – assumed equal to Consumption spending – is represented by a straight line rising to the right from the origin; its angle is the wage rate. Investment spending will be treated as exogenous in the short run, so will be marked off on the vertical axis. Aggregate demand will then be the line $C+I$, rising to the right from the $I$ point on the vertical axis; its slope is the wage rate (Figure 11.4).

The origin, here and in later diagrams, is the point at which labor cost absorbs all output. Employment in such an economy will depend only on effective demand; there is no marginal productivity adjustment.[18] Output will increase with the amount of labor employed (capacity utilized); all and only wages will be spent on consumption, and all profits will be saved as retained earnings. Investment can be taken as exogenous as a first approximation.[19] Expenditure is given by the $C+I$ line. (This ignores $G$, government spending, for the moment, although in the modern world it will be much greater than in the earlier forms of the capitalist economy.) But the output function will be a straight line rising from the origin with a slope equal to the average productivity

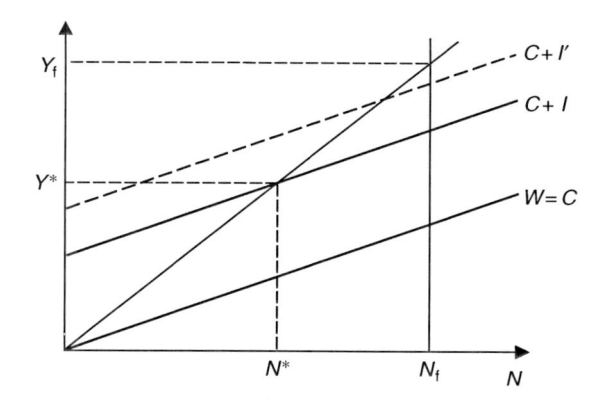

*Figure 11.4* Adjustment in the mass production economy.

of labor. Suppose Investment is exceptionally high; then employment will be increased, and Consumption will also be exceptionally high. Conversely, if Investment is low, employment will be low, and thus so will Consumption. Consumption adjusts in the same direction that Investment moves.[20] When investment rises, consumption, output and employment also increase in a definite proportion.

Simple as this is, it provides us with a number of powerful insights. Admittedly, they are derived on the basis of very great abstraction, so they cannot be expected to prove literally true – but they may nevertheless give us genuine guidance in investigating the way the world works. For example:

- Investment and profits are equal here; this suggests that we should expect to find them closely correlated in practice – as we do (Nell, 1998, Ch. 7; Asimakopulos, 1988).
- Investment determines profits here; investment is the driving force. We should expect to find something like this in reality – which many studies suggest we do.
- The multiplier here will equal $1/(1 - w/a)$, where w is the real wage. That is, the multiplier will reflect the distribution of income, and will not be very large. Again this seems plausible.
- Real wages and the level of employment and output are *positively* related. This can be seen by drawing in a steeper wage line, with the same level of investment. The $C + I$ line with then also be steeper; so it will intersect the output line at a higher level of output and employment. In fact most empirical studies of the post-war era do find real wages and employment to be positively related (Nell, ed. 1998; Blanchard and Fischer, 1989).
- Household savings *reduce* output, employment and realized profits! (Obviously, qualifications are needed, and it must be remembered that this is a short-run analysis – but the long-run may never come! If this proposition seems hard to accept, think about Japan in the 1990s – and even recently.)
- Unemployment is indicated by marking off the level of full employment on the horizontal axis. It clearly results from deficiency in demand. That is, either investment is too low or wages are too low; which implies that unemployment can be reduced by increasing either.

Finally money: Let household saving increase with the rate of interest (as consumer durable spending declines), while business investment declines as the rate of interest rises. (Neither influence is likely to be very great.) More precisely, when interest is relatively high, businesses are likely to curtail or postpone investment projects, and households may cutback on consumer durables. Thus when interest is high the investment line must shift down to a lower intercept, while the household consumption line will swing down, reducing its angle. When interest rates are relatively low, investment and household spending will be correspondingly higher. Thus we can construct a downward-sloping function (an analogue to the traditional IS) relating the rate of interest, $i$, to employment, $N$ (Figure 11.5).

This function will intersect a horizontal line representing the level of the rate of interest as pegged by the Central Bank; this will determine the level of employment (Figure 11.6).

There is no Classical Dichotomy here; monetary and real factors interact. Yet – not so fast! What about equation 8c? If we impose this condition, the structure of asset prices will have to adapt to the real

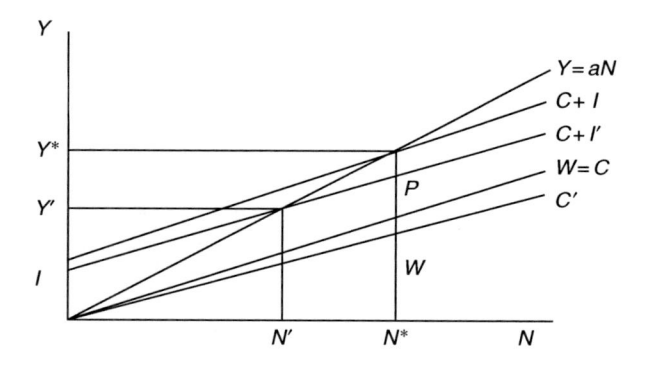

*Figure 11.5* Effects of interest on saving and investment.

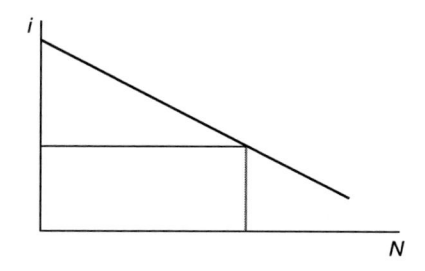

*Figure 11.6* The Central Bank's interest rate determines employment.

conditions of profitability – so the long rate will tend at times to move independently of the short. A form of the dichotomy may re-emerge. But this is another story.

## Conclusions

Keynes accepted the idea that the price mechanism did adjust to ensure that the real wage equaled the marginal productivity of labor. He did not, however, explain how this equality was brought about in labor market in which behavior responds to money wages. In his view the equality of the real wage and the marginal product justified calling the position an equilibrium; *but his argument shows that there will be a large number (on plausible assumptions, an infinite number) of such positions, besides the full employment level.* The way this works can be shown on a diagram in which it is clear that price changes tend to move the system to a profit-maximizing position, for a given level of investment.

But at first sight this appears to be a *stabilizing* pattern of adjustment. Each position of the economy will be a combination of a level of investment and a level of consumption (equal to the level of the real wage bill), such that higher investment (driving up prices, lowering real wages) would appear to be associated with lower consumption spending. This is stabilizing. When investment falls, for example, prices will fall, and consequently real wages and therefore consumption spending will rise, offsetting the decline in investment.

But such a pattern of adjustment puts the burden on profits; prices would fall in a slump, and firms would have to draw down their reserves. Accordingly firms should seek to develop greater flexibility to allow them to adjust the level of employment to market conditions, laying off and rehiring workers as demand changed. This provides an important incentive to innovate (Nell, 1998).

Keynes did not examine this. But what he saw is that price adjustment was *not* working to stabilize the system. On the contrary, fluctuations in investment appeared to set off destabilizing movements. A key point of his lectures was to explain this, showing that investment and consumption *moved together, not inversely*, thereby increasing volatility. This is a consequence of reducing the rate of diminishing returns, "flattening" the production function. Furthermore, he argued that investment was the active variable, the causative force, while consumption (and saving) simply re-acted passively. So prices and employment could adjust in such a way that the real wage and the marginal product of labor were brought into equality, thereby maximizing profits, while investment and consumption moved together, rather than inversely, creating "multiplier"-based volatility in the system. There is no pressure in this system to move to full employment, but each position can reasonably be considered "equilibrium."

## Notes

1. Both Davidson and Chick show how aggregate demand and aggregate supply in nominal terms interact (following Davidson and Smolensky) to determine employment and nominal output. Changes in money wages and prices will shift these aggregate functions, and a money wage–employment curve can be defined. But no process is defined showing how real wages and marginal productivity adjust (Chick, 1983).
2. *Modigliani and Hicks interpreted Keynes's premise that the real wage would equal the marginal product of labor as implying that employment would be determined in the labor market, unless that market were prevented from working by some kind of "imperfection". The claim here is that Keynes can be understood quite differently; it is consistent with his argument that prices could adjust *relative to* money wages, in order to bring the real wage into alignment with productivity at the margin. In this case there would be no "labor market" of the traditional type, but as we shall see such a system of price adjustment will tend to provide stabilization (Modigliani, 1944). (However – a point that Keynes certainly did not see – such a tendency to stabilize will be eroded as technology develops, since technological improvement will provide business with a greater ability to adjust employment and output to the variations in demand.)
3. Keynes always distinguished wage movements from price movements; wages and prices responded to different market pressures, so could adjust separately. Of course, they would also influence each other. But even over long periods they could move differently; accordingly, in the *Treatise*, he distinguished wage inflation and profit inflation.
4. Early capitalism, through the nineteenth century, appears to have had a weak built-in automatic stabilizer in a "price mechanism," which depended on technological inflexibility, and moved countercyclically, in tandem with the monetary system. This was swept away with the advent of mass production, and replaced by a volatile pattern of adjustment, in the multiplier augmented by the accelerator (or capital-stock adjustment process), so that the system came to rely on Government for stabilization. This has explored for six countries, the United States, the United Kingdom, Canada, Germany, Japan and Argentina, in which adjustment during the period 1870–1914 is contrasted with that in 1950–1990. Evidence of a weakly stabilizing price mechanism is found in all six in the early period; the transition to a multiplier-based adjustment is apparent in all but Argentina, which did not seem to fully accomplish the transition to a modern economy during the period studied (Nell ed., 1998; Modigliani, 1944).
5. This is a short-run relationship in which given plant and equipment is operated with more or less labor. Marshall and Pigou arguably operated with such a conception (Hicks, 1989). A "true" production function, Hicks (1963),

would require changing the technique when the amount of labor per unit capital varied. This is not a viable conception, as the "capital controversies" showed (Kurz and Salvadori, 1995; Laibman and Nell, 1977).
6. In post-War Mass Production (Nell, 1988, 1998), by contrast, constant returns prevail in the short run; to put it differently, unit costs are broadly constant. Workers need only be semi-skilled and teams can easily be broken up and re-formed; processes can be operated at varying levels of intensity in response to variations in demand, and they can easily be shut down and started up. It is likewise easy to layoff and recall workers. The widespread existence of constant unit costs came to light beginning with the debate on prices and pricing in the 1930s and 40s, cf. Hall and Hitch, 1938, Andrews, 1949, 1964. The suggestion here is that constant costs were the result of technological developments in manufacturing processes (Hunter, 1979). The evidence for constant costs is summarized and discussed in Lavoie, 1992, Chapter 3. Under constant costs, of course, the real wage will not be governed by marginal productivity.
7. To move from individual firms to the aggregate it is not necessary to hold the composition of output constant, so long as the movements are small. In both Craft and Mass Production the adjustment is better shown in two sectors. The aggregate function oversimplifies. When proportions of capital to consumer goods change in the Craft world, prices change; when they change in Mass Production the degree of utilization changes, but unit costs and prices are not affected.
8. The Penn World Tables provide data making it possible to plot output per head against capital per head with a large number of observations. When this is done for the advanced OECD economies, the scatter diagram shows no evidence of curvature. The same plot for the backward economies exhibits pronounced curvature, for middle-range economies moderate curvature. Of course this can be considered no more than suggestive.
9. Wages and salaries in the aggregate are closely correlated with Consumption spending, but do not fully explain it. Some obvious adjustments are easily made. Consumer spending also depends on the terms and availability of consumer credit. In addition it reflects transfer payments. Wealth and profitability are significant variables. But for the present purposes, which are purely illustrative, a simple "absolute income" theory will suffice.
10. This, of course, directly contradicts one of Modigliani's most celebrated contributions, the life cycle hypothesis. But half a century of empirical evidence has shown that in the United States (and other advanced countries) household consumption spending tracks wage and salary income "too closely" for any simple version of the life cycle hypothesis to be correct. Deaton, *Understanding Consumption*, Clarendon Press.
11. Nothing is implied in this discussion about the marginal product of capital. Since capital is given in amount and fixed in form, no change is possible, and its marginal product is not defined (Deaton, 1992).
12. It is tempting to set the model out in the form $Y = AN\alpha$, so that $w/p = \alpha A N^{\alpha-1}$. Then $\alpha$ becomes the parameter governing the rate at which returns diminish. However, the power function is only one of several forms that the relationship between $Y$ and $N$ might take. In particular the log form will be important.

13. Rymes, in *Keynes's Lectures, 1932–1935*, pp. 37–8 suggests that the real argument of the "Manifesto" by Robinson and Kahn concerned this effect. Rymes argues "If the increase in investment... results in a sufficient increase in demand, not only a higher price but also an increase in the costs of production facing the entrepreneur in the consumption goods sector, such that the new equilibrium, ..., entails a higher outlay on consumption goods, then it is possible the decline in the *output* of consumption goods could, in terms of effects on the volume of employment, more than offset the increase in the output of capital goods." Investment increases and consumption declines.
14. "Forced saving" was traditionally ascribed to the effects of an exceptional increase in the quantity of money, leading to a bidding up of prices, lowering consumption and so making an expansion of investment possible. One issue was whether the resulting increase in capital was permanent or temporary; another concerned the effect of the higher prices on rentiers. How the money supply was increased also became an issue, as did the relationship to interest rates. (See also Malthus, 1811; Ricardo, 1810; and Keynes, 1940, as well as those cited above.)
15. But the process cannot continue for too long, for with I rising and C falling, the ratio of capital goods to consumer goods will be moving further and further from its normal level. Nell, 1998, pp. 458–9. However, the monetary/credit system may support prices for too long, – "overshooting" – provoking a sharp crash.
16. Linear functions and plausible relations between parameters appear to provide unique positive solutions.
17. We can study these equations by writing them out with a Cobb–Douglas production function and linear coefficients in the other functions; the procedure for solution is simple. This will show that there is no partitioning of the model.
18. That is, employment is *not* determined in the labor market. It follows directly from the demand for output, given the output-employment function – as in Kalecki. Hicks, following Keynes, initially modeled effective demand by setting up the IS–LM system together with a labor market and a conventional production function. Later he came to feel that this was a mistake (Hicks, 1977, 1989). But if returns are constant and there is no marginal productivity adjustment, the markup must be explained. Cf. Rima, 2003.
19. On these assumptions Investment determines – and equals – realized Profits. When households save a certain percentage out of wages and salaries the Consumption line will swing below the Wages line – Profits will be reduced. When wealth-owning households (or businesses subsidizing top managers) add to their consumption spending in proportion to the level of activity, this swings the $C+I$ line upwards, increasing Profits.
20. The output multiplier in this simple example will be $1/(1-wn)$, where w is the real wage and n is labor per unit of output.

# References

Andrews, P. W. S. 1949. *Manufacturing Business*. London: Macmillan.
Andrews, P. W. S. 1964. *On Competition in Economic Theory*. London: Macmillan.

Asimakopulos, A. 1988. *Investment, Employment, and Income Distribution*. Boulder, CO: Westview Press.

Blanchard, O. and Fischer, S. 1989. *Lectures on Macroeconomics*. Cambridge, MA: MIT Press.

Chick, V. 1983. *Macroeconomics After Keynes*. Oxford: Philip Alan.

Davidson, P. 1994. *Post Keynesian Macroeconomic Theory*. Cheltenham: Edward Elgar.

Deaton, A. 1992. *Understanding Consumption*. Oxford: Clarendon Press.

Dunlop, J. H. 1938. "The Movement of Real and Money Wage Rates". *Economic Journal*, 48: 413–34.

Hall, R. and Hitch, C. 1938. "Price Theory and Business Behavior", in P. W. S. Andrews, (ed.) *Oxford Studies in the Price Mechanism*. Oxford: Oxford University Press.

Hayek, F. 1932. *Monetary Theory and the Trade Cycle*. Trans N. Kaldor and H. Croome. New York: Harcourt Brace.

Hayek, F. A. 1941. *The Pure Theory of Capital*. London: Routledge and Kegan Paul.

Hicks, J. R. 1989. *A Market Theory of Money*. Oxford: Clarendon Press.

Hicks, J. R. 1977. *Economic Perspectives*. Oxford: Clarendon Press.

Hicks, J. R. 1963. *A Theory of Wages, 2nd ed*. London: Macmillan.

Hunter, L. C. 1979. *A History of Industrial Power in the US*. 3 vols. Charlottesville: University of Virginia Press.

Keynes, J. M. 1930. *Treatise on Money*. London: Macmillan.

Keynes, J. M. 1936. *The General Theory of Employment, Interest and Money*. London: Macmillan.

Keynes, J. M. 1940. *How to Pay for the War*. Toronto: Macmillan of Canada.

Keynes, J. M. (1971–1989). *The Collected Writings of John Maynard Keynes*, 30 volumes, general editors D. E. Moggridge and E. A. G. Robinson, volume editors E. S. Johnson and D. E. Moggridge, London: Macmillan, and New York: Cambridge University Press, for the Royal Economic Society.

Kurz, H. and Salvadori, N. 1995. *Theory of Production*. Cambridge: Cambridge University Press.

Laibman, D. and Nell, E.J. 1977. "ReSwitching, Wicksell Effects and Neoclassical Production Function" *American Economic Review*, 63: 100–13.

Lavoie, M. 1992. *Post Keynesian Economics*. Cheltenham: Edward Elgar.

Malthus, T. R. 1811. "Depreciation of Paper Currency," *Edinburgh Review*, Vol. XVII, pp. 339–72, as reprinted in T. R. Malthus, *Five Papers on Political Economy*, ed. Cyril Renwick, No. 3 in a Series of Reprints of Works on Economics and Economic History Issued by the Faculty of Economics of the University of Sydney, Australia, 1953.

Modigliani, F. 1944. "Liquidity Preference and the Theory of Interest and Money" *Econometrica*, vol. 12, pp. 45–88.

Nell, E. J. 1988. *Prosperity and Public Spending*. Boston: Unwin Hyman.

Nell, E. J. 1992. *Transformational Growth and Effective Demand*. New York: New York University Press.

Nell, E. J. 1998. *The General Theory of Tranformational Growth*. Cambridge: Cambridge University Press.

Nell, E. J. (ed.) 1998. *Transformational Growth and the Business Cycle*. London and New York: Routledge.

Ricardo, D. 1810. *The High Price of Bullion, a Proof of the Depreciation of Bank Notes*, London: John Murray, as reprinted in *The Works and Correspondence of David Ricardo*, ed. P. Sraffa with M. H. Dobb, Vol. III, Cambridge, UK: Cambridge University Press for the Royal Economic Society, 1951.

Rima, I. 2003. "From Profit margins to Income Distribution: Joan Robinson's Odyssey from Marginal Productivity Theory". *Review of Political Economy*, 15(4).

Robertson, D. 1931. "Wage-Grumbles", in *Economic Fragments*, 42–57.

Rymes, T. K. 1989. (ed.) *Keynes's Lectures, 1932–35: Notes of a Representative Student*, Ann Arbor: University of Michigan Press.

Tarshis, L. 1938. "Real Wages in the United States and Great Britain". *Canadian Journal of Economics and Political Science*, 4(3): 362–76.

Tarshis, L. 1939. "Changes in Real and Money Wages". *Economic Journal*, 49: 150–4.

Thornton, H. 1802. *An Inquiry into the Nature and Effects of the Paper Credit of Great Britain*, London, as reprinted with introduction by F. A. Hayek, London: George Allen & Unwin, 1939.

# 12
# Keynes's Approach to Money: What can be Recovered?

L. Randall Wray

This chapter will first take a retrospective look at Keynes's *General Theory* approach to money. We next turn to the neoclassical synthesis approach to money to determine what was retained, and what was shed, from Keynes's approach. Finally, we examine what needs to be recovered to create a coherent and useful approach to money that synthesizes Keynes's early insights with more recent developments in monetary theory.

## Keynes's approach to money in the *General Theory*

Elsewhere I have argued that Keynes adopted two contradictory approaches to money in the *General Theory* (Wray 2006). The first approach is the more familiar "supply and demand" equilibrium model of Chapters 13 and 15, incorporated within conventional macroeconomics textbooks. The second is presented in Chapter 17, where Keynes drops money supply and demand in favor of a liquidity preference approach to asset prices. I argued that the supply and demand approach suffers from problems of interdependency, and is not consistent with his general approach, while the liquidity preference approach of Chapter 17 is critical to our understanding of the role money plays in causing unemployment. In this section, I will briefly summarize only the approach taken in Chapter 17.

In Chapter 17, Keynes presents a general theory of asset prices (Kregel 1997). The expected nominal return to holding any asset is $q-c+l+a$, where $q$ is the asset's expected yield, $c$ is carrying costs, $l$ is liquidity, and $a$ is expected price appreciation. This total return can be used to calculate a marginal efficiency for each asset, including money. The composition of returns varies by asset, with most of the return to illiquid assets (i.e. capital) consisting of $q-c$, while most of the return to liquid assets consists of the $l$. If a producible asset's return exceeds that on money, it is produced up to the point that its marginal efficiency falls back into line with money's return that rules the roost. If an asset that is not producible has a higher marginal efficiency, its price is pushed up and its return falls back in line. Finally, changing expectations about the future have differential impacts on the marginal efficiencies of different kinds of assets. Increased confidence raises the $q$s on capital while lowering the subjective values assigned to liquid positions (hence, the $l$ falls), so that the marginal efficiency of capital rises relative to that of liquid assets. Capital assets will be produced (investment rises, inducing the "multiplier" impact) and the full range of asset prices adjusts. Thus, expectations about the future go into determining the equilibrium level of output and employment – defined as a position in which firms hire just the amount of labor required to produce the amount of output they expect to sell.

Two important conclusions follow from the Chapter 17 approach. First, it is the existence of money that prevents the economy from coming to equilibrium (state of rest) at less than full employment; and, second, Keynes does not need an exogenously fixed money supply to explain the determination of interest rates. The first is important to make the theoretical case against neoclassical theory, while the second implies that unemployment is not due to misguided monetary policy. The supply/demand approach taken in Chapters 13 and 15 would seem to imply that the central bank could eliminate unemployment by increasing the money supply, pushing the interest rate down, and inducing interest-sensitive spending. However, according to Keynes, the problem is more fundamental and cannot be resolved through monetary policy alone. Keynes argued the existence of money is the cause of unemployment, because "in the absence of money...the rates of interest would only reach equilibrium when there is full employment" (Keynes, 1964, p. 235). Here, he is referring to the spectrum of own rates, equalized in the absence of money only at full employment. However, money sets a standard that is often too high for full employment. Further, he cautioned that an "increase of the money supply" is not necessarily a solution, as "there may be several slips between the cup and the lip" (ibid., p. 173). If liquidity preference is rising faster (or, the marginal efficiencies of producibles are falling faster) than the money supply, it will not be possible to stimulate employment. He was thus "somewhat skeptical of the success of a merely monetary policy directed toward influencing the rate of interest.... since it seems likely that the fluctuations in the market estimation of the marginal efficiency of different types of capital... will be too great to be offset by any practicable changes in the rate of interest" (ibid., p. 164).

What is the shape of the money supply function that is consistent with the Chapter 17 exposition? The forces that equalize marginal efficiencies do not depend on any particular money supply function – all that matters is the way in which financing terms affect forward-looking marginal efficiencies at the time individual decisions are taken, when the marginal efficiency of a particular capital asset is weighed against the marginal efficiency of money. Whether a higher scale of activity will affect interest rates is neither known nor considered by the individual taking the *ex ante* decision to invest. He will consider his finance costs but it would be illegitimate to presume that effects on interest rates resulting from greater aggregate spending matter in this decision. Thus, whether the money supply curve is vertical, as in the textbooks, or horizontal, as in a popular version of endogenous money (see below) does not matter. All that is necessary is that money has "peculiar characteristics" that cause its marginal efficiency to "rule the roost." Interdependence of money supply and money demand functions does not pose a problem for the Chapter 17 approach – where equilibrium is defined not as money demand equals money supply, but as equality among own rates of interest. As I will argue below, this is important because few economists today believe that the money supply can be exogenous.

## Money in the neoclassical synthesis

There is little need to go through the neoclassical synthesis approach to money in great detail, because it is too well-known. However it should be noted that it is closely based on the Chapters 13/15 approach of the *General Theory*. Three markets are treated: (1) a goods market, (2) a money market, and (3) a bond market. Equilibrium is defined as the income and interest rate combination at which saving equals investment, money demand equals money supply, and bond demand equals bond supply. By Walras's Law, the bond market is usually dropped in favor of a two equation IS–LM model. As in Chapters 13/15 of the GT, money demand consists of three motives and is both interest rate and income elastic. The IS–LM model adopts an exogenous money supply fixed by policy (the usual deposit multiplier approach is often invoked). Indeed, derivation of the LM curve requires independence of money supply and money demand functions.

It is well-known that Hicks had created a version of the IS–LM model to compare the "classical" approach to Keynes's approach. In his March 31, 1937 letter to Hicks, Keynes raised two important objections to this framework. First, he argued that "From my point of view it is important to insist that my remark is to the effect that an increase in the inducement to invest *need* not raise the rate of interest. I should agree that, unless the monetary policy is appropriate, it is quite likely to" (Keynes, CW 14, p. 80). He argued that while an increase of planned spending – as well greater actual spending – raises money demand, it will raise interest rates only if money supply does not increase. When Hicks clarified the presentation in a model, Keynes did not like the resulting implication that a shift of the IS curve will change the equilibrium interest rate so long as the LM curve (or, money supply) is independent of spending. This seems to be more evidence that Keynes's approach in Chapters 13 and 15 did not adequately represent the general argument he was trying to make because he would not accept the assumption that spending increases while the money supply is necessarily fixed.

Keynes's second point was that the Hicks treatment places too much emphasis on *current* income, while "in the case of the inducement to invest, expected income for the period of the investment is the relevant variable" (ibid.). Keynes said he is willing to take both liquidity preference (money demand) and saving as a function of current income, but investment is forward-looking, a function of expected future income as that will go into determining future effective demand. The usual investment function that lies behind the IS curve is far too stable to represent what Keynes had in mind, and what he had presented in Chapter 17. The IS curve makes investment and saving functions of income and interest rates, but Keynes argued that while that might be appropriate for saving, it misrepresents investment, which is a function of expected future profit income.

More importantly, Keynes noted in his letter that he was preparing a lecture on the rate of interest, which became a response to the views of Hicks as well as those held by the Swedish school (Ohlin) and Robertson. There he detailed his objections to the loanable-funds approach, as well as to Robertson's attempts to add saving plus bank loans to obtain a hybrid source of finance. Keynes argued that saving is not equivalent to finance, indeed, "Saving has no special efficacy, as compared with consumption in releasing cash and restoring liquidity... There is, therefore, just as much reason for adding current consumption to the rate of increase of new bank money in reckoning the flow of cash becoming available to provide new 'finance,' as there is for adding current saving" (ibid., p. 233). Indeed, "Increased investment will always be accompanied by increased saving, but it can never be preceded by it. Dishoarding and credit expansion provides not an *alternative* to increased saving, but a necessary preparation for it. It is the parent, not the twin, of increased saving" (ibid., p. 281). Investment, itself, cannot pressure interest rates because it returns to the "revolving fund of finance," creating equivalent saving (ibid., p. 208).

Further, "unless the banking system is prepared to augment the supply of money, lack of finance may prove an important obstacle to more than a certain amount of investment decisions being on the tapis at the same time. But 'finance' has nothing to do with saving" (ibid., p. 247). If banks do relax to satisfy the finance motive, interest rates will not rise as the scale of activity increases. In other words, while Keynes adopts equality between investment and saving (as in the IS–LM framework), he rejects the notion that saving "finances" investment. Rather, only a reduction of hoarding or expansion of credit can "finance" rising investment. Finally, he noted, "to the extent that the overdraft system is employed and unused overdrafts ignored by the banking system, there is no superimposed pressure resulting from planned activity over and above the pressure resulting from actual activity" (ibid., pp. 222–3). In an "overdraft" system, an increase of investment spending (or any other type of spending that has access to overdrafts) is associated with expansion of bank loans, and hence, with expansion of the money supply (as bank deposits grow with lending). Here Keynes has gone further, arguing that even "planned spending" can lead to increased lending, if there is an attempt to accumulate money in advance of spending it (the finance motive). What is important is Keynes's recognition that the "goods market" and "money market" are not independent – rising spending can be (indeed, normally is expected to be) met by rising money supply, so that there is no pressure on interest rates.

Recall from above that Keynes blamed money for the existence of unemployment. An IS–LM model with Pigou (or real balance) and Keynes effects that make spending a function of the real money supply will achieve equilibrium only at full employment. To be sure, a large number of "rigidities" has been proposed to explain persistence of unemployment – ranging from wage and price stickiness to coordination failures. Still, without rigidities, full employment would be attained. By contrast, Keynes argued that equilibrium – defined throughout the *General Theory* as the point at which effective demand equals income, and in Chapter 17 as the point at which the marginal efficiency of capital equals the marginal efficiency of money – can occur at any level of employment. In the IS–LM model, the equilibrium (real) rate of interest associated with the intersection of the curves is consistent with the full employment level of income (again, in the absence of frictions). In the *General Theory* there is a different equilibrium interest rate associated with each level of income and employment, only one of which represents full employment. This is because, as described above, Keynes argues that in the absence of money the own rates could come to equality only at full employment, while in the presence of money, its own rate sets a standard that is usually too high to allow production to proceed on the necessary scale to achieve full employment. It is money, not rigidities, that causes unemployment in Keynes's view.

While the neoclassical synthesis approach to money is based on Keynes's presentation in Chapters 13 and 14, it is not consistent with his general argument, thus, reaches different conclusions. First, IS–LM equilibrium is achieved at a unique interest rate/income combination. Moreover, the goods and money markets are dichotomized such that it is possible to increase spending while holding money supply constant; except for extreme values of parameters, increased spending will raise the equilibrium level of interest rates, while increased money supply will lower the equilibrium interest rate. The money supply is exogenous, under control of the authorities. In the absence of rigidities, involuntary unemployment is eliminated through effects on prices that in turn affect spending through Pigou and Keynes effects. While the IS–LM model does not adopt a loanable-funds approach, it is relatively silent on the finance process involved when spending rises with a constant money supply. This requires velocity to increase, induced by rising interest rates. However, many or even most practitioners of the neoclassical synthesis have at least implicitly adopted a loanable-funds approach, especially in discussing the long run and in growth models where investment is constrained by saving propensities.

## What needs to be recovered from Keynes?

### Liquidity preference and endogenous money

Even orthodoxy now rejects central bank control of the quantity of money, and some orthodox approaches explicitly assume that the money supply – broadly defined to include bank deposits – expands as spending grows, rejecting exogeneity in favor of endogeneity. How do we reconcile liquidity preference theory with the reality that central banks today operate with a short-term rate target? Even if we accept complete discretionary control over the overnight rate, as well as substantial influence over other interest rates on instruments such as government bonds, this still leaves a role for liquidity preference in determining all other own rates. Keynes never argued for mono-causality, rather, he singled out the role played by liquidity preference because he believed that to be the ultimate barrier to operation of the economy at full employment. The authorities can lower interest rate targets in response to unemployment, but if marginal efficiencies of producibles (assets produced by labor) are too low, even enlightened policy would not generate full employment.

We can distinguish between money as a stock, desired due to liquidity preference, and money as a flow used to finance spending (Wray, 1990). Rising spending will normally lead to an increase in the money supply (defined as an increase of bank liabilities as banks make loans). Whether the loan interest rate rises depends on numerous factors, including expected policy and liquidity preference of banks – but neither a completely elastic (horizontal) supply of loans nor a completely inelastic (vertical) loan supply curve is likely. On the other hand, rising liquidity preference is associated with a reduction of planned spending as marginal efficiencies of producible assets fall relatively to the return to liquid assets. For this reason, money demand (defined as demand for loans to spend) could even fall when liquidity preference rises. Money supply will not normally rise to meet rising liquidity preference; instead, asset prices adjust across the full spectrum of assets until wealth holders are satisfied to hold the existing set of assets. Hence, endogenous money is reconciled with liquidity preference, with money demand here defined not as a desire for a hoard of money in advance of spending but as a flow demand for finance of spending.

Others, including most prominently Moore (1988), have adopted a "horizontalist" approach. There are two aspects to the argument. First, the supply of reserves is horizontal at the interest rate target chosen by the central bank. For several reasons (some of which are explored below), central banks cannot control the quantity of reserves. In any event, it is now accepted by most theorists and practitioners that central banks should and do operate with interest rate targets. This means that the supply of reserves accommodates the demand so that the interest rate target can be hit (termed "accommodationist"). The second part of the argument is that private banks also accommodate the demand for loans and deposits, "horizontally." To put it as simply as possible, banks take the overnight interest rate target as a measure of the marginal cost of funds, then "mark-down" to set the deposit rate of interest and "mark-up" to set the loan rate. A distinction is made between "retail" and "wholesale" markets and interest rate determination in each, but that is not important to our argument. What is critical, however, is the recognition that the demand for loans and for deposits is linked to planned spending. Thus, the "money supply" expands "horizontally" as spending rises, with no pressure on interest rates.

In conclusion, if spending is normally financed by increased money supply, it is not legitimate to dichotomize "real" and "monetary" variables. Rather, production should be analyzed as "monetary production," as Keynes argued (see next section). Analysis should not begin with the presumption that money can be neutral – it is in a sense, the "engine" behind production. Further, if money expands "endogenously," it is not legitimate to treat the quantity of money as fixed or otherwise under control of the central bank. This is not to say that expansion of money is fully automatic, always accommodating any desire to spend. Lack of access to money can constrain spending; in the terminology of the approach developed by Clower and Leijonhuvud, absence of money prevents "notional demand" from becoming "effective demand." The central bank can play a role in influencing the willingness of financial institutions to expand the money supply – not through mechanistic control of bank reserves but by changing its overnight interest rate target as well as by adoption of various forms of credit constraints.

## The nature of money and the cause of unemployment

If money causes unemployment, why are economies organized around its use? According to orthodoxy, money originated to reduce transactions costs, a position that is at odds with Keynes's proposition that money prevents the economy from operating at its efficient, full capacity, level. Keynes clearly thought that money serves a more fundamental purpose than to "lubricate" the market mechanism. In the preparation of the GT, he wrote "In my opinion the main reason why the problem of crises is unsolved, or at any rate why this theory is so unsatisfactory, is to be found in the lack of what might be termed a *monetary theory of production*" (Keynes, CW 13, p. 408). This would be one that would deal

> with an economy in which money plays a part of its own and affects motives and decisions and is, in short, one of the operative factors in the situation, so that the course of events cannot be predicted, either in the long period or in the short, without a knowledge of the

behaviour of money between the first state and the last. And it is this which we ought to mean when we speak of a monetary economy.

(Keynes, CW 13, pp. 408–9)

He distinguishes this from a "real-exchange economy" that might use money, but "does not allow it to enter into motives or decisions" – in other words, one in which money is neutral (ibid.). By contrast, in Keynes's approach, money cannot be neutral, whether in the long run or the short run.

In the TOM, Keynes argued the "money of account comes into existence along with debts, which are contracts for deferred payment, and price lists, which are offers of contracts for sale or purchase.... [and] can only be expressed in terms of a money of account" (Keynes, CW 5, p. 3). That is, the money of account, money-denominated debts, and the price system emerged simultaneously. This is in contrast to the typical textbook presentation in which trade and relative prices exist before barterers settle on use of one commodity as a medium of exchange. In Keynes's view, prices are *nominal* and require a money of account in which they can be expressed. He distinguished between "money and money of account by saying that the money of account is the description or title and the money is the thing which answers to the description" (ibid.). Further, the state "claims the right to determine what thing corresponds to the name, and to vary its declaration from time to time – when, that is to say, it claims the right to re-edit the dictionary. This right is claimed by all modern States and has been so claimed for some four thousand years at least" (Keynes, CW 5, p. 4). Finally, "the age of chartalist or State money was reached when the State claimed the right to declare what thing should answer as money to the current money of account – when it claimed the right not only to enforce the dictionary but also to write the dictionary. Today all civilised money is, beyond possibility of dispute, chartalist" (ibid.).

Keynes got the "state money" or "chartalist" approach from Innes (1913) and Knapp (1924). The basic argument is that the state adopts a currency, imposes taxes in that currency, and issues the currency that it accepts in tax payment (Keynes, 1914). Taxpayers "redeem" the state's own money in payments made to the state. While we will not go into the history of money in detail, Keynes, Innes, and Knapp all argued that not only are modern money systems based on a state money, but that state money can be traced back through time to the earliest civilizations. This presents a challenge for the typical orthodox story about a commodity money replacing barter, with the money form slowly evolving to reduce private transactions costs. The most importance difference between the orthodox and the state money approaches concerns the role of the state – chartalism cannot imagine a monetary system without a state that imposes taxes to "back-up" the currency.

Hence, the state's money represents an obligation – the promise to "redeem" it in payment of taxes. Money and debt are inextricably linked – first because debts are denominated in the money of account, and second because all "money things" are created as liabilities of the issuers. The issuer is obligated to redeem the debt issued, either by canceling debts (including tax debts) owed by the redeemer, or in the case of convertible debt by delivering whatever has been promised for redemption. Except for money issued by the sovereign, most "money things" are convertible into other money things – often the liabilities of the sovereign treasury or central bank. On a gold standard, the sovereign promises to convert its liabilities to gold at a fixed exchange rate. While this is often called a "commodity money system," Keynes recognized that even gold standards are chartalist because the sovereign chooses the unit of account, issues state money or "money proper" denominated in that unit, and determines the rate of conversion of money proper into gold. Even if gold coins are used, it is not the value of the embodied gold that determines the value of the coin. The coin represents a state liability that happens to be stamped on gold, and will be accepted at government pay houses at a nominal value set by the state. There are complex historical reasons for the development of the gold standard, including a desire to constrain state spending, but the gold standard should not be taken as evidence that money used to take the form of commodities. Even gold coins are IOUs, redeemed in payments to the state.

While there remain some holes in our understanding of money's evolution and its essential nature, Goodhart concludes that "the chartalist/credit approach is historically valid, while the metallist/Mengerian/mainstream view of money arising as a means of reducing transactions costs is nothing but a pure myth, a fable" (Goodhart, 2005, p. 760). He goes on: "Does it matter? It can. Both Ingham and I have attributed part of the incorrect analysis of the European Monetary Union, and the current problems of relating (federal) monetary policies to (national) fiscal policies, to bad monetary theory" (Goodhart, 2005, p. 761; see also Goodhart, 1998 and Ingham, 2004). Orthodoxy focuses on money as a transactions-cost reducing medium of exchange, ignoring or downplaying its chartalist and credit nature, thereby pushing to the side other important roles played by money – most importantly the role played by money in causing unemployment as well as the possibility that government can use its sovereign power over money to implement policy in the public purpose, as explored in the next section.

### An alternative view of fiscal and monetary policy

Summarizing the argument to this point: rather than highlighting the "lubricating" role played by money in exchange, Keynes had emphasized the unit of account, as well as the role played by the state in "writing the dictionary." By imposing tax liabilities in the state's unit of account, payable in its own "money proper," the state establishes not only the conditions required for private creation of monetary contracts, but also for using government spending to raise effective demand. The significance is that the state is able to spend by emitting its own IOUs, required by the population to pay taxes (Wray, 1998). The important thing is that use of a state money makes it possible to implement Keynes's Chapter 24 fiscal policies to raise aggregate demand. Neither "money" nor "finance" needs to be a barrier to adopting full employment policy because sovereign government can spend on the necessary scale to mobilize resources.

This should not be misinterpreted as a call to "run the printing presses" in a manner that could cause hyperinflation. Virtually, all approaches to money at least since the time of Adam Smith have warned of the problems caused by "too much money," and almost all of them have emphasized the importance of using policy to "control money." Indeed, as alluded to above, part of the reason for enforcing a gold standard was to limit the creation of money. With the hands of government tied by a gold standard, the Currency School wanted to similarly control private bank note issue by forcing banks to hold 100% reserves against their liabilities. Later, the "real bills doctrine" sought to limit money creation to the needs of trade, while monetarism used a version of the quantity theory along with the notion of a deposit multiplier to advance the argument for a rule requiring the central bank to keep money growth to a constant rate to achieve price stability. There have always been dissenters to this tradition: the Banking School argued that the "law of reflux" would ensure that banks would not issue too many notes, so long as they were required to redeem them on demand for coin; Greenbackers demanded expansion of the supply of currency as well as easy credit; Kaldor, the Radcliffe Committee, and Gurley and Shaw all doubted that control over narrow money could limit spending because velocity is variable (Wray, 1990, 1998, and 2004). More recently, several versions of "endogenous money," including horizontalism, insist that the central bank has no control over reserves or the money supply (Moore, 1988; Lavoie, 1985). What is most interesting is how the terms of the debate moved gradually to focus almost exclusively on central bank activities while downplaying the effect of fiscal operations on the money supply.

Indeed, as noted above, the IS–LM framework dichotomizes fiscal and monetary policy, with fiscal policy having to do with the IS curve and monetary policy concerned with the LM curve. Hence, holding monetary policy unchanged, an increase of government spending shifts the IS curve and raises interest rates while money supply is not affected. Alternatively, holding fiscal policy constant, the central bank can increase the money supply (causing interest rates to fall, and/or causing prices to rise). Such an argument certainly would have appeared strange to either side in the Currency School-Banking School debates, which took it for granted that increased government spending would be accompanied by increased government notes (Wray, 1990, p. 106). The idea that a central bank, rather than a treasury, might make money drops from a helicopter would have also appeared bizarre! Central banks, of course, were viewed as profit-seeking institutions that had to be prodded to consider the public interest. In any case, even when central banks intervene they are cognizant of their balance sheets and provide reserves only against collateral or in exchange for outright ownership of assets. A treasury might flood markets with notes, but a central bank would not.

How should these issues be framed in the modern context, with the money of account established by sovereign government, with state money issued by government, and with more-or-less independent central banks? We can combine Keynes's approach with a version of the endogenous money approach that emphasizes the nondiscretionary nature of bank reserves.

A sovereign government spends by issuing liabilities denominated in its money of account; these are accepted by the nongovernment sector, ultimately, because they can be used in tax payment (of course other, subsidiary or derived, uses also create demand for the government's fiat money). When government receives tax payments, these are in the form of its own liabilities. This makes it clear that the taxes do not really "pay for" the government's spending, rather, government spending is the source of the means of tax payment – and, as discussed above, government liabilities are "redeemed" in payment of taxes. There is no reason for government spending and tax receipts to be equal over any particular period; the budget can be in deficit (outstanding government liabilities rise) or in surplus (outstanding government liabilities fall). However, a continuous government surplus would eventually eliminate all means of tax payment – unless an alternative to government spending exists whereby taxpayers can obtain government liabilities (such as through loans from the central bank). <u>On the other hand, a continuous budget deficit allows the nongovernment sector to accumulate net wealth in the form of government liabilities.</u>

Modern governments separate treasury operations from the operations of the central bank to some degree – through a combination of operating procedures as well as legal constraints. In the United States, the Treasury is required to write checks on its account at the Fed, in which it must have deposits to spend. It obtains deposits by transferring funds from its accounts at private banks; these funds are obtained either from tax payments or by selling treasuries. This makes it appear that the Treasury's spending is constrained by its "money in the bank." However, in practice, complicated procedures have been developed to ensure that the Treasury can always write checks when it needs to make payments. For example, if the flow of tax receipts is not sufficient, the Treasury sells bonds to special depositories that are allowed to buy the bonds *without having their reserves at the Fed debited* (Wray, 1998; Bell and Wray, 2002–2003).This is done to avoid undesired impacts on bank reserves that would occur when the Treasury shifts its deposits from the banks buying bonds to its deposits at the Fed. The Treasury can then cut checks; when these are deposited in private banks, reserves are credited to the receiving banks and simultaneously debited from the special banks that had previously bought treasury bonds.

The end result is that banks hold government bonds as assets and demand deposits as liabilities. It is as if money were created so that the Treasury could borrow and spend – evading any restrictions placed on the Fed that prevents it from "lending" to the Treasury. All of this is done to ensure that (a) the Treasury can spend and (b) fiscal operations will not affect banking system reserves. The overall effect, however, is equivalent to having the Treasury directly credit bank accounts (reserves on the asset side, bank deposits on the liability side) when it spends, and directly debiting them (reducing reserves and deposits) when taxes are paid. (See Bell, 2000 and Bell and Wray, 2002–2003 for details.)

Note that bond sales and purchases are required to achieve equilibrium in the interbank market for reserves. The Treasury sells bonds in the new issue market, and the Fed sells or buys them in open market operations; while the Treasury doesn't buy bonds, it retires them. It is commonly believed these Treasury operations are part of fiscal policy, while Fed operations are part of monetary policy. However, both achieve the same purpose: aligning the quantity of reserves with the desires of the banking system. As such, whether bond sales and purchases (or retirement) are undertaken by the Fed or Treasury, they are best conceived as accomplishing the goal of monetary policy, which is to hit an overnight interest rate target. Continuous budget deficits would generate excess reserve positions – and cause overnight rates to fall below target – unless they triggered bond sales, either in the new issue market or through open market sales. Continuous budget surpluses would drain reserves and place upward pressure on overnight rates, triggering bond purchases (or retirement). It is important to note that effects on interest rates are precisely the reverse of the comparative statics that come out of the simple IS–LM model – according to which an increase of government spending raises interest rates. The reason is because this model illegitimately holds the quantity of money constant. Indeed, even conventional analysis (e.g., by Ben Friedman, 1978) concluded that better treatment of stocks in the IS–LM framework could easily reverse these results, so that budget deficits could lower interest rates.

There is an enormous literature on central bank independence. It is presumed that the central bank can assert its independence, refusing to "monetize" treasury spending. Actually, this would require that the central bank "bounce" treasury checks or that it refuse to clear accounts among banks. This is never observed in any modern developed nation because reserves are supplied on demand to hit interest rate targets. The central bank always clears treasury checks and facilitates clearing among banks. The independence that modern central banks enjoy is the ability to set overnight interest rate targets, more or less free from interference by treasury officials or politicians. However, this independence actually requires that the central bank always maintains just the right amount of reserves in the banking system – fully accommodating demand. This, in turn, requires automatic accommodation to any adverse effects of fiscal operations on banking system reserves – eliminating any independence of the central bank to "choose" not to accommodate the treasury. Hence, "independence" only means ability to choose the overnight interest rate target.

## Keynes and the international monetary system

According to Keynes, state money may take any of three forms: "Commodity Money, Fiat Money and Managed Money, the last two being sub-species of Representative Money" (Keynes, 1971, Vol V of CW). Commodity money is defined as "actual units of a particular freely obtainable, non-monopolised commodity which happens to have been chosen for the familiar purposes of money," or "warehouse warrants for actually existing units of the commodity" (ibid.). Fiat money is representative money "which is created and issued by the State, but is not convertible by law into anything other than itself, and has no fixed value in terms of an objective standard" (ibid.). This is distinguished from managed money, which "is similar to Fiat Money, except that the State undertakes to manage the conditions of its issue in such a way that, by convertibility or otherwise, it shall have a determinant value in terms of an objective standard" (ibid., p. 8). Managed money is, according to Keynes, the most generalized form of money, which can "degenerate into Commodity Money on the one side when the managing authority holds against it a hundred per cent of the objective standard, so that it is in effect a warehouse warrant, and into Fiat Money on the other side when it loses its objective standard" (ibid.). Both the gold standard and the Bretton Woods system of fixed but adjustable exchange rates were managed money systems. Most developed countries now have fiat money systems – the dollar in the United States, the yen in Japan, and so on. While the euro is a fiat money in the sense that it is not "convertible by law into anything other than itself," the individual members of the EMU are users, not issuers, of the euro. Hence, the euro nations are operating toward the "commodity money" end of the managed money spectrum.

Keynes put forward an alternative "Bancor plan" to what became the Bretton Woods system that would have had fixed (but adjustable) exchange rates combined with a mechanism for penalizing both trade deficit as well as trade surplus nations, in order to promote "reflux" of international reserves. This would have reduced the "beggar thy neighbor" accumulation of hoards of international reserves that puts a downward bias on global effective demand. After the break-up of the Bretton Woods system, some believed that international market forces would produce balanced trade in floating rate regimes; in fact, not only has trade become more imbalanced, but international exchange rate crises have proliferated. Some Post Keynesians, and others, have returned to Keynes's original plan, calling for reinstatement of some sort of fixed exchange rate system. However, there appears to be very little political support for the level of international cooperation that would be required to reproduce anything like a Bretton Woods system.

One could argue that the world has come full circle since Keynes. In Europe, nations have pegged their fortunes to the euro, abandoning their own currencies. Similarly, many developing nations in Asia and

Latin and South America experiment with exchange rate pegs and mercantilists policies; a few nations have won at this game, but many others have suffered high unemployment, low growth, and periodic exchange rate crises (Goodhart, 1998; Wray, 1998). Abandoning national currencies severely constrains both fiscal and monetary policy as the government tries to build international reserves to protect exchange rates and to finance government spending. Chronic unemployment is often necessary to constrain aggregate demand in a hopeless competitive struggle for export markets. Most developed countries outside Euroland operate "fiat money" systems based on a sovereign and floating currency, but still use domestic policy to constrain effective demand, as in Keynes's day, to influence both the exchange rate and the trade balance.

Is there an alternative, Keynesian, strategy for the 21st century? In the GT, Keynes concluded that "under the system of domestic laissez-faire and an international gold standard... there was no means open to a government whereby to mitigate economic distress at home except through the competitive struggle for markets" (GT, p. 382). Under such a system, "the City of London gradually devised the most dangerous technique for the maintenance of equilibrium which can possibly be imagined, namely the technique of bank rate [adjusting the interest rate target to achieve the desired trade balance] coupled with a rigid parity of the foreign exchanges" (GT, p. 339). A "managed" but flexible exchange rate frees domestic policy to pursue internal stability. So long as a sovereign nation lets its currency float, it does have the possibility of using domestic policy to pursue full employment and economic growth: It can set its interest rate target without worrying about effects on exchange rates; and can adopt expansionary fiscal policy without worrying about effects of trade deficits on exchange rates or international reserve balances. In that case, "[I]nternational trade would cease to be what it is, namely, a desperate expedient to maintain employment at home by forcing sales on foreign markets... but a willing and unimpeded exchange of goods and services in conditions of mutual advantage" (GT, pp. 282–3). With a floating rate and domestic policy geared toward full employment, then the "real and substantial" advantages of trade, as Keynes put it, can be enjoyed. On the other hand, if domestic policy is geared to depress demand in order to run trade surpluses, the benefits of trade cannot be reaped.

In short, given current political realities that make international monetary system reform along the lines of Keynes's Bancor plan unlikely, sovereign currencies and floating rates are the best ways to promote fiscal and monetary policy independence.

### Role of government in causing – and curing – unemployment

What we can recover from Keynes as well as from other authors before him is the role played by the state in choosing the unit of account and in issuing money denominated in that account. Rather than dichotomizing "monetary" versus "real," we can recognize the necessary interdependence of spending and money. Government spending should be at the level required to achieve and maintain full employment. Its spending, in turn, essentially takes the form of crediting bank accounts. Because the "money supply" is not held constant as government spending rises, this will not pressure interest rates. Indeed, all else equal, increased government spending financed by crediting bank accounts will *lower* interest rates. This is why fiscal policy must be coordinated with monetary policy – offsetting behavior by the central bank to ensure banks have the level of reserves required (or desired) so that overnight interest rate targets are hit. While all of this might seem strange to the generations raised on the IS–LM model, it was quite obvious to economists who read the *General Theory* before it was filtered through Hicks and Hansen – see Lerner (1947) and Friedman (1948).

Indeed, we can go further. Recalling Keynes's claim that unemployment results because of the existence of money, and recalling his argument that money is and has been chartalist for at least the past 4000 years, it is difficult to avoid the conclusion that government is to blame for unemployment since it is responsible for money. Let us examine why.

While "Keynesian" policy has become nearly synonymous with "micro-management" and "fine-tuning," Keynes actually insisted that private markets perform tolerably well in allocating resources, given the level of effective demand:

> To put the point concretely, I see no reason to suppose that the existing system seriously misemploys the factors of production which are in use.... It is in determining the volume, not the direction, of actual employment that the existing system has broken down.
> (Keynes, 1964, p. 379)

Hence, "If we suppose the volume of output to be given, i.e. to be determined by forces outside the classical scheme of thought, then there is no objection to be raised against the classical analysis..." (Keynes, 1964, p. 378). The problem is that because the "classical" analysis has no role for money to play, it cannot explain unemployment, nor can it find a solution to the two "outstanding faults of the economic society in which we live," "its failure to provide for full employment and it arbitrary and inequitable distribution of wealth and income" (Keynes, 1964, p. 372). Both of these problems are linked to the existence of chartal money, whose origins can be traced to government.

If government refuses to spend by crediting bank accounts on the necessary scale to raise effective demand to the full employment level, then unemployment results. Further, because money's own rate sets the standard that must be achieved by all other assets, if interest rates are too high then private spending is too low to achieve full employment. Finally, a high interest rate rewards "no genuine sacrifice" but keeps capital scarce, resulting in "high stakes" and a "rentier aspect of capitalism" (Keynes, 1964, pp. 374, 376). Lower interest rates would euthanize the rentier, establishing a "basic rate of reward" for owners of capital, so that "if adequate demand is adequate, average skill and average good fortune will be enough" (Keynes, 1964, pp. 378, 381).

It is mostly the fiscal policy that exerts control over the quantity of state money, while monetary policy controls the "basic reward" to owners of assets. Proper fiscal policy will ensure that government spending and the quantity of money that results will be at the correct level to achieve full employment. Monetary policy will maintain a lower bar (low overnight rate) for the performance of assets so that own rates come to equality only when capital is no longer scarce. While the return to holding assets will be pushed to a lower level, returns will be more certain in an economy that operates at a higher level. With lower returns to "luck," excessive inequality will be reduced. Thus, the twin policies of expansionary fiscal policy (that increases money supply) and lower interest rates administered by the central bank (that encourages creation of producible assets) will attenuate the two extraordinary faults of the monetary production economy. Such "twin" expansionary thrusts are made possible by the use of state money, redeemed only in tax payment. This allows both fiscal policy and monetary policy independence to pursue domestic stability.

## References

Bell, Stephanie. "Do taxes and bonds finance government spending?" *Journal of Economic Issues*, 34: 2000, 603–20.

Bell, Stephanie and L. Randall Wray. "Fiscal impacts on reserves and the independence of the fed", *Journal of Post Keynesian Economics*, 25(2): Winter 2002–2003, 263–71.

Friedman, Benjamin, "Crowding out or crowding in? Economic consequences of financing government deficits", *Brookings Papers on Economic Activity*, 3: 1978, 593–653.

Friedman, Milton. "A monetary and fiscal framework for economic stability", *American Economic Review*, 38(June): 1948, 245–64.

Goodhart, Charles A. E. "Two concepts of money: implications for the analysis of optimal currency areas", *European Journal of Political Economy*, 14: 1998, 407–32.

Goodhart, Charles A. E. "Review of credit and state theories of money: the contributions of A. Mitchell Innes", *History of Political Economy*, 37(4): Winter, 2005, 759–61.

Innes, A. Mitchell. "What is money?" *Banking Law Journal*, 30(5): May 1913, 377–408, in Wray, L. R. ed. *Credit and State Theories of Money*, Northampton: Edward Elgar 2004, pp. 14–49.

Ingham, Geoffrey 2004. "The emergence of capitalist credit money". In Wray, L. R. ed. *Credit and State Theories of Money*, Northampton: Edward Elgar 2004, pp. 50–78.

Keynes, John M. "What is Money?" *Economic Journal* 24(95): September 1914, 419–21.

Keynes, John M. *The General Theory of Employment, Interest, and Money*, Harcourt Brace Jovanovich: New York and London 1964.

Keynes, John M. *"The Collected Writings of John Maynard Keynes"*, In D. E. Moggridge ed., London: Macmillan and New York: Cambridge University Press for the Royal Economic Society.

Keynes, John M. Vol. IV. *A Tract on Monetary Reform*, 1971a.

Keynes, John M. Vol. V. *A Treatise on Money*, vol. 1 *The Pure Theory of Money*, 1971b.

Keynes, John M. Vol. VI. *A Treatise on Money*, vol. 2 *The Applied Theory of Money*, 1971c.

Keynes, John M. Vol. XIII. *The General Theory and After Part I Preparation*, 1973a.

Keynes, John M. Vol. XIV. *The General Theory and After Part II Defense and Development*, 1973b.

Keynes, John M. Vol. XXVIII. *Social, Political and Literary Writings*, 1982.

Knapp, Georg F. *The State Theory of Money*. Reprint, Augustus M. Kelley, (1924) 1973.

Kregel, J. A. "The theory of value, expectations and Chapter 17 of *The General Theory*". In G. C. Harcourt and P. A. Riach eds., *A "Second Edition" of The General Theory*, vol. 1, London and New York: Routledge, 1997, pp. 261–82.

Lavoie, Marc. "Credit and money: The dynamic circuit, overdraft economics, and post Keynesian economics". In Jarsulic, Marc ed., *Money and Macro Policy*, Boston, Dordrecht, Lancaster: Boston-Dordrecht-Lancaster, 1985, p. 63.

Lerner, Abba P. 1947. "Money as a creature of the state", *American Economic Review*, 7: 312–17.

Moore, Basil. *Horizontalists and Verticalists: The Macroeconomics of Credit Money*, Cambridge: Cambridge University Press, 1988.

Wray, L. Randall. *Understanding Modern Money: The Key to Full Employment and Price Stability*. Cheltenham, UK: Edward Elgar, 1998.

Wray, L. Randall. *Money and Credit in Capitalist Economies: The Endogenous Money Approach*. Aldershot, UK: Edward Elgar, 1990.

Wray, L. Randall. "Keynes's approach to money: an assessment after seventy years", *Atlantic Economic Journal*, 34: 2006, 183–93.

# 13
# Keynes's Revolutionary and "Serious" Monetary Theory

*Paul Davidson*

> It seems to me that economics is a branch of logic: a way of thinking.... One can make some quite worthwhile progress merely by using axioms and maxims. But one cannot get very far except by devising new and improved models. This requires... vigilant observation of the actual working of our system. Progress is economics consists almost entirely in a progressive movement in the choice of models.
> – J. M. Keynes (1938, pp. 296–7)

> The terms in which contracts are made matter. In particular, if money is the goods in terms of which contracts are made, then the prices of goods in terms of money are of special significance. This is not the case if we consider an economy without a past or future... if a serious monetary theory comes to be written, the fact that contracts are made in terms of money will be of considerable importance (italics added).
> – Arrow and Hahn (1971, pp. 356–7)

> In the first place, the fact that contracts are fixed... in terms of money unquestionable plays a large part
> – Keynes (1936a, p. 236)

On New Years Day in 1935 Keynes (1973a, p. 492) wrote a letter to George Bernard Shaw stating:

> To understand my new state of mind, however, you have to know that I believe myself to be writing a book on economic theory which will largely revolutionize not I suppose at once but in the course of the next ten years the way the world thinks about economic problems....

I can't expect you or anyone else to believe this at the present stage, but for myself I don't merely hope what I say. In my own mind I am quite sure.

The first page of text of *The General Theory of Employment, Interest and Money* reveals what Keynes thought was the revolutionary aspect of his analysis

> I have called this book the *General Theory*... placing the emphasis on the prefix *general*. The object of such a title is to contrast the character of my arguments and conclusions with those of *classical* theory... the postulates (axioms) of the classical theory are applicable to a special case only and not to the general case.... Moreover the characteristics of the special case assumed by the classical theory happen not to be those of the economics society in which we actually live, with the result that its teaching is misleading and disastrous if we attempt to apply it to the facts of experience.
>
> (Keynes, 1936a, p. 3)

Vigilant observation of the actual working of the economic system led Keynes to his revolutionary analysis that required questioning existing theory and *throwing out three fundamental axioms underlying classical theory* as not applicable to the operation of the type of monetary economy in which we live.

A theory is more general compared to another theory if it is based on fewer restrictive axioms. In the German language edition of *The General Theory* (1936b, p. ix) Keynes specifically noted "This is one of the reasons which justify my calling my theory a *general* (emphasis in the original) theory. Since it is based on *fewer restrictive assumptions* ('weniger enge Voraussetzunger stutz') than the orthodox theory, it is also more easily adopted to a large area of different circumstances" (Second emphasis added).

What makes his analytical system revolutionary is that Keynes's general theory requires a smaller axiomatic foundation (fewer restrictive axioms) than classical (or more recent Arrow–Debreu–Walrasian general equilibrium) analysis. The latter then are special cases of Keynes's theory that impose additional restrictive axioms to the logical foundation of Keynes's general theory. The onus is, therefore, on those who add such axioms to the general theory to justify these additional axioms.[1] Those theorists who invoke a smaller axiomatic base of a general theory are not required, in logic, to prove a general negative, i.e., they are not required to prove the additional restrictive axioms are unnecessary.

The purpose of this chapter is to explain

(1) Why mainstream economists presumed Keynes's theory to be a special case of classical theory (where there were rigidities in wages and/or prices) rather than comprehending that the classical theory is a special case of Keynes's general theory where the classical analysis requires three additional restrictive axioms.
(2) Why flexible wages and prices are neither a necessary nor a sufficient condition to assure a full-employment equilibrium, while price or wage rigidities is not a necessary condition for involuntary unemployment. Rather the cause of Keynes's involuntary unemployment equilibrium is nested in the peculiar but essential properties possessed by money and other liquid assets and the desire of people to save income by purchasing liquid assets that can be sold in orderly and well-organized markets in a monetary economy.
(3) Why Keynes's revolutionary monetary theory was aborted immediately after World War II was for two reasons: (1) the inability of mainstream economists, especially those who called themselves Keynesians, to comprehend Keynes's message and (2) the political atmosphere of McCarthyism that was rampant in the United States why the political climate after World War II, especially in the United States, encouraged this perversion of Keynes's theoretical analysis.
(4) The axiomatic differences between Keynes's General Theory and "Keynesian" economics.
(5) Why Keynes's general theory axiomatic foundation requires the analysis to focus on the importance of the use of contracts written in terms of money and the resulting problems of liquidity (but not a problem of a liquidity trap). Keynes's monetary theory, therefore meets the criteria for a serious theory laid down by Arow and Hahn while mainstream monetary theory does not.

The failure of Keynes's analysis to revolutionize the way economists theorize would not have been surprising to Keynes. In his inaugural lecture before the British Academy on April 22, 1971, Austin Robinson, quoting from an unpublished early draft of Keynes's *General Theory*, indicated that Keynes had written:

> "In economics you cannot *convict* your opponent of error, you can only *convince* him of it. And even if you are right, you cannot convince him ... if his head is already filled with contrary notions that

he cannot catch the clues to your thought which you are throwing to him."

We shall show that, in the 1930s and 1940s, not only established economics professors, but even younger economists such as Nobel Prize winners Paul Samuelson and J. R. Hicks had their heads so full of the contrary notions of Walrasian general equilibrium theory that they could not recognize the thoughts that Keynes was sending to all who would listen.

## Fixed wages and the problem of unemployment

Keynes's biographer, Lord Skidelsky (1992, p. 512) has noted that "the validity of Keynes's 'general theory' rests on his assertion that the classical theory...is, as he put it in his lectures, 'nonsense.' If it (the classical theory) were true, the classical 'special case' would in fact, be the 'general theory,' and Keynes's aggregative analysis not formally wrong, but empty, redundant. It is worth noting...that mainstream economists after the Second World War treated Keynes's theory as a 'special case' of the classical theory, applicable to conditions where money wages...were 'sticky.' Thus his theory was robbed of its theoretical bite, while allowed to retain its relevance for policy."

If Keynes was merely arguing that unemployment was the result of price and wage rigidities, then Keynes was not providing a revolutionary theory of a monetary economy that experienced problems of unemployment. For even in the 19th century classical economists had argued that the lack of flexible wages and prices (supply side imperfections) is the cause of unemployment.

In *The General Theory*, Keynes specifically denied that the fundamental cause of unemployment is the existence of wage and/or price rigidities when he (Keynes, 1936a, p. 257) wrote: "the Classical Theory has been accustomed to rest the supposedly self-adjusting character of the economic system on an assumed fluidity of money wages; and when there is a rigidity, to lay on this rigidity the blame of maladjustment.... My difference from this theory is primarily a difference of analysis." Given this statement of Keynes, how could mainstream economists after World War II ever conceived that Keynes's theory required sticky wages, prices, or even an absolute liquidity trap (i.e., a fixed minimum interest rate[2]) to demonstrate the existence of involuntary unemployment?

A sage once said that the definition of a "classic" is a book that everyone cites but no reads. Mainstream economists who call themselves

"Keynesians," and yet attribute unemployment to wage, price or interest rate rigidities, must think of Keynes's *General Theory* as a literary classic that they can cite without bothering to read or understand Keynes's serious monetary theory.

Ever since World War II, in most prestigious universities' economics departments students are taught that Keynes's book *The General Theory of Employment, Interest and Money* is an obscure and confusing book[3] and therefore they need not read or comprehended. Instead, students are taught that it is supply side imperfections, especially in the labor market of the last half century where the "welfare" state has coddled workers, that is the basic cause of observed unemployment in the real world. Accordingly, today a hi-tech mathematical version of the 19th-century classical theory is the foundation of *all* mainstream economic models of the economy – and economic problems are always associated with the existence of some wage and/or price rigidity – and these rigidities are often associated with government policies that interfere with a free market environment.

In order to provide concrete evidence of why Keynes's revolution was never understood before it ever had a chance of entering the professional economic literature, initially we will use primarily the example of Paul Samuelson's attempt to propagate Keynesianism and compare it with Keynes's revolutionary monetary theory – where the latter meets Arrow and Hahn's criterion for developing "a serious monetary theory."

At the end of this chapter, we will explain why J. R. Hicks, who won the Nobel Prize in 1972 for his "pioneering contributions to general equilibrium theory," in the 1970s recognized that his classical general equilibrium analysis of Keynes – the IS–LM version of neoclassical Keynesianism was not representative of Keynes's general theory framework – and Hicks's 1980s admission that he was now "labeling my own point of view as *nonergodic*."

## Samuelson's neoclassical synthesis Keynesianism

For most students who studied economics in any American University during the last half of the 20th century, Samuelson was thought to be a direct disciple of Keynes and his revolutionary general theory analysis. Samuelson is usually considered the founder of the American Keynesian school which he labeled Neoclassical Synthesis Keynesianism because of the classical microeconomic theory that Samuelson had developed in his *Foundations of Economic Analysis* (1947) that Samuelson claimed was the micro foundation of Keynes's macro analysis. Unfortunately,

Samuelson's neoclassical synthesis brand of "Keynesianism" is not analytically compatible with Keynes's theoretical framework.

Given Samuelson's dominance of the American macroeconomic scene after World War II, the different axiomatic foundation of Samuelson's popularization of Keynesianism vis-à-vis Keynes's *General Theory* aborted Keynes's truly revolutionary analysis from being adopted as the basis of mainstream macro economics. Consequently in the 1970s academic literature, the Monetarists easily defeated Samuelson's "Keynesianism" on the grounds of logical inconsistency between its microfoundations and its "Keynesian" macroeconomic policy prescriptions. The effect of this defeat was to change the domestic and international choice of policies: (1) to prevent unemployment, (2) to promote economic development, and even (3) to finance government social security systems away from prescriptions founded on Keynes's revolutionary analysis and toward the age-old laissez-faire policies promoted by classical theory that had dominated 19th- and early 20th-century thought. Consequently, socially acceptable policies to prevent unemployment, etc. have regressed, with the result that the "golden age of economic development" experienced by both OECD nations and LDCs during the more than quarter century after World War II has disappeared[4] despite the technological advances in the study of economics.

As a result of the Monetarist victory over Samuelson's Keynesianism in the 1970s, New Keynesian theory as espoused by Mankiw and others tended to replace Samuelson's Keynesianism. Just as Friedman's Monetarism had conquered Samuelson's brand of Keynesianism, however, New Classical theory and its concept of rational expectations easily made a mockery of the New Keynesians approach which relied on the rigidity of wages and prices to achieve Keynesian-like results. Rational expectations required the ergodic axiom as a basis and therefore presumed that with free markets there already existed a full employment economic future that human actions and government policies could not alter. Accordingly, the New Classicists could argue that our economic problems were associated with supply-side problems primarily due to government interference that prevented free competition in the labor and product market place. The result was to lead policy makers to dance to the Panglossian siren song that "all is for the best in the best of all possible worlds provided we let well enough alone" (Keynes, 1936a, p. 33) by encouraging adoption of policies of "liberalizing" all domestic and international markets.

Accordingly, as we entered the 21st century, only the Post-Keynesian school remains to carry on in Keynes's analytical footsteps and develop

Keynes's theory and policy prescriptions for a 21st century real world of economic globalization.

## The coming of Keynesianism to America

In their wonderful book *The Coming of Keynesianism to America*, Colander and Landreth (1996, p. 23) credit Paul Samuelson with saving the textbook pedagogical basis of the Keynesian Revolution from destruction by the anti-communist spirit (McCarthyism) that ravaged America academia in the years immediately following World War II.

Lorie Tarshis, a Canadian who had been a student attending Keynes's lectures at Cambridge during the early 1930s had, in 1947, wrote an introductory textbook that incorporated Tarshis' lecture notes interpretation of Keynes's *General Theory*. Colander and Landreth note that despite the initial popularity of the Tarshis textbook, its sales declined rapidly as trustees of and donors to American colleges and universities, attacked Tarshis's book as preaching an economic heresy. The frenzy about Tarshis's textbook reached a pinnacle when William F. Buckley, in his book *God and Man at Yale* (1951), attacked the Tarshis analysis as communist inspired.

In August 1986 Colander and Landreth (hereafter C-L) interviewed Paul Samuelson (C-L, 1996, pp. 145–78) about his becoming an economist and a "Keynesian." Samuelson indicated that he recognized the "virulence of the attack on Tarshis" and so he wrote his textbook "carefully and lawyer like" (C-L, 1996, p. 172). The term "neoclassical synthesis Keynesianism" did not appear in the first edition of Samuelson's textbook, *Economics An Introductory Analysis* (1948), which was published after the early attacks on Tarshis's text. This neoclassical synthesis terminology, however, does appear prominently in the later editions of Samuelson's textbook. Samuelson's assertion that his brand of Keynesian macroeconomics is synthesized with (and based on) traditional neoclassical microeconomic assumptions made the Samuelson version of Keynesianism less open to attacks of bringing economic heresy into University courses on economics compared to Tarshis's Keynesian analysis.

Unlike Tarshis's analysis which was based on separate aggregate supply and demand functions, the analytical foundation of Samuelson's Keynesianism was imbedded in Samuelson's 45-degree Keynesian cross. Samuelson derived this cross analysis from a single equation aggregate demand function. This mathematical derivation in conjunction with the claimed synthesis of neoclassical theory made it more difficult to attack the Samuelson version of textbook Keynesianism as politically motivated. Thus for several generations of economists educated after World War II, Samuelson's name was synonymous with Keynesian theory as various editions of Samuelson's neoclassical Keynesian textbook – the best-selling economics textbook of all times with over a million copies sold – dominated the teaching of economics. Even those younger economists who broke with the old neoclassical synthesis Keynesianism and developed their own branch of New Keynesianism based their analytical approach on the Samuelson's *Foundation of Economic Analysis* (1947) and its classical microeconomic axiomatic foundations.

From an historical perspective it appears that Samuelson saved the textbook pedagogical basis of the Keynesian Revolution from McCarthyism destruction simply by ignoring the less restrictive axiomatic foundation of Keynes's analytic revolution.

## How did Samuelson learn Keynes's theory?

In his 1986 interview, Samuelson indicated that in the period before World War II, "my friends who were not economists regarded me as very conservative" (C-L, 1996, p. 154). Samuelson graduated from the University of Chicago in June 1935 and were it not for the Social Science Research Council fellowship that he received upon graduation, he would have done his graduate studies at the University of Chicago (C-L, 1996, pp. 154–5). It was the visible hand of a fellowship offer that placed Samuelson at Harvard when Keynes's *General Theory* was published in 1936. What information about Keynes's *General Theory* was Samuelson exposed to at Harvard?

Robert Bryce, a Canadian, had attended the same Keynes's Cambridge lectures as Tarshis between 1932 and 1935. In a 1987 interview with Colander and Landreth (1996, pp. 39–48), Bryce indicated that in the spring of 1935 he (Bryce) spent half of each week at the London School of Economics and half at Cambridge. At LSE Bryce used his Cambridge lecture notes to write an essay on Keynes's revolutionary ideas – without having read *The General Theory* – for the people at the LSE. Bryce's essay so impressed Hayek that Hayek let Bryce have four consecutive weeks of Hayek's seminar to explain Keynes's ideas as he had written them out in this essay. Bryce's lectures were a huge success at the LSE (C-L, 1996, p. 43).

In the fall of 1935, Bryce went to Harvard and stayed for two years. During that time, informal groups met during the evenings to discuss Keynes's book. Bryce, using the same pre-General Theory essay that he had used as the basis for his talks at the LSE, presented to these groups what he believed was Keynes's *General Theory* analysis – although he still had not read the *General Theory*. As Bryce put it "In most of the first academic year (1935–1936) I was the only one who was familiar enough with it (Keynes' theory) to be willing to argue in defense of it." (C-L, 1996, pp. 45–6). So in 1936, Bryce's essay became the basis of what most economists at Harvard, probably including Samuelson, thought was Keynes's analysis – even though Bryce had not read *the* book when he made his presentations. Even in 1987, Bryce stated that, "anyone who studies that book is going to get very confused. It was ... a difficult, provocative book" (C-L, 1996, pp. 44–6).

The immediate question therefore is: "Did Bryce ever really comprehend the basis of Keynes's analytical framework?" And if he did not, how did that affect how the young Samuelson and others at Harvard in 1936 learn about Keynes's analytical framework? Bryce's presentations at the LSE and Harvard were supposed to make Keynes's ideas readily understandable – something that Bryce believed Keynes could not do in his *General Theory* book. Bryce indicated that in his first year at Harvard "I felt like the only expert on Keynes's work around" (C-L, 1996, p. 45).

Samuelson has indicated that his first knowledge of Keynes's *General Theory* was gained from Bryce (C-L, 1996, p. 158). Moreover, even after reading *the General Theory* in 1936, Samuelson, perhaps reflecting Bryce's view of the difficulty of understanding Keynes's book, found the *General Theory* analysis "unpalatable" and not comprehensible (C-L, 1996, p. 159). Samuelson finally indicated that "The way I finally convinced myself was to just stop worrying about it (about understanding Keynes's analysis). I asked myself: why do I refuse a paradigm that enables me to understand the Roosevelt upturn from 1933 till 1937? I was content to assume that there was enough rigidity in relative prices and wages to make the Keynesian alternative to Walras operative" (C-L, 1996, pp. 159–60).

Obviously, Samuelson's mind was already so filled with contrary notions of Walrasian general equilibrium theory that he never made any attempt to catch the clues to Keynes's general theory analytical foundation that rested on removing three classical axioms. For in 1986 Samuelson was still claiming that "we (Keynesians) always assumed that the Keynesian underemployment equilibrium floated on a substructure of administered prices and imperfect competition" (C-L, 1996, p. 160). When pushed by Colander and Landreth as to whether this requirement of rigidity was ever formalized in his work, Samuelson's response was "There was no need to" (C-L, 1996, p. 161).

Yet, specifically in chapter 19 of *The General Theory* and even more directly in his published response to Dunlop and Tarshis, Keynes (1939b) had already responded in the negative to this question of whether his analysis of underemployment equilibrium required imperfect competition, administered prices, and/or rigid wages. Dunlop and Tarshis had argued that the purely competitive model was not empirically justified, therefore it was monopolistic and administered pricing and wage fixities that was the basis of Keynes's unemployment equilibrium. Keynes reply was simply: "I complain a little that I in particular should be criticised for conceding a little to the other view" (Keynes, 1939b, p. 411). In chapters 17–19 of his *General Theory*, Keynes explicitly demonstrated that even if a competitive economy with perfectly flexible money wages and prices existed ("conceding a little to the other side"), there was no automatic market mechanism that could restore the full employment level of effective demand. In other words, Keynes's general theory could show that, as a matter of logic, less than full-employment equilibrium could exist even in a purely competitive economy with freely flexible wages and prices.

Obviously Samuelson, who became the premier American Keynesian of his time, had either not read, or not comprehended, (1) Keynes's response to Dunlop and Tarshis or even (2) chapter 19, *The General Theory* which was entitled "Changes in Money Wages." As we have already noted, in chapter 19, Keynes explicitly indicates that the theory of unemployment equilibrium did not require "a rigidity" in money wages (Keynes, 1936a, p. 257).

Keynes (1936a, p. 259) indicated that to assume that rigidity was *the* sole cause of the existence of an unemployment equilibrium lay in accepting the argument that the micro-demand functions "can only be constructed on some fixed assumption as to the nature of the demand and supply schedules of other industries and as to the amount of aggregate effective demand. It is invalid, therefore to transfer the argument to industry as a whole unless we also transfer the argument that the *aggregate effective demand is fixed*. Yet, this assumption reduces the argument to an *ignoratio elenchi*."

An *ignoratio elenchi* is a fallacy in logic of offering a proof irrelevant to the proposition in question. Unfortunately, Samuelson invoked the same classical *ignoratio elenchi* when he argued that Keynes's general theory was simply a Walrasian general equilibrium system where, if there is an exogenous decline in effective demand, rigid wages and prices created a temporary disequilibrium that prevented full employment from being restored in the short-run[5].

As Keynes went on to explain, "whilst no one would wish to deny the proposition that a reduction in money wages *accompanied by the same aggregate effective demand as before* will be associated with an increase in employment, the precise question at issue is whether the reduction in money wages will or will not be accompanied by the same aggregate effective demand as before measured in term of money, or, at any rate, by an aggregate effective demand which is not reduced in full proportion to the reduction in money-wages" (Keynes, 1936a, pp. 259–60, see Davidson 1998 for an explicit diagrammatic analysis of this point). Keynes then spent the rest of chapter 19 explaining why and how a general theory analysis must look at the relationship between changes in money wages and/or prices and changes in aggregate effective demand – an analysis that, by assumption, is not relevant to either a Walrasian system[6] or Samuelson's neoclassical synthesis Keynesianism.

At the same time that Samuelson became a Keynesian by convincing himself not to worry about Keynes's actual analytical framework, Tarshis had obtained a position at Tufts University, a mere half-hour of travel from Harvard. Tarshis would often meet with a group at Harvard, including Bryce, who were discussing Keynes. Tarshis notes that "Paul Samuelson was not in the Keynesian group. He was busy working on his own thing. That he became a Keynesian was laughable" (C-L, 1996, p. 64).

Yet, Paul Samuelson has called himself a "Keynesian" and even a "Post Keynesian" in several editions of his famous textbook. Nevertheless, as we will explain *infra*, Samuelson's theoretical "neoclassical synthesis" axiomatic foundation is logically different from Keynes general theory of a monetary economy.

## The axiomatic differences between Samuelson's neoclassical Keynesianism and Keynes's theory of a monetary economy

At the same time that Samuelson was developing his neoclassical synthesis Keynesianism, he was working on his masterful *Foundations of Economic Analysis* (1947). In his *Foundations* Samuelson asserts certain specific classical axioms are the basis of classical micro theory and therefore by extension, his neoclassical synthesis Keynesian macroeconomic analysis. For example Samuelson noted that utility functions are homogeneous of degree zero (Samuelson, 1947, pp. 119–21) and in a purely competitive world it would be foolish to hold money as a store of value as long as other assets had a positive yield (Samuelson, 1947, pp. 122–4). These statements mean that (1) money is neutral and (2) any real producible capital goods that produce a positive yield are assumed to be *gross substitutes*. Thus at the same time Samuelson was promoting his pedagogical brand of Keynesianism in his textbook he was arguing that the gross substitution axiom and the neutral money axiom are the foundation upon which all economic analysis must be built. (We shall indicate *infra* where Keynes specifically rejected these two classical axioms as a foundation for his *General Theory*.)

Furthermore in an article published in 1969 Samuelson argued that the "ergodic hypothesis (axiom)" is a necessary foundation if economics is a hard science (Samuelson, 1969, p. 184). (As explained *infra*, Keynes also rejected this ergodic axiom.)

What is this ergodic hypothesis? If one conceives of the economy as a stochastic process, then the future outcome of any current decision is determined via a probability distribution. Logically speaking to make statistically reliable forecasts about future economic events, the decision maker should obtain and analyze sample data from the future. Since that is impossible, the assumption of an ergodic stochastic process permits the analyst to assert that samples drawn from past and current data are equivalent to drawing a sample from the future. In other words, the ergodic axiom implies that the outcome at any future date is the statistical shadow of past and current market data.

A realization of a stochastic process is a sample value of a multidimensional variable over a period of time, i.e., a single time series of recorded outcomes. A stochastic process provides a universe of such time series. *Time statistics* refers to statistical averages (e.g., the mean, the standard deviation, etc.) calculated from a singular realization over an indefinite time space. *Space statistics*, on the other hand, refers to statistical averages calculated at a fixed point of time observation and are formed over the universe of realizations (i.e., space statistics are calculated from cross-sectional data).

If, and only if, the stochastic process is ergodic, then for an infinite realization the time statistics and the space statistics will coincide. For finite realizations of ergodic processes, time and space statistics coincide except for random errors, i.e., they tend to converge (with the probability of unity) as the number of observations increase. Consequently, if the ergodic axiom is applicable, statistics calculated from either past time series or cross-sectional data are statistically reliable estimates of the space statistics that will occur at any specific future date.

The ergodic axiom therefore assures that the outcome associated with any future date can be reliably predicted by a statistical analysis of already existing data. The future is therefore never uncertain. The future can always be reliably predicted (actuarially known) by a sufficient statistical analysis of already existing data. Future outcomes, in an ergodic system, are probabilistically risky but are statistically reliably predictable from existing data. (In a nonstochastic deterministic orthodox economic model, the classical ordering axiom plays the same role as the ergodic axiom of classical stochastic models.[7])

Accordingly, in an ergodic stochastic world, in the long run, the equilibrium future is predetermined and can not be changed by anything human beings or governments do. It follows that any government market regulation or interference into normal competitive market (assumed ergodic) processes, may, in the short run, prevent the system from achieving the full employment level assured by the axioms of a classical Walrasian system. In an ergodic system where the future can be reliably predicted so that future positive yields of real capital producible assets can be known with actuarial certainty, and where the gross substitution axiom underlies all demand curves, then as long as prices are flexible, money must be neutral and the system automatically adjusts to a full-employment general equilibrium.

If, on the other hand, in such an ergodic world prices are sticky in the short run, then it will take a longer time for the gross substitution theorem to work its way through the system but, at least in the long run, a full-employment general equilibrium is still assured. Samuelson (C-L, 1996, p. 163) has stated that in his view Keynes's analysis is a "very slow adjusting disequilibrium" system where the "full Walrasian equilibrium was not realized" in the short-run because prices and wages do not adjust rapidly enough to an exogenous shock. Nevertheless the economic system would, if left alone, achieve full employment in the long run.

In Keynes's general theory analysis, on the other hand, a full-employment equilibrium is not assured in either the short-run or the long-run.

## Samuelson's neoclassical synthesis Keynesian axioms that Keynes threw over in his theory of a monetary economy

Keynes was primarily a monetary theorist. The words money, currency, and monetary appear in the titles of most of his major volumes in economics. Post-Keynesian monetary theory evolves from Keynes's revolutionary approach to analyzing a money using economy where money was never neutral even if a hypothetical pure competitive market conditions including instantaneously flexible wages and prices exists.

Keynes (1936a, p. 26) argued that even if a hypothetical economy with perfectly flexible wages and prices existed, it would not automatically achieve a full-employment general equilibrium in a money-using economy.

Keynes compared those economists whose theoretical logic was grounded on the classical special case additional restrictive axioms to Euclidean geometers living in a nonEuclidean world

> who discovering that in experience straight lines apparently parallel often meet, rebuke the lines for not keeping straight – as the only remedy for the unfortunate collisions which are taking place. Yet, in truth, there is no remedy except to throw over the axiom of parallels and to work out a non-Euclidean geometry. Something similar is required today in economics.
>
> (Keynes, 1936a, p. 16)

James K. Galbraith has noted that the first three words of the title of Keynes's 1936 book *The General Theory of Employment, Interest and Money* "are evidently cribbed from Albert Einstein" (Galbraith, 1996, p. 14). Einstein's general theory of relativity had displaced Newton's classical theory in physics where the latter had maintained the separation of time and space. Einstein's theory demonstrated that the time–space continuum is, in essence the extension of non-Euclidean Riemannian geometry of curved spaces. Keynes hoped to mimic Einstein's revolutionary general theory of relativity and displace the classical economic theory's neutral money axiom that assumed the separation of market outcomes and the money supply. Keynes wanted to replace this axiomatic separation of money and markets with the equivalent of a market-money curved-space continuum, i.e., where money and market outcomes continuously interact.

Post-Keynesian monetary theory has followed Keynes's fewer restrictive axiom analytical framework. In light of Keynes's analogy to geometry, Keynes's serious monetary theory might be called non-Euclidean economics.

To throw over an axiom is to reject what the faithful believe are "universal truths." For example, Blanchard (1990, p. 828) insists that all New Keynesian macroeconomic models must be based on "hard headed" microfoundations that "impose long-run neutrality of money as a maintained presumption (axiom). This is a matter of faith, based on theoretical considerations rather than on empirical evidence".

Keynes's revolutionary analysis, however, requires economists to "throw over" of three restrictive classical axioms – including the axiom that Blanchard accepts as "a matter of faith." The classical axioms that Keynes threw out in his revolutionary theory of a monetary economy were (1) *the neutrality of money axiom*, (2) *the gross substitution axiom*, and (3) *the axiom of an ergodic economic world*.

In 1935, Keynes explicitly noted that in his analytic framework money matters in both the long and short run, i.e., money is never neutral. Money affects real decision making. In 1935 Keynes wrote:

> the theory which I desiderate would deal...with an economy in which money plays a part of its own and affects motives and decisions, and is, in short, one of the operative factors in the situation, so that the course of events cannot be predicted either the long period or in the short, without a knowledge of the behavior of money between the first state and the last. And it is this which we mean when we speak of a monetary economy.... Booms and depressions are peculiar to an economy in which...*money is not neutral*.... I believe that the next task is to work out in some detail a monetary theory of production...that is the task on which I am now occupying myself in some confidence that I am not wasting my time.
>
> (Keynes, 1935, pp. 408–9)

As Keynes's developed his theory of liquidity preference he recognized that his theory of involuntary unemployment required specifying "The Essential Properties of Interest and Money" (1936a, Chapter 17) that differentiated his results from classical theory. These "essential properties" assured that money and all other liquid assets[8] are never neutral. These essential properties (Keynes, 1936a, pp. 230–1) are

(1) the elasticity of production of all liquid assets including money is zero or negligible, and
(2) the elasticity of substitution between liquid assets (including money) and reproducible goods is zero or negligible.

A *zero elasticity of production* means that money does not grow on trees and consequently workers can not be hired to harvest money trees when the demand for money (liquidity) increases. Or as Keynes wrote: "money...cannot be readily reproduced; – labour cannot be turned on at will by entrepreneurs to produce money in increasing quantities as its price rises" (Keynes, 1936a, p. 230). Thus, for example, suppose people decide to spend less out of any given level of income on space machines (automobiles) that are the products of industry and instead used these savings to purchase time machines (in the form of money and/or other liquid assets used to move purchasing power into the future) out of a given level of income. Employment in the auto industry will, *ceteris paribus*, decline while as the additional savings becomes an increased demand for nonproducible money and/or other liquid assets. Private sector entrepreneurs can not hire the industrial workers who have been fired in the auto industry to harvest money trees or produce more liquid assets to meet this increase in demand for nonreproducible (by industrial firms) liquid assets.

In classical theory, on the other hand, money is a reproducible commodity. In many neoclassical textbook models as well as in the Walrasian general equilibrium system, peanuts or some other reproducible product of industry is the money commodity or numeraire. Peanuts may not grow on trees, but they do grow on the roots of bushes. Thus if, in this general equilibrium world, if people reduce their demand for autos and use this saving to increase their demand for peanut money, then the supply of peanuts can easily be augmented by private sector peanut producing entrepreneurs hiring the laid-off workers from the auto industry. In this case the propensity to save creates jobs just as much as the propensity to consume.

Keynes's "essential property" zero elasticity of substitution between liquid assets and the products of industry assures that portion of income that is not spend on by the products of industry for consumption purposes, i.e., what Keynes defined as savings, will find, in Hahn's (1977, p. 31) terminology, "resting places" in the demand for nonproducibles. Some forty years after Keynes, Hahn rediscovered Keynes's point that a stable involuntary unemployment equilibrium could exist *even in a Walrasian system with flexible wages and prices* whenever there are "resting places for savings in other than reproducible assets" (Hahn, 1977, p. 31).

In Keynes's system, because of uncertainty, savings were held in the form of money and liquid assets that possess a zero elasticity of production. If the demand for nonproducibles increases (an increased demand for liquidity), then the market price would rise proportionately. If, however, the elasticity of substitution between these nonproducibles and the products of industry is zero, then this rising price of liquid nonproducibles will not spill over into a demand for the products of industry.

Keynes (1936a, p. 161) argued that the only "radical cure" for unemployment is "to allow the individual no choice between consuming his income and ordering the production of the specific capital asset which... impresses him as the most promising investment open to him. It might be that, at times when he was more than usually assailed by doubts concerning the future, he would turn in his perplexity toward more consumption and less investment.... But that would avoid the disastrous, cumulative and far reaching repercussions of its being open to him, when thus assailed by doubts, to spend his income neither on the one or the other."

Hahn rigorously demonstrated what was logically intuitive to Keynes. Hahn (1977, p. 37) showed that the view that with "flexible money wages there would be no unemployment has no convincing argument to recommend it.... Even in a pure tâtonnement in traditional models convergence to (a general) equilibrium cannot be generally proved" as long savings were held in the form of nonproducibles (e.g., money and other liquid assets). Hahn (1977, p. 39) demonstrated that "any non-reproducible asset allows for a choice between employment inducing and non-employment inducing demand." Accordingly, the existence of a demand for money and other liquid nonreproducible assets (that are *not* gross substitutes for the products of industries) as a store of "savings" means that all income earned by households engaging in the production of goods is not, in the short or long run, necessarily spent on the products of industry. Households who want to store that portion of their income that they do not consume (i.e., that they do not spend on the products of industry) in liquid assets are choosing, in Hahn's words "a non-employment inducing demand" for their savings.

If the gross substitution axiom was universally applicable, however, any new savings that would increase the demand for nonproducibles and therefore would increase the price of nonproducibles (whose production–supply curve is, by definition, perfectly inelastic). The resulting relative price rise in nonproducibles vis-à-vis producibles would, under the gross substitution axiom, induce savers to increase their demand for reproducible durables as a substitute for nonproducibles in their wealth holdings. Consequently, as in classical theory, nonproducibles could not be ultimate resting places for savings as they spilled over into a demand for producible goods (cf. Davidson, 1972).

Samuelson's assumption that *all* demand curves are based on a ubiquitous gross substitution axiom implies that everything is a substitute for everything else. In Samuelson's foundation for economic analysis, therefore, producibles must be gross substitutes for any existing nonproducible liquid assets (including money) when the latter are used as stores of savings. Accordingly, Samuelson's *Foundation of Economic Analysis* denies the logical possibility of involuntary unemployment[9] as long as all prices are perfectly flexible.

Samuelson's brand of Keynesianism is merely a form of the classical special case analysis that is "misleading and disastrous" (Keynes, 1936a,

p. 3) if applied to the operation of a monetary economy. In the absence of a restrictive universally applicable axiom of gross substitution, however, income effects (e.g., the Keynesian multiplier) can predominate and can swamp any hypothetical classical substitution effects. Just as in non-Euclidean geometry lines that are apparently parallel often crash into each other, in the Keynes-Post Keynesian non-Euclidean economic world, an increase demand for "savings" even if it raises the relative price of nonproducibles, will not spill over into a demand for producible good and hence when households save a portion of their income they have made a choice for "non-employment inducing demand."

Finally, Keynes argued that only in a money-using entrepreneur economy where the future is uncertain (and therefore could not be reliably predicted) would money (and all other liquid assets) always be nonneutral as they are used as a store of savings. In essence, Keynes viewed the economic system as moving through calendar time from an irrevocable past to an uncertain, not statistically predictable, future. This required Keynes to reject the ergodic axiom.

Keynes never used the term "ergodic", since ergodic stochastic theory was first developed in 1935 by the Moscow School of Probability and it did not become well known in the West until after the second world war and Keynes was dead. Nevertheless Keynes's main criticism of Tinbergen's econometric "method" (Keynes, 1939a, p. 308) was that the economic data "is not homogeneous over time." Non-homogenous data over time mean that economic time series are non-stationary, and non-stationary is sufficient (but not a necessary condition) for a nonergodic stochastic process. Consequently Keynes, with his emphasis on uncertainty had, in these comments on Tinbergen, specifically rejected what would later be called the ergodic axiom – an assumption that Samuelson has declared is a foundation necessary to make economics a hard science.

In sum, Samuelson theoretical foundations require three classical axioms that are the equivalent of the axiom of parallels in Euclidean geometry. Clearly then Samuelson's macroeconomics is not applicable to the "non-Euclidean" economics of a money-using entrepreneurial system that Keynes developed in his *General Theory*.

## Liquidity and contracts

Nevertheless, the question may remain "Does applying Keynes's smaller axiomatic base make any difference in our understanding of the real world in which we live vis-à-vis applying Samuelson's classical axiomatic foundation version of Keynesianism?" The answer is definitely yes because only if we overthrow these three classical axioms that are an essential part of Samuelson's foundations of economic analysis can the concept of liquidity play an important role in our analysis – as it does in our lives.

Important decisions involving production, investment and consumption activities are often taken in an uncertain (nonergodic) environment. Hiring inputs and buying products using forward contracts in money terms are a human institution developed to efficiently organize time-consuming production and exchange processes. Since the abolition of slavery[10] the money-wage contract is the most ubiquitous of these contracts. Unemployment, rather than full employment, is a common *laissez-faire* outcome in such a market oriented, monetary production economy.

The economy in which we live utilizes money contracts – not real contracts – to seal production and exchange agreements among self-interested individuals. The ubiquitous use of money contracts is an essential element of all real world entrepreneurial economies. Moreover *recontracting without income penalty* (an essential characteristic of the Walrasian system) whenever parties have entered into a contract at a price other than the implicit full employment general equilibrium price *is never permitted under the civil law of contracts*. Why, one might ask Samuelson, do economies continue to organize production and exchange on the basis of money contracts, if such use interferes with the rapid achievement of a socially optimal general Walrasian equilibrium?

The use of money contracts has always presented a dilemma to classical theorists. Logically consistent classical theorists must view the universal use of money contracts by modern economies as irrational, since such agreements fixing payments over time in nominal terms can impede the self-interest optimizing pursuit of real incomes by economic decision makers. Mainstream economists tend to explain the existence of money contracts by using non-economic reasons such as social customs, invisible handshakes, etc. – societal institutional constraints which limit price signaling and hence limits adjustments for the optimal use of resources to the long run.

For Keynes and Post Keynesians, on the other hand, *binding* nominal contractual commitments are a sensible method for dealing with true uncertainty regarding future outcomes whenever economic activities span a long duration of calendar time. In organizing production and exchange on a money contractual basis, buyers need not be as unduly worried about what events happen in the uncertain future as long as they have, or can obtain, enough liquidity to meet these contractual commitments as they come due. Thus liquidity means survival in a money-using contractual entrepreneurial directed market economy. Bankruptcy, on the other hand, occurs when significant contractual monetary obligations can not be met. Bankruptcy is the equivalent of a walk to the economic gallows.

Keynes's general theory that emphasizes money and liquidity implies that agents who planned to spend in the current period need not have earned income currently, or previously, in order to exercise this demand in an entrepreneur system. All these buying agents need is the liquidity to meet money contractual obligations as they come due. This means that investment spending, which we normally associate with the demand for reproducible fixed and working capital goods, is not constrained by either actual current income or inherited endowments – as long as there are unemployed resources available. Investment can be a form of exogenous spending that is constrained, in a money-creating banking system, solely by the expected but uncertain future *monetary* (not real) cash inflow (Keynes, 1936a, Chapter 17) upon which banks are willing to make additional loans.

In a world where money is created primarily only if someone increases their indebtedness to banks in order to purchase newly produced goods, then real investment spending will be undertaken as long as the purchase of newly produced capital goods are expected to generate a future of cash inflow (net of operating expenses) whose discounted present value equals or exceed the money cash outflow (the supply price currently needed to purchase the capital good).

For any component of aggregate demand not to be constrained by actual income, therefore, agents must have the ability to finance purchases by borrowing from a banking system that can create money. This Post Keynesian financing mechanism where increases in the nominal quantity of money are used to finance increased demand for producible goods results in increasing employment levels. Money, therefore, can not be neutral and can be endogenous.

To reject the neutrality axiom does not require assuming that agents suffer from a money illusion. It only means that "money is not neutral" (Keynes, 1935, p. 411) in the sense that; money matters in both the short and the long run, affecting the equilibrium level of employment and real output. If it weren't for Samuelson's (and Blanchard's) insistence on neutral money as a foundations for all macroeconomic theory, economists might recognize that in a money-using entrepreneurial economy that organizes production and exchange with the use of spot and forward money contracts, money is a real phenomenon. The money neutrality axiom must be rejected.

Arrow and Hahn (1971, pp. 356–7) implicitly recognized this necessity of overthrowing the neutral money axiom when they wrote:

> The terms in which contracts are made matter. In particular, if money is the goods in terms of which contracts are made, then the prices of goods in terms of money are of special significance. This is not the case if we consider an economy without a past or future.... *if a serious monetary theory* comes to be written, the fact that contracts are made in terms of money will be of considerable importance (italics added).

Moreover Arrow and Hahn demonstrate (1971, p. 361) that, if production and exchange contracts are made in terms of money (so that money affects real decisions) in an economy moving along in calendar time with a past and a future, then *all general equilibrium existence theorems are jeopardized*. The existence of money contracts – a characteristic of the world in which we live – implies that there need never exist, in the long run or the short run, any rational expectations equilibrium or general equilibrium market clearing price vector. Samuelson's Walrasian foundation is not a reliable base for real-world economies that use money and money contracts to organize economic activities.

## What about Hicks's IS–LM model?

Hicks (1939, pp. 1–4) wrote that he "had the fortune to come upon a method of analysis. The method of General Equilibrium...was specially designed to exhibit the economic system as a whole...(With this method) we shall thus be able to see just why it is that Mr. Keynes reaches different results from earlier economists." Hicks (1937) used this method to develop his IS–LM model where the real and monetary aspects of the economy are divided into independent subsets of equations. These independent subsets require the neutral money axiom. Accordingly, this IS–LM model is merely another classical theory version of Samuelson's neoclassical synthesis Keynesianism.

In 1971, I met John Hicks at a six day IEA conference on the microfoundations of macroeconomics. At the conference my participation (Davidson, 1977, pp. 313–17) emphasized the importance of contracts and the existence of spot and forward markets, the need for liquidity, and the fact that a classical "general equilibrium model was not designed to, and could not answer the interesting macroeconomic questions of money, inflation and unemployment...(and) if we insist on balancing Keynes's macroeconomic analysis on an incompatible general equilibrium base we would not make any progress in macroeconomics; we would also regress to the disastrous pre-Keynesian solutions to the macro-political–economic problems"[11] (Davidson, 1977, p. 392). By the end of the conference, Hicks informed me that the microfoundations of his approach to macroeconomics was closer to mine than to any one else at the conference (which included Nobel Prize winners Tinbergen and Stiglitz).

Over the next few years, Hicks and I met privately several times in the United Kingdom to continue our discussions regarding the microfoundation of Keynes's general theory. By the mid-1970's Hicks (1976, pp. 140–1) was ready to admit that his IS–LM model was a "potted version" of Keynes. By 1979, Hicks (1979) was arguing that economics is embedded in calendar time and a relationship that held in the past could not be assumed to hold in the future (Hicks, 1979, p. 38). In a 1981 article in the *Journal of Post Keynesian Economics* entitled "IS–LM: An Explanation," Hicks recanted his IS–LM model when he wrote (Hicks, 1980–81, p. 139): "As time has gone on, I have myself become dissatisfied with it (the IS–LM apparatus)." In this JPKE article, Hicks admitted that IS–LM did not describe Keynes's general theory approach at all.

Finally, after reading my paper on the fallacy of rational expectations (Davidson, 1982–1983), Hicks wrote to me in a letter dated February 12, 1983[12] "I have just been reading your RE (rational expectations) paper.... I do like it very much.... You have now *rationalized* my suspicions, and shown me that I missed a chance of labeling my own point of view as *nonergodic*. One needs a name like that to ram a point home."

Thus the author of the IS–LM renounced his famous formulation of Keynes's framework and accepted the Post-Keynesian view of what was the basic analysis of Keynes's *General Theory* analysis of the operation of a monetary economy.

## Conclusion

Paul Samuelson saved the term "Keynesian" from being excoriated from post–World War II textbooks by the McCarthy anti-communist movement at the time. But the cost of such a saving was to sever the meaning of Keynes's theory in mainstream economic theory from its *General Theory* analytical roots. Keynes's revolution was to demonstrate that in a money using, market-oriented economy, supply-side market imperfections including the fixity of money wages and/or prices or a liquidity trap are not necessary conditions for the existence of involuntary unemployment equilibrium, while flexible wages and prices and pure competition are not sufficient conditions to assure full-employment equilibrium, even in the long run.

Samuelson's view of Keynesianism resulted in aborting Keynes's revolutionary analysis from altering the foundation of mainstream macroeconomics. Consequently what passes as conventional macroeconomic wisdom of mainstream economists at the beginning of the 21st century is nothing more than a high-tech and more mathematical version of 19th-century classical theory.

In winning the battle against the forces trying to prevent the teaching of suspected communist inspired "Keynesian" economics in our universities, Samuelson ultimately lost the war that Keynes had launched to eliminate the classical theoretical analysis as the basis for real-world economic problems of employment, interest, and money. In 1986 Lorie Tarshis recognized this when he noted "I never felt that Keynes was being followed with full adherence or full understanding of what he had written. I still feel that way" (C-L, p. 72).

Mainstream economics – whether espoused by Old Neoclassical Keynesians, New Keynesians, Old Classical or New Classical theorists, etc.[13] – relies on the three classical axioms that Keynes discarded in his general theory attempt to make economics relevant to the real-world problems of unemployment and international trade and international payments. As a result these problems still plague much of the real world in the globalized economy of the 21st century.

Until mainstream journal of economics open their pages to the revolutionary (fewer axiomatic) base of Keynes's general theory of a monetary economy, mainstream economists will not be able to provide policy prescriptions for resolving the major economic problems (e.g., outsourcing, persistent US current account deficits, increasing inequality of income and wealth within nations as well as between nations, etc.) of the global economy of the 21st century.

## Notes

1. Walras and Arrow–Debreu general equilibrium model are built on three restrictive axioms that Keynes threw out in developing his theory of a maximum generality. Weintraub (2002, p. 113, emphasis added) has noted that Debreu, in his Bourbakian mathematical approach to economics has argued that *"good general theory does not search for the maximum generality, but for the right generality."* In other words, Bourbaki mathematicians do not accept Keynes's search for the "maximum" generality of a general theory, i.e., a

general theory that had the smallest axiomatic foundation that still provides a readily recognizable description of a real-world economy. According to Debreu's Bourbakian view, Keynes's general theory based on fewer axioms than Debreu's general equilibrium theory is not "good" theory. Instead, Debreu's general equilibrium theory of value which expresses itself in terms that few, if any would readily recognize as an apt description of a real-world economy (Weintraub, 2002, p. 114) provides the Bourbakian "right" level of generality – even if it not realistic. In other words, theories that are readily recognizable as descriptions of reality are not necessarily important, in Debreu's view of economics. Unfortunately Debreu, and other general equilibrium theorists, do not provide any criteria for what is the "right" level of generality. Weintraub notes that the Bourbakian case for the right level of generality is merely a matter "of style...and politics...and taste" (Weintraub, 2002, p. 125).
2. This sticky interest rate argument is called the "liquidity trap" where at some low, but positive, rate of interest the demand to hold money for speculative reasons is assumed to be perfectly elastic (i.e., horizontal). After the World War II, econometric investigations could find no evidence of a liquidity trap. Had mainstream economists read *The General Theory*, however, they would have known that on p. 202 Keynes specifies the speculative demand for money as a rectangular hyperbola – a mathematical function that never has a perfectly elastic segment. Moreover, eyeball empiricism led Keynes (1936a, p. 207) to indicate that he knew of no historical example where the liquidity preference function became "virtually absolute," i.e., perfectly elastic. In sum, both from a theoretical and an empirical view, Keynes denied the existence of a liquidity trap.
3. For example, Mankiw (1992) has written that the "*General Theory* is an obscure book...(it) is an outdated book.... We are in a much better position than Keynes was to figure out how the economy works.... Few macro economists take such a dim view of classical economics (as Keynes did)...Classical economics is right in the long run. Moreover, economists today are more interested in the long-run equilibrium.... (There is) widespread acceptance of classical economics."
4. For almost a quarter of a century after World War II, governments actively pursued the types of economic policies that Keynes had advocated in the 1930s and 1940s. The result was that per capita economic growth in the capitalist world proceeded at a rate that has never been reached in the past nor matched since. The *average* annual per capita economic growth rate of OECD nations from 1950 till 1973 was almost precisely double the previous *peak* growth rate of the industrial revolution period. Productivity growth in OECD countries was more than triple (3.75 times) that of the industrial revolution era.

The resulting prosperity of the industrialized world was transmitted to the less-developed nations through world trade, aid, and direct foreign investment. From 1950–1973, average per capita economic growth for all less-developed countries (LDCs) was 3.3 per cent, almost triple the average growth rate experienced by the industrializing nations during the industrial revolution. Aggregate economic growth of the LDCs increased at almost the same rate as that of the developed nations, 5.5 and 5.9 per cent,

respectively. The higher population growth of the LDCs caused the lower per capita income growth. (See Davidson, 2002, pp. 1–3.)
5. The particular proof that Keynes claimed was irrelevant was the classical assertion that a fixed and unchanging downward-sloping marginal product curve of labor was the demand curve for labor and so that falling wages must induce an increase in employment. In chapter 20 of *The General Theory*, Keynes specifically develops an "employment function" that is not the marginal product of labor curve and does not assure that aggregate effective demand is fixed.

What the marginal productivity of labor curve indicates is that if in response to an expansion of aggregate effective demand, private sector entrepreneurs hire more workers to produce an additional flow of output per period, then in the face of diminishing returns (with no change in the degree of competition), the rise in employment will be associated with a fall in the real wage rate. In other words, the marginal product of labor curve is, for any given the level of effective demand and employment, the real wage determining curve. For a complete analysis of this point see Davidson (1998) or Davidson (2002).
6. If the only things that provide utility are the reproducible products of industry, then Say's Law is operative and there is no barrier to the equilibrium point where there is the full employment of utility maximizing workers.
7. True uncertainty occurs whenever an individual cannot specify and/or order a complete set of prospects regarding the future, either because (i) the decision maker cannot conceive of a complete list of consequences that will occur in the future; or, (ii) the decision maker cannot assign probabilities to all consequences because "the evidence is insufficient to establish a probability" so that possible consequences "are not even orderable" (Hicks, 1979, pp. 113 and 115). In such cases the ordering axiom is not applicable.
8. Liquid assets are defined as nonproducible financial assets that are traded in well-organized and orderly markets (See Davidson, 1994, p. 49).
9. To overthrow the axiom of gross substitution in an intertemporal context is truly heretical. It changes the entire perspective as to what is meant by "rational" or "optimal" savings, as to why people save or what they save. It would deny the life-cycle hypothesis. Indeed Danziger *et al.* (1982–1983) have shown that the facts regarding consumption spending by the elderly are incompatible with the notion of intertemporal gross substitution of consumption plans which underlie both life cycle models and overlapping generation models currently so popular in mainstream macroeconomic theory.
10. There is never any involuntary unemployment of slaves.
11. Unfortunately, my prediction involving the progress in macroeconomics has come true.
12. This letter is available in the collection of my correspondence that is on deposit at the Duke University Library Archives of economists' correspondence and writings.
13. Some economists, e.g., behavioral theorists, have tried to erect *ad hoc* models suggesting that agents do not always act with the economic rationality of classical theory's decision makers although there is nothing in their analysis that denies the possibility that rational decision making is possible. Unfortunately, such theories have no unifying underlying general theory to explain

why such "irrational" behavior exists. Behavioral theorists can not explain why those who undertake non-rational behavior have not been made extinct by a Darwinian struggle with those real-world decision makers who take the time to act rationally.

Had behavioral theorists adopted Keynes's general theory as their basic framework, irrational behavior can be explained as sensible if the economy is a non-ergodic system. Or as Hicks (1977, p. vii) succinctly put it, "One must assume that the people in one's models do not know what is going to happen, and know that they do not know just what is going to happen." In conditions of true uncertainty, people often realize they just don't have a clue as to what rational behavior should be.

## References

Arrow, K. and Hahn, F. H. (1971), *General Competitive Analysis*, San Francisco: Holden-Day.
Blanchard, O. J. (1990), "Why Does Money Affect Output? A Survey" in *Handbook of Monetary Economics, II*, ed. B. M. Friedman and F. H. Hahn, New York: Elsevier.
Buckley, W. F. (1951), *God and Man at Yale*, Chicago: Henry Rigney.
Colander, D. C. and Landreth, H. (1996), *The Coming of Keynesianism To America*, Cheltenham: Elgar.
Danziger, S., Van der Gaag, J., Smolensky, E., and Taussig, M. K. (1982–1983) "The Life Cycle Hypothesis and The Consumption Behavior of the Elderly", *Journal of Post Keynesian Economics*, 5.
Davidson, P. (1972), *Money and The Real World*, London: Macmillan.
Davidson, P. (1982–1983), "Rational Expectations: A Fallacious Foundation for Studying Crucial Decision-Making Processes", *Journal of Post Keynesian Economics*, 5.
Davidson, P. (1994), *Post Keynesian Macroeconomic Theory*, Cheltenham: Elgar.
Davidson, P. (1998), "Post Keynesian Employment and Analysis and The Macroeconomics of OECD Employment", *The Economic Journal*, 108.
Davidson, P. (2002), *Financial Markets Money and The Real World*, Cheltenham: Elgar.
Galbraith, J. K. (1996), "Keynes, Einstein, and the Scientific Revolution" in *Keynes, Money and the Open Economy*, ed. Arestis, Cheltenham: Elgar.
Hahn, F. A. (1977), "Keynesian Economics and General Equilibrium Theory" in *The Microfoundations of Macroeconomics*, ed. G. C. Harcourt, London: Macmillan.
Hicks, J. R. (1937), "Mr. Keynes and the Classics: A Suggested Interpretation", *Econometrica*, 5 (April), pp. 147–9.
Hicks, J. R. (1939), *Value and Capital*. Oxford: Oxford University Press.
Hicks, J. R. (1976), "Some Questions of Time in Economics" in *Evolution, Welfare and Time in Economics*, ed. A. M. Tang et al., Lexington: Heath Books.
Hicks, J. R. (1977), *Economic Perspectives*, Oxford: Clarendon Press.
Hicks, J. R (1979), *Causality in Economics*, New York: Basic Books.
Hicks, J. R. (1980–1981) "ISLM: An Explanation", *Journal of Post Keynesian Economics*, 3.

Keynes, J. M. (1935), "A Monetary Theory of Production" in *The Collected Writings of John Maynard Keynes, XIII*, ed. D. Moggridge, London: Macmillan, 1973a. All references are to reprint.
Keynes, J. M. (1936a), *The General Theory of Employment, Interest, and Money*, New York: Harcourt, Brace.
Keynes, J. M. (1936b), *The General Theory of Employment, Interest, and Money*, German Language edition, Berlin: Duncker and Humboldt.
Keynes, J. M. (1937), "The General Theory", *Quarterly Journal of Economics* in *The Collected Writings of John Maynard Keynes, XIV*, ed. D. Moggridge, London: Macmillan, 1973b. All references are to reprint.
Keynes, J. M. (1938), "Letter to R F. Harrod reprinted in *The Collected Writings of J. M. Keynes, XIV*, ed. D. Moggridge, London: Macmillan 1973. All references are to reprint.
Keynes, J. M. (1939a), "Professor Tinbergen's Method", *Economic Journal*, 49, reprinted in *The Collected Writings of John Maynard Keynes, XIV*, ed. D. Moggridge, London: Macmillan, 1973b. All references are to reprint.
Keynes, J. M. (1939b), "Relative Movements of Real Wages and Output", *The Economic Journal*, 49, reprinted in *The Collected Writings of John Maynard Keynes, XIV*, ed. D. Moggridge. London: Macmillan, 1973. All references are to reprint.
Mankiw, N. G. (1992). "The Reincarnation of Keynesian Economics", *European Economic Record*, 36.
Samuelson, P. A. (1947), *Foundations of Economic Analysis*, Cambridge: Harvard University Press.
Samuelson, P. A. (1948), *Economics: An Introductory Analysis*, New York: McGraw-Hill.
Skidelsky, R. (1992), *John Maynard Keynes, The Economist as Saviour 1920–1937*, London: Macmillan.
Weintraub, E. R. (2002), *How Economics Became a Mathematical Science*, Durham: Duke University Press.

# 14
## Preliminary Draft: Was There a (Methodological) Keynesian Revolution?

*Sheila C. Dow*

> I believe myself to be writing a book on economic theory which will largely revolutionise – not, I suppose, at once but in the course of the next ten years – the way the world thinks about economic problems.
> – (Keynes, 1935)

### Introduction

The purpose of this chapter is to examine whether, how far, and in what sense we might say that there has been a Keynesian revolution at the level of methodology. This involves an interpretation of Keynes's expression "the way the world thinks about economic problems" as referring, not just to the content of economics, but also to the mode of thought and specific methodology employed in addressing that content. It is hard to separate content from methodology, at least here we put the accent on methodology.

The notion of a revolution in economic thought was given focus in the 1960s by the work of Thomas Kuhn (1962), who characterized the history of scientific thought more generally in terms of revolutionary transitions from one paradigm to the next. The notion of a paradigm is helpful in that it applies to scientific thought at a variety of levels. Kuhn's thesis was that scientific thought develops within scientific communities, which have shared foundations in terms of understanding of reality and principles for building knowledge, and thus methodology. The normal business of science therefore does not deal with foundational issues; these only emerge in times of "crisis," when anomalies between science and reality come to general attention. If a new paradigm becomes dominant, it is incommensurate with the old one, since the understanding of reality, the meaning of terms, and the way of building knowledge have all changed. The content of scientific activity will also have changed, but there is a limit to how far the content of the two paradigms can be compared, other than in terms of one paradigm or another.

These matters are of course of direct relevance to accounts of the history of economic thought. It is conventional now in the history of economic thought to recognize that, in order to understand as well as possible the writing of a particular author, great efforts should be made to understand the context and intentions of the author. Perfect understanding is beyond our grasp; indeed there is arguably no such thing – even authors themselves (including Keynes) have been charged with not fully understanding their own work. But some understanding, however contestable, can be achieved. Even Foucault (1969), who identifies the most fundamental shifts of anyone in modes of thought from one age to the next, still feels justified in providing historical accounts.

And we are fortunate in the extent of Keynes scholarship on which we can draw for considering our question. Some Keynesians (notably Joan Robinson, Kaldor, Davidson, Chick and Harcourt) continued to point out where post-war economics was departing from the methodology employed by Keynes. But following the publication of the *Collected Writings* in the early 1970s, the volume of methodological analysis multiplied, generally explicitly aiming at "what Keynes really meant," rather than imposing categories developed for application to modern economics. (This should be distinguished from categories developed in modern discourse for analysis of historical periods.) In particular, Chick (1983) and Harcourt and Riach (1997) explicitly set out to extrapolate from an understanding of what Keynes really meant in order to offer a modern Keynesian analysis (with explicit methodological content).

We are also fortunate, in comparing Keynes's mode of thought and methodology with those of modern economics, that he was more explicit than most about his views on the fundamental nature of the social world and of the economy, i.e. about his ontology. It is now conventional to read the *General Theory* bearing in mind that it was written by the author of *A Treatise on Probability* (Carabelli, 1988; O'Donnell, 1989). Having said that, Keynes only occasionally made explicitly methodological statements about the *General Theory*, so much of the discussion about his methodology is inferred, as it must be for most economists. But in what follows we will draw where possible on Keynes's own account.

In considering below whether or not there has been a methodological revolution, an account of the evolution of the methodology of economics since the *General Theory* is required. But of course any such account is also contestable. Further, there is the difficult question of how far any change in methodology has been due to Keynes. Also any influence from Keynes may or may not be what he intended; popular opinion has it, for example, that Keynes was a general advocate of deficit current spending, in contrast to what can be taken from a reading of Keynes himself.

In what follows, we start with an account of Keynes's methodology which is representative of the modern attempt to understand Keynes in his intentions, against the backdrop of his context. It represents what modern scholarship can do in terms of understanding what Keynes really meant (see Runde and Mizuhara's, 2003, collection on recent thinking). This is followed by an account of how the *General Theory* was received, in methodological terms, and how economics subsequently developed. In the process, we consider how current developments in economics relate to what we have identified as the way Keynes thought about economics. This chapter concludes with an assessment of the idea of a methodological Keynesian revolution.

## Keynes's methodology

In providing an account below of Keynes's methodology in such a way as to provide a comparison with modern methodology, we focus on a range of themes, which we address in turn.

### Philosophy of science

Before he engaged with economics, Keynes was concerned with the theory of probability, in the sense of reasonable grounds for belief (Keynes, 1921). The notion of "belief" reflected Keynes's close study of David Hume, who had resolved his skepticism about the scope for reason by arguing that reason requires a foundation in conventional belief. Keynes argued, like Hume, that reality, and in particular social systems, are organic (in the sense of evolving and complex, with interrelations which are also evolving). There is therefore very little scope for certain knowledge. Since most knowledge can only be held with uncertainty, how can we justify action?

> In metaphysics, in science, and in conduct, most of the arguments, upon which we habitually base our rational beliefs, are admitted to be inconclusive in a greater or lesser degree.
>
> (Keynes, 1921, 3)

Keynes set out the procedures employed (by philosophers, by policy makers and by agents) as follows (see further Dow, 2003). We have direct experience, and other sources of evidence. On the basis of this, we develop theories about the causal mechanisms at work in reality, applying reason as far as we can. But evidence and reason are inadequate as a basis for action. So we supplement them with conventional opinion, expert opinion, extrapolating from the past more than is justified (given our knowledge that structures evolve), and the critical ingredient of what Hume referred to as "sentiment," or what Keynes called instinct, or animal spirits. Where the body of evidence is particularly limited, and therefore confidence in our assessment of probability low, instinct or animal spirits will encourage inaction. However, if confidence in our assessment is high, decisions as to action are more readily taken.

Since Keynes understood economic knowledge as being built up in this way (economists too facing uncertainty), we will see how his theory of probability led him to a particular methodological approach. Questions of knowledge were fundamental to him. Further, as Coates (1997) explains, Keynes's thinking continued to progress beyond the *Treatise*, in line with that of philosophers such as Wittgenstein and Ramsey. But in applying this thinking to economics, Keynes (1936a, xxiii) had to contend with "habitual modes of thought and expression" in economics, notably what he identified as the Ricardian/Marshallian tradition. In communicating this in the *General Theory*, he was concerned to address fellow-economists. Keynes himself was engaged in a "long struggle of escape" (ibid.), and, as the letter to Shaw quoted above indicates, he did expect others would follow.

## Generality

It is no accident that the word "general" appeared in the title of the *General Theory*. The more obvious sense in which the theory was general was that it applied to the macroeconomy, in particular the determination of output (which was conventionally taken as given), and to the short period as well as the long period. Keynes was thus concerned to relax assumptions underpinning contemporary economics which he saw as unduly restrictive (Gerrard, 1997, 169). Full employment equilibrium for Keynes was a very special case; allowing output and employment to vary was more general.

But the *General Theory* was also general in the sense of Keynes's underlying theory of knowledge. The limited scope for certainty for economic actors meant that the state of confidence in expectations could shift discretely, changing the demand for money and long-term investment plans, for example. Without the foundation of rational individual behavior (based on certain knowledge) with scope for certain knowledge, the foundations of conventional microeconomics, as well as macroeconomics, were challenged. For the policy-maker, too, there was the underlying problem of being unable to predict with certainty the outcome of policy actions (O'Donnell, 1989). But at least policy could be addressed to the central issue of the state of confidence in market expectations, and knowledge of those economic relations which governments held with some confidence. The most important difference at the methodological level, that Keynes analyzed behavior under uncertainty as the general case, therefore had direct implications for theory and policy. But, as we shall see, it also had profound implications for Keynes's methodology. Prevailing theory, which he referred to as "classical" economics, therefore, in all these respects, referred to a special case.

## Open-system theorizing

It is common now to analyze Keynes's methodology in terms of open systems theorizing (e.g. Chick and Dow, 2001). Open systems are defined in different ways. Lawson (1997) for example defines them in opposition to closed systems. A closed system is one where there is both extrinsic closure (no force for change from outside the system) and intrinsic closure (no force for change within the system – the elements are atomic). It is characterized by event regularities, and yields invariant laws. Chick and Dow (2005) likewise define closed systems as satisfying all of these conditions. But open systems occur when one or more of these conditions is not met, so there is a range of possibilities for open systems – an open system is not the dual of a closed system. Thus any or all of unforeseen human creativity, non-deterministic interactions, evolving institutions, etc can make a real social system open. The implication is that economic relations cannot be captured in invariant laws. Keynes (1921) used the term "organic" for social systems, to explain why knowledge in the form of quantitative probabilities was not in general possible.

The appropriate system of knowledge, as presented in the *Treatise*, was itself an open system, given the role of conventions and human intuition, and the appropriate methodology was pluralist. Just as Keynes talked about non-quantitative probability being based variously on direct knowledge, indirect knowledge, convention, expert knowledge, and intuition, so indirect knowledge itself would draw on a range of incommensurate methods, and follow several different chains of reasoning (Gerrard, 1997, 189). Each chain of reasoning would involve some closure to segment it from other variables and mechanisms – completely open theorizing is not practicable. But these closures are permeable and provisional, rather than the fixed closures of closed-system reasoning. Thus for example Keynes discussed in turn the implications of different assumptions about short-term expectations and long-term expectations (Kregel, 1976). Similarly, Keynes took the money supply as given for the purposes of the *General Theory*, while he had analyzed the forces which shape it (as an endogenous variable) in the *Treatise on Money* (Dow, 1997). The key is that the models he employed to segment the analysis were partial; no formal argument was capable of providing a demonstrably determinate answer.

## Methodology and the role of formalism

The structure of the *General Theory*, with its multiple chains of argument reflects an open-systems methodology. It is helpful here to distinguish between axioms and principles. Axioms, understood as self-evident truths, are the fixed starting point for the deductive logic of a closed theoretical system. Keynes rather builds his argument on the basis of a range of principles (including notably his three psychological principles). These are best understood in the same way as Adam Smith's principles. Both after all were influenced by Newton's "experimental" methodology, whereby principles were formulated on the basis of experience, then employed in a provisional way to develop theory, always aware that further experience might require modifications to the principles. Thus, for example, Keynes's analysis of the consumption function was based on his psychological principle of the falling MPC, but was qualified by a range of possible disturbing factors which would need to be addressed in particular contexts.

But in considering reference to experience, Keynes was quite explicit about the ambiguity of evidence. He referred to direct knowledge based on experience in the following terms:

> Sensations which we may be said to *experience*, the ideas of meanings, about which we have thoughts which we may be said to *understand*, and facts and characteristics or relations of sense-data, or meanings which we may be said to *perceive*.
> (Keynes, 1921, 12, emphasis in original)

Given this imprecision at the level of experience, Keynes was wary, among other things, of analysis which presumed terms to have precise meaning. Indeed, Keynes wrote on a variety of occasions on the merits of vagueness in language (Coates, 1996, 1997; Davis, 1999). For example: "Much economic theorizing today suffers, I think, because it attempts to apply highly precise and mathematical methods to material which is itself much too vague to support such treatment" (Keynes, XIV, 379). The reasoning therefore referred to the nature of the subject matter, understood as an open system, such that the knowledge of agents as well as economists is held with uncertainty. The issue of meaning therefore had ontological roots, rather than being purely a matter of linguistic interpretation (as in the later Wittgenstein).

More generally, Keynes proposed an alternative to deductivist classical logic, which required fixed axioms which could be taken as true (This alternative, variously termed "human logic" and "ordinary logic," was adapted to analysis based on assumptions which were only provisional, and which could not be demonstrated to be true (Gerrard, 1992)). Rather than one deductivist chain of reasoning, ordinary logic involved several chains of reasoning, inevitably with different starting points (which may or may not be "principles"), and potentially employing different methods. While some of this reasoning might be mathematical, not all could be (otherwise the various chains would collapse into one formal model). While any one chain of reasoning (or model) would abstract from some aspect of reality, the important element, in putting the chains of reasoning together, was to bring to the fore those "necessary reserves and qualifications and the adjustments which we shall have to make later on" which we had kept "at the back of our heads" (Keynes, 1936a, 297–8). To do so is more feasible in ordinary language than in mathematics.

O'Donnell (1989, 1997) makes it clear that Keynes was not arguing against all use of mathematics in economics. Indeed in the Preface to the German edition, he addressed his inductivist readership by presenting the *General Theory* as "formalist." Rather he developed a logical argument that mathematical formalism should not account for all of economics. In a letter to Harrod on Champernowne's work in 1936, Keynes wrote as follows:

> I feel increasingly that one cannot think as an economist unless one's method of thought is capable of handling material which is not completely clear-cut and which is, so to speak, symptomatic thinking rather than a completely formal, watertight thinking. What one

hopes is that [economists] might learn to be mathematicians and economists simultaneously, capable of keeping in their minds at the same time formal thinking and shifting uncertain material.

(Keynes, 1936c)

Keynes applied the same logic to econometrics, notably in his critique of Tinbergen. O'Donnell (1997) shows that Keynes's objections were to Tinbergen's specific techniques, not to econometrics per se. His primary critique was of econometric analysis which requires an invariant structure; he argued that the onus should be on the econometrician to demonstrate that a particular case reasonably approximated a fixed structure, so that regression analysis was warranted. But he made other detailed critiques, which have proved to be influential in the development of econometrics.

**Rhetoric**

The fact that Keynes built up the argument of the *General Theory* using several chains of reasoning contributes to the fact that the book is not a straightforward read. Indeed Keynes himself was not satisfied with the way the argument was organized. Reflecting on the "various criticisms and particular points which want carrying further," Keynes indicated in a letter to Ralph Hawtrey that "the whole book needs re-writing and re-casting" (Keynes, 1936b).

Keynes was very conscious of how he expressed himself, tailoring his style to his audience. He was explicit about his attempts at persuasion. For example:

> In economics you cannot convict your opponent of error; you can only convince him of it. And, even if you are right, you cannot convince him, if there is a defect in your own powers of persuasion and exposition or if his head is already so filled with contrary notions that he cannot catch the clues to your thought which you are trying to throw to him.
>
> (Keynes, XIII, 470)

The importance of persuasion followed from the general difficulty he had explored in the *Treatise on Probability* with demonstrating the truth of arguments. This provided further justification for the range of styles in the *General Theory*. Thus, in Chapter 2, he sought to demonstrate how little it would take for the conventional model to allow involuntary unemployment. In later chapters he abandoned much of that framework, believing that he would have carried his readers with him.

Similarly, in Chapter 11 he used a conventional framework to discuss the investment decision, demonstrating in fact that, according to this framework, it would never be rational to invest since there would never be enough information to form expectations with certainty. The style of Chapter 12 is quite different, focusing on how financial markets and entrepreneurs actually behave under uncertainty.

In the absence of the conditions for demonstrable arguments, Keynes used his powers of persuasion to convince readers to accept his point of view. He accepted Harrod's arguments about how to present his theory in order to connect best with what economists already knew. He paid close attention to the criticisms of the *General Theory*, considering how better to put those arguments which he thought had been misunderstood. But, particularly given Keynes's premature death, his work proceeded to take its effect according to how it was subsequently interpreted, without further restatements from Keynes. And, given the complexities of his economics, there was scope for multiple interpretations. Further, since his *Collected Writings* were not published until the 1970s, the major impact was of the *General Theory* itself, without benefit of materials on his philosophical work.

## The methodology of economics following Keynes

Clearly, Keynes did have a powerful effect on economics. He is regarded by many as the greatest economist of the twentieth century. But what exactly that effect was at the methodological level is more difficult to pin down. In what follows we focus on how far Keynes influenced the way in which economics was conducted and understood, i.e. its methodology. We do this in terms of the same themes as in the previous section.

### Philosophy of science

It was only in the 1980s that the relevance of the *Treatise on Probability* for Keynes's economic methodology became accepted. The *General Theory* was thus taken at face value by fellow economists outside his circle, and in isolation from Keynes's philosophy. That is, it was understood, arguably, in terms of the meanings and habits of thought from which Keynes was trying to escape. This was the case even among those normally identified as Keynesians, such as Harrod (Kregel, 1980). Keynes was writing at the same time as the growth of logical positivism, the philosophy based on the proposition that only testable statements are meaningful. As we have seen, Keynes was cautious about the scope for econometrics as a means of testing theories. Indeed, his philosophy emphasized the general inability to demonstrate arguments with evidence. Nevertheless the macroeconomics which Keynes encouraged to grow, with all its data requirements, suited the logical positivist age. Keynes of course was not the sole force behind this trend; institutionalists (as in the NBER) were pursuing an agenda of data gathering, and there were other forces for government intervention (as in the New Deal) which required data. If anything, the strength of support for logical positivism can be seen as a major influence on how Keynesian economics developed.

There was a blossoming of activity around the building of macromodels and their empirical application. Meanwhile, the philosophy of science continued to evolve, as did economists' view of its implications for them. Popper, with his critique of logical positivism, was widely referred to as the main influence on economics. But, as Blaug (1980) argued, economists predominantly practiced verificationism rather than Popper's falsificationism. However, Popper had also exempted the axioms of rational individual behavior from the testing requirement, and this provided influential support for a continuation at the microeconomic level of the axiomatic approach. As the 1970s progressed, the microfoundations movement extended the role of the axioms to macroeconomics. These axioms were very different from Keynes's provisional principles, in that they were not provisional, but rather taken as self-evident. Further the general equilibrium program, following Debreu and Hahn, deliberately detached analysis from empirical application.

Reference to Popper and Lakatos subsequently declined among economists. The conclusion has been drawn by methodologists that their relevance to economics had become very limited (de Marchi, 1988; de Marchi and Blaug, 1991). The emergence of constructivism in the 1960s and 1970s led to doubts about the scope for empirical testing as a meaningful exercise. Nevertheless, the balance has been shifting from pure theory to applied economics. In particular, experimental economics and use of surveys have been generating evidence which challenges the traditional rationality axioms and thus provokes change to pure theory. The content of the rationality axioms is now being treated by some as provisional.

## Generality

While Keynes had presented his theory as general, with the classical theory a special case, leading economists quickly moved to attempt to demonstrate that the reverse was true. But the arguments were conducted at a different level from Keynes. Keynes had seen his theory as general not only in its scope with respect to the economy, but also its scope in terms of knowledge. Issues of knowledge however did not attract significant attention, relative to the *General Theory* result of the general possibility of persistent involuntary unemployment. The focus then was on showing that persistent involuntary unemployment was only possible as a special case: either because the economy was caught in a liquidity trap, or in the less special case of nominal wages being sticky downward. In terms of the model employed, these arguments held good. But the model itself involved restrictions which were at odds with Keynes's system. This is something which has been widely discussed, both in terms of the contemporary alternatives to Hicks's IS–LM system put forward by Champernowne and Meade (Young, 1987) and the later reinterpretation of IS–LM by Hicks himself (1980–1981), where he admitted that inadequate attention had been paid to shifting expectations. The issue is the status of the model – is it part of a wider argument, involving additional strands of reasoning, or is it the whole argument? Is there scope for shifting expectations or not? To address the latter requires that Keynes's discussion of uncertainty be taken seriously.

The Keynes-as-a-special-case argument has evolved over the years, but always colored by being conducted within a particular model as the full argument. Thus New Keynesian models provide a more elaborate account of market imperfections as an explanation for unemployment equilibrium. Yet this literature scarcely refers to Keynes's own work. Indeed Keynes had emphasized the positive role played by the kind of institutional arrangements and conventions which New Keynesians regard as market imperfections (Davis, 1994, 1997). These elements of social structure provide stability for decision-making in the absence of certain knowledge about the future (Shapiro, 1997).

The role of expectations was brought to the fore with the Rational Expectations Hypothesis, but without any scope for uncertainty. There was limited reference back to Keynes's work as an influence (Lucas, 1980) and indeed the quantification of uncertainty was represented as a sign of technical progress. More recently, robust control theory, based on the rational expectations hypothesis, has attempted to grapple with model uncertainty (uncertainty about what the true model of the economy is). But effectively the uncertainty disappears in its mathematical specification, becoming risk. And since the issue is posed in terms of the goal of identifying the "true model," it rests on a very different methodology to Keynes's methodology. For Keynes, the nature of the economy was such that no model (i.e. no one chain of formal reasoning) could represent it. Yet the issue which prompted this literature is a very Keynesian one: how do central banks make monetary policy decisions in the face of uncertainty about the causal mechanisms at work in the economy?

## Closed-system theorizing

To think of a model as sufficient for argument is to consider a closed system as an adequate representation of the economy, which most economists would accept as being in fact an open system. A closed-system approach involves the view that relevant variables are known (or are known to be random), and can be classified as endogenous or exogenous. A deductive axiomatic system such as general equilibrium theory is an archetypical closed system, and is the system into which Keynesian economics was squeezed in the postwar years. Any model of course is closed: variables are specified, and classified as endogenous or exogenous. It is the *role* of the model which is significant. Does it yield partial arguments or full, definitive arguments? Are the restrictions (assumptions) regarded as provisional or as fixed? Is the theory more than the model?

Much of the misunderstanding of Keynes in the neoclassical synthesis period can be said to have arisen from treating a particular model as the entire theoretical system. Thus Keynes was for long thought to have taken the money supply as exogenous, when in fact he had taken it as given (having discussed its determination in the *Treatise on Money*). Yet macroeconomics for decades was built on models which took the money supply as exogenous. As the complete argument, these models gave the money supply great causal power, and the money supply became a central policy variable. Similarly, by incorporating the explicit modeling of expectations, they too were incorporated into the closed system. Keynes had analyzed expectations (as in Chapter 12) separately from his comparison of the *mec* and the rate of interest (in Chapter 11), without any attempt to combine them. The Chapter 11 account was typical of a business plan, by which "saves our faces as rational economic men" (Keynes, XIV, 114), i.e. of rhetorical significance, relative to the way in which expectations are actually formed in practice under uncertainty. Yet one of the contributions Lucas (1980) claims for the rational expectations approach is that it can "operationalize" expectations analysis, bringing it into the (closed) system (see Vercelli, 1991, for an analysis of Lucas in relation to Keynes).

In the early years following the *General Theory*, economics was segmented into partial chains of reasoning, notably in the form of macroeconomics and microeconomics. Then it evolved into a singular, general equilibrium, system (Weintraub, 1985). Now economics is seen widely as becoming more fragmented (Colander, 2000; Goodwin, 2000), into game theory, experimental economics, evolutionary economics, behavioral economics, complexity economics, and so on, drawing increasingly on a range of outside disciplines, such as psychology, sociology, and neurology (Davis, 2006). Further, new types of evidence based on experiments and surveys are being applied to a rethinking of the characterization of individual behavior. This can be interpreted as treating the rationality axioms as provisional in the face of experience. The ingredients seem to be there for a return to a more open theoretical system. What transpires will be influenced significantly by how thinking evolves on the question of formalism.

### Methodology and the role of formalism

Those who have noted an increasing fragmentation in the content of mainstream economics, to the extent that Colander (2000) announced the death of neoclassical economics, have also noted homogenization in terms of method. Others had discussed the emergence of mathematical formalism as an organizing principle for economics since the 1950s (see, e.g. Blaug, 1999). But what was being noted was that, rather than being identified by content (as in general equilibrium theory), mainstream economics was now defined by its method. Thus any analysis which was not mathematically formalist, and thus not expressible in terms of a closed system, could not be classed as economics. Given what we have identified as Keynes's position on mathematics and economics, his analysis would thus be excluded. In this sense it is clear that there has not been a Keynesian methodological revolution.

In a closed system, it is important to combine all elements of the analysis in a commensurate form in order to yield, ideally, a single equilibrium outcome. It is one of the chief attractions of mathematics that it presents all arguments in a commensurate manner. But, as Keynes had argued, this is also its main shortcoming; only those elements of reality which can be expressed mathematically remain in the argument. Mathematization is not neutral (Chick and Dow, 2001). The challenge then, as Hahn has often pointed out, is in drawing any implications for a reality to which the analysis does not directly apply.

The outcome of current developments in mainstream economics will thus depend crucially on how far mathematization continues to be regarded as the *sine qua non* of theory. If individual behavior is still to be represented formally in a deterministic way, then the outcome will be rationality axioms which are more complex and deal more directly with observed behavior. Nevertheless, as the starting point for deductive classical logic, they will simply alter the content of closed-system analysis, not its form. On the other hand, if there is a new willingness to allow multiple chains of different types of reasoning, justified by a willingness to take on board the kind of creative individual behavior and indeterminate institutional evolution which makes the future uncertain, then Keynes's way of thinking about economics will be carried forward.

## Keynes, modernism and postmodernism

We have noted already, however, that Keynes contributed to the growth of logical positivism in economics by providing an ideal research agenda for the purpose: macroeconomics. How far this is regarded as an unintended consequence of Keynes's economics depends on how far Keynes is understood as a modernist – and on what that means. In considering Keynes's influence for modern economics, this implies that we also consider Keynes in relation to postmodernism.

Keynes has been characterized as modernist by association with the Bloomsbury Group, which encouraged his self-referential, psychologistic account of human behavior (Phelps, 1990; Klamer, 1995; Klaes, 2006). Yet the resulting idea of the fragmented self is now more commonly associated with postmodernism (Amariglio, 1988). And modernism as a philosophy of science is also associated with logical positivism, and the idea of science as a closed expert system. In comparing Keynes's style of reasoning with Samuelson, Klamer finds Keynes the closer to postmodernism. And indeed Keynes's open-system approach seems to fit better with a postmodern approach to economics.

But this kind of discussion quickly becomes mired in different understandings of modernism and postmodernism; indeed for postmodernism this is inevitable in that it sets itself up against common understandings. The reason for raising the issue here is two-fold. First, however it is classified itself, Keynes's new macroeconomic theory and the scope for using it for policy intervention fed into a growing (modernist) confidence in science as an activity which could yield certain knowledge as a result of empirical testing. Keynesian theory in the neo-classical synthesis shed Keynes's concerns with expectations and problems of knowledge in order to become what Coddington (1976) termed hydraulic Keynesianism.

It was the failure ultimately for this approach to survive a series of structural changes in the 1970s that eroded confidence in large macroeconomic models and in activist macro policy. Expectations and information limitations came to the fore, and policy impotence stressed. As postmodernism took hold more widely in society, economics also became more modest about its own knowledge. Keynes had addressed knowledge problems and worked out an approach to building knowledge which were aimed at dealing with them. Just as with an entrepreneur, the absence of certain knowledge does not paralyze action. But in the 1990s, much of economics reacted dualistically to a loss of certainty by retreating from activism.

Most significant for our purposes was the changing attitude to methodological discussion, just as methodology itself was changing. McCloskey's pivotal 1983 article argued that, while the official discourse of economics was formalist, the informal discourse was much more pluralistic. But, while this might have been the basis for a useful debate on methodology, and the relative merits of a pluralist methodology in particular, the reverse transpired. McCloskey put the case (which Kuhn had made many years before) that there was no independent basis for any set of methodological rules. But, unlike Kuhn, for whom there is one set of methodological rules particular to each paradigm, McCloskey argued that theories succeed or fail according to how persuasively or otherwise they are presented. Methodology as a field establishing a single set of rules thus had no place. In fact methodology was already moving beyond this traditional activity to a much richer array of analyses. But the message that was absorbed more widely was that there was no point in discussing methodology. Thus, while mainstream economics is facing a number of exciting challenges which have the potential to point economics in a new methodological direction – including the kind of direction which Keynes had sought – there is a marked unwillingness to discuss it.

## Conclusion

We have set out the modern understanding within Keynes studies of the way that Keynes thought about economics. We have found that this account differs from how the *General Theory* was received and understood at the time, and what developed as the dominant methodology in modern economics. This does not mean that Keynes had no methodological influence. Keynes in fact provided the impetus for the important development of macroeconomics in the twentieth century.

The questions he posed and the model of effective demand he developed provided exciting new material for an application of logical positivism to economics. Initially this analysis was partial, segmented from microeconomic theory, somewhat in line with an open systems approach to economics as advocated by Keynes. But the axiomatic structure of conventional microeconomic theory and the subsequent general equilibrium move to derive macroeconomics from the same structure moved economics in the direction of a closed system, whereby one modeling structure could be expected to yield definitive answers. Central to this development was the growing importance of mathematical formalism as defining the subject matter of economics.

It is therefore concluded that, on balance, there has not been a Keynesian revolution at the level of methodology that is consistent with Keynes's approach to economics. The methodology of economics evolved after Keynes, with the conventional interpretation of Keynes's macroeconomic innovations playing an important part. But the growth of mathematical formalism meant a significant divergence from Keynes's approach. He has often been characterized as rejecting mathematics outright, which, as we have seen, misrepresents Keynes's view that mathematical modeling has a role, but only a partial role, in economic thinking. The very idea of treating the issue in dualistic terms (math or no math) is in fact a further reflection of closed-system thinking (Dow, 1990).

Nevertheless there are currents in modern economics which might draw anew, to great effect, on Keynes's methodology, were it more widely understood and appreciated. The fact that experimental and survey evidence is being taken seriously in discussions about individual rationality, for example, suggests that what were regarded a self-evident axioms of rational individual behavior may now be being thought of as provisional. The very public discussion of the model uncertainty of central banks, as markets attempt to interpret signals of central bank thinking, puts the focus on the limitations of single formal models in providing reliable forecasts. There is the possibility here for a change in the way in which we think about economic problems.

The critical issue, in my view, is how far economics continues to be defined by its (mathematical formalist) method. It is that which will determine whether thinking does change in the way Keynes had advocated, with formal argument being treated as only partial alongside other (incommensurate) forms of argument. There are significant difficulties in incorporating into rationality axioms the type of behavior which these new types of evidence are suggesting, just as it has proved impossible to incorporate model uncertainty, in its true sense, into a modeling framework. Keynes's "way of thinking" addressed the actual behavior and actual knowledge problems we face in a non-deterministic social system. If these are really to be taken seriously as economics moves forward, and Keynes's thinking taken on board, then there is still scope for a methodological Keynesian revolution.

## References

Amariglio, J (1988) "The Body, Economic Discourse, and Power. An Economist's Introduction to Foucault", *History of Political Economy*, 20, 583–613.
Blaug, M (1980) *The Methodology of Economics*. Cambridge: Cambridge University Press.
Blaug, M (1999) "The Formalist Revolution or What Has Happened to Orthodox Economics after World War II", in *From Classical Economics to the Theory of the Firm*, R E Backhouse and J Creedy (eds). Cheltenham: Edward Elgar, 257–80.
Carabelli, A (1988) *On Keynes's Method*. London: Macmillan.
Chick, V (1983) Macroeconomics After Keynes. Oxford: Philip Allan.
Chick, V and Dow, S C (2001) "Logic, Formalism and Reality: A Keynesian Analysis", *Cambridge Journal of Economics*, 25, 705–21.
Chick, V and Dow, S C (2005) "The Meaning of Open Systems", *Journal of Economic Methodology*, 12 (3), 363–82.
Coates, J (1996) *The Claims of Common Sense*. Cambridge: Cambridge University Press.
Coates, J (1997) "Keynes, Vague Concepts, and Fuzzy Logic," in G C Harcourt and P A Riach (eds), *A "Second Edition" of The General Theory*, London and New York: Routledge, Vol. 2, 244–57.
Coddington, A (1976) "Keynesian Economics: The Search for First Principles", *Journal of Economic Literature*, 14 (4), 1258–73.
Colander, D (2000) "The Death of Neoclassical Economics", *Journal of the History of Economic Thought*, 22 (2), 127–43.
Davis, J B (1994) *Keynes's Philosophical Development*. Cambridge: Cambridge University Press.
Davis, J B (1997) "J. M. Keynes on History and Convention," in G C Harcourt and P A Riach (eds), *A "Second Edition" of The General Theory*, London and New York: Routledge, Vol. 2, 203–21.
Davis, J B (1999) "Common Sense: A Middle Way between Formalism and Poststructuralism", *Cambridge Journal of Economics*, 23 (4), 503–15.
Davis, J B (2006) "The Turn in Economics: Neoclassical Dominance to Mainstream Pluralism?", *Journal of Institutional Economics* 2 (1), 1–20.
de Marchi, N (ed.) (1988) *The Popperian Legacy in Economics*. Cambridge: Cambridge University Press.
de Marchi, N and Blaug, M (eds) (1991) *Appraising Economic Theories*. Aldershot: Edward Elgar.
Dow, S C (1990) "Beyond Dualism", *Cambridge Journal of Economics* 14 (2), 143–57.
Dow, S C (1997) "Endogenous Money", in Harcourt and Riach (eds).

Dow, S C (2003) "Probability, Uncertainty and Convention: Economists" Knowledge and the Knowledge of Economic Actors', in Runde and Mizuhara.
Foucault, M (1969) *The Archeology of Knowledge*. London: Routledge, 2002.
Gerrard, B (1992) Human logic in Keynes's thought: escape from the Cartesian vice' in P Arestis and V Chick (eds) *Recent Developments in Post-Keynesian Economics*. Cheltenham: Edward Elgar.
Gerrard, B (1997) "Method and Methodology in Keynes's *General Theory*," in G C Harcourt and P A Riach (eds), *A "Second Edition" of The General Theory*, London and New York: Routledge, Vol. 2, pp. 166–202.
Goodwin, C (2000) Comment: It's the Homogeneity, Stupid!', *Journal of the History of Economic Thought*, 22(2), 179–84.
Harcourt, G C and Riach, P (1997) *A Second Edition of the General Theory*. London: Routledge.
Hicks, J R (1980–81) "IS-LM: An Explanation", *Journal of Post Keynesian Economics*, 3 (2), 139–54.
Keynes, J M (1921) *A Treatise on Probability*. Collected Writings Vol. VIII. London: Macmillan, 1973.
Keynes, J M (1930) *A Treatise on Money*. Collected Writings Vols V and IV. London: Macmillan, 1971.
Keynes, J M (1935) Letter to G B Shaw, 1 January. Collected Writings Vol. XIII, *The General Theory and After Part I: Preparation*. London: Macmillan, 1973, pp. 492–3.
Keynes, J M (1936a) *The General Theory of Employment, Interest and Money*. Collected Writings Vol. VII. London: Macmillan, 1973.
Keynes, J M (1936b) Letter to R G Hawtrey, 31 August. Collected Writings Vol. XIV, *The General Theory and After Part II: Defence and Development*. London: Macmillan, 1973, p. 47.
Keynes, J M (1936c) Letter to Harrod, 2 July. Collected Writings Vol. XIV, *The General Theory and After Part II: Defence and Development*. London: Macmillan, 1973.
Klaes, M (2006) "Keynes Between Modernism and Post Modernism", in R Backhouse and B Bateman (eds), *The Cambridge Companion to Keynes*. Cambridge: Cambridge University Press 2006.
Klamer, A (1995) "The Conception of Modernism in Economics: Samuelson, Keynes and Harrod", in S C Dow and J Hillard (eds), *Keynes, Knowledge and Uncertainty*. Cheltenham: Edward Elgar.
Kregel, J (1976) "Economic Methodology in the Face of Uncertainty", *Economic Journal*, 86, 209–25.
Kregel, J (1980) "Economic dynamics and the theory of Steady Growth: An Historical Essay on Harrod's 'Kinfe-edge'", *History of Political Economy*, 12 (1), 97–123.
Kuhn, T S (1962) *The Structure of Scientific Revolutions*. Chicago: University of Chicago Press.
Lawson, T (1997) *Economics and Reality*. London: Routledge.
Lucas, R E Jr (1980) "Methods and Problems in Business Cycle Theory", *Journal of Money, Credit and Banking*, 12, 696–715.
McCloskey, D N (1983) "The Rhetoric of Economics", *Journal of Economic Literature*, 21.
O'Donnell, R (1989) *Keynes: Philosophy, Economics and Politics*. London: Macmillan.

O'Donnell, R (1997) "Keynes and Formalism," in G C Harcourt and P A Riach (eds), *A "Second Edition" of The General Theory*. London and New York: Routledge, Vol. 2, 131–65.

Phelps, E S (1990) *Seven Schools of Macroeconomic Thought*. Oxford: Oxford University Press.

Runde, J (1997) "Keynesian Methodology", in G C Harcourt and P A Riach (eds), *A "Second Edition" of The General Theory*. London and New York: Routledge, Vol. 2, 222–43.

Runde, J and Mizuhara, S (eds) (2003) *The Philosophy of Keynes's Economics*. London: Routledge.

Shapiro, N (1997) "Imperfect Competition and Keynes," in G C Harcourt and P A Riach (eds), *A "Second Edition" of The General Theory*, London and New York: Routledge, Vol. 1, 83–92.

Vercelli, A (1991) *Methodological Foundations of Macroeconomics: Keynes and Lucas*. Cambridge: Cambridge University Press.

Weintraub, E R (1985) *General Equilibrium Analysis*. Cambridge: Cambridge University Press.

Young, W (1987) *Interpreting Mr Keynes*. Oxford: Polity Press.

# 15
# What Keynesian Revolution? A Reconsideration Seventy Years After *The General Theory*

*Robert W. Dimand*

## It's that man again: The continuing fascination of keynes

Economists and non-economists are more inclined to read about John Maynard Keynes than about other eminent dead economists, and such terms as New Classical, New Keynesian, and Post Keynesian indicate that the issues that divided Keynes from those he labeled as classical still inspire research, however distant and hazy may be the historical awareness of such recent mainstream writers as Mankiw (1992). Widely read biographies by Don Moggridge and Robert Skidelsky reveal both a fascinating life and a public career of historical significance from the critique of the Versailles peace treaty to the Bretton Woods negotiations, and a more specialized literature considers Keynes's views on philosophy and probability (and will undoubtedly be revived when Rod O'Donnell's long-awaited supplement to Keynes's *Collected Writings* finally appears), but most of all the continuing attention to Keynes focuses on his repute as the man who revolutionized economics.

Even before the concept of a "Keynesian revolution" appeared as the title of Klein (1947), Keynes himself suggested in his famous 1935 letter to George Bernard Shaw in which he declared himself on the verge of publishing a book that would over the next decade or so revolutionize how economists thought about the economy, knocking out the Ricardian foundations of orthodox economics (and in Keynes's mind, also of Marxian economics). But commentators continue to grapple with the nature of that revolution. Francis X. Diebold proclaimed that "A striking and easily forgotten fact is that, before Keynes and Klein, *there really was no macroeconomics*" (in Adams 1992, p. 31, Diebold's emphasis). In contrast, David Laidler's *Fabricating the Keynesian Revolution* (1999) stresses the rich heritage of monetary economics and business cycle theory, and argues that Keynesian macroeconomics, as embodied in the IS–LM framework, emerged from a process of evolution rather than revolution during two decades of intellectual development in which Keynes was a major figure, but by no means the only important contributor, and with Keynes's contributions being not only *The General Theory* but also the quantity theoretic *Tract* on the inflation tax, covered interest parity, and the social cost of inflation. In this view, Keynes (1936) did not mark a radical break with previous economic thinking, but rather a highly selective synthesis of themes that had permeated economics since the World War I and before.

I consider Diebold's sweeping assertion untenable, supportable only by a quibbling claim that monetary economics and business cycle theory do not count as macroeconomics until the term macroeconomics was coined (or else I would not have given the title *The Origins of Macroeconomics* to a ten-volume anthology of material extending back half a century before *The General Theory*). Laidler's contrasting view, buttressed by careful and wide-ranging scholarship, raises the question of why, beyond accidents of political circumstance, Keynes's *General Theory* received, and receives, so much attention. An answer is given by Laidler himself, in his chapter on "Keynes and the birth of modern macroeconomics" in *The Cambridge Companion to John Maynard Keynes* (Backhouse and Bateman 2006, p. 48): "The *General Theory* was by no means the first work to argue that: (a) the co-ordination of saving and investment at full employment by the rate of interest might break down because of the working of the monetary system; and that (b) this breakdown would probably result in unemployment. Earlier work, however, had failed to explain just how (b) in fact followed from (a)." Laidler then cites Keynes's own *Treatise on Money* as an example of such earlier work, but the statement is equally applicable to the writings of his contemporaries and predecessors in monetary and business cycle analysis. Laidler next refers to Keynes's use of the spending multiplier as how he derived (b) from (a). However, Keynes's account of how deficiency of aggregate demand can cause unemployment to arise and persist in a monetary economy involved much more than the spending multiplier (or, moving from changes to levels, the goods market equilibrium condition), and provided a new analytical focus crucial to transforming the rich and variegated heritage of business cycle analysis and the quantity theory of money into modern macroeconomics, even though (as Laidler 2004 emphasizes) recent mainstream macroeconomics (post-modern macroeconomics?) has narrowed its focus to exclude much of Keynes's message.

Laidler (1999) is subtitled *Studies of the Inter-War Literature on Money, the Cycle, and Unemployment*. The literature on money and on the cycle is indeed treated fully and with great insight. Pre-Keynesian British writing on unemployment is discussed in Laidler's Chapter 7, but more peripherally to his main story. Writing on money and on the cycle was already unmistakably macroeconomic before Keynes, but the literature on unemployment was what would later be termed microeconomic and partial equilibrium, analyzing unemployment as a problem of one market, that for labor.

## A benchmark for interpreting Keynes: Samuelson in 1946

In his 1946 *Econometrica* memorial article on Keynes, Paul Samuelson held that "until the appearance of the mathematical models of Meade, Lange, Hicks, and Harrod, there is reason to believe that Keynes himself did not truly understand his own analysis" (in Lekachman 1964, p. 316). The sorting-out of the differences between Keynes and classics, and the introduction of the formal modeling of the macro-economy in small, aggregated systems of simultaneous equations, was thus situated by Samuelson in the October 1936 Econometric Society session in Oxford in which Harrod, Hicks, and Meade presented their systems of equations for Keynesian economics (see Lekachman 1964, Young 1987), accompanied in the case of Hicks (1937) with diagrams that shaped the trained intuition of the profession (especially after Alvin Hansen replaced Hicks's diagrams for capital goods and consumer goods with a diagram for goods market and money equilibrium in a one-good economy). According to Samuelson, "except for his discussion of index numbers in Volume I of the *Treatise* and for a few remarks concerning "user cost," which are novel at best only in terminology and emphasis, [Keynes] seems to have left no mark on pure theory" (in Lekachman 1964, p. 326). Reflecting in 1963 on subsequent developments, Samuelson credited A. C. Pigou and Gottfried Haberler, and following them Oskar Lange, Don Patinkin, and Franco Modigliani, with "the demonstration that within a Keynesian system full employment can in all probability be fully restored" through the real balance effect of driving down money wage rates and prices, increasing the real value of outside money, hence of net wealth, stimulating consumption even in a liquidity trap (in Lekachman 1964, pp. 332–3). Unsuccessful as a challenge within pure theory to Pigou's Marshallian orthodoxy, and with Keynes's theoretical contribution reduced in this stylized history to an arbitrary but empirically plausible assumption that money wages are sticky downward (perhaps because of irrational money illusion on the part of workers), Keynesianism (as formalized by Samuelson's generation, more attuned to model-building than was Keynes) was nonetheless a breakthrough in policy. Like his first doctoral student Lawrence Klein (*The Keynesian Revolution*, 1947, pp. 45–6, 53), Samuelson mocked Ralph Hawtrey's Macmillan Committee testimony for arguing that government spending would crowd out private spending, except to the extent that it was financed by the creation of new money, which would have been just as expansionary without the government spending (in Lekackman 1964, p. 330n). Samuelson's 1946 verdict on Keynes was promptly reprinted in Harris (1947), and echoed both in Samuelson's best-selling introductory textbook and in Klein's dissertation (which had a second edition in 1966, and was the subject of a conference volume, Adams 1992). Samuelson's eloquent and long-influential 1946 interpretation, from which I have (quite unfairly to Samuelson) selectively cited only judgments that later proved problematic, provides a convenient straw man as a backdrop for changing readings of Keynes.

## Keynes and IS–LM

The IS–LM formalization of Keynes's *General Theory*, presented in small systems of equations in journal articles by Champernowne, Reddaway, Ellis, Harrod, Hicks, and Meade in 1936 and 1937 and in the Hicks–Hansen diagram (see Young 1987), shaped the trained intuition of the economics profession for decades more strongly than did direct contact with Keynes's own writings, and continues (together with its open-economy extension by Mundell and Fleming) to have a leading role in the teaching of intermediate undergraduate macroeconomics and in short-term policy analysis even after the monetarist and New Classical challenges to Keynesianism (Young and Zilberfarb 2000). Just as price theory (thereafter microeconomics) had Marshall's scissors diagram of supply and demand, so the emerging sub-discipline of macroeconomics found in IS–LM a common reference point for argument and analysis, augmented by use of IS–LM to derive the AD curve on the Aggregate Demand/Aggregate Supply diagram and of the 45-degree "Keynesian cross diagram" for derivation of the IS goods market equilibrium curve (see Axel Leijonhufvud's "Life Among the Econ," in Leijonhufvud (1981), on the totem of the Macro and the totem of the Micro). One of the uses of the IS–LM framework was to stifle the great debate between Keynesian liquidity preference and Robertsonian loanable funds theories of the interest rate. To ask whether the interest rate is determined by equality of money supply and money demand (liquidity preference) or by equality of saving and investment (loanable funds) is to ask whether it is set by the LM curve or the IS curve, which, as Marshall said of whether supply or demand determines price, is like asking which blade of the scissors cut the paper.

But *The General Theory* has only one diagram (suggested by Harrod), and its few equations are not gathered into a system of simultaneous equations. Paul Samuelson claimed that Keynes did not understand his own theory until his saw it translated into the language of IS–LM. To the contrary, Keynes's closest associates among the younger Cambridge economists, Joan Robinson (1975) and Richard Kahn (1984), vehemently denied that IS–LM was anything more than a travesty of Keynes's message, offering a tidy, mechanical determination of equilibrium levels of income and interest that obscured Keynes's emphasis on fundamental uncertainty, lack of knowledge of the future, and volatile private investment (an emphasis particularly notable in Keynes (1937), responding to reviews in the *Quarterly Journal of Economics*). Robinson and Kahn saw Keynes's theory as describing an economy moving through historical time, not a set of simultaneous equations for a static equilibrium.

However, the first two published presentations of small, aggregate models equivalent to IS–LM in articles published in June 1936 by David Champernowne and W. Brian Reddaway (both reprinted in Lekachman (1964), with subsequent reflections by the authors) were written by Cambridge students who had attended Keynes's lectures, tutorial supervisions, and Political Economy Club. T. K. Rymes's compilation and synthesis of notes taken by students attending Keynes's lectures (Rymes 1987, 1989) revealed that the first representation of Keynes's theory in the form of a general equilibrium model of four simultaneous equations was made by John Maynard Keynes himself on December 4, 1933, in the concluding lecture of his series of eight lectures on "The Monetary Theory of Production" (see Dimand 1988, 2007). Champernowne and Reddaway attended the lectures. The student notes on Keynes's lectures are particularly interesting, because, after resigning from a salaried lectureship upon his return from the wartime and postwar Treasury in 1919, Keynes lectured only on the subject of whichever he was writing at the time. The exceptional nature of Keynes's lectures is shown by the continued attendance of some listeners year after year: we have notes taken by Lorie Tarshis for four successive years, 1932 to 1935, and by Robert Bryce for three years, 1932 to 1934 (see also Tarshis 1987).

In his concluding lecture in the Michaelmas Term of 1933, Keynes summarized his theory as:

$$M = A(W, \rho) \text{ money supply} = \text{liquidity preference (money demand)}$$
$$C = \varphi 1(W, Y) \text{ consumption function}$$
$$I = \varphi 2(W, \rho) \text{ investment function}$$
$$Y = C + I = \varphi 1(W, Y) + \varphi 2(W, \rho) \text{ aggregate demand}$$

where rho ($\rho$) is the interest rate and $W$ is the "state of the news." The level of national income ($Y$) did not appear along with the interest rate as an argument in the liquidity preference function until Lorie Tarshis's notes on Keynes's lecture on November 25, 1935.

The IS–LM representation of Keynes, which became the trained intuition of generations of macroeconomists, thus originated in Keynes's own lectures, and first reached print in articles on Keynes by two of his students, Champernowne and Reddaway, who had attended his lectures in 1933 and subsequent years. This disposes of the claim by Paul Samuelson (1946) that "until the appearance of the mathematical models of Meade, Lange, Hicks, and Harrod, there is reason to believe that Keynes himself did not truly understand his own analysis" and also of the argument of Joan Robinson (1975) and Richard Kahn (1984) that Keynes would never have countenanced representing his theory as a system of simultaneous equations. Axel Leijonhufvud (1968) viewed IS–LM as the core of the "Keynesian economics" that missed the point of "the economics of Keynes", because it concealed from view the crucial importance of expectations, information, and barriers to interest rate adjustment. It is thus striking that the four-equation model of Keynes's December 1933 lecture differs from the subsequent IS–LM model by having "the state of the news" ($W$), treated as an exogenous variable (like the animal spirits underlying long period expectations in *The General Theory*) as an explicit argument in the liquidity preference, consumption, and investment functions. Keynes did not publish his system of equations himself: as a good Marshallian, he followed Marshall's celebrated advice to use mathematics as an aid to thought, translate the mathematical analysis into English, illustrate with examples relevant to actual life, and then burn the mathematics. He did, however, assure his readers that "if we have all the facts before us, we shall have enough simultaneous equations to give us a determinate result" (1936, p. 299).

## Did Pigou win out in theory?

The verdict of Don Patinkin (1965) was that Keynes's King's College colleague A. C. Pigou won the theoretical debate with Keynes: if money wages were flexible, market forces would automatically restore full employment after a negative demand shock. Both Pigou and Patinkin denied that this theoretical conclusion had any relevance for practical policy, and defended Keynesian management of aggregate demand in a real world in which money wages are sticky downward. Pigou (1943) argued that lower money wages and a lower price level would increase aggregate expenditure even in a liquidity trap. Even if a liquidity trap prevented an increase in the real money supply from lowering the interest rate and stimulating investment, a lower price level would, by increasing the purchasing power represented by the money supply, increase real wealth and thereby increase consumption. Gottfried Haberler (1941) made a similar argument in the third edition of his *Prosperity and Depression*, but this attracted little notice: the *Economic Journal* published Kahn's hostile review of the first edition, Haberler's reply, a note by Keynes denied Haberler's claim that Kahn had misinterpreted Keynes, and a short unsigned review by Keynes of the second edition, but no review of the wartime third edition. Michal Kalecki, in a 1944 comment on Pigou, pointed out that the Pigou (or Pigou–Haberler–Scotivsky) real-balance effect only applied to outside money (cash plus non-interest-bearing reserve deposits held by the banks at the central bank), not to inside money, bank deposits backed by liabilities of other agents. In editorial correspondence about Kalecki's *Economic Journal* comment on Pigou, Keynes argued that the real-balance effect also does not apply to government bonds, whose market value is the present discounted value of interest and dividends that will have to be paid by taxpayers in the future (Dimand 1988), but this anticipation of Barro's Ricardian debt neutrality was not published. But granting that the monetary base (outside money) is much smaller than the sum of all money and government bonds, a real-balance effect remained, and the economics discipline agreed with Patinkin (1965) that, as a matter of pure theory, a sufficient reduction in money wages and prices could restore full employment after any demand shock. Keynes's *General Theory* was reduced to a theoretically trivial, albeit practically important, assumption of rigid wages.

But this controversy concerned the effect of a lower price level (comparing two equilibria that differ only by one having a lower price level and money wage rate), not a falling price level, even if economists spoke loosely of changes in response to a demand shock. The neutrality of a change in the real value of inside debts was also taken for granted. The literature ignored two crucial contributions, neither published in an obscure place: Chapter 19 of Keynes's *General Theory*, on "Changes in Money-Wages," and Irving Fisher's "Debt-Deflation Theory of Great Depressions," published in 1933 in the first volume of *Econometrica* by the founding president of the Econometric Society (reprinted in Fisher 1997, Volume 10). The appendix to Keynes's Chapter 19, attacking Pigou's *Theory of Unemployment* (1933), was much noticed; not so the message of the chapter itself. Keynes (1936, Chapter 19) argued that deflation reduces effective demand, by creating expectation of further deflation which increases liquidity preference (money demand), offsetting the effect of lower prices in increasing the real quantity of money. His analysis, he claimed, was not dependent on taking money wages as given (or at least rigid downward), the simplifying assumption made in his first 18 chapters. Fisher, writing from bitter personal experience, stressed that an unanticipated deflation redistributes real wealth from borrowers to creditors, and sets off a scramble for liquidity by those with debts fixed in nominal terms (including banks) that pushes prices (including asset prices) down even further. The possibility of costly illiquidity and bankruptcy introduces an asymmetry between inflation and deflation when there are outstanding debts denominated in money: deflation increases perceived lender's risk and borrower's risk, raising the risk-adjusted cost of capital. According to Fisher, the deflation that began in 1929 led to a great depression while the rapid deflation of 1920–21 did not because the volume of outstanding nominal debt was much higher in 1929.

In a simple model with adaptive expectations, an expectations-augmented Phillips curve, and aggregate demand depending on both the price level and the expected rate of change of prices, James Tobin (1975) posed the issue as whether aggregate demand increases when the economy is operating below potential output. A lower price level would increase aggregate demand, through the Pigou real-balance effect on consumption and through the Keynes effect of a larger real quantity of money shifting the LM curve down, reducing the interest rate, which stimulates investment. But, following Keynes (1936, Chapter 19), expected deflation increases liquidity preference by reducing the opportunity cost of holding real money balances, shifting the LM curve up (if nominal interest is on the vertical axis). If the nominal interest rate cannot fall because of a liquidity trap at or slightly above zero, faster deflation pushes real interest up point for point, swamping a real balance effect that acts only on the small amount of outside money. Tobin (1980, 1993) and Hyman Minsky (1975) added the Fisher effect of deflation, causing a scramble for liquidity and redistributing wealth to lenders from borrowers who became borrowers because they have higher propensities to spend, as strengthening the contractionary effect of deflation. The more flexible money wages and prices are, and so the faster the deflation resulting from a negative demand shock, the more likely is the economy to move further away from potential output in the wake of a really large negative demand shock, even if the system is self-adjusting for smaller shocks (Tobin 1975, 1980, 1993, see also Tobin "writing as J. M. Keynes" in Harcourt and Riach 1997). The issue of self-adjustment or stability becomes an empirical one of the size of the coefficients on the price level and expected deflation in the aggregate demand function, and the responsiveness of speed of adjustment of prices to the size of the output gap, as well as a question of how dependent Tobin's result was on the specifics of his model (e.g. adaptive expectations versus rational expectations). Regardless of the progress of these investigations, it is clear that it can no longer be maintained that Pigou (1943) won out over Keynes (1936) on the battleground of theory. Pigou's real balance effect did not reduce Keynes's *General Theory* to the practically relevant but theoretically banal case of a fixed money wage.

Robert Clower (1967, 1984) and Axel Leijonhufvud (1968, 1981) argued, contrary to Samuelson and Patinkin, that Keynes's rejection of what he labeled Say's Law of Markets (in aggregate, supply creates its own demand, so aggregate demand deficiency cannot cause a general glut) be taken seriously as an innovation in economic theory by Keynes, regardless of its accuracy as an account of the version of Say's Law held by any individual classical economists such as John Stuart Mill. Walras's Law (so named by Oskar Lange, six years after Keynes's *General Theory*) holds that the value of aggregate demand for the whole economy summed across all markets (including money) must add to zero for any price vector (not just equilibrium prices), because budget constraints (plus local non-satiation) keep the sum over all markets of the value of each individual's excess demands to zero. Clower and Leijonhufvud pointed out that, if the labor market does not clear, the amount of labor that a quantity-constrained household cannot sell, multiplied by the wage rate at which it cannot sell that labor, should not be counted as part of that household's budget constraint for determining its effective demand for goods. The "reappraisal of Keynesian economics" initiated by Clower and Leijonhufvud in the late 1960s attracted considerable attention at first (see Hines 1971), but was not absorbed into the mainstream of macroeconomics (see Leijonhufvud 1998). Their reformulation of Keynes's rejection of Say's Law implied that if all firms expanded hiring (for instance, because of pump-priming government spending), households might spend the resulting wages in ways that justified the expansion of output, moving the economy to a new, Pareto-superior equilibrium, even if it would not have been in the interest of any one firm to expand alone. This was intuitively appealing to Keynesians, but not easy to model persuasively. Similarly, Adam Smith's attribution of the gains from trade to increasing returns to scale (the division of labor is limited by the extent of the market), the subject of the first three chapters of *The Wealth of Nations*, was well known but did not influence international trade theory until the 1980s, when means were found to make increasing returns tractable in formal modeling. The game-theoretic concept of strategic complementarity (Cooper 1998) may provide a comparable resurgence of interest in modeling coordination problems (in contrast to New Classical models that exclude the possibility of coordination problems by assuming the existence of a representative agent).

## A revolution in policy?

The belief that Keynes's *General Theory* contributed no more to pure theory than an arbitrary assumption of sticky wages was accompanied by a myth of Keynes as a lone advocate of expansionary fiscal and monetary policy in response to the Great Depression. Mark Blaug (1991, 178) points out that "there was a pre-Keynesian orthodoxy on policy matters in Britain – free trade, the gold standard, balanced budgets, debt redemptions, and structural reforms – but it was a creed of bankers, businessmen, civil servants, and politicians, not of academic economists". A few economists, notably Lionel Robbins (1934), Friedrich Hayek (1931), and their LSE colleagues, shared that orthodoxy (see also Mises 1935), and, when serving with Robbins on the Committee of Economists, Keynes ironically complimented Robbins on being one of the few classical economists whose policy prescriptions were consistent with his theoretical position. Keynes sharply criticized Pigou's *Theory of Unemployment*, which emphasized the demand for and supply of labor in terms of real wages, abstracting from bargaining in money terms, but he also made clear, when responding when Kahn sent Keynes a copy of a popular, policy-oriented book by Pigou in 1937, that he saw little difference between himself and "The Prof" on matters of practical policy: "why do they insist on maintaining theories from which their own practical conclusions cannot follow? It is a sort of Society for the Preservation of Ancient Monuments" (Keynes 1971–89, Vol. XIV, 259). Terrence Hutchison (1977, 1978) showed that later British Keynesians erred in depicting Pigou as anti-Keynesian in his policy recommendations and in attributing to Keynes a determination to push for demand expansion to reduce unemployment to very low rates.

The identification of Keynes's revolution as one in policy has led to all too many reported sightings of precursors of Keynes, whenever someone is found to have proposed public works as a response to unemployment – a criterion which, as Hutchison shows, would make Jean-Baptiste Say himself an early Keynesian. Advocacy of public works did not necessarily imply a Keynesian understanding of aggregate demand, let alone Abba Lerner's "functional finance": Rexford Tugwell proposed an anti-Depression public works program to be financed by cutting other government spending. Herbert Hoover, while Secretary of Commerce, endorsed a plan for a reserve of public works projects to be kept for hard times, but did not put such public works programs into effect when he was President during the Great Depression (even halting work on the half-finished Commerce Department building), because they would have increased the budget deficit. L. Albert Hahn (1949) claimed that everything that was mistaken and exaggerated in *The General Theory* was stated earlier and more clearly in his own works. Since Hahn was an outspoken proponent of the real stimulus obtainable from easy money in the early days of the German hyperinflation (when Keynes was analyzing the social costs of inflation in his *Tract on Monetary Reform*), and then took an equally strong hard-money, balanced budget line during the Great Depression, Hahn's claim to have anticipated Keynes may be doubted, and his attempts to match policy advice with economic events were, to say the least, unfortunate.

The idea that an initial round of spending, such as a public works project, leads to secondary rounds of spending goes back at least to a speech by Pericles, as recorded by Plutarch, and was noted by Walter Bagehot in *Lombard Street* in 1873 and by Alfred and Mary Marshall in their *Economics of Industry* in 1879. What was new was the derivation between 1928 and 1933 of a spending multiplier that would have a finite value because of leakages from successive rounds of spending, explaining why spending a shilling would not produce an unbounded expansion. Ralph Hawtrey in an unpublished 1928 Treasury memorandum (see excerpt in Dimand 1988) and L. F. Giblin in a published 1930 inaugural lecture in Melbourne derived a finite multiplier with leakage only into imports, which would still yield an unbounded multiplier for the world economy as a whole. In the *Economic Journal* in 1931, Keynes's younger Cambridge associate Richard Kahn provided the first published derivation of a finite-valued multiplier with leakages into imports, reduced unemployment benefits ("the dole"), and increased unspent corporate profits (Kahn labeled the equality of injections and leakages "Mr. Meade's relation"), with the Danish economist Jens Warming extending the leakages to personal saving in a comment on Kahn the next year. Keynes's (1933) pamphlet *The Means to Prosperity* used Kahn's multiplier analysis, for changes in income where Kahn had worked in terms of changes in employment (see Hawtrey, Giblin, Kahn, Warming, Meade, and Keynes reprinted in Dimand 2002b, Vol. 2).

J. Ronnie Davis (1971), and Gordon Tullock in his introduction to that volume, made much of the supposed independent discovery of the income–expenditure theory (the multiplier process) in the United States by Paul H. Douglas and John Maurice Clark before the publication of *The General Theory*. Mark Blaug (1991, 178n) rebuked Keynes for ignoring Douglas (1934) and Clark, finding the failure to cite Clark, a "co-discoverer of the multiplier," "particularly striking." But there is nothing in Douglas (1934) or in Clark's (1935) writings that goes beyond Keynes's (1933) pamphlet *The Means to Prosperity*, which was cited by both Douglas and Clark. Indeed, Clark's (1935) article (reprinted in Dimand 2002b, Vol. 2) referred to the multiplier as "the Kahn-Keynes theory", and contrasted it with his own analysis, which emphasized changes in velocity of circulation. Attempts by Joseph Dorfman and Luca Fiorito to read a derivation of a finite multiplier into a 1931 book by Clark have been shown to depend on not quoting the passage in question (Dimand 2002a).

## A fabricated revolution?

The working title for David Laidler's *Fabricating the Keynesian Revolution* (1999) was "*The Synthetic Revolution*. The word 'synthetic' is ambiguous. It first of all suggests that the Keynesian revolution was largely a matter of synthesizing earlier ideas into a manageable framework, which I think is true; and it also suggests that the notion that there had been a great revolution in 1936, in the sense that a previous orthodoxy was destroyed, was a manufactured idea. So those two senses of synthetic capture the ambiguity of my attitude to Keynes's accomplishments" (Laidler interviewed by Christof Rühl 1998). The first sense brings out an important aspect of *The General Theory*, the crucial function of synthesis that is easily overlooking when attention is paid to the origin of the multiplier or another specific concept. As Joseph Schumpeter (1954) stressed, many of the ideas in *The Wealth of Nations* can be traced to David Hume, Richard Cantillon, A. R. J. Turgot, Francis Hutcheson, or other eighteenth-century writers, but Adam Smith created that a synthesis that proved to be a manageable and enormously influential framework. In evaluating Keynes's work of synthesis, it should be recalled that even the IS–LM system of simultaneous equations, first published by Champernowne and Reddaway, originated in Keynes's lectures. That is another parallel with Smith: the discovery in the 1890s of notes taken by students attending Smith's lectures in the 1760s revealed the extent of Smith's originality and priority relative to the Physiocrats and, concerning the four-stages theory of historical development, Adam Ferguson.

More than many of his followers, Keynes recognized that, like Newton, if he saw further, it was because he stood on the shoulders of giants. In the 1937, *Economic Journal* exchanges with Hawtrey, Robertson, and Ohlin over alternative theories of the rate of interest, Keynes emphasized that he did not consider Hawtrey or Robertson as classical economists: "On the contrary, they strayed from the fold sooner than I did. I regard Mr. Hawtrey as my grandparent and Mr. Robertson as my parent in the paths of errancy, and I have been greatly influenced by them. I might also meet Professor Ohlin's complaint by adopting Wicksell as my great-grandparent, if I had known his works in more detail at an earlier stage in my own thought and also if I did not have the feeling that Wicksell was *trying* to be 'classical.' As it is, so far as I am concerned, I find, looking back, that it was Professor Irving Fisher who was the great-grandparent who first influenced me strongly towards regarding money as a 'real' factor" (Keynes 1971–80, Vol. 14, pp. 202–3n). In his *Banking Policy and the Price Level* (1926), Robertson stated that his discussions with Keynes while writing the book were so extensive that he could not be sure which of them had originated any idea in the book. The connection with Wicksell's natural and market rates of interest is more prominent in the "fundamental equations" of Keynes's *Treatise on Money* than in *The General Theory*, and, when writing a chapter for a *Festschrift* for Irving Fisher in 1937 (reprinted in Keynes 1971–89, Vol. 14, pp. 101–8), Keynes was no doubt inclined by the occasion to exaggerate the resemblance between his marginal efficiency of capital and Fisher's rate of return over costs (contrast Keynes on Fisher in the lecture notes edited by Rymes 1987, 1989). Later textbook Keynesianism dismissed

Robertson, Hawtrey, and Fisher as anti-Keynesian classical quantity theorists believing in an implicitly vertical aggregate supply curve, not as the parent, grandparent, and great-grandparent of Keynes's *General Theory*. Nonetheless, Keynes was conscious of drawing on a rich heritage of monetary theory, and, although in *The General Theory* he paid more attention to such outsiders as Hobson, Gesell, and the mercantilists, over the following year (until his first heart attack) he paid tribute to that heritage in the *Economic Journal* exchange, in the *Festschrift* chapter for Fisher, and in his statement in his rough notes for his 1937 lectures that, compared to Ohlin's Marshall Lectures, "I'm more classical than the Swedes, for I am still discussing the conditions of short-period equilibrium" (Keynes 1971–89, Vol. 14, p. 183).

In his 1971, Ely Lecture on "The Keynesian Revolution and the Monetarist Counter-Revolution" (in Johnson and Johnson 1978), a work that influenced Laidler (1999), Harry Johnson listed among the factors responsible for the success of both Keynesian revolution and monetarist counter-revolution, "the production of an apparently new theory that nevertheless absorbed all that was valid in the existing theory while so far as possible giving these valid concepts confusing new names" and "a degree of difficulty of understanding just sufficient to deter the old and to challenge and reward the young, and hence to reopen the avenues of professional opportunity for the ambitious." Another criterion for success was "the advancement of a new and important empirical relationship, suitable for estimation by the budding econometrician... since intelligent and gifted young men and women will persevere until they succeed in finding statistical validation of an allegedly important theoretical relationship, and will then interpret their results as evidence in favour of the theory that originally suggested the relationship, their efforts will inevitably be extremely favourable to the theory in question." Laidler (2004) notes that Johnson's analysis can also be applied to understand the success of New Classical macroeconomics and also of Johnson's own monetary approach to the balance of payments. However, Johnson's first criterion for success of a theoretical revolution was "a central attack, on theoretically persuasive grounds, on the central proposition of the orthodoxy of the time. In the case of the Keynesian revolution, that proposition was the automatic tendency of the economy to full employment" (Johnson and Johnson 1978, 194). Johnson accepted that, in attacking that classical proposition, Keynes did genuinely set himself apart from the prevailing theoretical orthodoxy.

## The four building blocks of Keynes's theory

I have argued previously (Dimand 1988) that Keynes's synthesis in *The General Theory* had four building blocks, and that, beyond the process of synthesis, Keynes made crucial contributions to each of these four building blocks, although he was by no means the only person to do so. First, the goods market equilibrium condition, with the level of income, not just the interest rate, bringing saving and investment into equality, with the multiplier as the corollary for changes in spending and income. Second, the money market equilibrium condition, with money demand (liquidity preference) a function of national income and the interest rate. Third, the volatility of private investment, reflecting shifting long-period expectations about a fundamentally uncertain future. Fourth, Keynes analyzed why the labor market does not clear (including Chapter 19 of why flexible money wages may not clear the labor market). Taken together, Keynes's synthesis yielded a theory of the role of aggregate demand in determining the level of employment and real output in a monetary economy, not just prices and nominal income.

In *A Treatise on Money* (1930), Keynes followed Wicksell (1898) is treating the interest rate as the variable equating desired investment and saving. As long as the monetary authority and banking system set the market rate of interest at something other than the natural rate of interest, a cumulative inflation or deflation would continue. In Keynes's (1930) parable of a thrift campaign in a closed economy producing and consuming only bananas, planned saving would exceed investment by the amount of windfall losses, causing investment to be reduced, increasing the gap between planned saving and investment. The only limit to the ensuing deflation would be when all production ceased and the whole population starved to death, a corner solution that Don Patinkin's secretary famously rendered as a "coroner solution" – unless, as Keynes remarked in a throwaway line, the contraction of income reduced saving. Patinkin (1982) identified the working out of the implications of that insight, the goods market equilibrium condition ("the principle of effective demand") with the level of income as the equilibrating variable equating saving to desired investment (and setting undesired investment, unintended inventory changes, to zero), as the "central message" to the economics profession of Keynes's *General Theory*. Hawtrey, Giblin, Kahn, Meade, and Warming all contributed, between 1928 and 1933, to working out the multiplier relationship between a change in autonomous spending (exports, investment, or government spending) and the resulting change in equilibrium income, and all five were in contact with Keynes during those years (although Giblin's inaugural lecture may not have come to Keynes's attention, despite their correspondence when Giblin was reviewing Keynes's *The Means to Prosperity* for the *Economic Record*). Keynes synthesized these contributions, but here too he added something original, writing the goods market equilibrium condition for levels of spending and income where the multiplier discussions had dealt only with changes. Patinkin (1982) distinguished Keynes's principle of effective demand from Michal Kalecki's contrasting emphasis on mathematical models of the dynamics of business cycles (including Kalecki 1935, published in English in *Econometrica*). However, Simon Chapple (1991, p. 260) notes that one paper published by Kalecki in Polish in 1933 (translated in Kalecki 1967, pp. 16–25) did "show how changes in exports, the budget deficit, and investment, in a loose two-period framework, cause a rise in profits and production to equilibrate savings and investment." Patinkin (1982, p. 69n) dismissed that paper by Kalecki in a single sentence in a longer footnote as not being part of Kalecki's central message because it appeared in a semi-popular magazine on economics.

In contrast to Patinkin, Sir Ralph Hawtrey, discussing Keynes's aggregate supply analysis in the 1950s, identified the liquidity preference function as Keynes's crucial innovation (see Deutscher 1990). Keynes, in *The General Theory*, was the first to write money demand explicitly as a function of income and the interest rate. Irving Fisher had, in *The Theory of Interest* in 1930 (Fisher 1997, Vol. 9, 216), given what would now be considered a correct statement of the marginal opportunity cost of holding money, but had not stated the money demand function. Fisher had mentioned in passing the rate of interest as an influence on the velocity of circulation in 1896 in an article on the meaning of capital (Fisher 1997, Vol. 1), but not when systematically cataloguing determinants of velocity in *The Purchasing Power of Money* in 1911 (Fisher 1997, Vol. 4), even though just four years before he had written a book entitled *The Rate of Interest*. Passing mentions in verbal discussions, also common in Cambridge monetary theory before *The General Theory*, are no substitute for including a variable in a formal analysis. It is significant that Hawtrey should regard including the interest rate in the money demand function as something new and important contributed by Keynes. Hawtrey was one of the shapers of the "Treasury view" that public works spending would only crowd out private investment (see Hawtrey's 1925 article reprinted in Dimand 2002b, Vol. 2), and so he has been interpreted, notably by Samuelson (1946) and Klein (1947), as implicitly believing in a classical vertical aggregate supply curve. This, however, would make nonsense of Hawtrey's emphatic belief in the effectiveness of monetary policy. Furthermore, Hawtrey helped develop the finite-valued spending multiplier, providing a numerical example with leakage into imports alone in a 1928 Treasury memorandum, a numerical example with leakage into saving in a 1930 Macmillan Committee working paper commenting on Keynes's *Treatise*, and an algebraic version in 1932 (Hawtrey 1932, Dimand 1988, Deutscher 1990, Eric Davis 1990). But if including the interest rate as an argument in the money demand function was news to Hawtrey in 1936, then he would have been perfectly consistent, taking money demand as completely interest-inelastic, to consider monetary policy effective and fiscal policy completely ineffective in stimulating aggregate demand and output, even while fully understanding the multiplier process through which an increase in investment, due to monetary expansion, increases the equilibrium level of national income by a finite amount. Don Patinkin (1981), Harry Johnson (see his 1971 Ely Lecture in Johnson and Johnson 1978), and David Laidler (1999) have caused considerable offense in Chicago by emphasizing how much Milton Friedman's money demand function owes to Keynes's liquidity preference, not just to Chicago oral tradition. The money market equilibrium condition of Keynes's lectures and *General Theory*, with the monetary authority setting the quantity of money, has been largely supplanted in recent years by a recent to the Wicksellian tradition of Keynes's *Treatise on Money*, in which the monetary authority and the banking system set the interest rate, not the quantity of money (Wicksell 1898, Keynes 1930, Moore 1988, Taylor 1993, Woodford 2003).

Post Keynesians such as Paul Davidson (1991) stress the third component of Keynes's theory, the role of fundamental uncertainty in making liquidity preference and private investment volatile, as did Keynes in his 1937 reply to reviews in the *Quarterly Journal of Economics* (in Keynes 1971–89, Vol. XIV). It is noteworthy that Keynes's simultaneous equations summary of his theory in his December 1933 lecture differed from the subsequent IS–LM framework of Harrod, Hicks, Meade, Hansen, and Modigliani by Keynes's explicit inclusion of the "state of the news" as an argument in the investment, consumption, and liquidity preference functions. Again, Keynes was not the only person thinking along such lines: Frank Knight (1921) also distinguished measurable risk from unmeasurable uncertainty, but used the distinction for a very different purpose. Knight was concerned with the existence of entrepreneurial profit, Keynes with macroeconomic instability due to fluctuating expectations and investment. Pigou's *Industrial Fluctuations*

(1927) attributed the trade cycles to investment swings due to waves of optimism and pessimism similar to Keynes's "animal spirits." Keynes's exogeneity of long-period expectations proved particularly troubling to mainstream macroeconomists, with New Classical economists opting for the radically different hypothesis of rational expectations. Bayesians (and Coddington 1983) question the distinction between risk and uncertainty, positing a subjective probability distribution over what the true probability distribution may be, with "any other outcome" as a residual classification that sidesteps the problem of not being to able to list all possible outcomes.

The fourth component of Keynes's theory, the rejection of automatic readjustment to full employment, was singled out by Harry Johnson as crucial to the Keynesian revolution. Chapter 2 of *The General Theory* presented a model that accepted the "first classical postulate" that the economy is on the labor demand curve with the real wage equal to the marginal product of labor, but rejecting the "second classical postulate" that the economy is on the labor supply curve, with the utility of the wage equal to the marginal disutility of labor, the two "classical postulates" being Keynes's summary of Pigou (1933). If the money wage is sticky downward (because workers care about relative wages, and not all money wages would be changed at the same time, given staggered contracts), changes in the price level move the economy along the labor demand curve, with employment inversely related to the real wage. Keynes's Chapter 2 concern with relative wages and overlapping contracts as sources of downward wage stickiness was revived by John Taylor (1980). Given that workers care about relative wages, and that not all contracts are renegotiated at the same time, no money illusion is needed for workers to resist cuts in their money wages (when other workers with unexpired contracts for similar jobs continue to receive unchanged wages), yet acquiesce in a rise in the price level that reduces the real wages of all workers at the same time. Already by 1939, Lorie Tarshis and John Dunlop had presented evidence that forced Keynes to accept that the cyclical pattern of real and money wages was an open question (see Tarshis, Dunlop, Keynes, Ruggles, and Tsiang in Dimand 2002b, Vol. 8). Subsequent data on real wages fail to show either the clear countercyclical pattern predicted by Keynes's Chapter 2 and by Robert Lucas's monetary misperceptions version of New Classical economics, or the clear pro-cyclical pattern predicted by real business cycle theory. But *The General Theory* also included Chapter 19 (discussed above) on why even flexibility of money wages might fail to ensure restoration of full employment after a negative demand shock.

Sir William Beveridge's *Unemployment: A Problem of Industry, 1909 and 1930* (1930) treated unemployment as a microeconomic problem of frictional, seasonal, and structural unemployment (see Darity 1981–82, Dimand 1999a, b), a view reiterated by Beveridge in a series of three *Economica* articles in 1936–37 (reprinted in Dimand 2002b, Vol. 8). Mark Casson (1983) claimed to find a sophisticated Pre-Keynesian structural analysis of unemployment in the writings of Edwin Cannan, Sir Henry Clay, and A. C. Pigou, but this argument depended on looking at a book review by Cannan to the exclusion of Cannan's 1932 Royal Economic Society presidential address on "The Demand for Labour" (in Dimand 2002b, Vol. 8) and on excluding Pigou's *Theory of Unemployment* from Pigou's relevant writings (see Dimand 1988 on Casson). Such interwar British monetary theorists as Hawtrey, Lavington, and Robertson contributed much to the ideas synthesized in *The General Theory*, as Laidler (1999) shows, but the leading British authorities on unemployment as a labor market problem, such as Beveridge (1930), Cannan, Clay, and Pigou (1933), were far removed from Keynes's Chapter 19 analysis of the failure of the automatic adjustment mechanism.

These four elements together comprised Keynes's synthesis, rather than any one of them alone being Keynes's "central message" to economists. On each of these four aspects of his framework, Keynes added something of his own to the important work of others, but his crucial contribution was the synthesis of these four elements into a persuasive and influential framework. Others, notably J. R. Hicks (1935, 1937, 1939), took part in the work of synthesis, without capturing all of Keynes's system (Keynes's fundamental uncertainty is much less visible in Hicks's presentation of IS–LM), but notes taken by students attending Keynes's lectures establish his priority and his influence on early articles by Champernowne and Reddaway.

## Conclusion

The roots of modern macroeconomics are much more varied than just *The General Theory* (see Dimand 2003, Hoover 2003). The Swedish school of Dag Hammarskjold, Karin Kock, Erik Lindahl (1939), Erik Lundberg (1937, 1994, 1996), Gunnar Myrdal (1939), and Bertil Ohlin built their macrodynamics on Wicksellian foundations (see Jonung 1991, 1993), while Michal Kalecki's intellectual debts were to Marx and Rosa Luxemburg. Keynes himself acknowledged Hawtrey, Fisher, and Wicksell as his intellectual ancestors. He encouraged the work of Colin Clark, Erwin Rothbarth, James Meade, and Richard Stone on national income and product accounts, but the at least equally important parallel development of national accounts by Simon Kuznets at NBER was independent of Keynes, and had its roots in the empiricism of Wesley Mitchell. The postwar macro-econometric modeling of Lawrence Klein owed much to Klein's reading of Keynes and to the IS–LM framework, but also to the pioneering econometrics of Ragnar Frisch, Jan Tinbergen, and Trygve Haavelmo. Had there been no Keynes, there would still have been national accounts from Kuznets and macro-econometrics from Frisch, Tinbergen, Haavelmo, and Koopmans (see Tinbergen, Frisch, Haavelmo, Koopmans, and Klein in Dimand 2002b, Vol. 7). Keynes responded very skeptically to Tinbergen's *Statistical Testing of Business Cycle Theories* (1939), as did Frisch and Milton Friedman, but accepted the presidency of the Econometric Society. Already by 1939, Keynes acknowledged empirical and theoretical doubts raised by Dunlop, Tarshis, and Kalecki about the cyclical pattern of real and money wages implied by Chapter 2 of *The General Theory*.

Nonetheless, Keynes's *General Theory*, both through Keynes's individual contributions and through his work of synthesis, was crucial to the emergence of modern macroeconomics. Keynes, and not just such interpreters of Keynes as Hicks and Hansen, gave economists a usable macroeconomic framework, with roles for the goods market and money market equilibrium conditions, for expectations, uncertainty, and volatile investment, and for an analysis of why the labor market may not clear and nominal shocks can have real consequences. All four components were fundamental to the framework. To single out any one of the four as Keynes's "central message" obscures the powerful synthesis that they jointly comprise. Keynes provided macroeconomics with a focus on the determination of the equilibrium levels of income and employment that differed both from the focus of business-cycle theory on dynamic movements and of the focus of monetary theory on prices, albeit with considerable attention to short-run non-neutrality. Much had been written on unemployment, for instance Fisher (1926) correlating unemployment with a distributed lag of past price-level changes (reprinted in 1973 as "I Discovered the Phillips Curve"), but neither Fisher nor his contemporaries went beyond such empirical correlations to offer any macroeconomic theory of the level of employment, unemployment, or output. Pigou's *Theory of Unemployment* (1933) was a microeconomic theory of supply and demand in one market, with unemployment simply meaning that the wage was too, as in Edwin Cannan's (1932) presidential address to the Royal Economic Society (in Dimand 2002b, Vol. 8) – with the difference that Cannan, unlike Pigou, accepted the conclusion that wage cutting would cure unemployment.

Yes, Virginia – and yes, Chicago – there was a Keynesian Revolution in macroeconomics theory. Many contributed to the emergence of modern macroeconomics from its rich heritage of business cycle analysis and monetary theory, but Keynes's *General Theory* altered the focus and the basic analytical framework of the field. The "Keynesian Revolution" was a synthesis, but not a fabrication.

## References

F. Gerard Adams, ed. (1992) *Lawrence Klein's The Keynesian Revolution 50 Years After*. Philadelphia, PA: Department of Economics, University of Pennsylvania.
Roger E. Backhouse and Bradley W. Bateman, eds. (2006) *The Cambridge Companion to John Maynard Keynes*. Cambridge, UK: Cambridge University Press.
W. H. Beveridge (1930) *Unemployment: A Problem of Industry (1909 and 1930)*. London: Longmans, Green.
Mark Blaug (1991) "Second Thoughts on the Keynesian Revolution," *History of Political Economy* 23, Summer, 171–92.
Mark Casson (1983) *Economics of Unemployment: An Historical Perspective*. Oxford: Martin Robertson.
Simon Chapple (1991) "Did Kalecki Get There First? The Race for the General Theory," *History of Political Economy* 23, Summer, 243–61.
John Maurice Clark (1935) "Cumulative Effects of Changes in Aggregate Spending as Illustrated by Public Works," *American Economic Review* 25, March, 14–20.
Robert W. Clower, ed. (1967) *Monetary Theory*. Harmondsworth, UK: Penguin.
Robert W. Clower (1984) *Money and Markets*, ed. Donald Walker. Cambridge, UK: Cambridge University Press.
Alan Coddington (1983) *Keynesian Economics: The Search for First Principles*. London: George Allen & Unwin.
Russell Cooper (1998) *Coordination Games*. Cambridge, UK: Cambridge University Press.
William Darity, Jr. (1981–82) "Beveridge and the New Search Unemployment," *Journal of Post Keynesian Economics* 4, Winter, 171–80.
Paul Davidson (1991) "Is Probability Theory Relevant for Uncertainty? A Post Keynesian Perspective," *Journal of Economic Perspectives* 5, Winter, 129–43.
Eric G. Davis (1990) "The Correspondence between R. G. Hawtrey and J. M. Keynes on the *Treatise*: The Genesis of Output Adjustment Models," *Canadian Journal of Economics* 12, 716–24.
J. Ronnie Davis (1971) *The New Economics and the Old Economists*. Ames, IA: Iowa State University Press.
Patrick Deutscher (1990) *R. G. Hawtrey and the Development of Macroeconomics*. London: Macmillan.
Robert W. Dimand (1988) *The Origins of the Keynesian Revolution*. Aldershot, UK: Edward Elgar Publishing, and Stanford, CA: Stanford University Press.

Robert W. Dimand (1999a) "Beveridge on Unemployment and Cycles Before *The General Theory*," *History of Economic Ideas* 7, Fall, 33–51.

Robert W. Dimand (1999b) "The Beveridge Retort: Beveridge's Response to the Keynesian Challenge," in Luigi L. Pasinetti and Bertram Schefold, eds., *The Impact of Keynes in the 20th Century*, Cheltenham, UK, and Lyme, NH: Edward Elgar Publishing, 221–39.

Robert W. Dimand (2002a) "John Maurice Clark's Contribution to the Genesis of the Multiplier: A Response to Luca Fiorito," *History of Economic Ideas* 10, 29–36.

Robert W. Dimand, ed. (2002b) *The Origins of Macroeconomics*, 10 volumes. London and New York: Routledge.

Robert W. Dimand (2003) "Interwar Monetary and Business Cycle Theory," in W. Samuels, J. Biddle, and J. Davis, eds., (2003) *The Blackwell Companion to the History of Economic Thought*, Oxford and Malden, MA: Blackwell, 325–42.

Robert W. Dimand (forthcoming 2007) "Keynes, IS-LM, and the Marshallian Tradition," *History of Political Economy*, 39(1), 785–92.

Paul H. Douglas (1934) *Controlling Depressions*. New York: W. W. Norton.

Fisher, I. (1926) "A Statistical Relation Between Unemployment and Price Changes," *International Labour Review* 13(6), 785–92, reprinted as "Lost and Found: I Discovered the Phillips Curve – Irving Fisher," *Journal of Political Economy* 81 (1973), 496–502.

Irving Fisher (1997) *The Works of Irving Fisher*, 14 volumes, ed. William J. Barber assisted by Robert W. Dimand and Kevin Foster, consulting ed. James Tobin. London: Pickering & Chatto.

Gottfried Haberler (1941) *Prosperity and Depression*, 3rd ed. Geneva: League of Nations.

L. Albert Hahn (1949) *The Economics of Illusion*. New York: Squier Publishing.

Geoffrey C. Harcourt and Peter A. Riach, eds. (1997) *A "Second Edition" of The General Theory*, 2 volumes. London and New York: Routledge.

Harris, S. E., ed (1947) *The New Economics: Keynes' Influence on Theory and Public Policy*. New York: Alfred A. Knopf.

R. G. Hawtrey (1932) *The Art of Central Banking*. London: Longman.

Friedrich A. von Hayek (1931) *Prices and Production*. London: Routledge (2nd ed. 1935).

J. R. Hicks (1935) "A Suggestion for Simplifying the Theory of Money," *Economica* n.s. 2, February, 1–19.

J. R. Hicks (1937) "Mr. Keynes and the Classics: A Suggested Interpretation," *Econometrica* 5, April, 147–59.

J. R. Hicks (1939) *Value and Capital*. Oxford: Clarendon Press (2nd ed. 1946).

A. G. Hines (1971) *On the Reappraisal of Keynesian Economics*. Oxford, UK: Martin Robertson.

Kevin D. Hoover (2003) "A History of Postwar Monetary Economics and Macroeconomics," in W. Samuels, J. Biddle, and J. Davis, eds., (2003) *The Blackwell Companion to the History of Economic Thought*, Oxford and Malden, MA: Blackwell, 410–27.

T. W. Hutchison (1977) *Keynes v. the "Keynesians"...? An Essay in the Thinking of J. M. Keynes and the Accuracy of Its Interpretation by His Followers*. London: Institute of Economic Affairs.

T. W. Hutchison (1978) *On Revolutions and Progress in Economic Knowledge*. Cambridge, UK: Cambridge University Press.

Elizabeth S. Johnson and Harry G. Johnson (1978) *The Shadow of Keynes*. Chicago: University of Chicago Press.

Lars Jonung, ed. (1991) *The Stockholm School of Economics Revisited*. Cambridge, UK: Cambridge University Press.

Lars Jonung, ed. (1993) *Swedish Economic Thought*. London and New York: Routledge.

Richard F. Kahn (1984) *The Making of Keynes's General Theory*. Cambridge, UK: Cambridge University Press.

Michal Kalecki (1935) "A Macrodynamic Theory of Business Cycles," *Econometrica* 3, July, 327–44.

Michal Kalecki (1967) *Studies in the Theory of Business Cycles 1933–1939*. Oxford: Basil Blackwell (reprinted in Dimand 2002b, Vol. 5).

John Maynard Keynes (1923) *A Tract on Monetary Reform*. London: Macmillan.

John Maynard Keynes (1930) *A Treatise on Money*, 2 volumes. London: Macmillan.

John Maynard Keynes (1933) *The Means to Prosperity*. New York: Harcourt Brace.

John Maynard Keynes (1936) *The General Theory of Employment, Interest and Money*. London: Macmillan.

Keynes, J. M. (1937) "The General Theory of Employment," *Quarterly Journal of Economics* 51, 209–223.

John Maynard Keynes (1971–89) *The Collected Writings of John Maynard Keynes*, 30 volumes, general editors D. E. Moggridge and E. A. G. Robinson, volume editors Elizabeth S. Johnson and D. E. Moggridge. London: Macmillan, and New York: Cambridge University Press, for the Royal Economic Society.

Lawrence R. Klein (1947) *The Keynesian Revolution*. New York: Macmillan.

Frank H. Knight (1921) *Risk, Uncertainty and Profit*. Boston: Houghton Mifflin.

David Laidler and Christof Rühl (1998) "Perspectives on Modern Macroeconomic Theory and its History: An Interview with David Laidler," *Review of Political Economy* 10:1, 27–56.

David Laidler (1999) *Fabricating the Keynesian Revolution: Studies of the Inter-War Literature on Money, the Cycle, and Unemployment*. Cambridge, UK: Cambridge University Press.

David Laidler (2004) *Macroeconomics in Retrospect: The Selected Essays of David Laidler*. Cheltenham, UK, and Northampton, MA: Edward Elgar Publishing.

Axel Leijonhufvud (1968) *On Keynesian Economics and the Economics of Keynes*. New York: Oxford University Press.

Axel Leijonhufvud (1981) *Information and Coordination: Essays in Macroeconomic Theory*. New York: Oxford University Press.

Axel Leijonhufvud (1998) "Mr. Keynes and the Moderns," *European Journal of the History of Economic Thought* 5, Spring, 169–88.

Robert Lekachman, ed. (1964) *Keynes' General Theory: Reports of Three Decades*. New York: St. Martin's.

Erik Lindhal (1939) *Studies in the Theory of Money and Capital*. London: George Allen & Unwin.

Erik Lundberg (1937) *Studies in the Theory of Economic Expansion*. London: P. S. King.

Erik Lundberg (1994) *Studies in Economic Instability and Change*, ed. R. G. H. Henrikson. Stockholm: SNS Forlag.

Erik Lundberg (1996) *The Development of Swedish and Keynesian Macroeconomic Theory and its Impact on Economic Policy*. Cambridge, UK: Cambridge University Press.

N. Gregory Mankiw (1992) "The Reincarnation of Keynesian Economics," *European Economic Review* 36, 559–65.
Hyman P. Minsky (1975), *John Maynard Keynes*. New York: Columbia University Press.
Ludwig von Mises (1935) *The Theory of Money and Credit*, trans. H. Batson. London: Jonathan Cape.
Basil Moore (1988) *Horizontalists and Verticalists: The Macroeconomics of Credit Money*. Cambridge, UK: Cambridge University Press.
Gunnar Myrdal (1939) *Monetary Equilibrium*, trans. R. B. Bryce and N. Stolper. London: W. Hodge.
Don Patinkin (1965) *Money, Interest and Prices*, 2nd ed. New York: Harper & Row.
Don Patinkin (1981) *Essays on and in the Chicago Tradition*. Durham, NC: Duke University Press.
Don Patinkin (1982) *Anticipations of the General Theory? And Other Essays on Keynes*. Chicago: University of Chicago Press.
A. C. Pigou (1927) *Industrial Fluctuations*. London: Macmillan.
A. C. Pigou (1933) *Theory of Unemployment*. London: Macmillan.
A. C. Pigou (1943) "The Classical Stationary State," *Economic Journal* 53, December, 343–51.
Dennis H. Robertson (1926) *Banking Policy and the Price Level*. London: P. S. King.
Joan Robinson (1975) "What Has Become of the Keynesian Revolution?" in Milo Keynes, eds., *Essays on John Maynard Keynes*, Cambridge, UK: Cambridge University Press.
Lionel Robbins (1934) *The Great Depression*. London: Macmillan.
Thomas K. Rymes, ed. (1987) *Keynes's Lectures, 1932–35: Notes of Students*. Ottawa, ON: Department of Economics, Carleton University.
Thomas K. Rymes, ed. (1989) *Keynes's Lectures, 1932–35: Notes of a Representative Student*. London: Macmillan, and Ann Arbor: University of Michigan Press.
Paul A. Samuelson (1946) "The General Theory," *Econometrica* 14, July, as reprinted in Lekachman (1964), 315–31.
Joseph A. Schumpeter (1954) *History of Economic Analysis*. New York: Oxford University Press.
Lorie Tarshis (1987) "Keynesian Revolution," in John Eatwell, Murray Milgate, and Peter Newman, eds., *The New Palgrave: A Dictionary of Economics*, London: Stockton Press (Macmillan).
John B. Taylor (1980) "Aggregate Dynamics and Staggered Contracts," *Journal of Political Economy* 88, February, 1–24.
John B. Taylor (1993) *Macroeconomic Policy in a World Economy*. New York: Norton.
Jan Tinbergen (1939) *Statistical Testing of Business-Cycle Theories*, 2 volumes. Geneva: League of Nations; reprinted in 1 volume, New York: Agathon Press, 1968.
James Tobin (1975) "Keynesian Models of Recession and Depression," *American Economic Review: AEA Papers and Proceedings*, 65, May, 195–202.
James Tobin (1980) *Asset Accumulation and Economic Activity*. Oxford: Basil Blackwell, and Chicago: University of Chicago Press.
James Tobin (1993) "Price Flexibility and Output Stability: An Old Keynesian View," *Journal of Economic Perspectives* 7, Winter, 45–65.
Knut Wicksell (1898) *Interest and Prices*, trans. R. F. Kahn with an introduction by Bertil Ohlin. London: Macmillan for the Royal Economic Society, 1936.

Michael Woodford (2003) *Interest and Prices: Foundations of a Theory of Monetary Policy*. Princeton, NJ: Princeton University Press.

Warren Young (1987) *Interpreting Mr. Keynes: The IS-LM Enigma*. Cambridge, UK: Polity Press, and Boulder, CO: Westview Press.

Young, W., and Zilberfarb B. Z., eds. (2000) *IS-LM and Modern Macroeconomics*. Boston, Dordrecht, and London: Kluwer Academic Publishers.

# Index

aesthetics, 3, 101–18
aggregate
   demand, 5, 21, 24, 32, 64, 139–40, 151, 166, 197–216, 232, 237, 247, 288, 290, 292–303
   supply, 140, 247, 290, 295, 300, 302
algebra, 21, 95, 303
ancient monument, 17, 297
animal spirit, 11, 117, 139, 146, 149, 271, 292, 304
anthropology, 3–4, 120–4, 129
anti-Keynesian, 8, 66, 78–80, 84, 157, 164–6, 168, 172, 175, 179–80
anti-liberal, 32
anti-trust, 94
architect, 9, 109, 134
attitude, 9, 12, 15–17, 20, 50, 70–1, 87, 95, 109, 180, 282, 298
auctioneer, 10, 161–4, 170, 182
authority, 8, 11, 14, 21, 30

Backhouse, Roger, 2, 8–27, 60, 288
balanced budget, 12, 296
ballet, 101–3, 110
Barro, Robert, 8, 11, 173–4, 293
Bateman, Bradley, 2, 8–27, 32, 121, 288
beauty, 3, 50, 104–16
Bell, Clive, 102, 106, 110, 116–17
Bell, Vanessa, 101–2, 116
Besomi, Daniele, 35, 37
biographer, 2, 28–9, 34–5, 38–9, 244
biography, 2, 29, 30, 34, 37, 38, 60, 117
Blaug, Mark, 37–8, 277, 280, 296, 298
Bloomsbury, 18–19, 24–5, 56, 101–16, 129, 281
BrettonWoods negotiations, 103, 123, 134, 236, 287
Brittan, Samuel, 36
Bryce, Robert, 15, 53, 248–9, 251, 291
Buchanan, James, 8, 12, 58

budget deficits, 12, 15, 234–5, 297, 302
business cycle analysis, 1, 6, 7, 288, 307

*Cambridge Daily News*, 45
Cannan, Edwin, 305–6
capitalism, 3, 18, 21, 47, 50–1, 53, 59, 73, 83, 91–9, 108–34, 239
capitalist society, 16, 129
Circus, the (Cambridge), 33–4
civilization, 31, 60, 108–9, 117, 230
classical liberalism, 3, 67–73, 81–3, 87
classics, 3, 30, 63–4, 71, 73, 75, 83–154, 168, 289
Clower, Robert, 10–11, 159, 229, 295
Coase theorem, 81–2
Colander, David, C., 15, 25, 54, 159, 247–9, 280
*Collected Writings of John Maynard Keynes*, 29, 33, 141, 269, 276, 287
collectivism, 83, 88
commodity (-ties), 11, 149, 160, 169, 178, 230–1, 235–6, 256
Communism, 31, 123, 134
comparative system, 4, 120, 124, 126
competition, 10, 63, 67, 69, 84, 86–8, 93, 94, 122, 162–87, 246, 250, 263
consumption, passim
Cooper, Richard N., 4, 9, 133–5
coordination, 10–11, 147, 238
corporatism, 3, 103–12
Council for the Encouragement of Music and the Arts (CEMA), 103–9
counter revolution, 8, 54, 58, 80–1, 84, 172, 300
craft economy, 5, 197, 203–5, 210
criticism, 14, 29, 33–4, 37, 65, 82–3, 104, 110, 172, 174–6, 258

Davidson, Paul, 5–6, 241–63, 269, 303
deficit, 12, 151, 159, 233, 234, 236, 270, 297, 302
democracy, 12, 31, 53, 79, 92

deregulation, 81–3, 94
De Vroey, Michel, 4, 157–95
Dimand, Robert W., 6–7, 25, 33, 37–9, 150, 287–311
diminishing returns, 35, 198, 201, 203, 206–7, 210, 216
disequilibrium, 10–12, 64, 75, 77–9, 82, 87, 144, 158, 169, 173–87, 198–9, 250, 253
doctrine, 9, 13, 37, 65, 134, 207, 232
dogma, 18–20, 112
Dostaler, Gilles, 3, 101–17
Dow, Sheila C., 6, 25, 268–84

econometrics, 9, 75, 77, 94, 166–7, 188, 258, 275, 289, 294, 306
*Economic Consequences of the Peace* (Keynes), 43, 45, 47–50, 54, 56
*Economic Journal*, 20, 30, 45–6, 121, 293, 298–300
economic liberalism, 3, 64–6, 69, 71–6, 83–8
*Economist, The*, 2, 44–46
economy,
  self-adjusting, 1, 138–9, 142, 151, 244, 295
effective demand, passim
employment, passim
equilibrium, passim
*Essays in Persuasion* (Keynes), 46, 48, 51–2
exchange rate, 30, 92, 126, 134, 151, 231, 236–7

Fabian, 70
fascism, 31, 134
fiscal policy, passim,
fine tuning, 9, 129, 133, 151, 238
Fisher, Irving, 150, 294–5, 299–300, 302, 305–6
Forstater, Mathew, 3–4, 25, 120–3
freedom, 31, 59, 66–7, 69, 73, 97, 127–8
free-market, 68, 70, 83, 87, 91, 126–8, 165, 245–50
free trade, 45, 68, 71, 296
Friedman, Milton, passim
Fry, Roger, 18, 102, 106, 110, 116
full-employment, 73, 76–7, 147, 151, 197, 243, 250, 253–4, 263

gap, 16, 66–7, 84, 86–8, 106, 185, 295, 301
*General Theory of Employment, Interest and Money* (Keynes), passim
generation, 1–3, 8, 20, 22, 31, 36, 48, 50, 53, 57, 59, 70, 86, 104, 126, 145, 169, 175, 185, 238, 248, 290, 292
Gerrard, B., 39, 271, 273–4
Goodwin, Craufurd D. W., 18, 25, 75, 280
Grant, Duncan, 44–7, 101–2, 116
great depression, 3, 46, 60, 77, 134, 166–7, 294, 296–7
Grossman, Herschel, 11, 173–4

habitual modes of thought, 19, 52, 271
Hansen, Alvin, 9, 54, 238, 289, 290, 303, 306
Harcourt, G. C., 38, 60–1, 269, 295
Harrod, Roy F., 2, 10, 14, 15, 28, 30–8, 75, 144, 146, 167, 274, 276, 289–92, 303
Hawtrey, Ralph G., 34, 275, 290, 297–305
Hayek, Friedrich A., 15–16, 18, 29, 65, 94–5, 175, 207, 212, 248, 296
Heilbroner, Robert L., 4, 129
Henderson, Hubert, 29, 46, 52
heritage, 1, 6, 140, 288, 300, 307
Hicks, John R., 10, 14, 37, 64, 75, 152, 165, 167–8, 171, 173, 175, 179, 181–4, 188, 202, 225, 238, 244–5, 261–2, 266, 278, 289, 290, 292, 303, 305, 306
Hubbard, Glenn R., 44, 54–5
Hydraulic Keynesianism, 16, 281

ideological, 13, 86, 127, 185
ideology, 44, 185
individualism, 31, 76, 87, 92, 127
inferior good, 3, 98
inflation, 11, 16, 22–3, 46, 50–1, 77, 82, 159, 262, 288, 294, 297, 301
inflationary gap, 16, 22
instability, 1, 82, 85, 114, 212, 303
intuition, 16, 20, 22, 23–4, 36, 105–7, 272–3, 289, 290, 292

investment, passim
invisible hand, 63, 66, 67, 69, 85–8, 176, 259
involuntary unemployment, 5–6, 14, 17, 19, 71–2, 77, 122, 166, 168, 176, 180, 182, 188, 199, 227, 243–4, 255–6, 263, 275, 278

Kahn, Richard F., 17, 30–7, 211, 291–8, 301
Kalecki, Michal, 293, 302, 306
Kasper, Sherry D., 3, 25, 43–60
Keynesian, passim
  adjustment, 5, 197
  conceptual apparatus, 5, 157, 165, 171, 173–5, 179, 185–6, 188
  economics, 5, 8, 10–14, 54, 75, 78, 121, 137, 145, 152, 180, 182, 243, 262–3, 277, 279, 289, 292, 295
  policy, 5, 11, 36, 77, 164, 168, 172, 182, 238
  revolution, 1, 6–7, 8–9, 12–13, 23, 43, 53–4, 58, 74, 83, 122, 152, 167, 247–8, 268, 270, 283, 287, 298, 300, 304, 307
Keynes, John Maynard, passim
  intellect, 36, 56
  legacy, 1, 4, 8, 53
  puzzles, 10, 98, 137
King's College, Cambridge, 17, 117, 293
Klein, Lawrence, 9, 75, 134, 167, 169, 198, 287, 290, 302, 306
Knapp, Georg F., 121–2, 124, 230
Knight, Frank H., 136–9, 153, 303

labour market, 5, 14, 74, 77, 166
Laidler, David, 38, 287–9, 298, 300, 303, 305
laissez-faire, 32, 63–5, 69, 71, 79–80, 84, 108, 123, 126–8, 137–51, 165, 184, 237, 246, 259, 298, 300, 303, 305
Lange, Oskar, 10, 37, 289, 292, 295
legacy, Keynes's, 1–2, 4, 8–16, 48–60, 98, 120, 123, 133–5, 153
Leijonhufvud, Axel, 10–11, 140, 159, 290, 292, 295–6

Lerner, Abba P., 9–10, 14–15, 37, 238
liberalism, passim
  classical, 3, 67–73, 81–3, 87
liberal party, 46, 51
liquidity, 5, 13, 21, 35, 74, 76, 143–9, 202, 207, 222–5, 227–8, 243–5, 255–62, 278, 289–95, 301–3
long-period equilibrium, 137–46, 170
Lucas, R.E., 12–13, 57–8, 73, 78–84, 162, 164–5, 170, 172, 174, 176–87, 278–9, 304
Lydia, Lopokova, 2, 31, 101–2, 104

macrodynamics, 305
macroeconomics, passim
mainstream, 9, 22, 57, 63, 65, 73, 75–6, 83, 144, 209, 231, 243–6, 259, 262–5, 280, 282, 287–8, 296, 304
management, 9, 14–16, 20–1, 96, 122, 149, 151, 153, 238, 293
*Manchester, Guardian, The*, 46
Marcuzzo, Maria Cristina, 2, 28–39
marginal
  efficiency, 21, 34, 35, 74, 129, 137, 139–51, 222–6, 299
  productivity, 5–6, 35, 95, 197–217, 265
  product of labor, 5–6, 197–201, 203, 205, 209–10, 216, 304
  propensity to consume, 21, 73
marginalist, 9, 35, 69, 198–200
Marshall, Alfred, passim
Marshallian, passim
Marshall-Walras divide, 5, 63, 157, 160, 168, 182
Marx, Karl, 31, 121, 129, 212, 287, 305
mathematics, 21–2, 36, 44, 120, 274, 280, 283, 292
Meade, James, 16, 37, 167, 278, 289, 290, 292, 298, 301, 303, 305
methodology, passim
Michaelmas term, 23, 33, 292
microeconomics, 93, 159–60, 167, 171, 272, 280, 290
middle-class, 44, 51
Mills, C. Wright, 44, 97
modern macroeconomics, 1, 4, 6, 175, 191, 288, 305–7

Modigliani, Franco, 10, 75, 134, 169, 198–202, 208, 289, 303
Moggridge, Don, 2, 15–16, 20, 28–39, 287
monetarism, 78, 83, 158, 172, 175, 232, 246
monetary, passim,
  analysis, 4, 139–41, 145–7, 152
  economy, 1, 5, 10, 77, 82, 137, 139–50, 202, 230, 242–4, 251, 253, 258, 262–3, 268, 301
  expansion, 185, 303
  policy, 1, 13, 67, 73–4, 83, 139, 148–53, 172, 176, 184, 186, 223–5, 232–9, 279, 296, 303
  theory, passim,
money
  demand, 5, 224–5, 228, 291–2, 294, 301–3
  supply, 5–6
  wages, 5, 6, 75, 78, 122, 138, 142, 147, 197–209, 216, 244, 250–1, 257, 262, 289, 293–5, 301, 304, 306
monopoly, 82, 93, 125, 149, 162
Moore, George E., 50, 104, 110, 112, 149, 228, 233, 303
  *Principia Ethica*, 50, 104, 110
multiplier, 73–5, 210, 214, 217, 223–4, 232, 258, 288, 297–303

*Nation, The*, 46, 52, 55, 110
national accounts, 133, 135, 306
national income, 16, 108, 292, 301, 303, 305
natural evolution, 32, 36
Nazi, 31
Nell, Edward J., 5, 197–221
neoclassical, 5, 9, 11, 13, 63, 65, 75–8, 80, 83–4, 92–3, 121, 158, 160, 164, 171, 173–4, 176, 179, 181–7, 222–4, 227, 245–8, 251, 253, 256, 261, 263, 279–80
neo-Keynesian, 2, 8
neoliberal (-lism), 80–3, 87–8
New Classical Economics, 78, 134, 304
new-Keynesian, 2, 8, 13, 14, 150, 158, 176, 180, 182, 184, 198–9, 246, 248, 254, 263, 278, 287

*New Quarterly*, 45
*New Statesman*, 18, 46
*New York Times*, 30, 43, 45, 50
nominal shocks, 6, 185, 306
non-neutrality of money, 7, 180, 306

oligopoly, 82, 162
orthodoxy, 2, 9, 18–19, 25, 144, 227, 229, 231, 289, 296, 298, 300

Paris Peace Conference, 43, 45, 47–9, 297
  *see also* Versailles peace treaty
Patinkin, Don, 10, 33, 46, 53, 75, 76, 289, 293, 295, 301–3
patron, 24, 102, 110
perfect-competition market, 63, 86, 88
Phelps, Edmund S., 3, 25, 78, 91–9, 281
Phillips curve, 77–8, 172, 184, 294, 306
philosophy, 64, 76, 83–4, 105, 114, 120–1, 270, 276–7, 281, 287
Pigou, A.C., 17, 29–30, 32, 70, 74, 76, 82–3, 150, 217, 226–7, 289, 293–7, 304–7
policy making, 10, 15, 36
political economist, 3–4, 129, 160
political science, 3, 120, 122–3, 129
Pollard, Sidney, 38
Posner, Richard, 44, 54–9
Post Keynesian, 2, 5, 8, 11–12, 37, 122, 149, 197, 199, 236, 246, 251, 253–4, 258–60, 262, 287, 303
post-war, 22, 23, 25, 66, 77, 92, 123, 137, 151, 212, 214, 269
practitioner, 13, 39, 227–8
pre-Keynesian, 63, 262, 289, 296, 305
*Principia Ethica* (Moore), 50, 104, 110
productivity, 5, 35, 94–6, 147, 197–217
propensity to consume, 21, 73, 137, 141–2, 146, 148, 256
public intellectual, 2, 3, 43–60

quantity theory of money, 7, 22, 232, 288

Ramsey, Frank P., 3, 21, 95, 98, 271
readership, 29, 31, 274

real analysis, 4, 139–40, 145–6, 150, 152
real wage, passim
recession, 11, 19
Reddaway, Brian, 15, 37, 290–2, 299, 305
relative wage, 304
revolution, passim
Ricardian, 19, 52, 68, 271, 287, 293
Robbins, Lionel, 29, 68, 71, 296
Robertson, Dennis H., 17, 29, 30, 32, 136, 150, 152, 207, 225, 299–300, 305
Robinson, Austin, 23, 211, 243
Robinson, Joan, 11, 15, 17, 22–4, 30, 37, 144, 198, 211, 243, 269, 291–2
Rogers, Colin, 4, 25, 136–5
root, 9, 77, 142, 152, 166, 256, 262, 274, 305–6
Royal Commission, 4, 45, 133
Royal Economic Society, 30, 305–6
Rymes, T. K., 21, 23, 33, 38, 201, 211–12, 291, 299

Samuelson, Paul A., 9–10, 17, 54, 57, 75, 78, 210, 244, 245–53, 257–63, 281, 289–92, 295, 302
Sargent, Thomas, 12, 13, 110, 172
Say's law of markets, 3, 64, 73, 137, 140, 143, 145–6, 295–6
scarcity, 51, 59, 117
Schumpeter, Joseph A., 1, 94, 139–41, 299
self-regulate, 64
Shackle, G. L. S., 11, 145–6, 148
Shaw, George Bernard, 18, 232, 241, 271, 287
Skidelsky, Robert, 2–3, 20, 28–9, 31, 34–9, 45–8, 52, 56–7, 244, 287
Smith, Adam, passim
social sciences, 3–4, 120–248
Sociology, 3, 120–3, 129, 280
solidarism, 92, 97
stability, 1, 68–9, 82, 85, 92, 114, 123, 135, 145, 148, 161, 212, 232, 237, 239, 278, 295, 303
stabilization, 13, 92, 212

stagflation, 11, 17
statism, 83, 88
statistics, 120–1, 252
stickiness, 10, 13, 14, 148, 173, 226, 304
symbol (-lic, lize), 21, 55, 92, 115
synthesis, 9, 11, 13, 65, 68, 75–8, 80, 83–4, 158, 184, 186–7, 222, 224, 227, 245–8, 251, 253, 261, 279, 281, 288, 291, 298–301, 305–7

Temporary National Economic Committee (TNEC), 94
testimony, 4, 30, 102, 127, 133, 290
totalitarianisms, 31
*Tract on Monetary Reform, A* (Keynes), 20, 51, 288, 297
Treasury, 45–8, 60, 108–9, 149, 231, 233–5, 291, 297, 302–3
*Treatise on Money, A* (Keynes), 46, 301
Turnell, S., 38

unemployment, passim
unreconstructed Keynesian, 17
utility, 5, 9, 63, 83, 163, 198–200, 251, 304

Vercelli, Alessandro, 3, 31, 63–90, 279
Versailles peace treaty, 287
  *see also* Paris Peace Conference

wage rate, 11, 21, 203–4, 213, 289, 293, 295
Wagner, Richard, 8, 12
Walrasian, 10, 11, 157, 159–87, 198, 242, 244, 249–53, 259, 261
*Wealth of Nations, The* (Smith), 66–7, 129, 296, 299
welfare liberalism, 75
Wicksell, Knut, 140–1, 143, 299, 301, 303, 305
Woolf, Virginia, 19, 101–17
World War I, 20, 45, 47, 50, 60, 288
World War II, 16, 44, 46, 54, 56, 59, 92, 244–8, 262
Wray, L. Randall, 5, 25, 121, 122, 222–40